Canon 5D Mark III:
From
Snapshots to
Great Shots

Ibarionex Perello

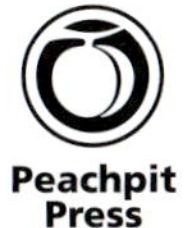

Peachpit Press

Canon 5D Mark III: From Snapshots to Great Shots
Ibarionex Perello

Peachpit Press
1249 Eighth Street
Berkeley, CA 94710
510/524-2178
510/524-2221 (fax)

Find us on the Web at: www.peachpit.com
To report errors, please send a note to: errata@peachpit.com
Peachpit Press is a division of Pearson Education.
Copyright © 2013 by Peachpit Press

Acquisitions Editor: Rebecca Gulick
Development and Copy Editor: Elizabeth Kuball
Production Coordinator: Myrna Vladic
Compositors: David Van Ness, Myrna Vladic
Proofreader: Patricia Pane
Indexer: Valerie Haynes-Perry
Interior Design: Riezebos Holzbaur Design Group
Cover Design: Aren Straiger
Cover Image: Ibarionex Perello
Back Cover Author Photo: Ted Waitt

13-digit ISBN: 978-0-321-85685-2
10-digit ISBN: 0-321-85685-6

9 8 7 6 5 4 3 2 1

Printed and bound in the United States of America

DEDICATION

Para Raquel, Pablo y Margarita. Te quiero con todo mi corazon.

ACKNOWLEDGMENTS

I consider myself very blessed to make a living practicing something I love. Photography has been in my blood since Mike Cohen of the Boys Club of Hollywood introduced me to it. From the moment that I saw an image reveal itself in a developing tray, I have been captivated by the possibilities that photography promises and often delivers.

My journey has been the result of being able to take advantage of opportunities as opposed to some well thought-out plan. As I result, I consider myself very lucky to be able to make a living from using a camera and putting words on a page. But I'm under no illusion that I've achieved this on my own. It's clear to me that any achievements that I may lay claim to are the result of the many people who have supported and encouraged me, even when I wasn't sure I was deserving of it.

There are many people to thank for helping me walk this path, not least of whom is my wife, whose continued support and love is invaluable to me, though I may not always acknowledge it. She is my rock.

I'm very grateful to my family, particularly my parents, whose sacrifices I've appreciated even more as I've gotten older. It's their hope for a better life that has helped make my accomplishments, such as this book, possible.

My friends continue to be important in my journey as a photographer. From them I continue to derive inspiration and the pleasure of their company. People including Martin Bailey, Emilio and Elena Banuelos, Dana Barsuhn, RC Concepcion, Jeff Curto, Tony DiZinno, Charlie Holland, Seth Joel, Dennis Keeley, Eric Kim, Tony Luna, Chris Marquardt, Martin Taylor, Marco Torres, and Everard William have been gifts to my life, and I thank them for their continued friendship.

The Peachpit Press team has been great to me and I've truly enjoyed collaborating with them on each successive project. Rebecca Gulick, Ted Waitt, Elizabeth Kuball, Sara Todd, Gary-Paul Prince, Scott Cowlin, and the rest of the staff are the best team anyone could ask for.

Lastly, I want to thank the many people who have been helped in some way through the work that I do as an author, a teacher, and a podcaster. Though I will never meet all of them, their accepting what I have to offer helps to make some of the special moments in my life possible. I am humbled and grateful for all of it.

Contents

CHAPTER 4: THAT WONDERFUL FACE 81

Settings and Features to Make Great Portraits

CHAPTER 5: MOVING TARGETS 109

Tricks to Capturing Motion

CHAPTER 6: LANDSCAPE PHOTOGRAPHY 137

Getting the Most Out of Your Landscape Photography

Introduction

Buying a new camera is always exciting. Of course, you get the thrill of holding a new piece of photographic equipment and appreciating its styling and functionality. But the real excitement comes from the promise that it offers to your photography. It's how this new tool will help you to fulfill your vision that makes such an investment truly worthwhile.

This book on the Canon EOS 5D Mark III aims to tell you much more than just how to set a particular control on your camera. Instead, I share the when, why, and how to help you make the most of this exciting DSLR. I think there is no better way to do that than by sharing with you how *I* use the camera and how it makes a difference in my own photography.

This book is not a comprehensive and exhaustive guide to every feature that the 5D Mark III offers—you have the user's manual for that. Instead, I focus my attention on those controls and features that I believe make the biggest difference in my photography and, hopefully, in yours. Regardless of whether you shoot portraits, travel, landscapes, sports, or still life, the words and images that I share in this book will help you gain confidence in how to make great photographs.

Whether this is your first DSLR or you're upgrading from a previous model, this book will provide you a valuable context for the many features found on the 5D Mark III. But before I delve into the meat of things, I want to answer some common questions that I believe will help you to make the most of what this book has to offer.

WHAT DOES THIS BOOK COVER THAT I WON'T FIND IN THE USER'S MANUAL?

The user's manual provides concise information on how to enable or change a particular control or function, but it's often lacking a sense of when and why you would want to use a specific feature. Though the manual may give some general examples of when you might want to use evaluative metering versus center-weighted metering or Auto White Balance versus a custom white balance, it isn't really rooted in the kinds of images that people like you and me make every time we bring the camera to our eyes. This is what you'll find in this book.

Because I'm writing much of what I share based on my own personal experience with the 5D Mark III, you'll find a point of view that you'd never find in a user's manual. It's the kind of information that I'd provide you if we were out together shooting together.

As such, it's important to remember that although this is the way *I* use the camera, it isn't necessarily the way *you* should use it. Every photographer is different. However, I think you'll find that my discussion of the camera and its features and how it impacts my photography will make the camera more accessible to you. This will eventually evolve into a level of confidence that will allow you to handle and use the camera in a way that's unique to you and the way you make images.

DOES THIS BOOK COVER EVERY FEATURE OF THE CAMERA?

No, but what it does emphasize are those features and controls that will have the biggest impact on the quality of your photographs. Not only do I go into detail on what I consider the key features of the camera that will impact almost every photograph you make, but I also delve into controls that you'll periodically use to handle difficult and challenging shooting conditions.

As you shoot, you'll use certain features over and over again, regardless of the subject matter of your photos. These features are the ones that I help you to understand and eventually master. As you gain this understanding, the importance (or lack of importance) of other features will become clearer to you.

So, instead of someone else telling you what's best, you'll be making informed decisions on these controls based on your own images and what you need as a photographer.

SHOULD I READ THE BOOK STRAIGHT THROUGH OR CAN I JUMP AROUND AND USE IT AS A REFERENCE?

You can use it in both ways, but I encourage you to at least read the first few chapters, even if you believe it's information that you're already familiar with. As I said earlier, I'm sharing my own perspective on the camera and its key features, so these chapters are written from a point of view that may provide you fresh insight to a familiar feature or control.

I suggest that you approach the information in this book at a modest pace. I know you're eager to get out and shoot and produce some amazing photographs, but don't pressure yourself to master this camera overnight. If you buy a Steinway piano today, you won't be ready to perform at Carnegie Hall tomorrow. As with anything, mastering your 5D Mark III will take practice—but the good news is, practice can be fun!

HOW IMPORTANT ARE THE ASSIGNMENTS AT THE END OF EACH CHAPTER?

The assignments can make a big difference. Regardless of how clear the chapters are, you won't really understand what you're reading until you put it into practice. It's only when you put down the book, grab your camera, and start making photographs that you'll take the information and tips found here and make it something of your own.

All the manuals and videos in the world, though informative and entertaining, won't make you or me a better photographer. If that were the case, we'd all be world-famous by now.

Instead, it's the act of going out and making images that makes us better photographers. And it's practicing with specific goals and assignments in mind that provides us the opportunity to learn those small but important lessons that help us not only master a new camera, but also make better photographs.

In other words, we stop *taking* photographs and we start *making* them.

HOW CAN I MAKE THE MOST OF THIS BOOK AND MY CAMERA?

Slow down. Impatience has likely produced more bad photography than any cheap camera or poorly written instruction manual.

We're all eager to make better photographs, especially when we hold brand-new cameras in our hands, but there's something to be said for practicing patience. Patience is valuable not only as you're trying to understand a new tool, such as the 5D Mark III, but especially when it comes time to making photographs.

When I'm patient and thoughtful about what I'm doing with my camera, I'm much more consistent with the images I produce. When I'm impatient and rushing, the only thing I do consistently is make lackluster photographs or, worse yet, ruin great photographs with poor technique.

The joy of photography comes from making photographs that complete my vision of the person, the scene, and the moment. And I can repeatedly do that by knowing my instrument, practicing, and remembering to have fun.

I hope that this book helps you to discover that joy for yourself.

Share your results with this book's Flickr group!

Join the group here: www.flickr.com/groups/ Canon5DMarkIIIFromSnapshotstoGreatShots

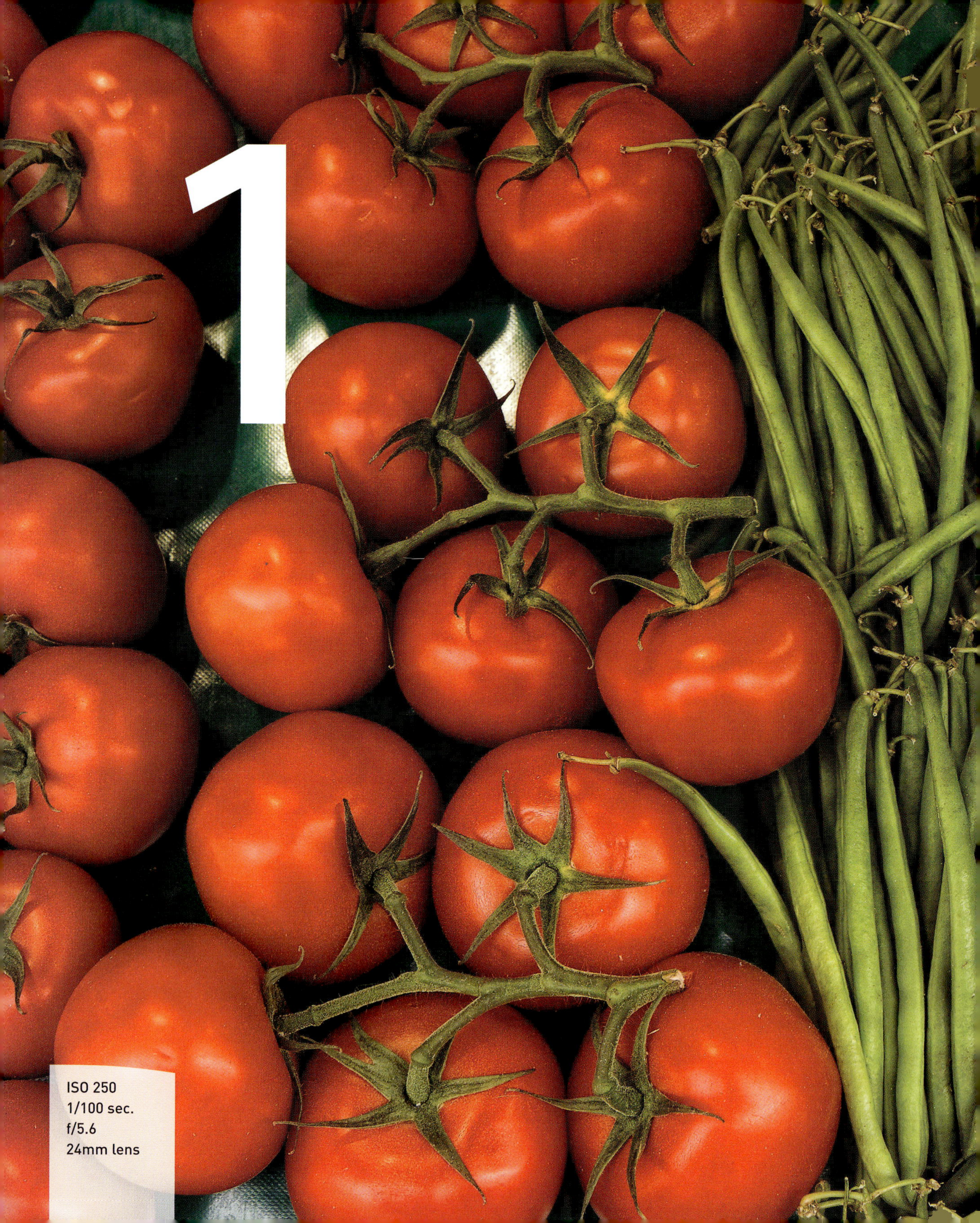
1
ISO 250
1/100 sec.
f/5.6
24mm lens

The 5D Mark III Top Ten List

TEN TIPS TO GET YOU STARTED

Like you, I felt the giddy satisfaction of pulling the camera out of the box, inserting the battery, and hearing that sharp snap as I released the shutter the first time. It was like music to my ears. And yes, despite any claims of professionalism I embrace, I began making photographs around the studio, even before cracking open the first few pages of the manual. I'm only human.

I still read the manual. With a camera as sophisticated as the 5D Mark III, this small, 404-page booklet is as invaluable and indispensable as the battery that powers the camera. Yet, I was as eager as anyone to see what this new camera could deliver.

So, with that in mind, I thought I would share ten tips that I believe will help you make the most of the camera straight out of the box, in case you're as eager as I was.

CAMERA FRONT

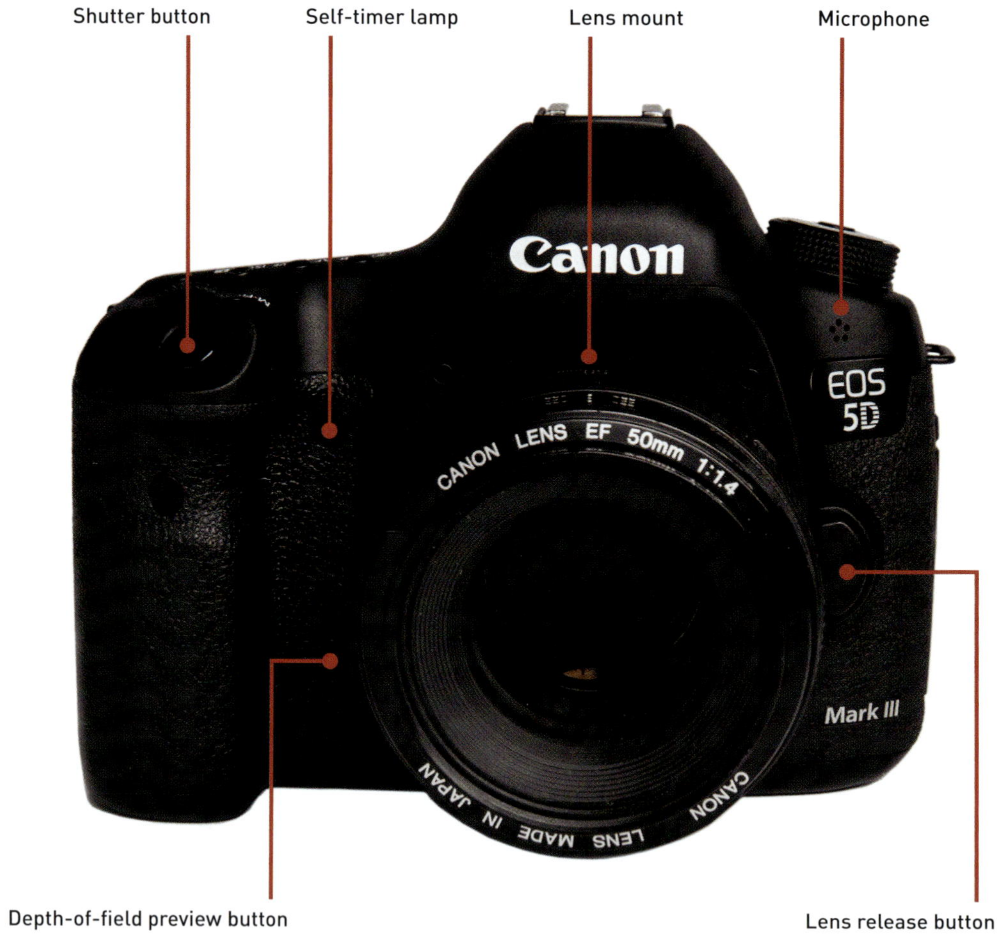

CAMERA BACK

Creative Photo/Comparative playback
(Two-image display)/Direct print button
Menu button
Info button
Viewfinder eyepiece
Live View shooting/
Movie shooting switch
Multi-controller
AF start button
AE lock button
AF point
selection button
Card slot
cover
RATE
Erase
button
Magnify/Reduce
button
LCD monitor
Multi-function
lock switch
Access lamp
Playback button
Rating button
Quick Control
button
Setting button
Quick Control Dial

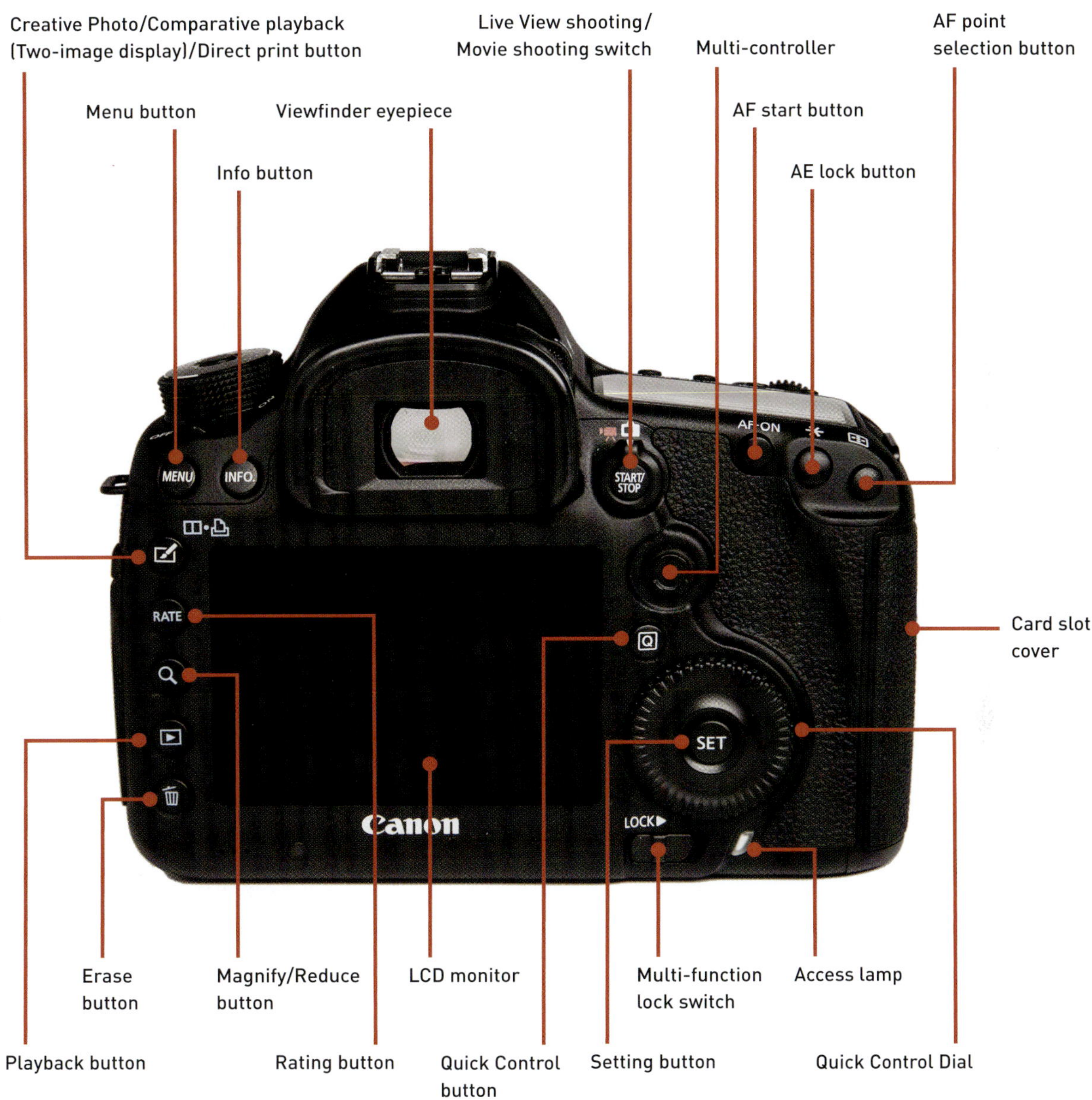

CAMERA TOP

Metering mode selection/
White balance selection button
AF mode selection/
Drive mode selection button
Lens mount
AF area selection mode/
Multi-function button
Shutter button
Mode Dial
Main Dial
Strap mount
Strap mount
M-Fn
Power switch
Hot shoe
Dioptric
adjustment knob
LCD panel
LCD panel
illumination button
Flash-sync contacts
ISO speed setting/Flash exposure
compensation button

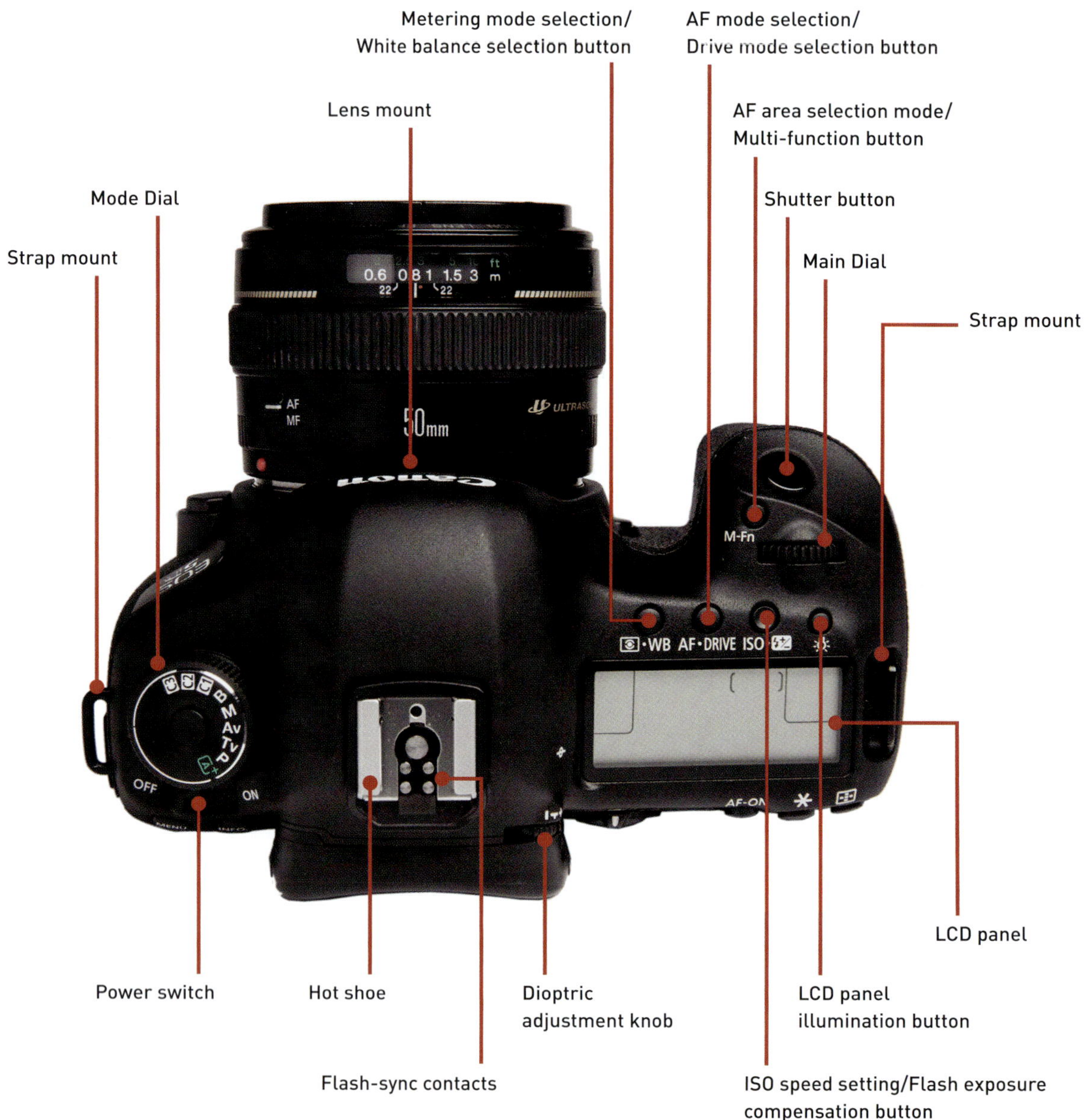

1. CHARGE YOUR BATTERY

The battery packaged with your camera is only partially charged out of the box. So, it's important to place the LP-E6 battery pack in the LC-E6 charger. A full charge should take approximately two-and-a-half hours under normal conditions.

I shoot fairly regularly, so I always charge my batteries the night before a shoot. Even if the battery indicator shows that I have a good amount of juice left, I'll charge it up to full capacity. This is especially important if you go days or weeks between uses. Even if the camera isn't being used, power will dissipate from the battery, and you don't want to be in a situation where your camera is no longer functioning due to lack of power.

You can check the status of your battery by referencing the battery check in the lower-right corner of the 5D Mark III LCD panel or the Battery Info screen (**Figure 1.1**).

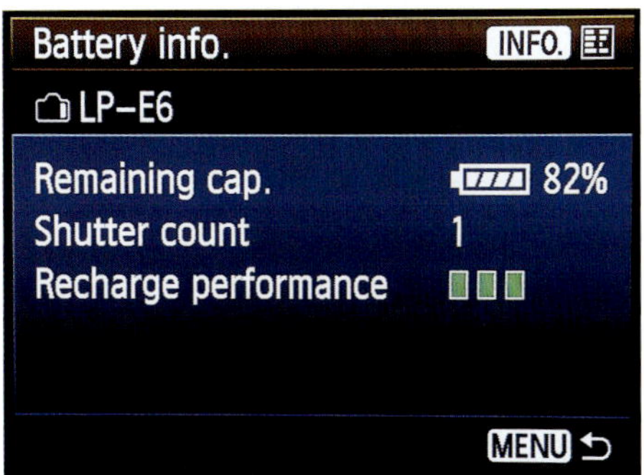

FIGURE 1.1
Make sure to fully charge your battery the night before a shoot. You can check the battery status on both the LCD Panel and the Battery Info screen, the latter of which provides the remaining charge capacity, frame count, and recharge performance.

KEEPING A BACKUP BATTERY

The first thing I always purchase with a new camera is a second battery. This not only provides a reliable backup but also extends my shooting time. According to the user's manual, each battery can deliver up to 950 exposures under normal operating temperatures. However, this number can be impacted by variables such as temperature, lens choice, and exposure time. I don't have to worry about such variations because I have a second battery in my bag, which provides more than enough power for a typical day of shooting.

2. SET YOUR ISO

One of the most important settings on your camera is the ISO. ISO is the control that allows you to adjust the camera's sensitivity to light, which by default on the 5D Mark III ranges from 100 to 25,600. This range can be expanded to 50 to 102,400.

Low ISO numbers require less light in order to produce a good exposure. So, on a bright sunny day, an ISO of 100 or 200 would be more than adequate to capture a good image. As light levels decrease, a higher ISO may be needed. So, a cloudy day may require an ISO of 200 or 400. When shooting indoors under fluorescent or tungsten light, the ISO might need to be set at 800 or higher.

The 5D Mark III has an automatic ISO feature, which results in the camera dynamically changing ISO as light levels change. This mode is automatically enabled when you're in the Scene Intelligent Auto mode. It also can be used in any other exposure mode, including Manual. However, I prefer to set my ISO manually in order to maintain control over this all-important feature.

Higher ISOs do increase the presence of noise, which appears as speckles, especially in areas of shadow. However, the 5D Mark III's full-frame sensor and processing engine keep noise levels very low, even at higher ISOs. So, although it's true that lower ISOs will deliver better image quality, I don't hesitate to increase my ISO if I need to, especially if it helps ensure that I have a shutter speed that's fast enough for me to handhold the camera and achieve a sharp photograph, free of camera shake.

TIP

Camera shake is the number-one reason for less-than-sharp photographs. Increasing the ISO is one way of remedying this, by allowing you to choose a faster shutter speed under low-light conditions.

I'd rather have a sharp image with noise than a noiseless image that's blurry. The former I can do something about; the latter ends up being just another failed and deleted image.

TO SET THE ISO, FOLLOW THESE STEPS:

1. Activate the camera by lightly pressing the shutter button.

2. Press the ISO speed-setting button on the top of the camera (refer to the "Poring over the Camera" diagram, earlier in this chapter).

3. Use the Main Dial to select an ISO between ISO 100 and 51,200.

4. Lightly press the shutter button again to lock in your change.

3. SET YOUR WHITE BALANCE

Light has color to it, from the warm glow of a sunset to the cool bluish hue right before the sun rises in the east. Our eyes and brains automatically adjust to this, so we sometimes don't pick up on the nuances of color when it happens. This is why, when you walk from outside on a bright sunny day into a fluorescent-lit office, the color remains amazingly consistent, even though the light sources are different.

The camera's Auto White Balance (AWB) feature attempts to correct for such variation in lighting, but as with any automatic feature, it's not infallible. Although AWB can provide acceptable results, I find that I achieve more accurate and consistent results by setting the white balance to a preset or by creating a custom white balance.

When saving images as JPEGs, getting the white balance right is very important, because it's difficult to correct color after the fact. Raw files provide greater flexibility because you can correct white balance easily in your photo-editing application without compromising image quality. However, it's always faster and simpler to get the white balance correct at the moment of capture.

Here are the white balance modes you can choose from (**Figure 1.2**):

- **Auto:** The default setting for your camera. It's the only white balance setting available to you when using the Scene Intelligent Auto mode.

- **Daylight:** Used for general daylight/sunlit shooting.

- **Shade:** Best suited for shaded areas on days that are bright and sunny.

- **Cloudy, twilight, sunset:** The choice for overcast or very cloudy days. This and the shade setting will eliminate the blue colorcast from your images.

- **Tungsten light:** For when you're using regular household-type bulbs for your light source. Tungsten is a very warm light source and will result in a yellow/orange cast if you don't correct for it.

- **White fluorescent light:** This setting gets rid of the green-blue cast that can result from using regular fluorescent lights as your dominant light source. Some fluorescent lights are actually balanced for daylight, which may allow you to use the daylight white balance setting.

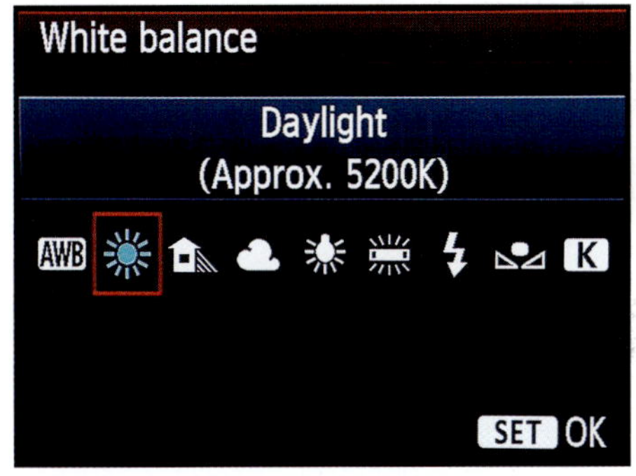

FIGURE 1.2
Though AWB promises convenience, it doesn't always provide the most accurate results. Most of the time, a preset white balance or a custom white balance will deliver more consistent color.

- **Flash use:** Select this white balance whenever using a flash or strobe. You also can use the daylight setting when using flash, because they share the same color temperature.

- **Custom:** Allows you to use a customized white balance that is adjusted for a particular light source. If you know what the color temperature of your light source is, you can manually create a white balance setting that is specific for that light source.

- **Kelvin:** This choice allows you to set a specific color temperature from 2500 to 10,000 degrees Kelvin, thus providing both control and precision. This provides an excellent option when neither the AWB or a preset can deliver accurate color, such as when shooting under mercury vapor lights.

TO SET YOUR WHITE BALANCE, FOLLOW THESE STEPS:

1. Activate the camera by lightly pressing the shutter button.
2. Press the Metering mode selection/White balance selection button on the top of the camera (refer to the "Poring Over the Camera" diagram, earlier in this chapter).
3. Rotate the Quick Control Dial to select the preferred white balance method.
4. Lightly press the shutter button and check the LCD panel to confirm the white balance method.

4. SET YOUR EXPOSURE MODE

After your ISO setting, the next two crucial controls for achieving an accurate exposure are shutter speed and aperture. The shutter speed controls the duration that the shutter remains open, often measured in increments of a fraction of a second (for example, 1/500 second). The aperture refers to the opening of the lens, commonly referred to as an f-stop (for example, f/5.6).

The interplay of ISO, shutter speed, and aperture determine the camera's ability to achieve an accurate exposure, with each setting having an impact on the other.

The 5D Mark III offers several exposure modes, which provide varying levels of control of the shutter speed and aperture and can have a dramatic impact on the look of a photograph:

- **Scene Intelligent Auto (A$^+$):** This is a fully automatic exposure mode, which allows the camera to control ISO, white balance, shutter speed, and aperture. It also dynamically adjusts sharpness, contrast, and color saturation for specific types of scenes or photographs it believes you're trying to make.

- **Program (P):** In this mode, the camera controls both shutter speed and aperture, while providing you the ability to manually adjust ISO, white balance, and other settings. Program can serve as your general-purpose exposure mode.

- **Aperture Priority (Av):** In this mode, you have control over the aperture, while the camera changes the shutter speed based on the light levels and the ISO. This allows for complete control over depth of field.

- **Shutter Priority (Tv):** This exposure mode provides you the ability to control the shutter speed, while the camera sets the aperture. You also have the flexibility of changing the ISO. This is a good choice when you want to freeze or blur action.

- **Manual (M):** This mode gives you complete control over your shutter speed, aperture, and ISO. This is a good mode to use not only when the automatic exposure modes are unable to provide an accurate result, but also when you want to keep exposure consistent.

- **Bulb (B):** For long-time exposure, the Bulb mode will leave the shutter open for as long as the shutter button is depressed. You can set your aperture and ISO as needed for long time exposures of star trails.

1. Press the Mode Dial lock release button.
2. Rotate the Mode Dial (refer to the "Poring Over the Camera" diagram, earlier in this chapter) to set your preferred exposure mode.

5. SET YOUR AUTOFOCUS MODE AND FOCUS POINT

The focusing system on the 5D Mark III has been dramatically improved from what was designed into its predecessor, the Mark II. In addition to increasing the individual focus points to 61 focus sensors, the camera's autofocus speed is significantly improved. The camera also provides much more extensive controls for customizing the camera autofocus performance, particularly when using the image to capture sports action.

You still need to understand that the camera's advanced autofocus system—while speedy and often accurate—is not sophisticated enough to always know what you're trying to make a photograph of. The autofocus system can, more often than not, detect focus on your subject, but there will be times when you'll need to take control.

One of the first considerations to make is which autofocus (AF) mode to use. The camera offers three:

- **One Shot:** This mode is best suited for static or still subjects. Once focus is detected and while maintaining halfway pressure on the shutter button or the AF start button, focus is locked. To refocus, you have to release pressure from the button and depress it again. This is the ideal setting for portraits, macro, or still life.

- **AI Servo:** This provides you the advantage of both One Shot and AI Focus. The camera starts off in One Shot mode, but if it detects that the subject is moving, it will automatically switch to AI Focus and begin to track your subject.

- **AI Focus:** In this focus mode, the camera is constantly adjusting for the movement of the subject. It's ideal for fast action and sports because the camera continually evaluates the autofocus data to maintain focus on the subject from shot to shot.

TO SET YOUR AF MODE, FOLLOW THESE STEPS:

1. Activate the camera by lightly pressing the shutter button.

2. Press the AF mode selection/Drive mode selection button located on the top of your camera (refer to the "Poring Over the Camera" diagram, earlier in this chapter).

3. Turn the Main Dial to select the preferred autofocus mode.

4. Confirm the autofocus mode by looking at the upper-right corner of the LCD panel.

You can use all 61 points for autofocus detection or just a single point. This provides great flexibility in telling the camera what areas of the frame you want it to pay attention to for the purpose of autofocus detection. You may prefer to use fewer autofocus points to eliminate problems (for example, when you're shooting through a fence or when there are momentary obstructions between the camera and the subject).

Here are the AF area selection modes:

- **Single-point Spot AF (manual selection):** This option provides pinpoint focus detection, even narrower than the Single-point AF.

- **Single-point AF (manual selection):** The camera uses a single sensor for focus detection.

- **AF point expansion (manual selection):** Focus detection is based on a single focus point and four adjacent sensors (above, below, right, and left).

- **AF point expansion (manual selection, surrounding points):** A single focus point, as well as all adjacent focus points, are utilized for focus detection.

- **Zone AF (manual selection of zone):** The 61 AF sensors are divided into 9 different zones of focus.

- **61-point automatic selection AF:** All 61 sensors are utilized for focus detection, with emphasis often going to the object or element closest to the camera.

TO SET YOUR AF AREA SELECTION MODE, FOLLOW THESE STEPS:

1. Activate the camera by lightly pressing the shutter button.

2. Press the AF point selection button located on the rear of your camera (refer to the "Poring Over the Camera" diagram, earlier in this chapter).

3. Repeatedly press the M-Fn (AF area selection mode/Multi-function button) to cycle through the various AF area selection modes.

4. Confirm the AF mode by looking at the glowing red indicators displayed in your viewfinder.

TIP

As a general rule, the less depth of field that I'm working with, the fewer sensors I use for focus detection. For example, if I'm making a portrait with a 50mm f/1.2 lens set at its widest aperture, I have a razor-thin amount of depth of field. So, to ensure that I get the subject's eyes sharp, I'll use the Single-point Spot AF or the Single-point AF to specifically target the eyes. Using a larger grouping of sensors may result in another area of the face being sharper than the eye, which I definitely don't want.

If I'm shooting action with a fast-moving subject, I'll use more sensors in order to ensure that the camera can detect and track the subject. My choice of AF area selection mode may be influenced by whether there are elements between the subject and the camera, such as another player who may occasionally interfere with focus detection on my subject.

6. SET THE IMAGE RECORDING QUALITY

Now, here's a topic that has likely erupted in a couple of bar fights: shooting RAW versus JPEG.

When you shoot in JPEG mode, your camera takes the image file and tweaks it for color, contrast, sharpness, and more. The camera's built-in image processor optimizes the image. The files are noticeably smaller than raw files, because they're compressed, which means some data is lost in order to make the file size smaller. As long as the quality setting remains relatively high, a JPEG can produce a good image.

Raw files are unprocessed files—they're what the camera's sensors captured. Instead of the camera processing the image, the photographer uses a photo-editing application (such as Adobe Photoshop or Lightroom) to make enhancements to color, sharpness, white balance, or contrast. Raw files provide the greatest image quality, because unlike JPEGs, they aren't compressed.

Raw files hold the promise of better image quality, but they don't look that great out of the camera as compared to JPEGs, because they haven't had the benefit of in-camera processing. So, if you want to make the image look great, you'll need to do some work in your photo-editing application. This is especially helpful if your images are underexposed or were captured with an incorrect white balance. Such corrections can be made easily, with no sacrifice of image quality.

I shoot RAW most of the time, but occasionally I shoot in RAW + JPEG mode if I want to produce images straight out of the camera that I can e-mail or post online. For example, when I'm at a party or on a day trip with my family, I produce JPEGs (along with my raw files), because I don't want to work on every image that I may have made during the day, but I want to have the option to work on the raw file if I happen to capture a great image.

TIP

If you're new to the idea of raw files, set your camera for JPEGs at the highest quality setting. Otherwise, choose the RAW setting.

The 5D Mark III offers three options for saving your images as raw:

- **RAW:** Allows you to save the files at their full 22-megapixel resolution of 5760 x 3840

- **MRAW:** Produces a 10-megapixel file at a resolution of 3960 x 2640

- **SRAW:** Produces a 5.5-megapixel file at a resolution of 2880 x 1920

The lower-resolution files are for photographers who know they don't need the full resolution provided by the 5D Mark III, but who still want the flexibility provided by shooting with a raw file. For example, some wedding photographers who know that most of their images won't be enlarged beyond 8-x-10-inch prints, may choose to use MRAW. Personally, I stay with the maximum-resolution raw files, because I want to make sure that I can always take advantage of the full resolution of the camera.

JPEGs are available in eight degrees of compression, with greater compression providing smaller files (and lower image quality). To achieve this greater compression (and smaller file size), the camera discards data. When significant amounts of data are tossed out, the image will exhibit signs of pixelization, which can limit the size of the enlargement. When shooting JPEGs, I always choose the highest quality setting (the one on the far left of the screen shown in **Figure 1.3**).

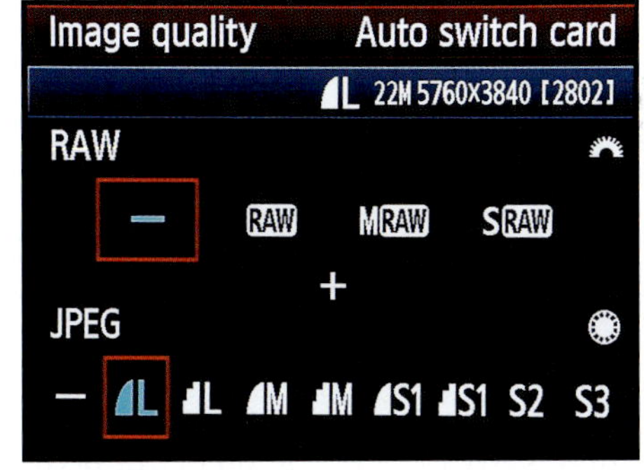

FIGURE 1.3

You can save your images as raw files, JPEGs, or both.

To set your image recording quality, follow these steps:

1. Press the Menu button on the back of the camera (refer to the "Poring Over the Camera" diagram, earlier in this chapter) to bring up the menu list.

2. Use the Quick Control Dial to select the Shoot 1 menu screen.

3. Use the Quick Control Dial to select Quality Option and press the Setting button.

4. Use the Main Dial to set your RAW Quality. You'll move the dial all the way to the left if you want to shoot only producing JPEGs.

5. Use the Quick Control Dial to set your JPEG Quality. Select the first L on the far left for the highest-quality JPEGs. (This will render a 22-megapixel image with a dimension of 5760 x 3840 pixels.)

7. MANAGE YOUR MEMORY CARDS

Formatting my memory card is one of the ways I reduce the chance of data corruption and the loss of images. Though I only use high-quality, name-brand memory cards, the way that I prepare my Compact Flash (CF) or Secure Digital (SD) cards is an important part of my process.

Every time I insert a card in my camera, I reformat it, which means that not only are the preexisting files deleted, but the whole directory structure of the card is rebuilt. This is better than selectively deleting files to create more space on the card. Over time, if the card isn't formatted, there is a risk of data corruption. It may be a small risk, but it's worth the few seconds it takes to reformat the card to reduce this risk.

After a shoot, I make sure that I've downloaded my files to my computer and to a backup hard drive before reformatting my card.

To format your memory card, make sure that you've downloaded your images to your computer and then follow these steps:

1. Press the Menu button and turn the Main Dial to get to the Set-up 1 menu screen.

2. Use the Quick Control Dial to select Format card (**Figure 1.4**).

3. If you have only one card in the camera, it will already be selected. If you have both a CF and an SD card in your camera, use the Quick Control Dial to select the card you want to format. Press the Setting button.

4. Use the Main Dial to select OK and press the Setting button.

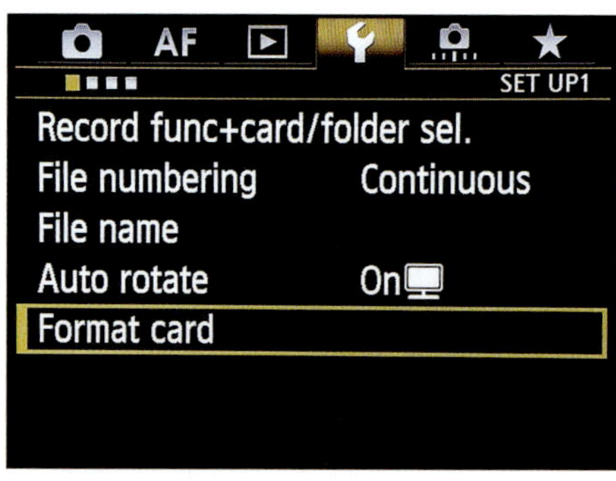

FIGURE 1.4

Make sure to format your memory cards before each shoot. Don't forget to download all the images on your cards before you format them.

One of the great advantages of the 5D Mark III is the ability to use two memory cards. This not only gives you increased capacity for memory storage but also can be a convenient way of creating automatic backups of your photographs in-camera.

There are four modes you have to choose from:

- **Standard:** The images will be recorded to a single installed card or the primary card, which you designate.

- **Auto switch card:** This works the same as the standard setting, except when the primary card becomes full, the camera automatically begins recording to the second card. A new file folder is created automatically.

- **Rec separately:** If you're shooting in RAW + JPEG mode, the respective files can be saved to different memory cards.

- **Rec to multiple:** Every image made by the camera will be recorded to both memory cards, creating an automatic backup. If you choose this option, you should use memory cards with the same capacity so that one doesn't fill up before the other.

Though recording to multiple cards can slow down the performance of the camera, I use this feature if the photographs are especially important. Otherwise, I use the auto switch card mode so that I don't have to replace a memory card in the middle of a shoot.

TO SET UP YOUR MEMORY, CARDS FOLLOW THESE STEPS:

1. Press the Menu button and rotate the Main Dial to get to the Set-up 1 menu screen. Press the Setting button.

2. Rotate the Quick Control Dial, select Recording Function, and press the Setting button.

3. Rotate the Quick Control Dial, select the Record/Play setting, and press the Setting button.

4. If you're using multiple cards, rotate the Quick Control Dial to select your primary memory card. The first icon refers to the CF card; the second, to the SD card (**Figure 1.5**). Press the Setting button to confirm the setting.

5. View the small window at the bottom of the LCD monitor to confirm which format will be saved to the respective cards.

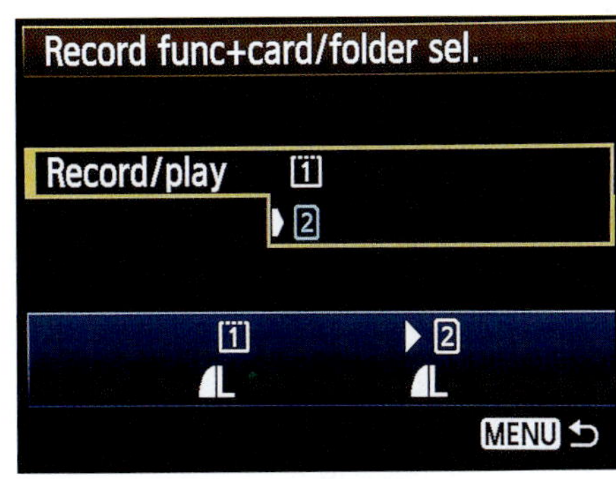

FIGURE 1.5
Check what file format is being saved to an installed memory card before you begin your shoot.

8. CHOOSE A COLOR SPACE AND PICTURE STYLE

Color space is the range of colors that a camera captures and records. It can influence the accuracy of color when reproduced either on-screen or on paper. The 5D Mark III offers two color space options—sRGB and Adobe RGB 1998 (**Figure 1.6**). These options are important when shooting JPEGs. (With RAW files, you have the option to change the color space freely in your photo-editing application.)

sRGB is a color space that closely matches the color range available on your computer monitor. It covers a smaller range, or *gamut,* than Adobe RGB 1998. But sRGB is the best choice if your images are destined for the web. sRGB is also often the color space used by many commercial labs. So, by shooting sRGB, it increases the likelihood that your prints will closely match what you captured with your DSLR.

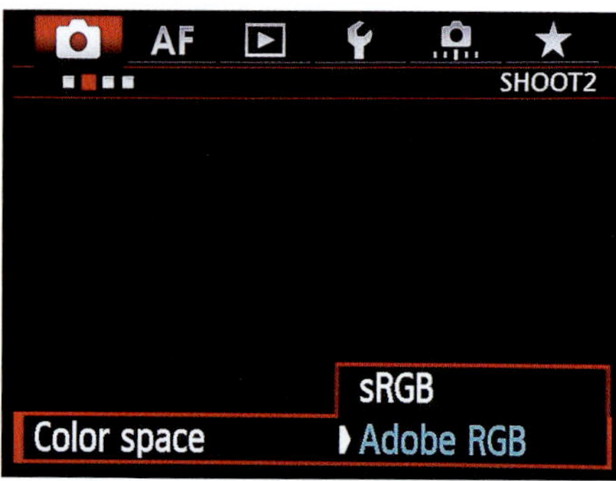

FIGURE 1.6

The choice of color space is largely based on how you intend to output your images. If they're designated for the web or a local photo lab, sRGB is recommended. If you expect to edit your own images and output them using an inkjet printer, Adobe RGB 1998 is the better option.

Adobe RGB 1998 encompasses a wider gamut, making it possible to reproduce certain colors more accurately on many inkjet or high-end printers, such as those found at commercial printing services. If you make your own prints or intend to work with your images extensively in your photo-editing software, the Adobe RGB 1998 color space is the best choice.

TO SET THE COLOR SPACE, FOLLOW THESE STEPS:

1. While pressing the Menu button, turn the Main Dial to select the Shoot 2 menu screen. Then use the Quick Control Dial to scroll down to Color Space.

2. Press the Setting button, and then highlight your desired color space and press the Setting button again.

3. Press the Menu button to leave the menu and begin shooting with your new color space.

Picture styles on the 5D Mark III allow you to enhance your images in-camera, depending on the type of photo you're taking. There are six picture styles to choose from, along with three additional user-defined styles.

- **Auto:** This picture style uses aspects of the camera's scene recognition technology to automatically choose one of the following picture styles:
  - **Standard:** This general-purpose picture style is used to create crisp images with bold, vibrant colors. It's suitable for most scenes.
  - **Portrait:** This picture style enhances the colors in skin tone and is used for a softer-looking image.
  - **Landscape:** This picture style enhances blues and greens, two colors that are typically visible in a landscape.
  - **Neutral:** This picture style creates natural colors and subdued images and is a good choice if you want to do a lot of editing to your photos on the computer.
  - **Faithful:** This picture style is similar to the neutral style but creates better color when shooting in daylight (with a color temperature of 5200L). It's also a good option if you prefer to edit your photos on the computer.
  - **Monochrome:** This picture style creates black-and-white images. It's important to note that if you use Monochrome style and shoot in JPEG, you can't revert the image to color.
  - **User-Defined:** This picture style lets you create your own customized picture style by adjusting contrast, sharpness, saturation, and color tone.

TO SET THE PICTURE STYLE, FOLLOW THESE STEPS:

1. Activate the camera by lightly pressing the shutter button.
2. Press the Creative Photo/Comparative playback (Two-image display)/Direct print button on the back of the camera.
3. Use the Main Dial to select the Picture Style mode and press the Setting button.
4. Use the Quick Control Dial to scroll through the styles.
5. Press the Setting button to lock in this change.

9. CHOOSE A METERING MODE

One of the biggest concerns that we have as photographers is exposure. Thankfully, the 5D Mark III not only offers an improved evaluative metering system, but also provides three other options for handling difficult and challenging lighting conditions:

- **Evaluative:** This 63-zone evaluative metering mode serves as a general-purpose meter, which can handle the great majority of situations. It can sometimes handle backlit subjects and provide a good overall exposure. It uses color and focus data to refine the exposure.

- **Partial:** This metering mode utilizes only 6.2 percent of the viewfinder area for metering. This restrictive metering is good when you're faced with severely backlit subjects.

- **Spot:** Utilizing only 1.5 percent of the viewfinder area at the center frame, spot metering is the most restrictive of the metering modes, allowing precise measurement of the subject or other areas of the frame.

- **Center-weighted:** This metering mode emphasizes the center area of the frame, which is then averaged with what exists in the rest of the frame.

I use the evaluative metering system over 90 percent of the time, but occasionally I use the other metering modes when I'm faced with a scene that has a very bright or dark background or when I know that the evaluative metering will likely be fooled.

TO SET YOUR METERING MODE, FOLLOW THESE STEPS:

1. Activate the camera by lightly pressing the shutter button.

2. Select one of the shooting modes, such as P. (You can't choose anything other than evaluative metering when using the Scene Intelligent Auto mode.)

3. Press the Metering mode selection/White balance selection button on the top of the camera (refer to the "Poring Over the Camera" diagram, earlier in this chapter) to bring up the metering menu.

4. Use the Main Dial to select the preferred metering method for your shooting situation. The selected meter icon will appear in the lower-right portion of the LCD panel.

5. Check the camera display to ensure that the proper metering mode is selected.

10. SET YOUR INFORMATION DISPLAY

The LCD monitor on the back of the camera provides wonderful feedback on image exposure and color quality, but if your screen happens to be set too bright or too dark, the image you're seeing may be deceptive. When you take a photograph, you usually want to keep detail in the highlight areas of the image and don't want to "blow out" anything (that is, you don't want certain areas of your image to be completely white). For example, if you were to use your flash while photographing a person and the image were overexposed, the light could flood her face. One way to prevent this loss of detail is by enabling Highlight Alert.

TO ENABLE HIGHLIGHT ALERT, FOLLOW THESE STEPS:

1. Press the Menu button and use the Main Dial to select the Play 3 menu screen.

2. Use the Quick Control Dial to select Highlight Alert and press the Setting button.

3. Turn the Main Dial to enable the Highlight Alert function and press the Setting button (**Figure 1.7**).

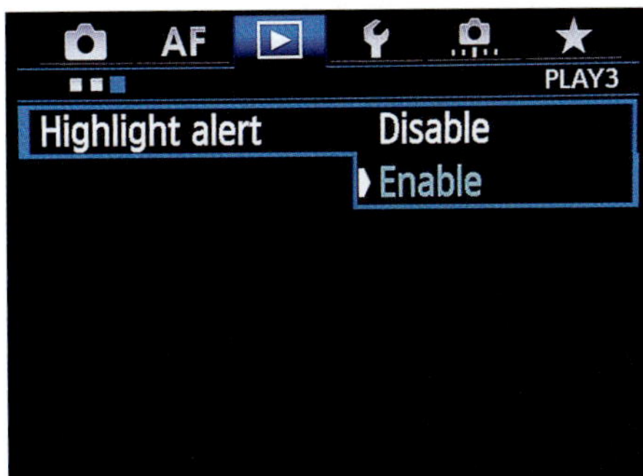

FIGURE 1.7
When the highlight warning is enabled, any area that is severely overexposed will blink between black and white as an exposure warning. The exposure will need to be corrected in order to retain detail in this bright area.

4. Press the Menu button to leave the menus and continue shooting.

Now that you've enabled Highlight Alert, you'll see a difference in your images while you review them. If you photograph something that is pure white (255, 255, 255 on the RGB color model), then that part of the image will blink black on the LCD monitor when you review your shot. At first you might find this a bit annoying, but trust me, it's extremely useful. This is feedback that will help you properly expose your images. It's very difficult to pull in detail from the areas that blink black, so if it's blinking somewhere you don't want it to, you'll need to reduce the exposure using exposure compensation if you're shooting in an automatic exposure mode.

Chapter 1 Assignments

Let's begin our shooting assignments by setting up and using all the elements of the top-ten list. This will allow you to interact with the various settings and menus that have been covered thus far.

Basic Camera Setup

Charge your battery to 100 percent and insert it in the camera. Reformat your card and set your camera for your preferred exposure mode, evaluative metering, one-shot AF mode, and JPEG recording.

Select the Proper White Balance

Choose a scene or subject that's in open shade and make several different photographs using each of the various white balance settings. Compare the results.

Focus on a Subject

Photograph a family member or friend with your camera in Aperture Priority (Av) mode and with the lens set to its widest aperture (f/4 or wider). Then take several images using each of the available focus methods, ranging from the 61-point automatic selection AF method to Single-point Spot AF. Compare the image to see how sharp the eyes are in each shot.

Play with the Manual Focus Mode

Change your focus mode from Autofocus to Manual focus and practice. Get familiar with where the focus ring is and how to use it to achieve sharp images.

Play with Picture Styles

Find one thing to photograph and take six different photos—one for each picture style. Compare the images to see how the style changes the colors and tones.

Evaluate Your Pictures with the LCD Monitor

Set up your image display properties and then review some of your previous assignment images using the different display modes. Review your shooting information for each image, and take a look at the histograms to see how the content of your photo affects their shapes.

Share your results with this book's Flickr group!

Join the group here: www.flickr.com/groups/Canon5DMarkIIIFromSnapshotstoGreatShots

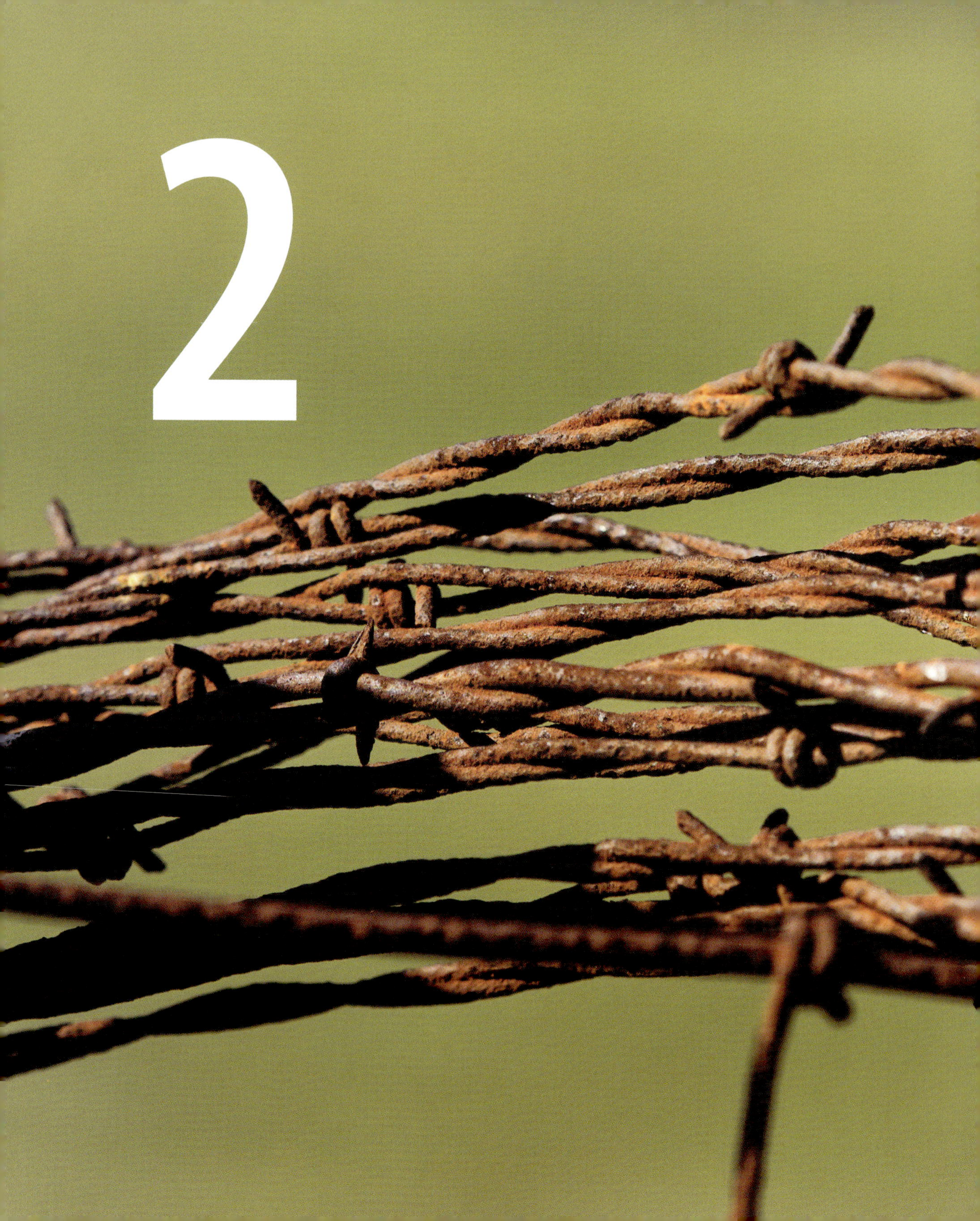

2

First Things First

WHAT TO KNOW BEFORE YOU BEGIN TAKING PICTURES

It's important not to be intimidated by the camera. That might be a little easier said than done, though, because even a cursory glance at the 5D Mark III's many features and controls can be overwhelming. It doesn't have to be that way, though.

The truth is that regardless of how many features are in the camera, there are only a few that you'll return to over and over again. It's these controls that make the biggest difference in most of my photography and that are the focus of this chapter.

This isn't to say that the other features of the camera aren't important. In certain situations and conditions, those features are invaluable and make the difference between getting the shot and not getting it. However, by paying attention and mastering these core features, you can make the 5D Mark III produce amazing photographs, without having to set it to an automatic mode and "shooting and praying."

ISO 200
1/500 sec.
f/8
180mm lens

Sometimes I include a static subject in my composition, but I like to include something to serve as an element of contrast. In this case, it's the legs of this pedestrian who was crossing the street at this downtown intersection. The fact that the color of his pants closely mimic the color of the hydrant is a bonus.

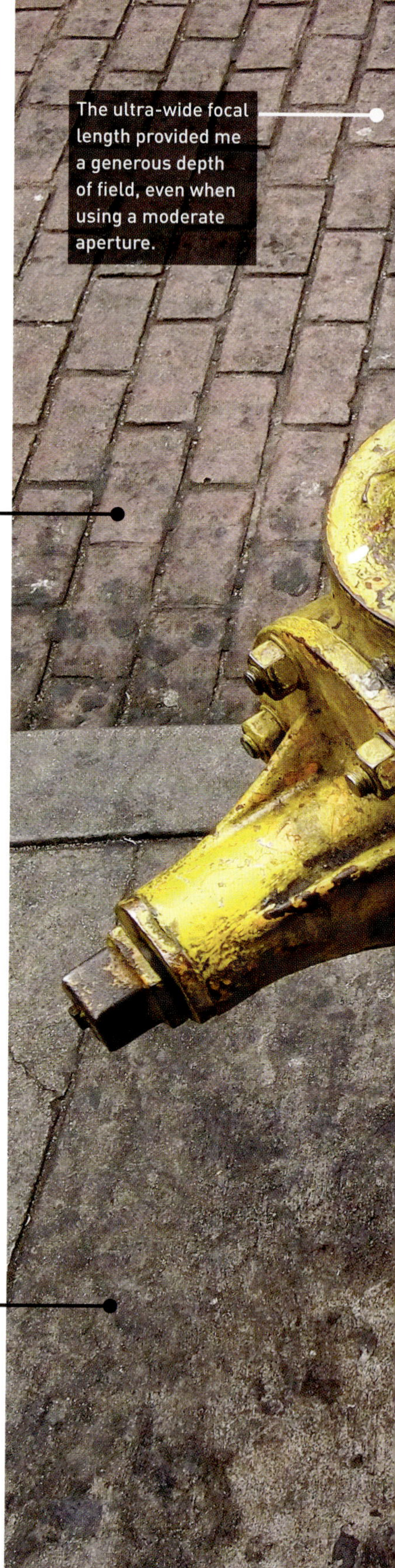

When using a wide focal length, be sure to consider everything that's included in the frame to ensure that distracting elements are kept out.

The heavily overcast day suggested that I should increase the ISO to 800 in order to be able to use a shutter speed fast enough to not only freeze motion, but also counter any potential camera shake.

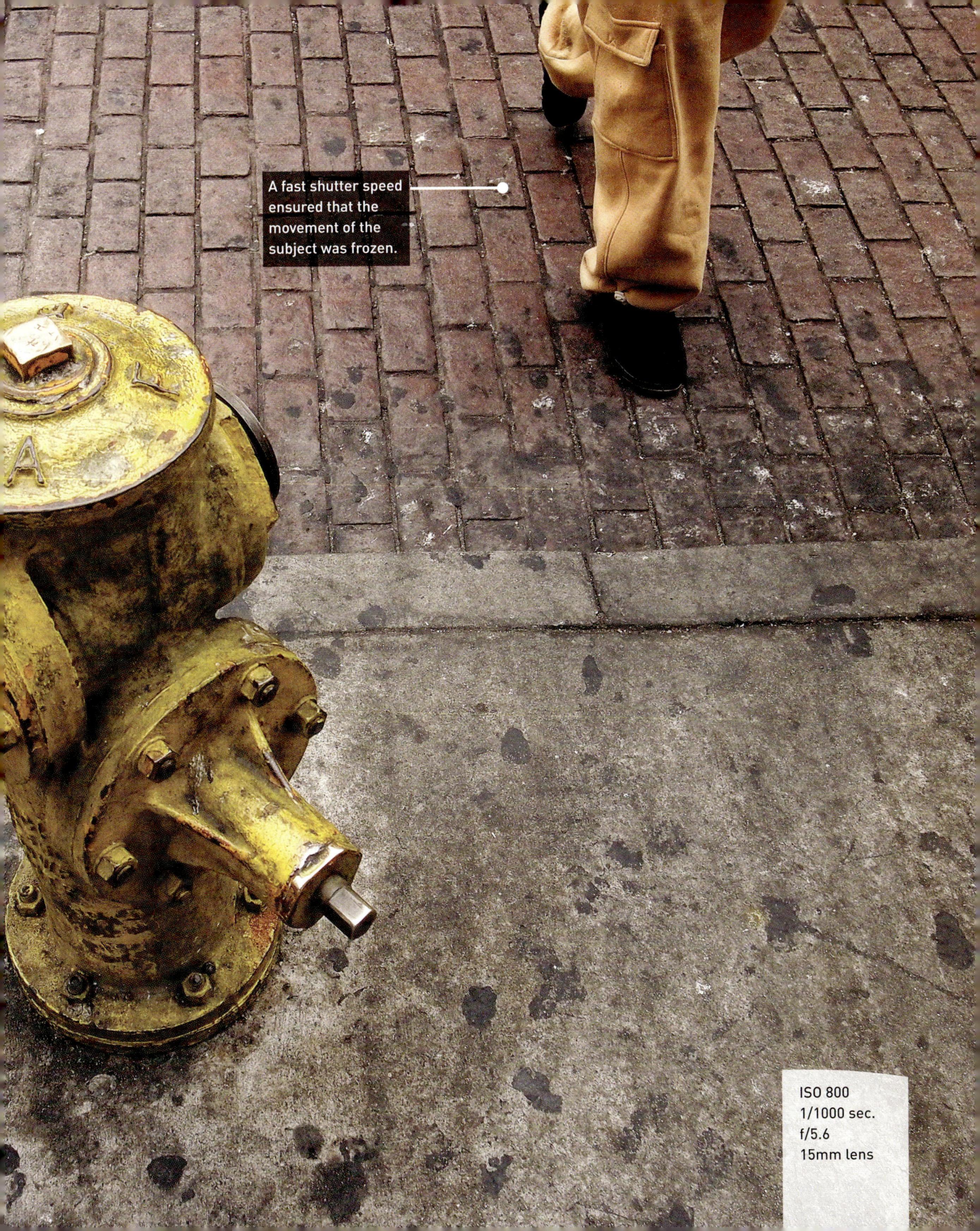
A fast shutter speed ensured that the movement of the subject was frozen.
ISO 800
1/1000 sec.
f/5.6
15mm lens

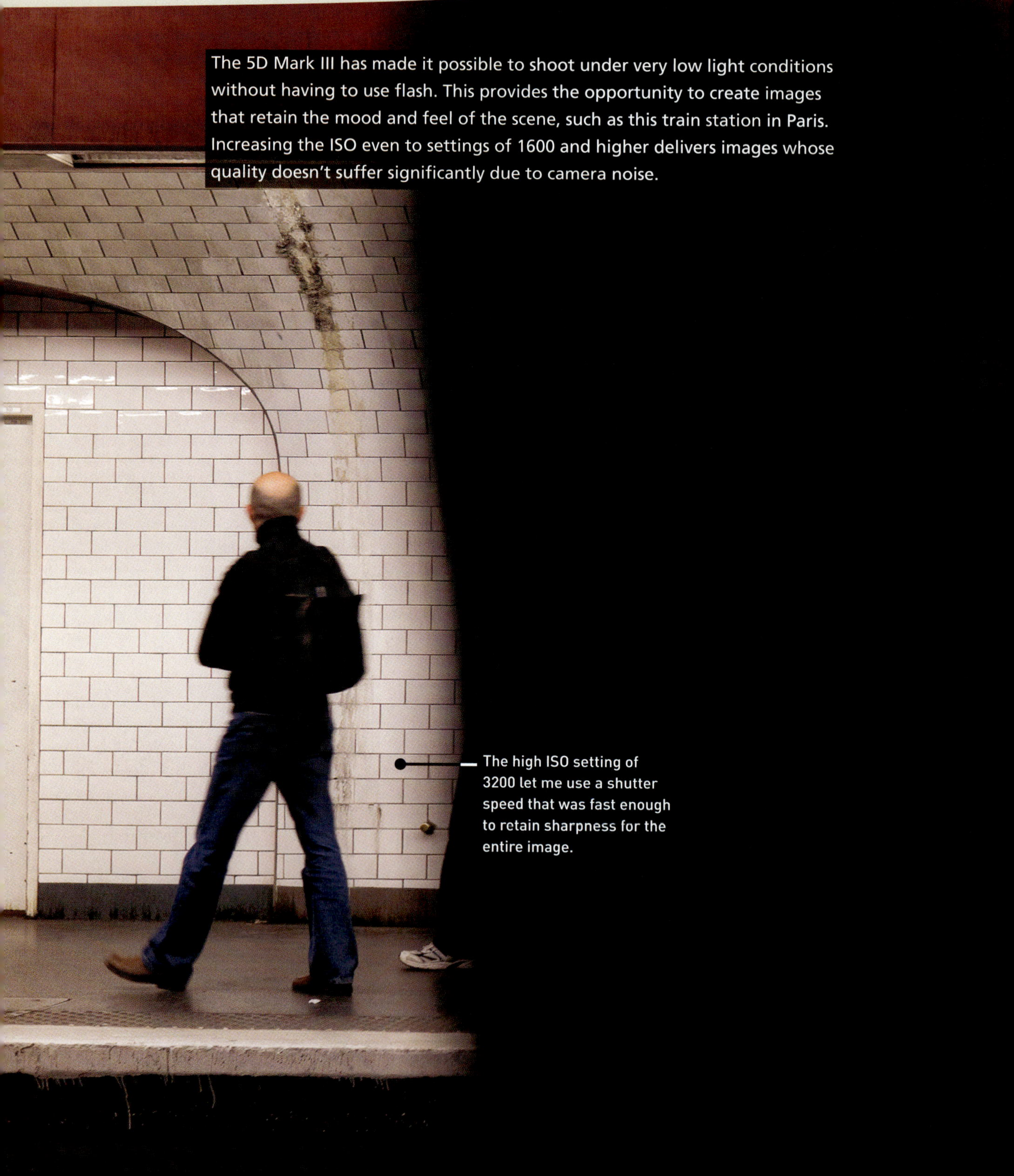

The 5D Mark III has made it possible to shoot under very low light conditions without having to use flash. This provides the opportunity to create images that retain the mood and feel of the scene, such as this train station in Paris. Increasing the ISO even to settings of 1600 and higher delivers images whose quality doesn't suffer significantly due to camera noise.

The high ISO setting of 3200 let me use a shutter speed that was fast enough to retain sharpness for the entire image.

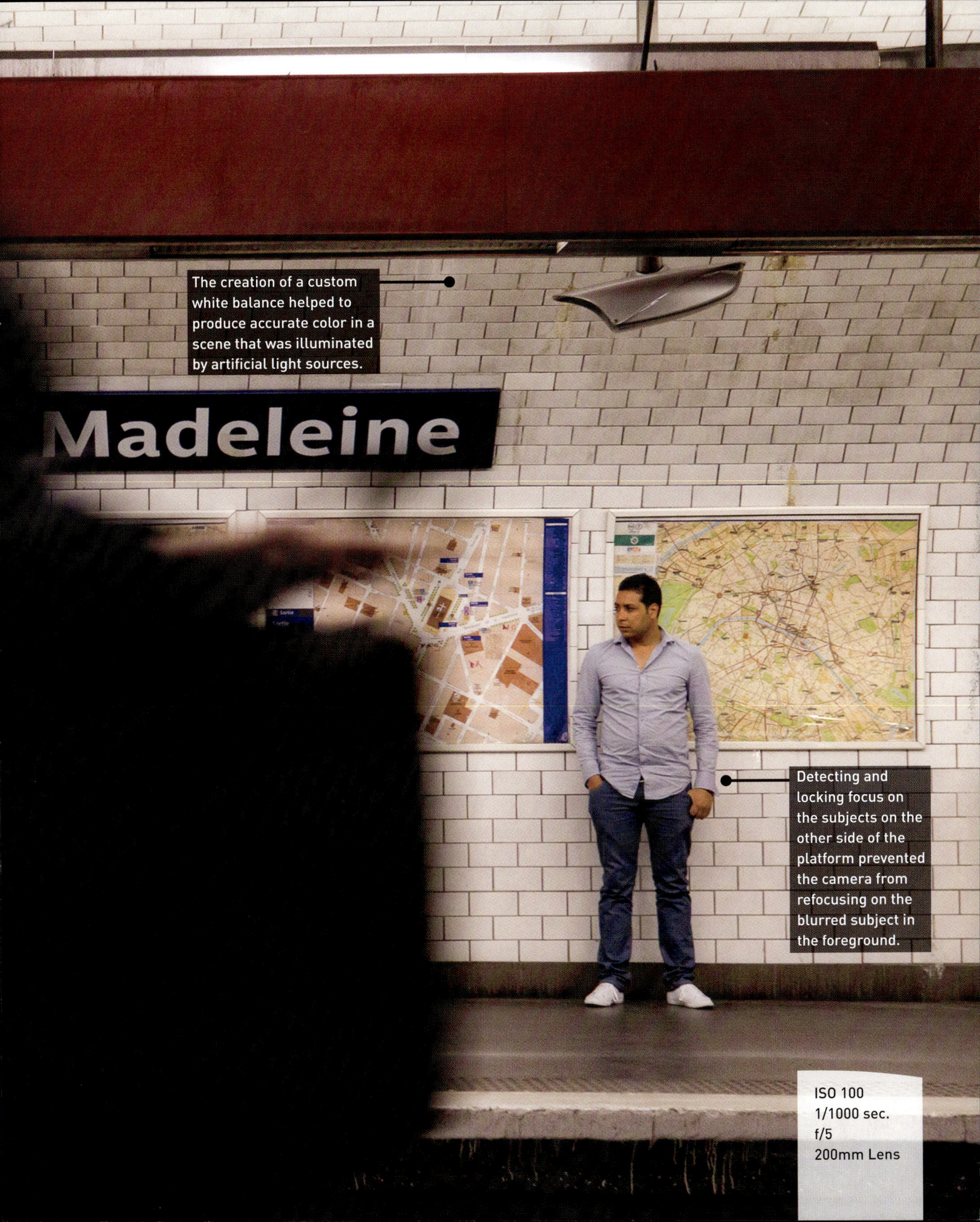

The creation of a custom white balance helped to produce accurate color in a scene that was illuminated by artificial light sources.
Madeleine
Detecting and locking focus on the subjects on the other side of the platform prevented the camera from refocusing on the blurred subject in the foreground.
ISO 100
1/1000 sec.
f/5
200mm Lens

I carry a camera with me everywhere I go. I find that my ability to make great pictures is helped significantly by having a camera. Go figure. And though I'm increasingly shooting with my cameraphone, I still enjoy the flexibility and control offered to me by a DSLR.

Because I'm always on the hunt for photographs, it's important that my camera be at the ready. I don't have the camera stuffed in a camera bag. Instead, I often have it slung over my shoulder with the lens cap off, ready to capture a moment immediately as it happens. In order to be able to do this, I can't be preoccupied with whether the settings on my camera are correct. I need to have my camera set up so that I can capture the image virtually instantaneously.

So, in order to do this, there are certain settings that I change in order to prepare my camera for any shooting opportunity that may arise. That's why I initially focus on ISO, shutter speed, and white balance.

EXPOSURE

Every camera uses three elements to control exposure: ISO, shutter speed, and aperture. These three elements are at the heart of every photograph you'll make.

ISO

The ISO setting controls the camera sensor's sensitivity to light. This has a direct impact on the shutter speed/aperture combination the camera uses in order to achieve the correct exposure.

So, in order to provide myself a good starting point, the first question I ask is, "How much light do I have to work with?" This initial assessment allows me to make a choice as to how high an ISO I need to set in order to achieve a well-exposed and sharp image.

If it's a bright and sunny day, I set my ISO for 100 or 200. On a cloudy or overcast day, or if I'm in a shaded area, the ISO will increase to 400. If I'm indoors and in a room that's illuminated by tungsten or fluorescent lights, the ISO might increase to 800, 1600 (**Figure 2.1**), or even higher. As the light source changes and the illumination levels drop, I have to increase the ISO sensitivity of the camera in order to ensure a good photograph.

ISO is the foundation for how I achieve a correct exposure using a combination of shutter speed and aperture.

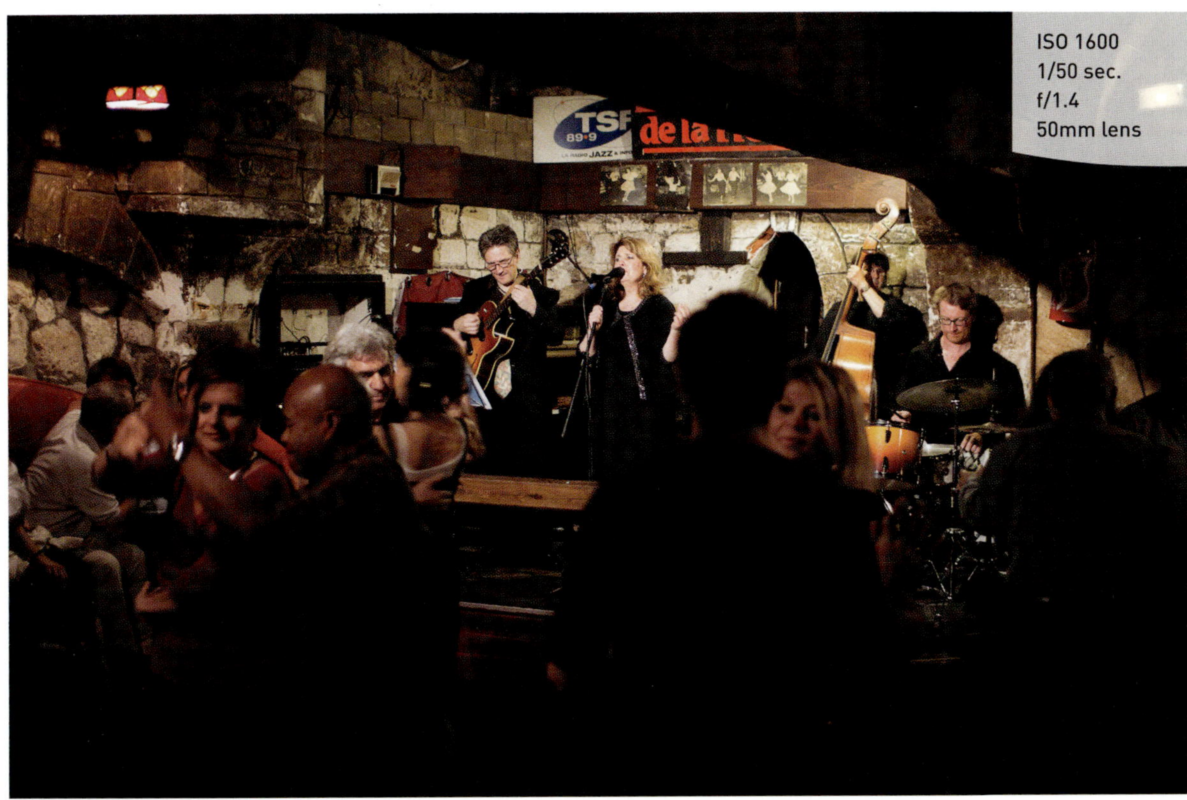

FIGURE 2.1
Setting the camera for a high ISO in a low-light situation helps to produce a sharp and well-exposed image without concern for camera shake due to a too-slow shutter speed.

SHUTTER SPEED

Your camera has a shutter that blocks the light from the sensor. Every time you depress the shutter button to take a photograph, you're releasing the shutter. The shutter moves out of the way, allowing the light to make the photograph. Shutter speeds are measured, for the most part, in fractions of a second. The 5D Mark III offers a shutter speed range of 1/8000 second to 30 seconds. It also offers a Bulb mode, in which the shutter remains open as long as you hold down the shutter button.

Traditionally, shutter speeds have been adjusted in full-stop increments: 1/1000, 1/500, 1/250, 1/125, 1/60, 1/30, 1/15, 1/8, 1/4, and 1/2 second. So, when you increase the shutter speed from 1/60 second to 1/125 second, you're letting half as much light hit the sensor. When you decrease the shutter speed from 1/60 second to 1/30 second, you're letting twice as much light hit the sensor. The 5D Mark III allows you to choose intermediate shutter speeds, such as 1/45 second or 1/90 second. These intermediate shutter speeds allow you to refine your exposure in increments as small as one-third or one-half of a stop (**Figure 2.2**).

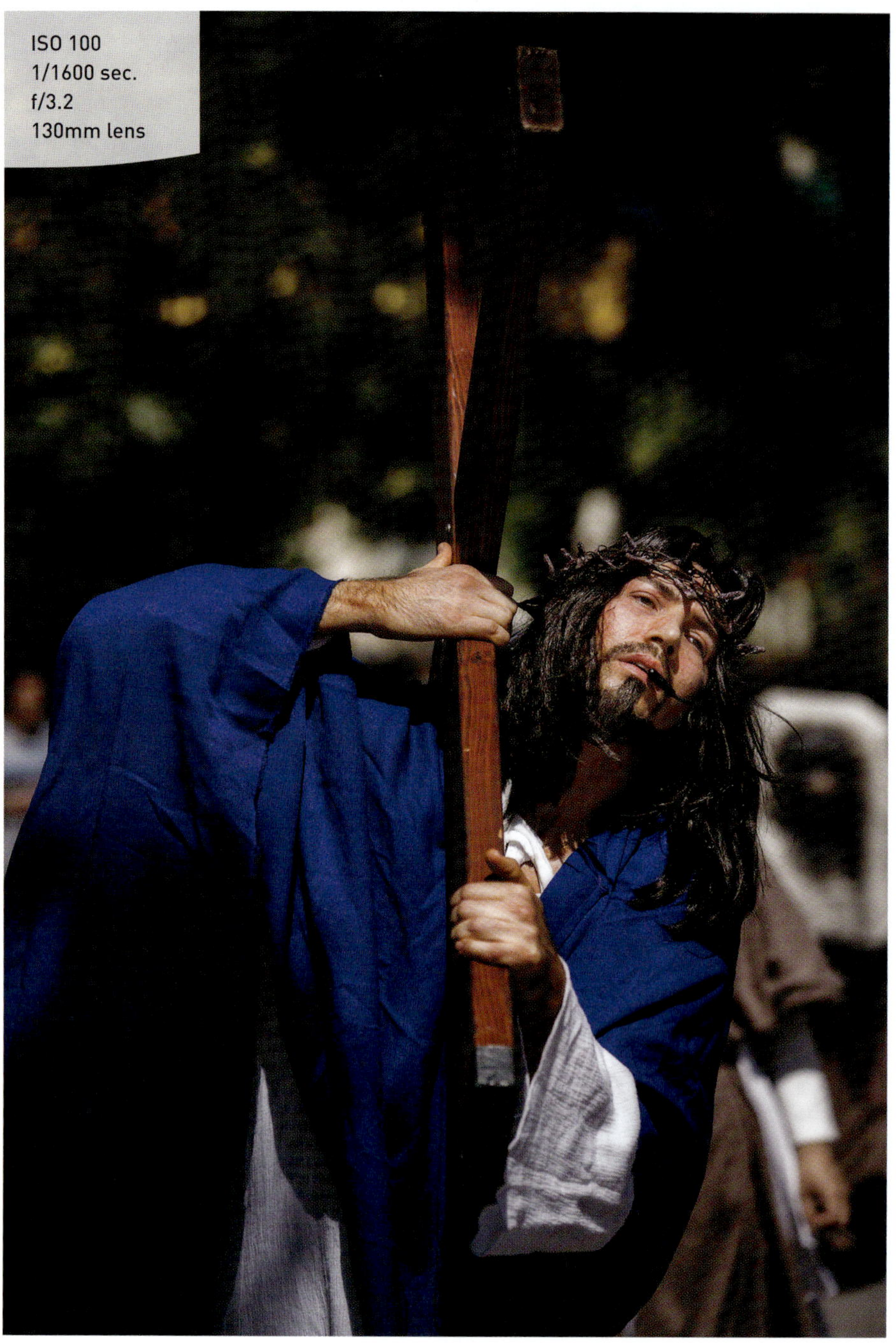

APERTURE

The aperture or f-stop of a lens controls the amount of light that passes through it. But unlike the shutter speed, which controls the duration that the shutter remains open, the f-stop controls the size of the lens opening.

Most lenses have a choice of aperture that can range from anywhere between f/22 to f/1.2. Not every lens extends for this full range, but every lens has a range of some sort. Small numbers, such as f/1.8 or f/2, represent a very large aperture that allows more light to pass through the lens. Larger numbers, such as f/16 or f/22, represent a smaller opening that restricts the amount of light passing through the lens.

As with shutter speed, a change in aperture doubles or halves the amount of light. The full aperture stops are f/2, f/2.8, f/4, f/5.6, f/8, f/11, f/16, and f/22. So changing the aperture from f/8 to f/11 halves the amount of light, while changing the aperture from f/8 to f/5.6 doubles it.

You also can adjust aperture in one-third or one-half stops. Apertures such as f/7.1 or f/3.2 allow you to make more precise changes to exposure. As with shutter speed, the choice of aperture influences the look of your image beyond the exposure. The aperture impacts the depth of field, which is how sharp elements in front or behind your point of focus appear in the image (**Figure 2.3**).

FIGURE 2.3
To emphasize
the reflection of
the building in
the water glass,
I selected a large
aperture, which
minimized depth of
field and blurred
the surroundings.

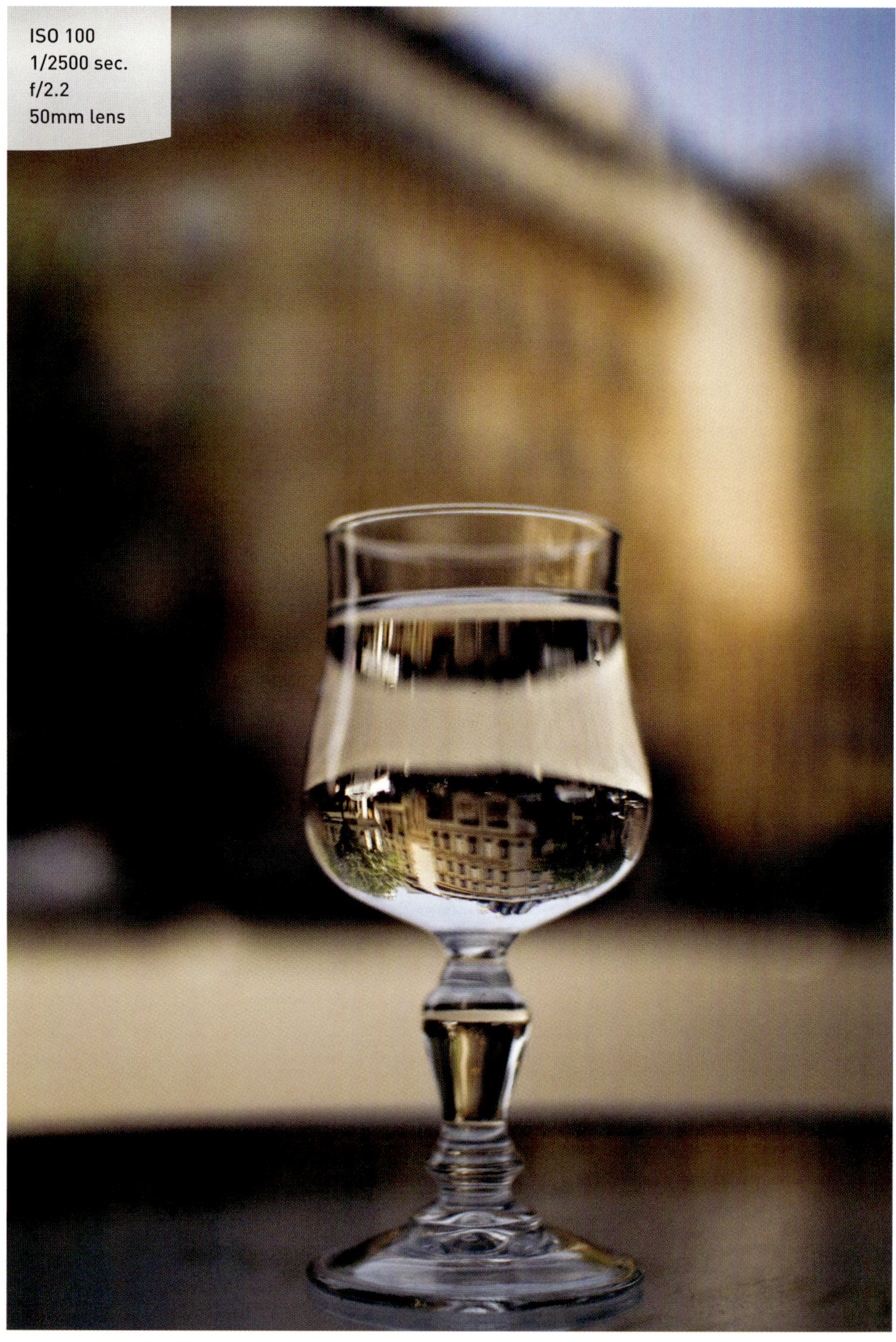

ISO 100
1/2500 sec.
f/2.2
50mm lens

HOW EXPOSURE IS CALCULATED

Now you know about the exposure triangle—ISO, shutter speed, and aperture—
so it's time to put all three together to see how they relate to one another and how
you can change them as needed.

When you point your camera at a scene, the light reflecting off your subject enters the
lens and is allowed to pass through to the sensor for a period of time as dictated by
the shutter speed. The amount and duration of the light needed for a proper exposure
depends on how much light is being reflected and how sensitive the sensor is.

To figure this out, your camera utilizes a built-in light meter that looks through the
lens and measures the amount of light. That level is then calculated against the sensitivity of the ISO setting, and an exposure value is rendered. Here's the tricky part: There
is more than one way to achieve a perfect exposure because the f-stop and shutter
speed can be combined in different ways to allow the same amount of exposure.

Following is a list of reciprocal settings that would all produce the same exposure
result. If you were to use any one of these combinations, they would each have the
same result in terms of the exposure (how much light hits the camera's sensor). Also
take note that every time the f-stop is cut in half, the shutter speed doubles.

RECIPROCAL EXPOSURES: ISO 100

APERTURE	2.8	4	5.6	8	11	16	22
SHUTTER SPEED	1/1600	1/800	1/400	1/200	1/100	1/50	1/25

Now that we know this, we can start using this information to make intelligent
choices in terms of shutter speed and f-stop. Let's bring the third element into this
by changing our ISO by one stop, from 100 to 200.

RECIPROCAL EXPOSURES: ISO 100

APERTURE	2.8	4	5.6	8	11	16	22
SHUTTER SPEED	1/3200	1/1600	1/800	1/400	1/200	1/100	1/50

Notice that, since we doubled the sensitivity of the sensor, we now need half as much
exposure as before.

So, why not just use the exposure setting of f/16 at 1/100 second? Why bother with all
these reciprocal values when this one setting will give us a properly exposed image?

The answer is that the f-stop and shutter speed also control two other important aspects of the image: motion and depth of field.

SUNNY 16

The sunny 16 rule says that on a bright, sunny day, you'll achieve the right exposure by setting your aperture to f/16 and your shutter speed to 1/ISO. In other words, if your ISO is 100, the proper exposure would be f/16 at 1/100 second. If your ISO is 200, the proper exposure would be f/16 at 1/200 second.

THE SHUTTER SPEED REFERENCE

One of the ways I determine whether the ISO is high enough is by referencing my shutter speed. For example, if I'm indoors and my ISO is 100, my shutter speed may be as low as 1/8 second, which is too slow to reliably handhold the camera. So, one option would be to increase my ISO to 800 to achieve a shutter speed of 1/60 second. This is because by increasing the ISO from 100 to 800, I gain three additional stops of light, which becomes the equivalent of 1/60 second, a shutter speed at which I can more reliably handhold.

More often than not, the reason a photograph isn't sharp has nothing to do with the quality of the lens or the camera. The softness of the image is often the result of a too-slow shutter speed. As a result, even the slightest vibration of the camera created by depressing the shutter button is enough to reduce the sharpness of the image. I've lost more shots than I care to admit to this simple and avoidable mistake.

If I've already set my ISO appropriately for the light levels that I'm working with, it increases the likelihood that I'm working with a fast-enough shutter speed to produce a sharp photograph. Because I'm often using Aperture Priority mode, I'll set my f-stop to f/4 or f/5.6, which is a moderate-to-wide aperture. This results in the camera choosing a relatively fast shutter speed for me. So, if my aperture is set for f/5.6 and my camera is set to an ISO of 100, and I step outside on a bright, sunny day, the camera would likely shoot at a shutter speed of 1/500 second, a shutter speed at which I'm more than capable of handholding.

WHITE BALANCE

Color accuracy is critical for a successful photograph. Though you can control and adjust color in your favorite photo-editing application, it isn't easy to correct color in a photograph, particularly if you don't have a lot of experience doing so.

This is why getting as accurate color as possible at the moment of capture is important. One of the ways of doing this is by controlling white balance.

AUTO WHITE BALANCE

Some photographers read the word *automatic* and think that now they don't have to worry about a particular aspect of the camera because the camera will handle it for them. I wish it were that easy.

What Auto White Balance (AWB) tries to do is evaluate the scene in front of the lens and determine the appropriate color temperature of all the light that's illuminating the scene. Granted, this feature does a pretty good job in many cases, but if you're hoping to get the best and most consistent results possible from the 5D Mark III, AWB may not be all that it's cracked up to be.

This is because the colors and tones in a scene can influence the accuracy of the white balance. A simple shift of the camera or any change in composition can be enough to change the white balance slightly. So, even though you're shooting the same subject in the very same scene, there may be some slight variability in the white balance, which will create a lack of consistent color from frame to frame. This may not be a big deal for snapshots, but if color accuracy is important as part of your shoot, you create more work for yourself later by having to correct individual shots for color accuracy.

Though AWB can serve in a pinch, when you're faced with a mixed lighting situation (**Figure 2.4**) or when lighting is changing rapidly, it shouldn't be the standard choice in your photography.

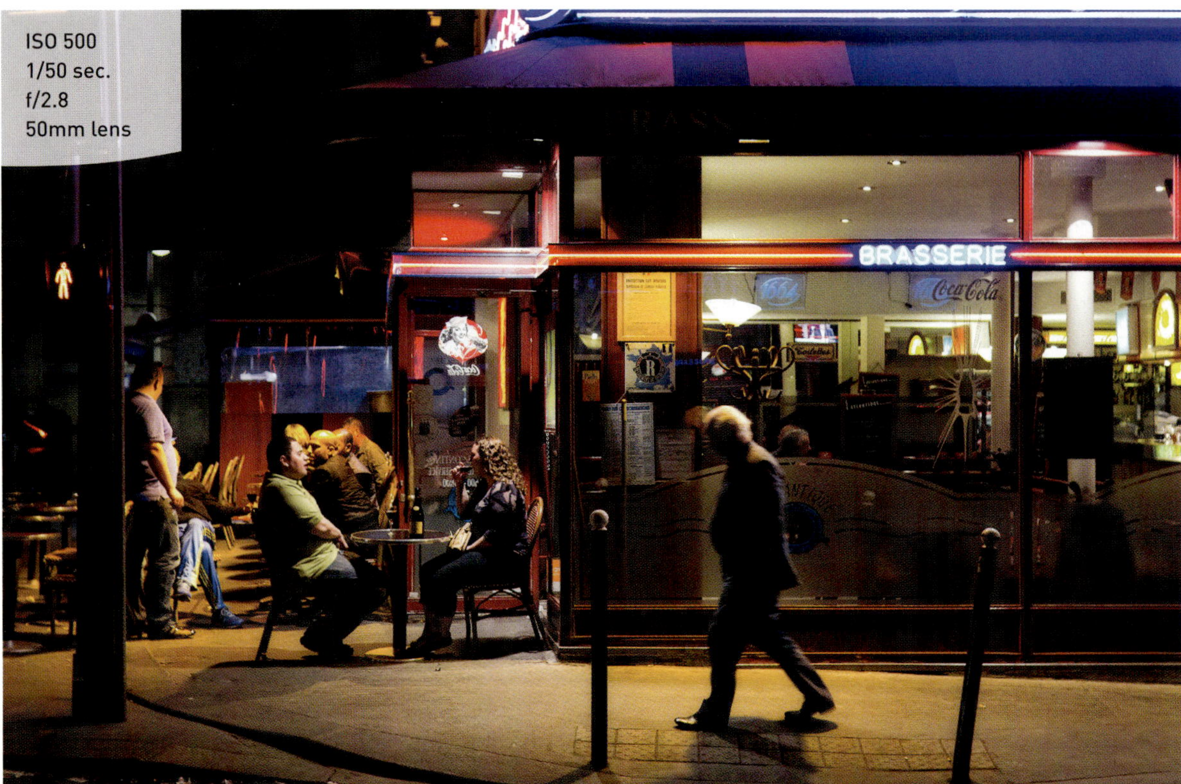

FIGURE 2.4
Shooting at night easily reveals the different quality and color temperature of light when the scene is illuminated by a variety of light sources. Scenes like this are a good time to use AWB because there is no single dominant light source.

Often, the best choice is a preset white balance, which is set for a specific color temperature. (For a full list of the white balance modes available on the 5D Mark III, turn to Chapter 1.) So, if you're shooting scenes at the beach on a bright, sunny day, you'll choose the Daylight white balance mode. If you move into the shade of a building to take a portrait, you'll set your camera to the Shade white balance setting.

White balance presets are the best starting point for accurate color. You have to be aware of the lighting before you begin shooting, but you'll easily and quickly develop that skill. Not only will looking at the light help you to get the most accurate color for your images, but it'll provide the knowledge you need when you want to intentionally introduce colorcasts to your images for creative effects.

CUSTOM WHITE BALANCE

Sometimes you'll want to create a custom white balance. For example, if you're shooting a line of clothing or a new breed of roses for which precise colors are important, a custom white balance setting will provide the best results. You can achieve a custom white balance by taking a photograph of a white or gray surface with the lighting conditions under which you'll be shooting. The camera uses this file to establish a precise white balance setting, which you can use for the entirety of the shoot, assuming that the lighting doesn't change. This option is especially useful for studio photographers whose lighting remains constant.

When measuring a custom white balance with a white or gray card, place your camera in Manual focus mode—it may not be able to autofocus because of the lack of contrast or detail. Also, fill the frame with the card or surface to ensure that you get accurate results.

TIP

Custom white balance is the best option when you're photographing in a room illuminated using energy-efficient bulbs. There are currently no existing white balance presets for these newer light sources. AWB may provide a good overall result for snapshots, but if color accuracy is critical and you can't control the lighting, a custom white balance is the best alternative.

RAW AND WHITE BALANCE

Raw files allow you to change the white balance without any loss of quality, well after you've created the photograph. This is a big advantage if you mistakenly have the camera set to an incorrect white balance or when you're faced with a complicated, mixed-lighting condition. Unlike JPEGs, in which the white balance is "baked in," raw files give you the flexibility to change the white balance for an individual image or a batch of images in the raw converter software.

Some photographers use this as an excuse to simply use AWB with the intent of "fixing it in Photoshop." You can certainly do this, but it's my experience that it takes longer to fix the white balance in photo-editing software than it takes to simply choose the appropriate preset in the camera. It may not be a big deal for a single image, but imagine the time it'll take you to adjust the white balance for dozens or hundreds of images. I prefer to spend my time making pictures rather than fixing easily correctable problems.

Though I may still work with the white balance of my raw images, it's often very minor tweaks that I'm making to those images. Most important, the process of setting the white balance when I'm shooting trains me to pay careful attention to the kind and quality of the light that I'm shooting with, which informs so much of what I do with the camera. For example, **Figure 2.5** was made in a bar with a variety of different light sources, including fluorescents, tungsten, and even neon. I shot it with a custom white balance and saved it as a raw file, which resulted in only minimal adjustments in Photoshop to get the color I desired.

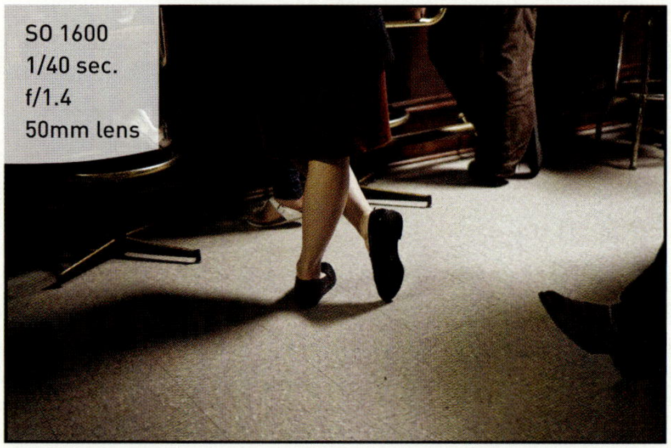

This process of evaluating the light helps me to make the connection between it and the important settings on my camera. Seeing the light helps me to make informed decisions about my ISO, shutter speed, and aperture. Understanding that lower light levels indoors will have a specific effect on my choice of ISO, shutter speed, aperture, and white balance helps me to make sense of what I need to do to ensure a good photograph.

FIGURE 2.5

The lighting in a bar can be especially challenging to achieve accurate color because of the variety of different light sources. Because I shot in RAW mode, I was able to refine the color in Photoshop to ensure that I got accurate color.

I could depend on AWB, auto exposure, and auto ISO to handle these things for me, but the resulting photograph may not be exactly what I was hoping to capture when I raised the camera to my eye. It's only when I start taking control of the camera to serve my own personal vision of the scene that the camera becomes more than just a device to document what's in front of me and transforms into a way to express my own personal vision.

CLEANING THE SENSOR

Cleaning camera sensors used to be a nerve-wracking process that required leaving the sensor exposed to scratching and even more dust. Now cleaning the sensor is pretty much an automatic function. Every time you turn the camera on and off, the sensor in the camera vibrates to remove any dust particles that might have landed on it.

There are three choices for cleaning in the camera setup menu: Auto Cleaning, Clean Now, and Clean Manually. By default, the camera is set to automatically clean the sensor every time you power on and off. You can disable this function, but it's best to leave it on.

The one cleaning function that you'll need to use via this menu is the Clean Now feature. Every time you remove the lens from the camera body and put a new lens on, you should clean the sensor. Removing or changing a lens will leave the camera body open and susceptible to dust sneaking into the body. If you never change lenses, you shouldn't have too many dust problems. But the more often you change lenses, the more opportunity you're giving dust to enter the body.

TO USE THE CLEAN NOW FEATURE, FOLLOW THESE STEPS:

1. Press the Menu button and use the Main Dial to get to the Set-up 2 menu screen.

2. Use the Quick Control Dial to highlight Sensor Cleaning, and then press the Setting button.

3. Use the Quick Control Dial to select Clean Now, and then press the Setting button.

4. Press the Setting button one more time to start the cleaning function.

5. To return to shooting mode, just lightly press the shutter button.

> **TIP**
>
> I have the Clean Now function added to the custom My Menu list (see Chapter 10) because I change lenses often and want to keep dust to a minimum.

Every now and then, a dust spot will be impervious to the shaking of the Auto Cleaning feature. This will require manual cleaning of the sensor. When you activate this feature, it raises the camera mirror and gives you access to the sensor so that you can use a blower or other cleaning device to remove the stubborn dust speck. The camera will need to be turned off after cleaning to allow the mirror to reset.

If you choose to manually clean your sensor, use a device that has been made to clean sensors (not a cotton swab from your medicine cabinet or compressed air). There are dozens of commercially available devices, such as brushes, swabs, and blowers, that will clean the sensor without damaging it.

The camera sensor is an electrically charged device. This means that when the camera is turned on, there is a current running through the sensor. This electric current can create static electricity, which attracts small dust particles to the sensor area. For this reason, it's always a good idea to turn off the camera prior to removing a lens. You also should consider having the lens mount facing down during lens removal so that there is less opportunity for dust to fall into the inner workings of the camera.

TO USE THE MANUAL CLEANING FEATURE, FOLLOW THESE STEPS:

1. Press the Menu button and use the Main Dial to get to the Set-up 2 menu screen.

2. Use the Quick Control Dial to highlight Sensor Cleaning, and then press the Setting button.

3. Use the Quick Control Dial to select Clean Manually, and then press the Setting button.

4. Use the Quick Control Dial to select OK, and press the Setting button.

5. Remove your lens, carefully clean the sensor, and then replace the lens or put on the body cap.

6. Turn the camera off to reset.

LENSES AND FOCAL LENGTHS

If you ask most photographers what they believe to be their most critical piece of photographic equipment, they'll tell you that it's their lens. The technology and engineering that goes into your camera is a marvel, but it isn't worth anything if it can't get the light from the outside world onto the sensor. The 5D Mark III uses the lens for a multitude of tasks, from focusing on a subject, to metering a scene, to delivering and focusing the light onto the camera sensor. The lens also is responsible for the amount of the scene that will be captured (the frame). With all this riding on the lens, let's take a more in-depth look at the camera's eye on the world.

Lenses are comprised of optical glass that is both concave and convex in shape. The alignment of the glass elements is designed to focus the light coming in from the front of the lens onto the camera sensor. The amount of light that enters the camera also is controlled by the lens, the size of the glass elements, and the aperture mechanism within the lens housing. The quality of the glass used in the lens has a direct effect on how well the lens can resolve details and the contrast of the scene (the ability to deliver great highlights and shadows). Most lenses now routinely include things like an autofocus motor and, in some cases, an image-stabilization mechanism.

The primary consideration of photographers when choosing a lens is often the focal length, which determines the angle of view delivered through the lens. Lenses are typically divided into three or four groups depending on the field of view they cover:

- **Wide-angle lenses:** *Wide-angle lenses* cover a field of view from around 110 degrees to about 60 degrees (**Figure 2.6**). There is a tendency to get some distortion in your image when using extremely wide-angle lenses. This will be apparent toward the outer edges of the frame. Anything 35mm or smaller could be considered wide.

  Wide-angle lenses can display a large depth of field, which allows you to keep the foreground and background in sharp focus. This makes them very useful for landscape photography and street photography. They work well in tight spaces, such as indoors, where there isn't much elbow room available. They also can be handy for large group shots, but due to the amount of distortion, not so great for close-up portrait work.

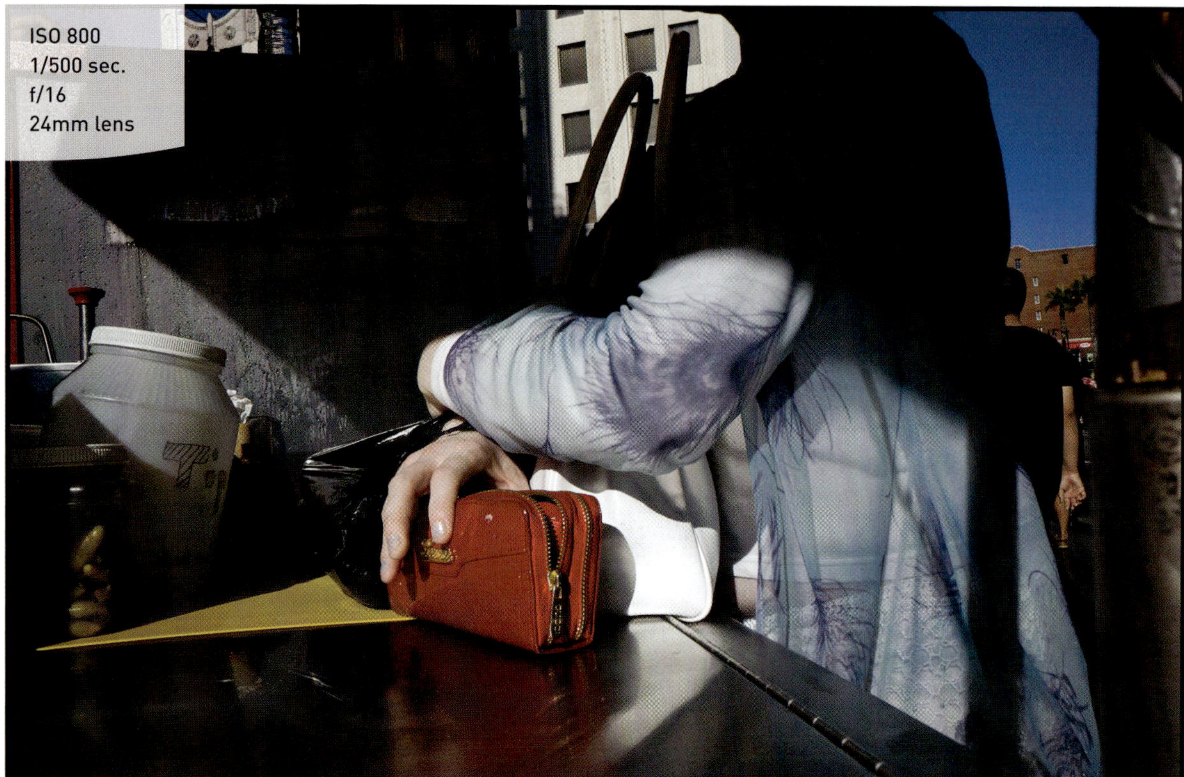

FIGURE 2.6
To use wide-angle lenses effectively, it's often best to get in close. Though there is some distortion to be aware of at the edges of the frame, the increased proximity can result in a very dramatic final shot.

- **Normal lenses:** Lenses with a normal focal length, around 50mm, are useful for photographing people (**Figure 2.7**), architecture, and for most other general photographic needs. They have very little distortion and offer a moderate range of depth of field.

- **Telephoto lenses:** Most longer focal length lenses are referred to as *telephoto* lenses. They can range in length from 135mm up to 800mm or longer and have a field of view that is about 35 degrees or smaller. These lenses have the ability to greatly magnify the scene, allowing you to capture details of distant objects, but the angle of view is greatly reduced. You'll also find that you can achieve a much narrower depth of field with telephoto lenses. In addition, they demonstrate something called *distance compression,* which means they make objects at different distances appear to be much closer together than they really are (**Figure 2.8**).

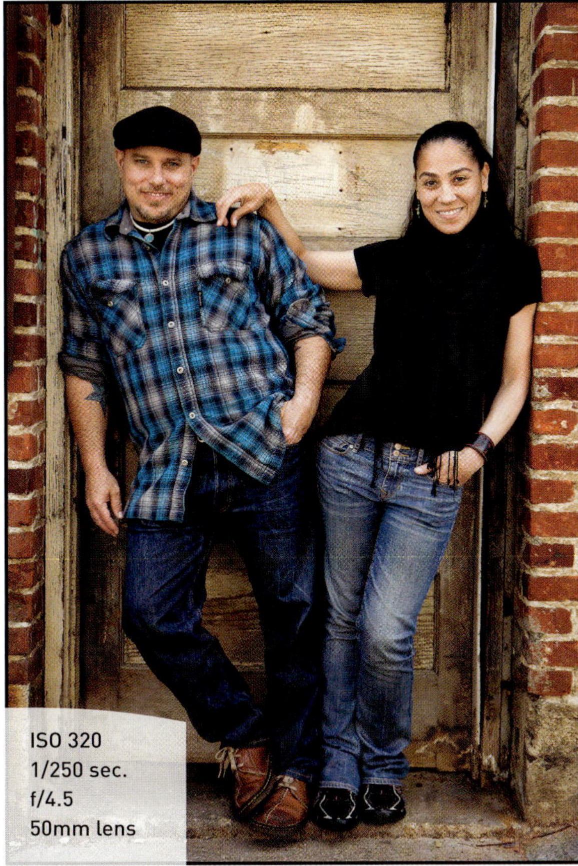

FIGURE 2.7

A standard 50mm lens is a great lens to include in your camera bag. A close equivalent to how the human eye sees, this focal length can be used for a wide variety of photography, from portraits to close-ups to scenics. Its speed and compact size make it a great everyday lens.

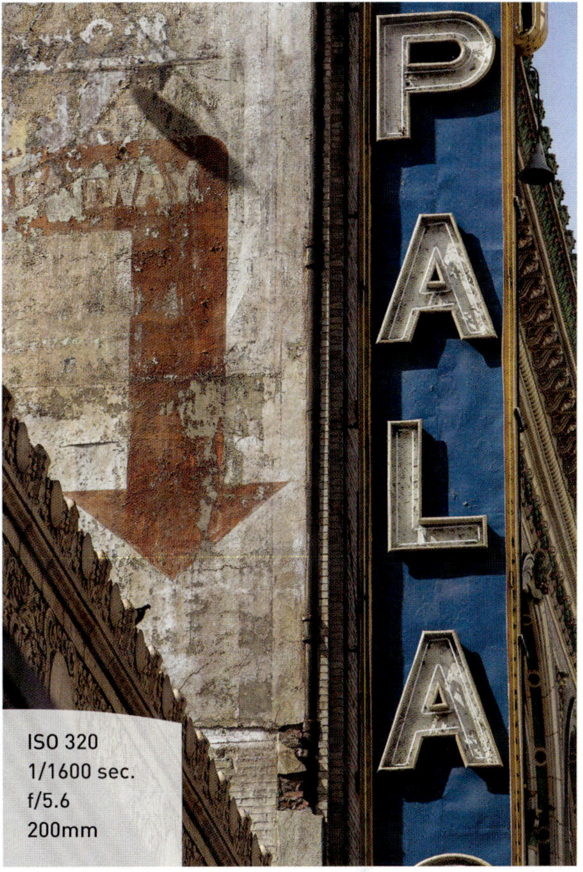

FIGURE 2.8

A telephoto lens is for more than making something far away appear closer. It also can emphasize important details and create the appearance that separate objects are closer to each other than they actually are. This can help produce very dynamic photographs, especially when controlling depth of field.

- **Zoom lenses:** A *zoom* lens is a great compromise to carrying a bunch of single focal length (prime) lenses (**Figure 2.9**). Zoom lenses can cover a wide range of focal lengths because of the configuration of their optics. However, because it takes more optical elements to capture a scene at different focal lengths, the light must pass through more glass on its way to the image sensor. The more glass, the less sharp the image. The other sacrifice that's made is in aperture. Zoom lenses typically have smaller maximum apertures than prime lenses, which means they can't achieve a narrow depth of field or work in lower light levels without the assistance of image stabilization, a tripod, or higher ISO settings.

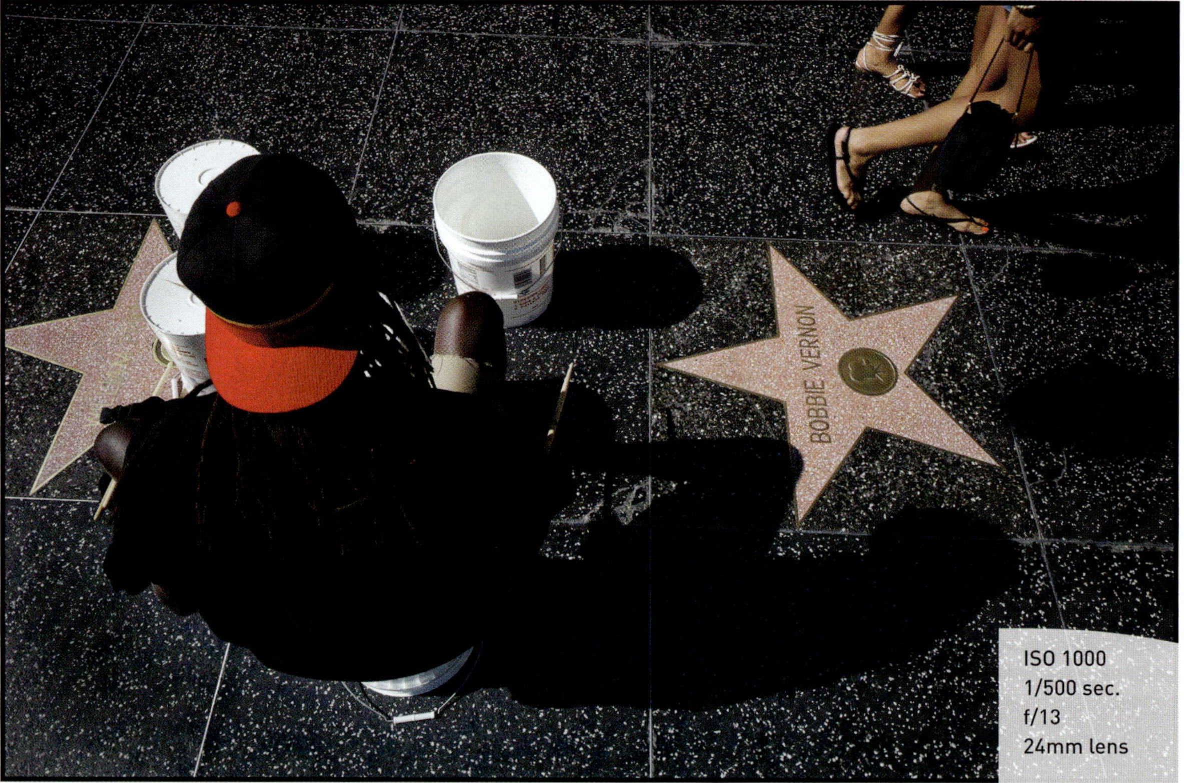

FIGURE 2.9

A zoom lens such as a 24–105mm provides great versatility and eliminates the need to repeatedly remove and attach lenses. Zoom lenses are great for keeping gear to a minimum and having the flexibility to capture fast-changing scenes.

Chapter 2 Assignments

Experiment with White Balance

Shoot under a variety of lighting conditions and experiment with different white balance choices, including AWB, a preset, and a custom white balance. Review the images on your computer to determine which settings provided you with the most accurate color.

Clean Your Sensor

You probably noticed the sensor-cleaning message the first time you turned your camera on. Make sure you're familiar with the Clean Now command so you can perform this function every time you change a lens.

Monitor Exposure

Go outdoors and photograph a subject from a variety of angles and perspectives. Keep an eye on how the exposure changes as you move around your subject and the lighting or the content of the frame changes. Make sure that your shutter speed isn't too slow for you to handhold the camera; if it is, change your ISO or aperture.

Explore Your Lens

If you're using a zoom lens, spend a little time shooting with all the different focal lengths, from the widest to the longest. See just how much of an angle you can cover with your widest lens setting. How much magnification will you be able to get from the telephoto setting? Try shooting the same subject with a variety of different focal lengths to note the differences in how the subject looks, as well as the relationship between the subject and the other elements in the photo.

Share your results with this book's Flickr group!

Join the group here: www.flickr.com/groups/Canon5DMarkIIIFromSnapshotstoGreatShots

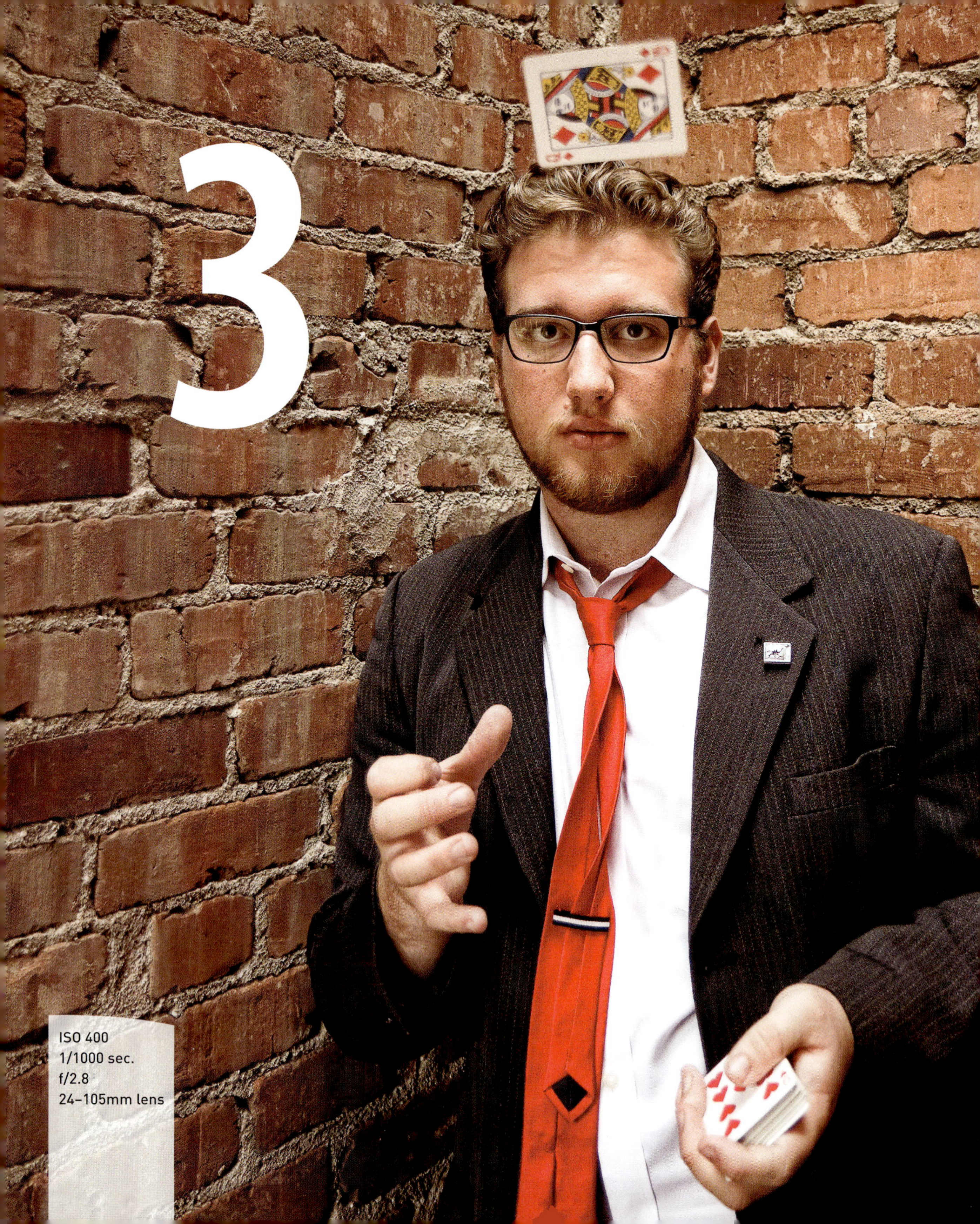
3
ISO 400
1/1000 sec.
f/2.8
24–105mm lens

The Exposure Zone

EXPOSURE MODES AND METERING

The 5D Mark III's exposure modes offer more than the ability to achieve a well-exposed photograph—they also provide a starting point for creativity. The camera offers some sophisticated technology beneath its shell, making it very tempting to rely on its automatic features (such as Scene Intelligent Auto mode and Program mode) for the majority of your shots. However, if you've invested in the 5D Mark III, I assume that you want something more than a glorified, expensive point-and-shoot.

Fully automatic exposure modes certainly have their place, but I encourage you to explore and experiment with the Aperture Priority, Shutter Priority, and Manual exposure modes. More often than not, these exposure modes will allow you to achieve the look and feel that you're striving for.

PORING OVER THE PICTURE

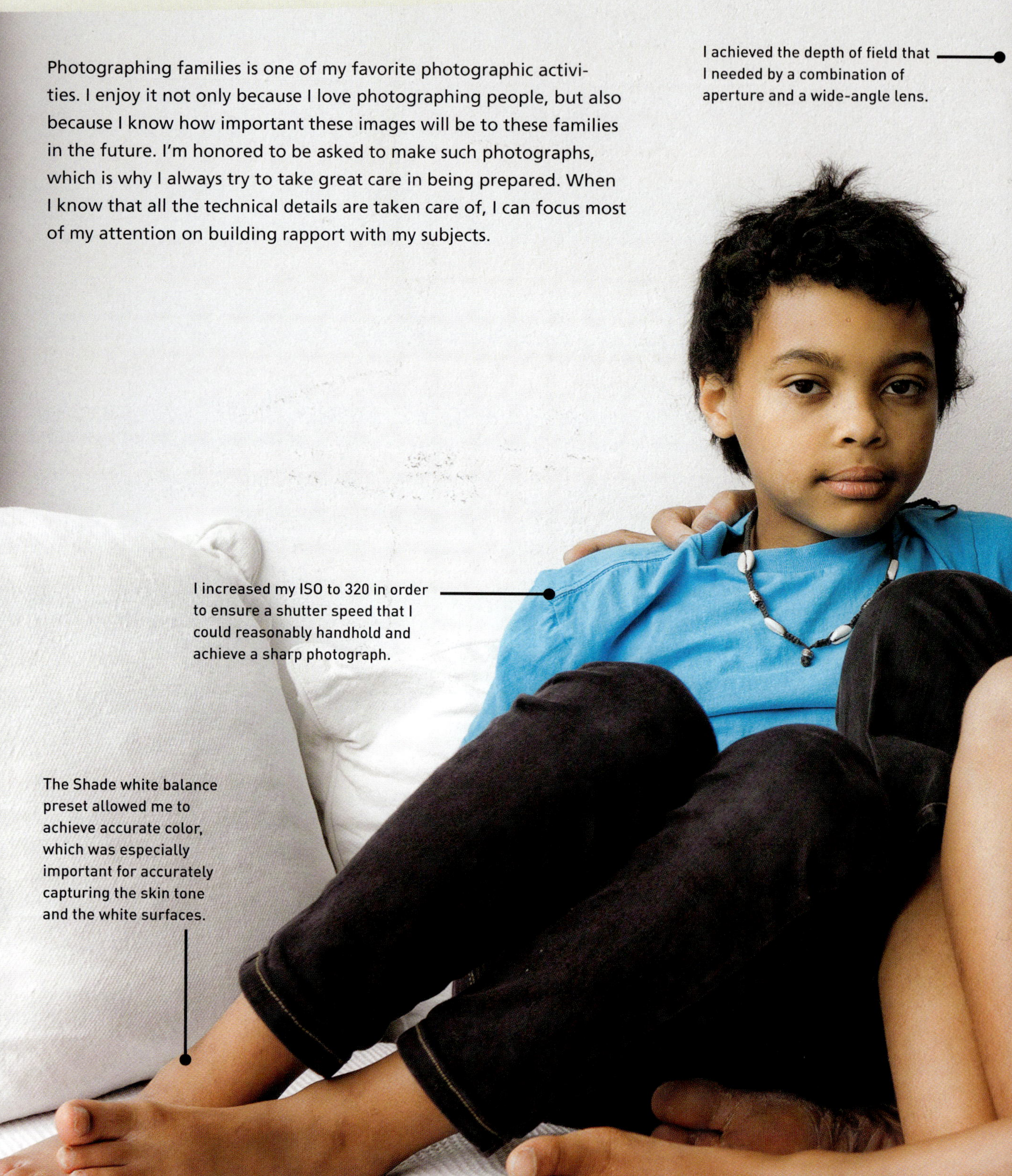

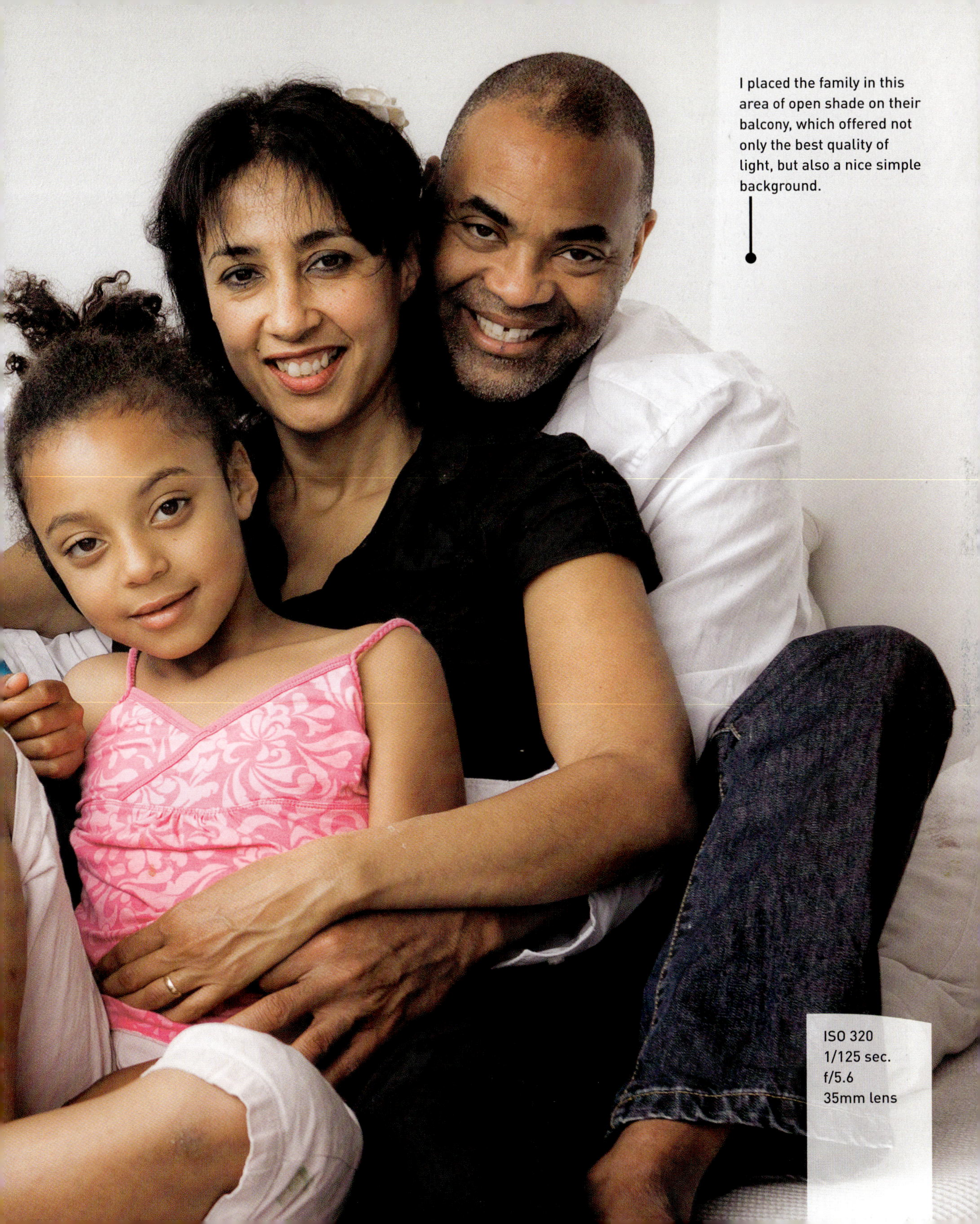
I placed the family in this
area of open shade on their
balcony, which offered not
only the best quality of
light, but also a nice simple
background.
ISO 320
1/125 sec.
f/5.6
35mm lens

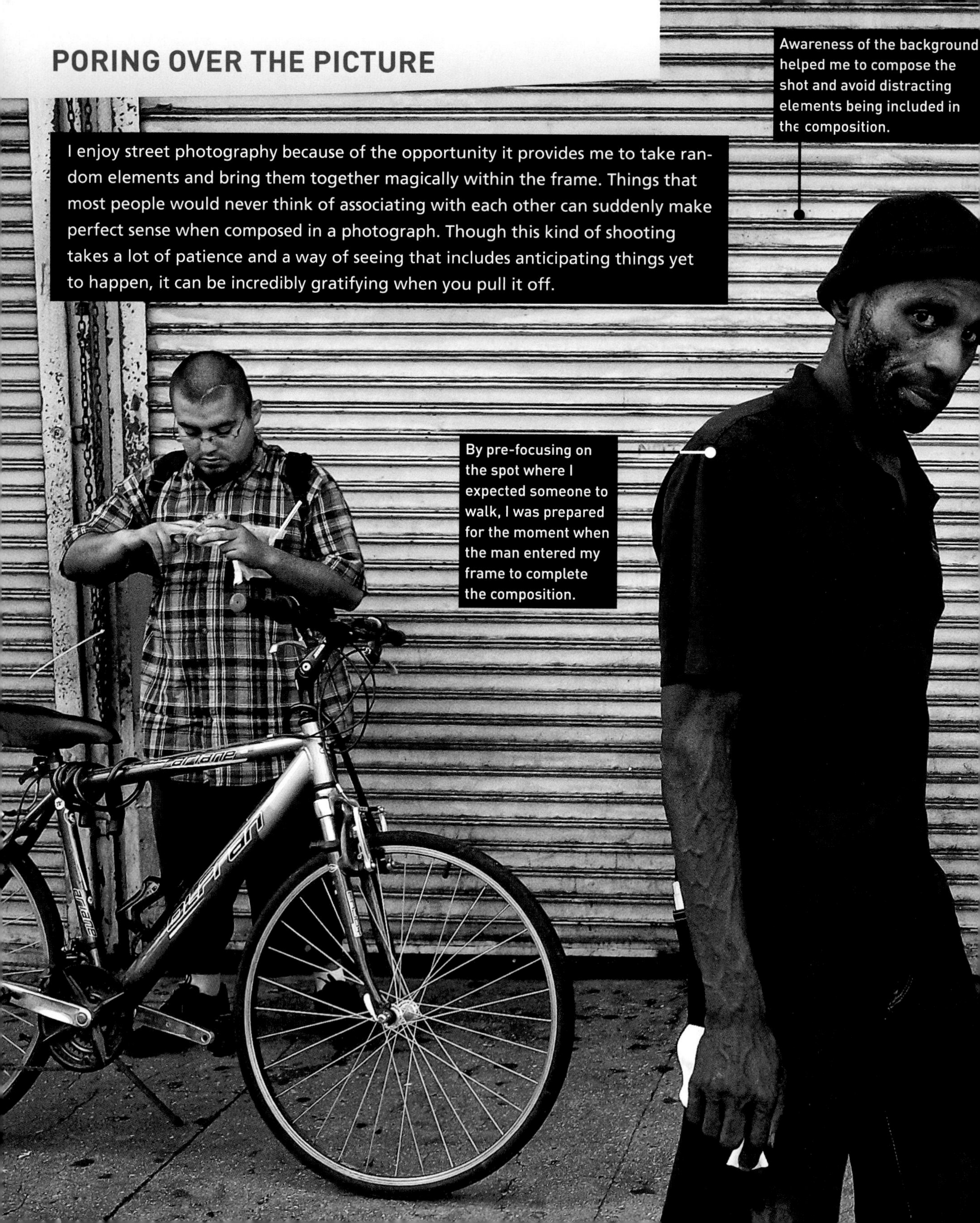

PORING OVER THE PICTURE

Awareness of the background helped me to compose the shot and avoid distracting elements being included in the composition.

I enjoy street photography because of the opportunity it provides me to take random elements and bring them together magically within the frame. Things that most people would never think of associating with each other can suddenly make perfect sense when composed in a photograph. Though this kind of shooting takes a lot of patience and a way of seeing that includes anticipating things yet to happen, it can be incredibly gratifying when you pull it off.

By pre-focusing on the spot where I expected someone to walk, I was prepared for the moment when the man entered my frame to complete the composition.

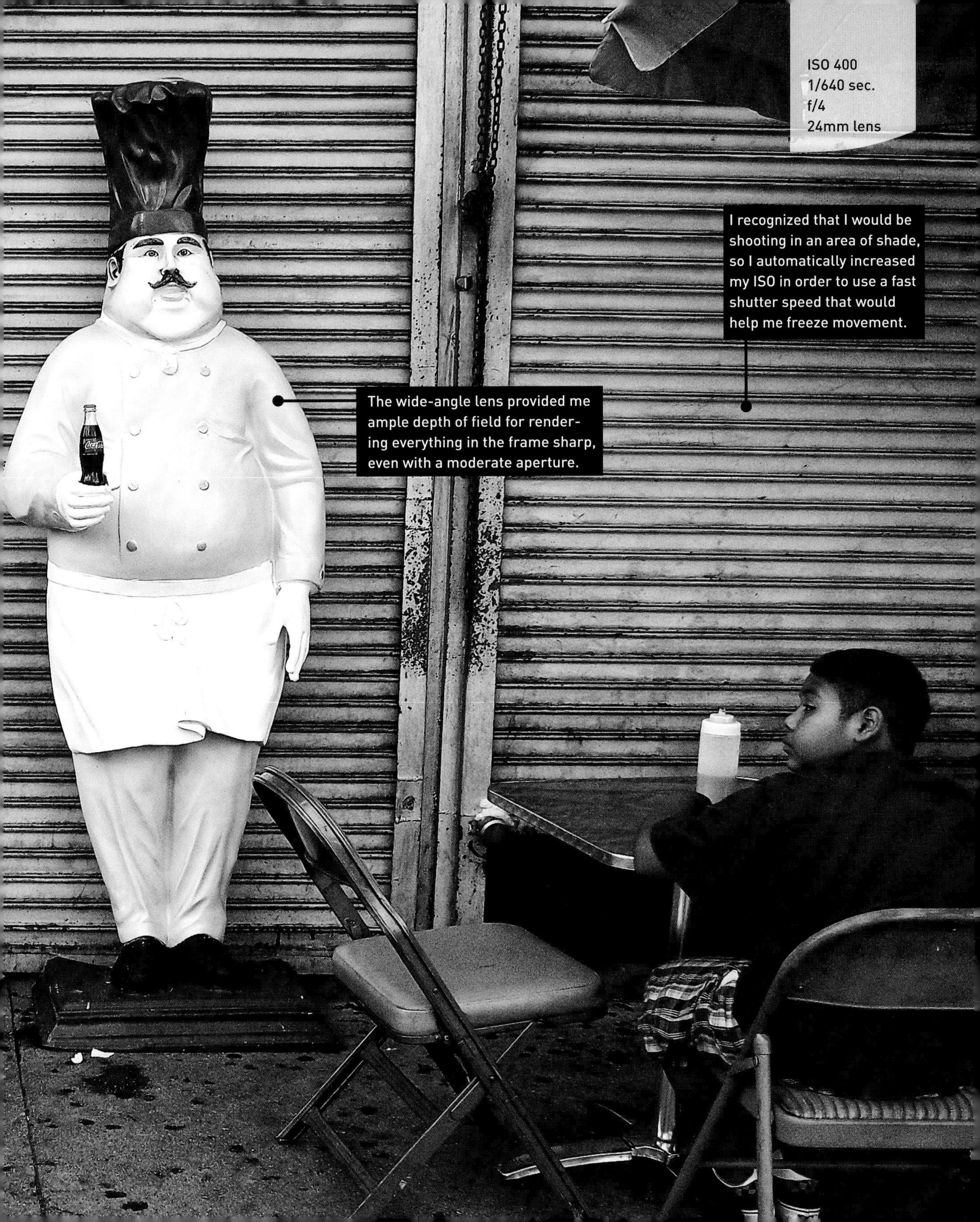

ISO 400
1/640 sec.
f/4
24mm lens

I recognized that I would be shooting in an area of shade, so I automatically increased my ISO in order to use a fast shutter speed that would help me freeze movement.

The wide-angle lens provided me ample depth of field for rendering everything in the frame sharp, even with a moderate aperture.

A⁺: SCENE INTELLIGENT AUTO MODE

Scene Intelligent Auto is a completely automatic exposure mode that combines several of Canon's automated photo enhancement technologies, including Picture Style Auto, Automatic Lighting Optimizer, Auto White Balance, Autofocus, and Automatic Exposure. By analyzing the content of the frame, the camera tries to assess the kind of image that you're trying to create and optimize the settings to produce a good result.

Because Scene Intelligent Auto mode will produce only JPEGs, some photographers choose not to use this exposure mode. Don't be dissuaded from using Scene Intelligent Auto just because it doesn't save raw files. A well-captured photograph saved as a JPEG can provide excellent results, even for an enlargement (**Figure 3.1**).

If these images are destined for a social networking website such as Facebook or Flickr or for modest sized-prints, such as 11 x 14 or smaller, the JPEG quality of these files will provide more than enough resolution.

WHEN TO USE SCENE INTELLIGENT AUTO MODE

- When you want to make casual snapshots of family events or a weekend outing

- When you want to produce good-quality JPEGs for printing through your local lab

- When you want to produce images that you can immediately share online with minimal enhancements in photo-editing software

- When you want to hand the camera to another person to make a photograph

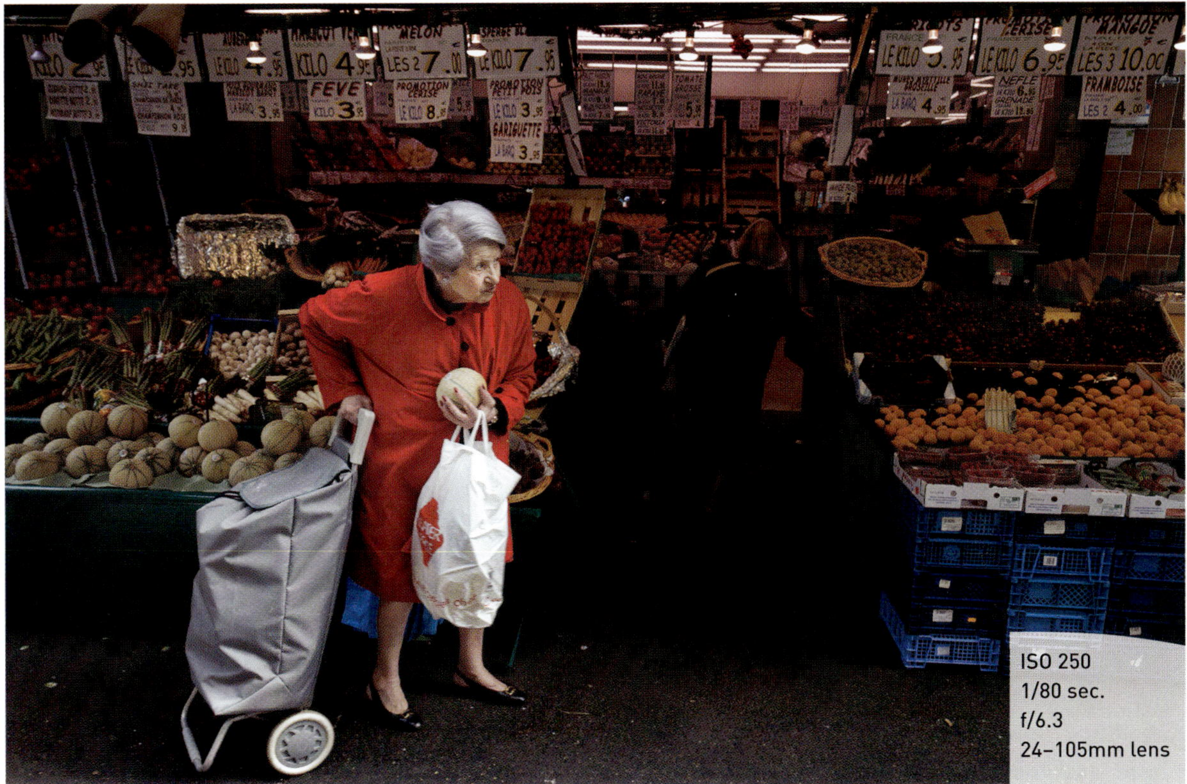

TO SET UP AND SHOOT IN SCENE INTELLIGENT AUTO MODE, FOLLOW THESE STEPS:

1. Turn on your camera, press the Mode Dial lock release button, and then turn the Mode Dial to align the A+ with the indicator line.

2. Point the camera at your subject, and then activate the camera meter by pressing the shutter button halfway. The camera will detect focus.

3. Press the shutter button fully to make a photograph.

P: PROGRAM MODE

Program Mode leaves the control of the shutter speed and aperture with the camera but allows you to change other important camera controls. The camera evaluates the scene and provides you a shutter speed/aperture combination that is suitable for many general shooting situations.

I opt for Program mode when I'm shooting in widely changing lighting conditions and I don't have the time to think through all my options, or I'm not very concerned with having ultimate control of the scene, such as this candid moment on the street of a man looking through an opening in a wall (**Figure 3.2**). I often use this mode when photographing an important family moment, rather than a new image for my portfolio. So, if that's the scenario, why choose Program over Scene Intelligent Auto mode? Because Program mode gives me choices and control over metering, ISO, and white balance, and most important, it gives me the ability to save my images as raw files.

Assuming that you aren't using the Auto ISO function of the 5D Mark III, you'll find that ISO is one of the key ways of influencing your shutter speed or aperture. If you find that your shutter speed is too slow, it's a good time to increase your ISO until you achieve a reasonable shutter speed that you can reliably handhold.

Don't make the mistake of using too low of an ISO because you're trying to preserve image quality, only to produce a soft image because the shutter speed is too slow. The 5D Mark III produces amazingly clean images even at ISO 1600. So, take advantage of that ability.

In addition to the ability to select the ISO, in Program mode you also can change the shutter speed/aperture combinations using Program Shift. By rotating the Main Dial, you can change the aperture or shutter speed and the camera will automatically adjust to ensure an accurate exposure. With Program Shift, you can influence what the shot will look like by controlling depth of field or by freezing or blurring the movement of the subject.

WHEN TO USE PROGRAM MODE INSTEAD OF SCENE INTELLIGENT AUTO MODE

- When shooting in a casual environment where quick adjustments are needed

- When you want control over the ISO and white balance

- When you want to record raw files

- When you want or need to shoot in the Adobe RGB color space

Do you need faster shutter speeds in order to stop the action? Just turn the Main Dial clockwise. Do you want a smaller aperture so that you get a narrow depth of field? Then turn the Main Dial counterclockwise until you get the desired aperture. The camera shifts the shutter speed and aperture accordingly in order to get a proper exposure, and you'll get the benefit of your choice as a result.

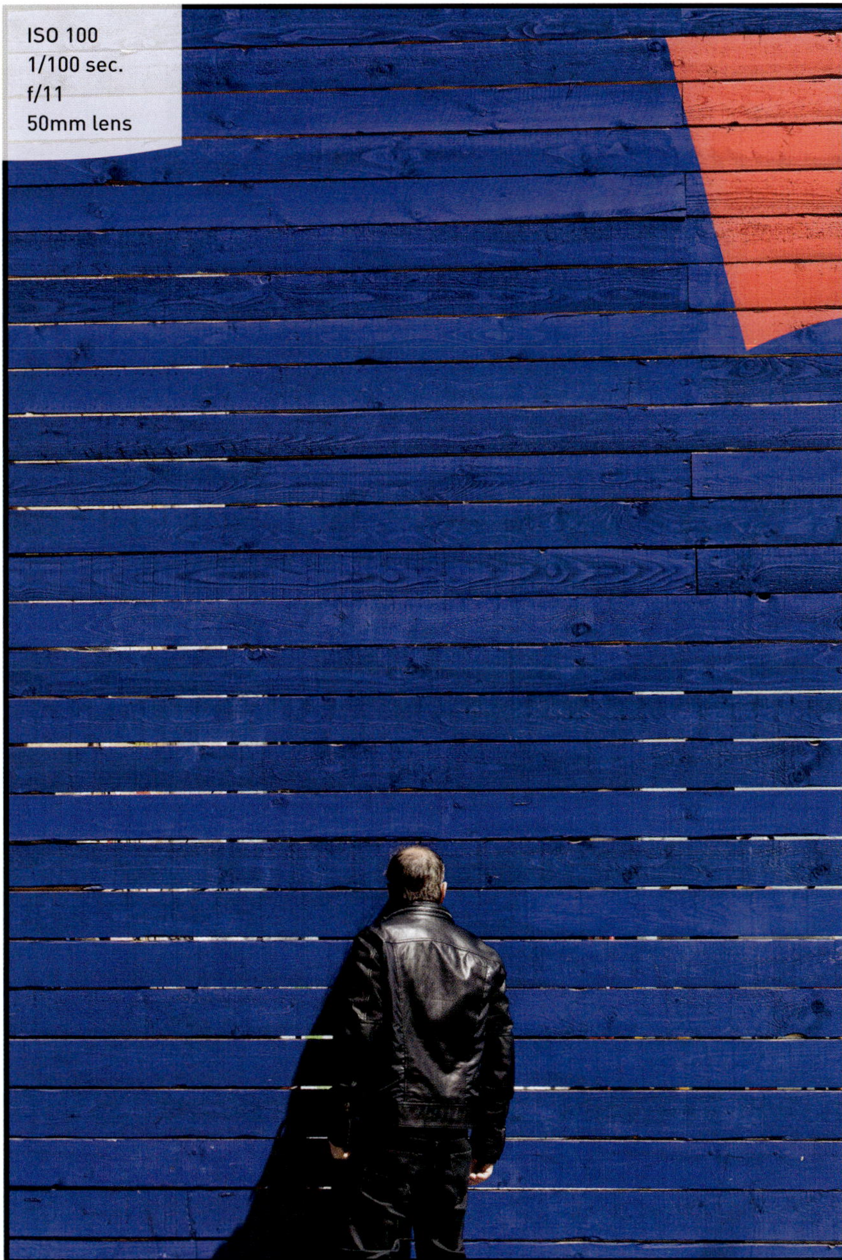

FIGURE 3.2
When I have an abundance of light, I have confidence that the camera will provide me both a fast shutter speed and a small aperture for a good exposure.

1. Turn on your camera, press the Mode Dial lock release button, and then turn the Mode Dial to align the P with the indicator line.

2. Select your ISO by pressing the ISO button on top of the camera, and then turning the Main Dial to the desired setting and pressing the ISO button again. The ISO selection will appear near the center of the LCD panel.

3. Point the camera at your subject and then activate the camera meter by pressing the shutter button halfway.

4. View the exposure information in the bottom of the viewfinder.

5. While the meter is activated, use your index finger to roll the Main Dial left and right to see the changed exposure values.

6. Select the exposure that's right for you, and start shooting. Don't worry if you aren't sure what the right exposure is. I fill you in on making the right choices for those great shots beginning with Chapter 4.

TV: SHUTTER PRIORITY MODE

Shutter Priority (Tv) mode gives you more freedom to control your photography. The shutter speed you select determines how long you expose your camera's sensor to light. The longer the shutter remains open, the more time your sensor has to gather light. The shutter speed plays a big part in determining how sharp your photographs are, as with this image of two kids running (**Figure 3.3**). When photographs aren't sharp, it may be because they aren't focused properly, but more often than not, it's because of camera shake (the camera moving while the shutter is open). A photograph also may be blurry if something in the photograph is moving.

The subject of your photo usually determines whether you'll use Shutter Priority mode. You need to visualize the result of using a particular shutter speed. If you're not sure how to do that, you're in luck: The great thing about shooting with digital cameras is that you get instant feedback by checking your shot on the LCD monitor. But what if your subject won't give you a do-over? That's often the case when you're shooting sporting events. It's not like you can go ask the quarterback to throw that touchdown pass again because your last shot was blurry because of a slow shutter speed. This is why it's important to know what those shutter speeds represent in terms of their abilities to stop the action and deliver a blur-free shot.

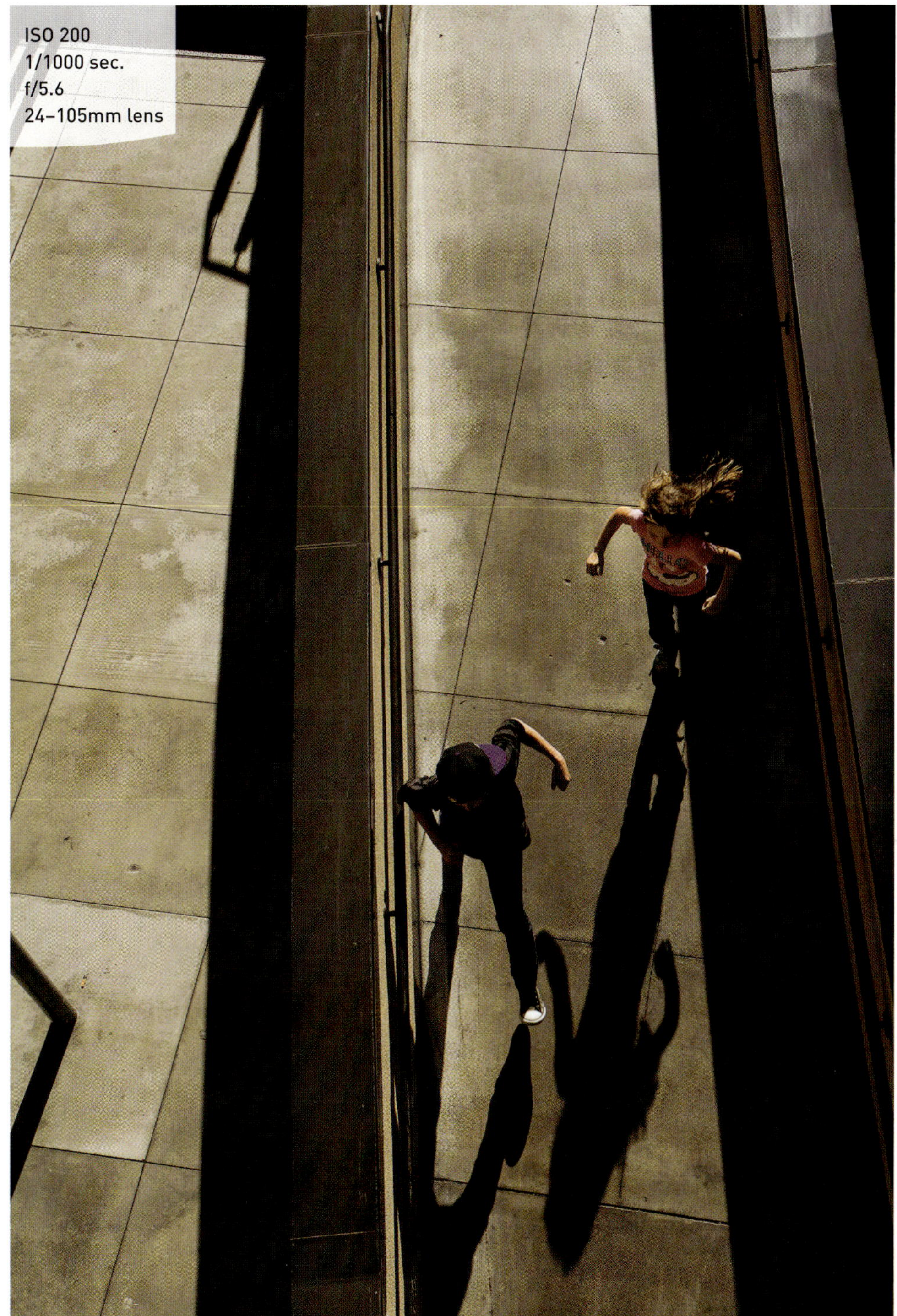

ISO 200
1/1000 sec.
f/5.6
24–105mm lens

FIGURE 3.3
A fast shutter speed allowed me to freeze the movement of these two kids. By capturing them midstride, I was able to use their bodies and the shadows to create a graphic composition.

Let's examine just how much control you have over the shutter speeds. The 5D Mark III has a shutter speed range from 1/8000 second all the way down to 30 seconds. With that much latitude, you should have enough control to capture almost any subject.

The other thing to think about is that Shutter Priority mode is considered a "semiautomatic" mode. This means that you're taking control over one aspect of the total exposure (the shutter speed) while the camera handles the other (aperture). This is important to keep in mind because you may want to use a particular shutter speed, but your lens won't be able to accommodate your request.

For example, you might encounter this problem when shooting in low-light situations: If you're shooting a fast-moving subject that will blur at a shutter speed slower than 1/125 second but your lens's largest aperture is f/3.5, you might see that your aperture display in your viewfinder and the LCD monitor will begin to blink. This is your warning that there won't be enough light available for the shot—due to the limitations of the lens—so your picture will be underexposed (too dark).

Another time when you might run into this situation is when you're shooting moving water. To get that look of silky, flowing water, you usually have to use a shutter speed of at least 1/15 second, if not longer. If your waterfall is in full sunlight, you may get that blinking aperture display because the lens you're using only closes down to f/22 at its smallest opening. In this instance, your camera is warning you that you'll be overexposing your image (it'll be too light). There are workarounds for these problems, which I discuss later, but for now just keep in mind that there can be limitations when using Shutter Priority mode.

SLOW VERSUS FAST: SHUTTER-SPEED TERMINOLOGY

A shutter speed is said to be "slow" if the shutter is open for a long period of time—like 1/30 second or longer. A shutter speed is said to be "fast" if the shutter is open for a very short period of time—like 1/250 second or less.

WHEN TO USE SHUTTER PRIORITY MODE

- When you're working with fast-moving subjects and you want to freeze the action

- When you want to emphasize movement in your subject with motion blur

- When you want to use a long exposure to gather light over a long period of time

- When you want a waterfall to have that silky look you see in many landscape photos

TO SET UP AND SHOOT IN SHUTTER PRIORITY MODE, FOLLOW THESE STEPS:

1. Turn on your camera, press the Mode Dial lock release button, and then turn the Mode Dial to align the Tv with the indicator line.

2. Select your ISO by pressing the ISO button on top of the camera, and then turning the Main Dial to the desired setting and pressing the ISO button again. The ISO selection will appear near the center of the LCD panel.

3. Point the camera at your subject and then activate the camera meter by pressing the shutter button halfway.

4. View the exposure information in the bottom of the viewfinder.

5. While the meter is activated, use your index finger to roll the Main Dial left and right to see the changed exposure values. Roll the dial to the right for faster shutter speeds and to the left for slower shutter speeds.

AV: APERTURE PRIORITY MODE

Aperture Priority (Av) mode is a semiautomatic mode because it allows you to control one factor of exposure (aperture) while the camera adjusts for the other (shutter speed).

Aperture Priority is a favorite exposure mode among many photographers, including myself, because the aperture helps to control depth of field. Depth of field, along with composition, is a major factor in how you direct people's attention to what's important in your image. It's the controlling factor when it comes to how much of your image is in focus. If you want to isolate a subject from the background, such as when shooting a portrait (**Figure 3.4**), you can use a large aperture to keep the focus on your subject and make both the foreground and the background blurry. If you want to keep the entire scene sharply focused, such as with a landscape scene, using a small aperture will render the greatest amount of depth of field possible.

FIGURE 3.4
When making portraits, I often use Aperture Priority mode because it provides full control of my depth of field. This allows me to keep my subject sharp, while also control-ling my overall depth of field.

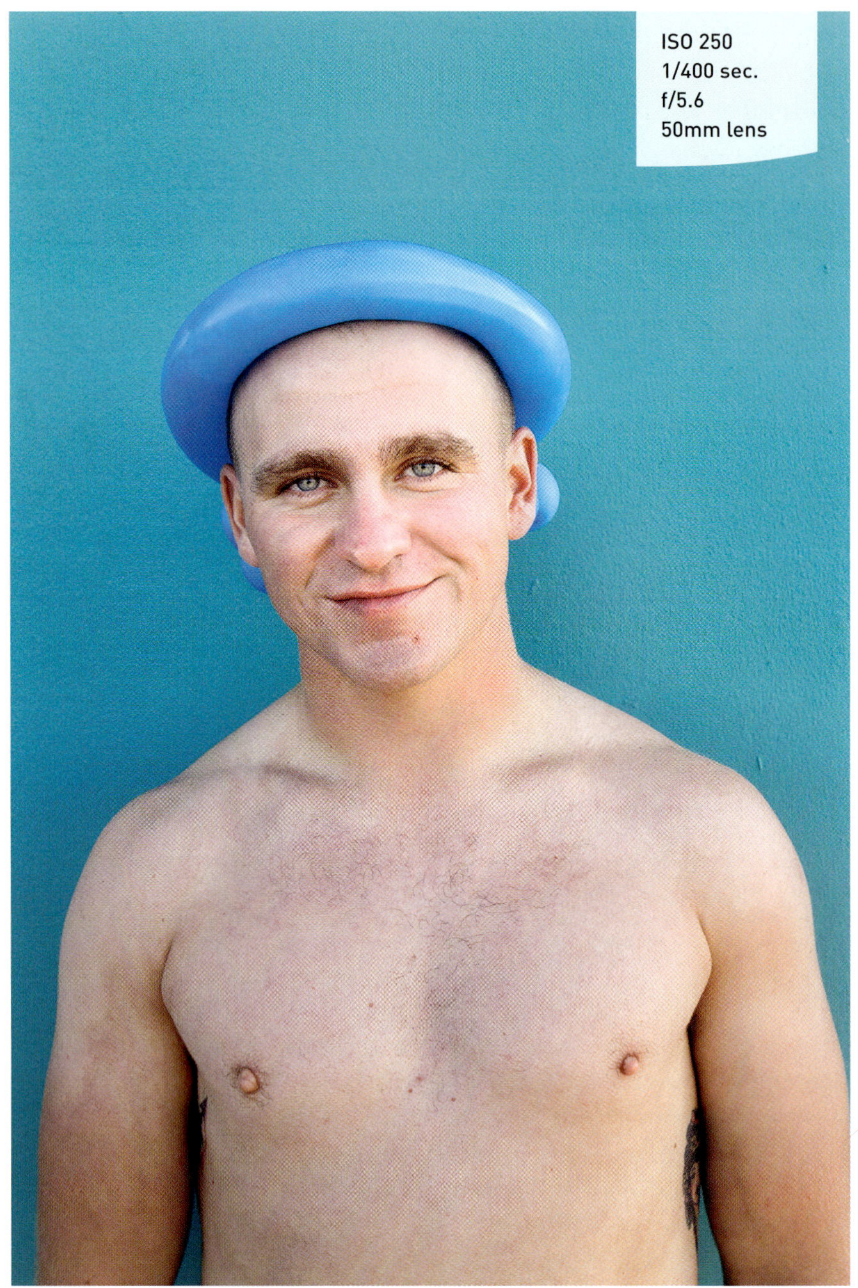

Aperture Priority mode is highly useful in controlling the depth of field in your image, but it's also pivotal in determining the limits of available light that you can shoot in. Different lenses have different maximum apertures. The larger the maximum aperture, the less light you need in order to achieve a properly exposed image. You'll recall that, when in Shutter Priority mode, there is a limit at which you can handhold your camera without introducing movement or camera shake, which causes blurriness in the final picture. If your lens has a larger aperture, you can let in more light all at once, which means that you can use faster shutter speeds. This is why lenses with large maximum apertures, such as f/1.4, are called "fast" lenses.

On the other hand, bright scenes require the use of a small aperture (such as f/16 or f/22), especially if you want to use a slower shutter speed. That small opening reduces the amount of incoming light, and this reduction of light requires that the shutter stay open longer.

WHEN TO USE APERTURE PRIORITY MODE

- When shooting portraits or wildlife

- When shooting most landscapes

- When shooting macro, or close-up, photographs

- When shooting architecture, which often benefits from a large depth of field

F-STOPS AND APERTURE

The numeric value of lens apertures are described as *f-stops.* The f-stop is an old photography term that relates to the focal length of the lens (for example, 200mm) divided by the effective aperture diameter. These measurements are defined as "stops" and work incrementally with your shutter speed to determine proper exposure. Older camera lenses used one-stop increments to assist in exposure adjustments (such as f/1.4, f/2, f/2.8, f/4, f/5.6, f/8, f/11, f/16, and f/22). Each stop represents about half the amount of light entering the lens iris as the larger stop before it. Today, most lenses don't have f-stop markings because all adjustments to this setting are performed via the camera's electronics. Also, today the stops are typically divided into 1/3-stop increments to allow much finer adjustments to exposures, as well as to match the incremental values of your camera's ISO settings, which also are adjusted in 1/3-stop increments.

1. Turn on your camera, press the Mode Dial lock release button, and then turn the Mode Dial to align the Av with the indicator line.

2. Select your ISO by pressing the ISO button on top of the camera, and then turning the Main Dial to the desired setting and pressing the ISO button again. The ISO selection will appear near the center of the LCD panel.

3. Point the camera at your subject and then activate the camera meter by pressing the shutter button halfway.

4. View the exposure information in the bottom of the viewfinder.

5. While the meter is activated, use your index finger to roll the Main Dial left and right to see the changed exposure values. Roll the dial to the right for a smaller aperture (higher f-stop number) and to the left for a larger aperture (smaller f-stop number).

ZOOM LENSES AND MAXIMUM APERTURES

Some zoom lenses (like the 70–300mm f/4–5.6 lens) have a variable maximum aperture. This means that the largest opening will change depending on the zoom setting. In the example of the 70–300mm zoom, the lens has a maximum aperture of f/4 at 70mm and a maximum aperture of only f/5.6 when the lens is zoomed out to 300mm. Fixed-aperture zoom lenses maintain the same maximum aperture throughout the zoom range. They're typically much more expensive than their variable-aperture counterparts.

M: MANUAL MODE

Manual (M) mode provides you control over the shutter speed and the aperture. This mode holds great appeal for photographers who want complete control over all aspects of exposure. Other photographers are intimidated by that very same quality, and they avoid using Manual mode altogether. Like any other feature of the camera, Manual mode is merely another tool that can be learned and mastered.

When you have your camera set to Manual (M) mode, the camera meter will give you a reading of the scene you're photographing. It's your job, though, to set both the aperture and the shutter speed to achieve a correct exposure. If you need a faster shutter speed, you'll have to make the reciprocal change to your aperture. Using any other mode, such as Shutter Priority or Aperture Priority, would mean that you just have to worry about one of these changes, but Manual mode means you have to do it all yourself. This can be a little challenging at first, but after a while you'll have a complete understanding of how each change affects your exposure, which will, in turn, improve the way that you use the other modes. This is especially important when shooting subject that are largely dark or light (**Figure 3.5**).

I recommend always starting with the value that's more important to you. If depth of field is primary, you set the aperture first. If rendering motion is more important, then you set your preferred shutter speed. With that as your base point, you can control the shutter speed or aperture respectively in order to produce a good exposure using the exposure level indicator located at the bottom of the viewfinder or at the lower left-hand corner of the LCD panel.

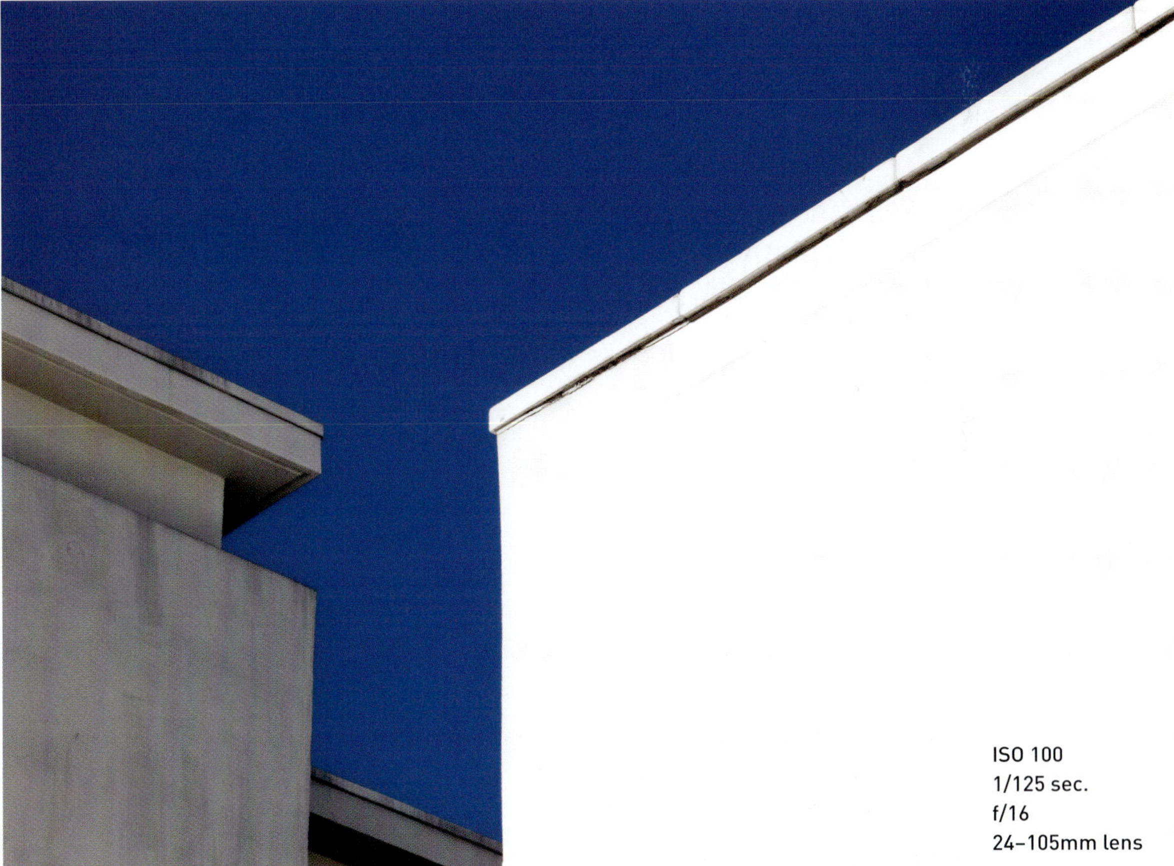

- When you're learning how each exposure element interacts with the others

- When your environment is fooling your light meter and you need to maintain a certain exposure setting

- When you're shooting silhouetted subjects, which requires overriding the camera's meter readings

- When autoexposure modes can't provide precise and consistent results

TO SET UP AND SHOOT IN MANUAL MODE, FOLLOW THESE STEPS:

1. Turn on your camera, press the Mode Dial lock release button, and then turn the Mode Dial to align the M with the indicator line.

2. Select your ISO by pressing the ISO button on top of the camera, and then turning the Main Dial to the desired setting and pressing the ISO button again. The ISO selection will appear near the center of the LCD panel.

3. Point the camera at your subject and then activate the camera meter by pressing the shutter button halfway.

4. View the exposure information in the bottom of the viewfinder.

5. While the meter is activated, use your index finger to roll the Main Dial left and right to change your shutter speed value until the exposure mark is lined up with the zero mark. The exposure information is displayed by a scale with marks that run from –3 to +3 stops. A "proper" exposure will line up with the arrow mark in the middle. As the indicator moves to the left, it's a sign that you'll be underexposing (there isn't enough light hitting the sensor to provide adequate exposure). Move the indicator to the right and you'll be providing more exposure than the camera meter calls for; this is overexposure.

6. To set your exposure using the aperture, press the shutter button until the meter is activated. Then, using your thumb, hold in the Av button on the back of the camera and use your index finger to turn the Main Dial right for a smaller aperture (large f-stop number) or left for a larger aperture (small f-stop number).

CUSTOM USER MODES C1, C2, AND C3

The 5D Mark III's Mode Dial also offers three custom user-mode settings. These allow you to save a combination of settings for such things such as white balance, picture style, drive mode, metering, and more. If you have certain settings that you return to frequently for particular types of shooting (such as portraiture, black and white, or close-up photography), you'll find the custom user modes handy.

EXPOSURE LOCK

The camera's meter is constantly active. So, as you move the camera, the shutter speed/aperture combination will adjust as the contents of the scene change when you're in Program, Aperture Priority, and Shutter Priority modes. (In Manual mode, the meter indicator will change, but the shutter speed and aperture will remain unchanged.) This change is a good thing in most situations, but sometimes you'll want to recompose the image without it resulting in a change of exposure. You can achieve this by locking the exposure.

When you depress the AE lock button, the exposure will be locked, resulting in the shutter speed and aperture remaining fixed, even if the light levels change. Locking the exposure is a good choice if you want to compose your subject off-center, but you don't want a bright or dark area in the balance of the frame to adversely influence the exposure. The exposure lock will remain active even after releasing the AE lock button and until the camera goes to sleep. When it's active, you'll see an asterisk symbol to the right of the battery indicator in the viewfinder. Exposure lock can help you handle high-contrast situations that may otherwise fool the camera's meter (**Figure 3.6**).

This street cleaner would have been overexposed in a composition with so much shadow. But by metering the scene using the camera's spot metering mode and locking the exposure, I achieved the look I was hoping for.

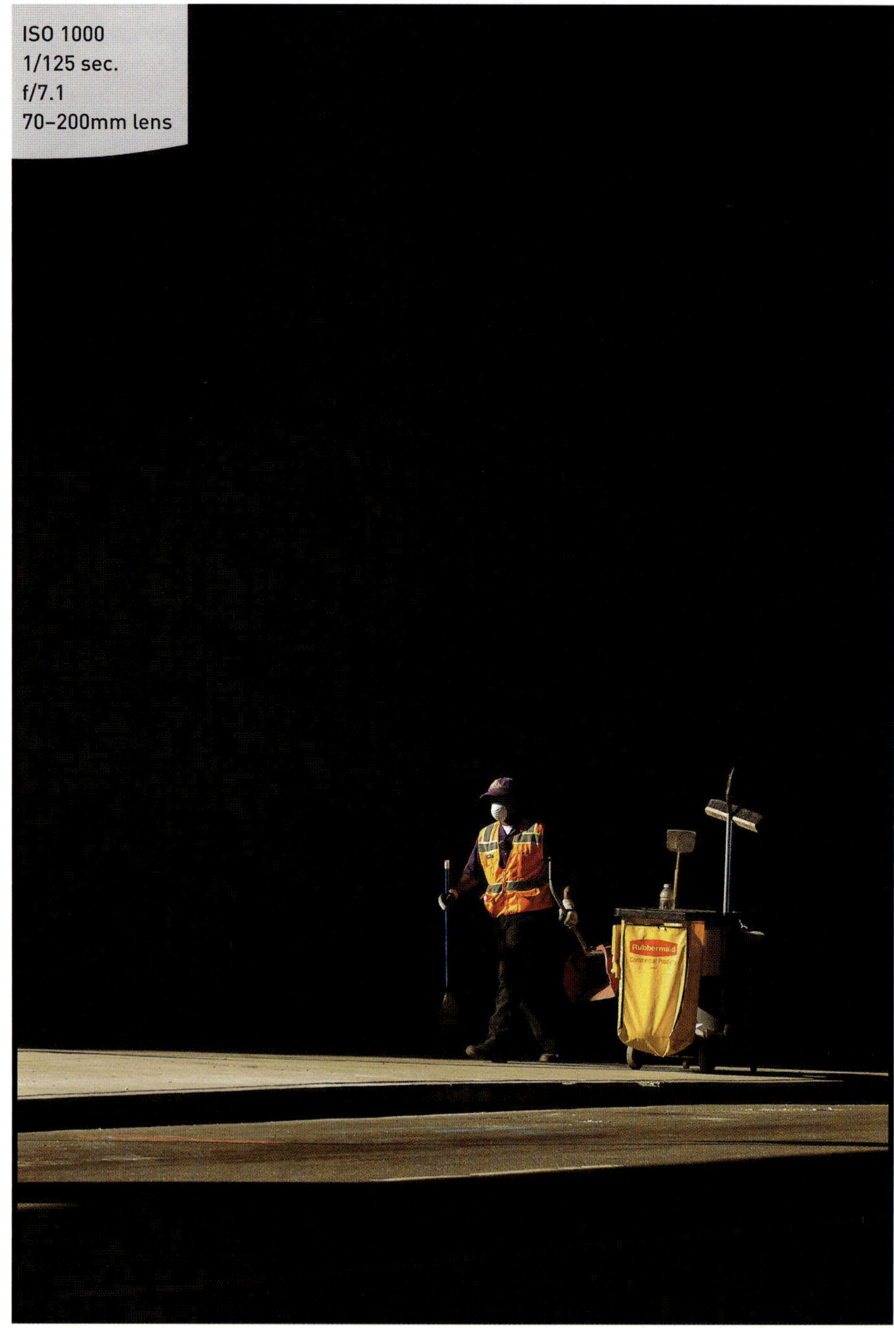

1. Turn on your camera, press the Mode Dial lock release button, and then turn the Mode Dial to your preferred automatic exposure mode (P, Av, or Tv).

2. Press the shutter button halfway to activate the meter and note the shutter speed/aperture combination being suggested by the camera's metering system.

3. Press and release the AE lock button to lock the current exposure.

4. Press the shutter button to make your photographs.

EXPOSURE COMPENSATION

The 5D Mark III metering options can be amazingly accurate, but sometimes they can be fooled. The camera may deliver an exposure that's quite good but doesn't fit with how you want the final image to look. In such situations, you have the ability to adjust the exposure when using Program, Aperture Priority, or Shutter Priority modes. This is called exposure compensation.

Using the Quick Control Dial on the back of the camera, you can decrease or increase the exposure in increments of 1/3 stop. Rotating the Quick Command Dial counter-clockwise reduces the exposure; rotating it clockwise increases the exposure. The amount of compensation that's being applied can be seen both in the viewfinder, as well as on the LCD panel.

When you're in Program mode, the amount of compensation may impact both the shutter speed and aperture. In Aperture Priority, the camera will apply the compensation by changing the shutter speed; in Shutter Priority, the camera will change the aperture. For example, let's assume you're in Aperture Priority mode and the camera is providing an exposure of 1/125 second at f/5.6, but when you review the image, the subject looks too dark. By increasing the exposure by +1 using exposure compensation, the shutter speed is reduced to 1/60 second, the equivalent of one stop of exposure. So, now the image is shot at 1/60 second at f/5.6.

If you're using Manual mode, you have complete autonomy over the shutter speed and aperture, so neither exposure value will be adjusted automatically for you. However, you can still apply exposure compensation to bias the meter if you want to purposefully bias the exposure. So, by setting a +1, as you refer to the meter when adjusting your shutter speed and aperture, your final exposure will reflect the +1 compensation that you dialed in, as you would do with a subject or scene that is pre-dominantly white (**Figure 3.7**).

FIGURE 3.7
This white wall and
futon could have
easily fooled the
camera's meter,
resulting in an
underexposed
image. By adjust-
ing the exposure
using the camera's
exposure compen-
sation feature, I
could easily achieve
a spot-on exposure
for this portrait.

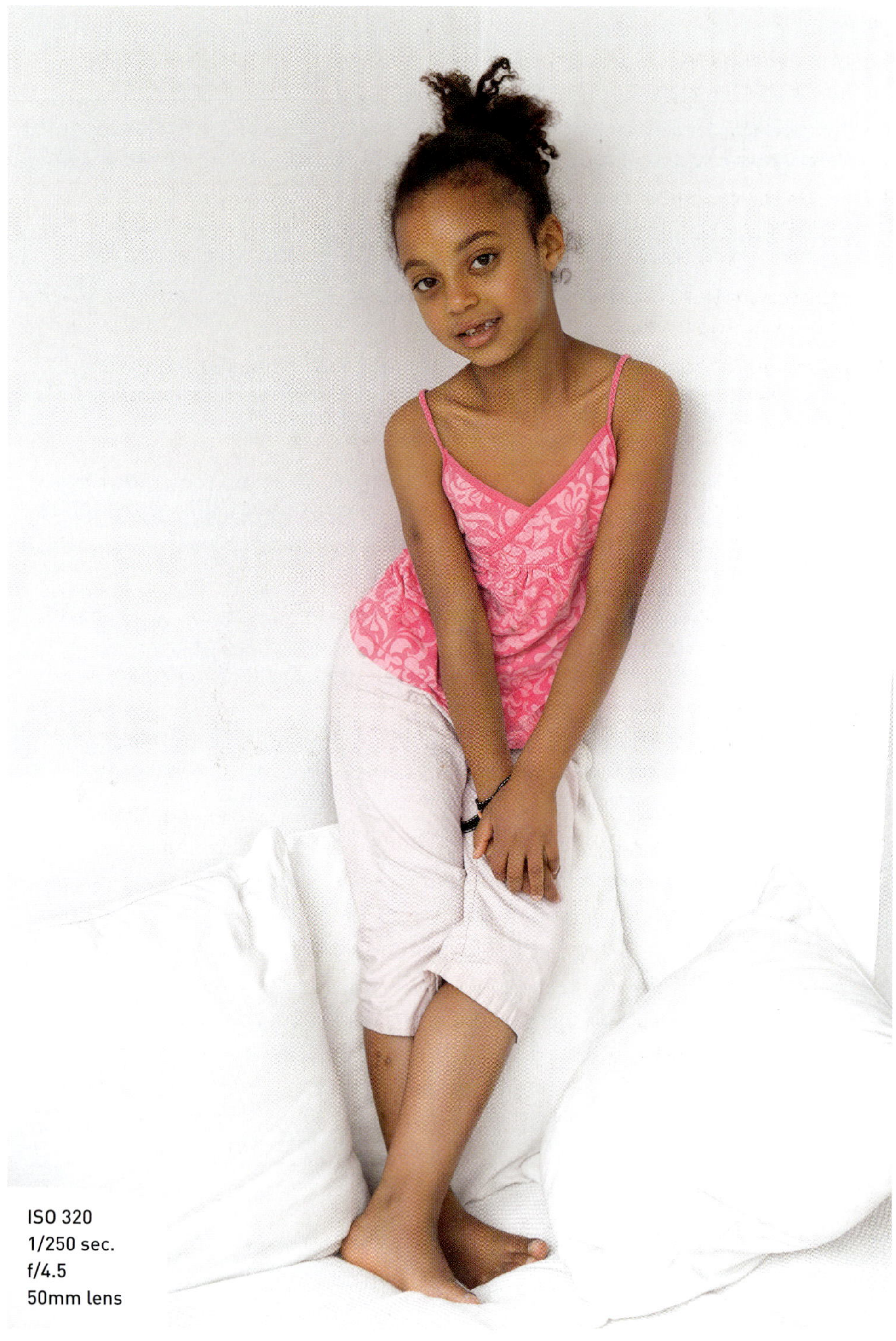

ISO 320
1/250 sec.
f/4.5
50mm lens

TO SET UP EXPOSURE COMPENSATION, FOLLOW THESE STEPS:

1. Turn on your camera, press the Mode Dial lock release button, and then turn the Mode Dial to your preferred automatic exposure mode (P, Av, or Tv).

2. Press the shutter button halfway to activate the meter and note the shutter speed/aperture combination being suggested by the camera's metering system.

3. Rotate the Quick Control Dial clockwise or counterclockwise to increase or decrease the exposure value in 1/3-stop increments. The arrow indicator in the viewfinder and LCD panel will reflect the applied amount of compensation.

4. Press the shutter button to make a photograph and review the captured image by pressing the Playback button.

5. When you're satisfied with the result, reset exposure compensation to its default setting to prevent other images from receiving the same amount of compensation.

EXPOSURE COMPENSATION AND HIGHLIGHT ALERT

Knowing exactly how much to compensate is often a matter of experience, as well as an evaluation of your scene and subject matter. In my experience, when I'm compensating for exposure, it's more about fine-tuning than it is about major corrections. Rarely do I have to adjust my exposure by more than +/–1 stop of exposure. I typically apply exposure compensation to reduce overexposure, which I can easily detect using Highlight Alert (see Chapter 1).

When Highlight Alert is enabled and you're playing back the image on the LCD monitor, areas of overexposure will blink black and white. This is a warning that these areas of the image will likely be overexposed. You can eliminate this problem by simply applying a minus compensation by rotating the Quick Control Dial counterclockwise to the desired amount. Reshoot the scene and when the "blinkies" have disappeared, the area is no longer at risk of overexposure.

Not all overexposure highlights are created equally. If the highlight alert is noting a high reflection on a metallic surface such as the chrome of a car, I ignore it, because there isn't important detail there that I want to retain. If, however, the highlight alert is located on a bride's dress, I apply some amount of exposure compensation in order to retain the important detail that exists in her gown.

Highlight Alert provides important information, which can reduce incidents of exposure, but always think about whether the area that it's warning you about is particularly important to your photograph. If the highlight exists from a metallic surface, where you expect it, the amount of compensation needed to retain the highlight there may severely underexpose the rest of your image.

METERING MODES

The 5D Mark III offers four metering methods: evaluative, partial, spot, and center-weighted average. Each provides a distinctive way of metering the scene.

- **Evaluative:** The evaluative meter is what I use for the majority of my photography (**Figure 3.8**). It uses a 63-zone TTL (through-the-lens) metering system, which includes data from the active focusing point(s) in order to determine the best exposure. It does more than just average the scene, though. It looks at tonality, color, and focus data to determine the best exposure for the scene, even with subjects that are backlit. I'm often pleasantly surprised with the results this provides, even under complicated lighting. Evaluative has become my preferred metering mode.

FIGURE 3.8

When faced with a wide range of tone and color, the evaluative metering system of the camera has no problem handling exposure, retaining good detail in both the highlights and the shadows.

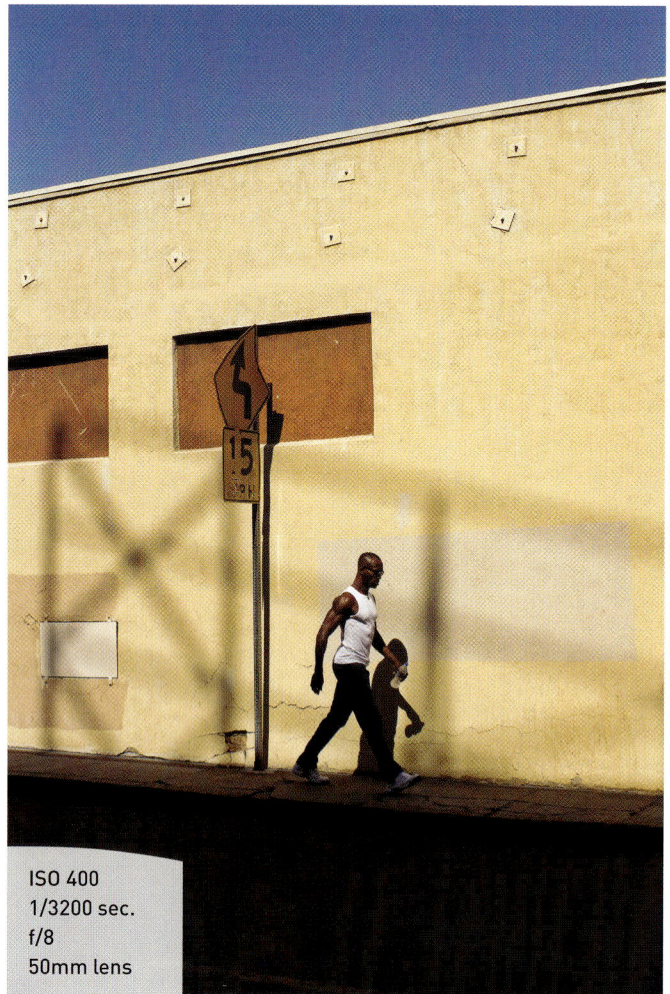

ISO 400
1/3200 sec.
f/8
50mm lens

- **Center-weighted average:** The center-weighted average meter is weighted more for the center area and then averaged for the entire scene. This is a good exposure mode when I want to emphasize my subject more than the background (**Figure 3.9**).

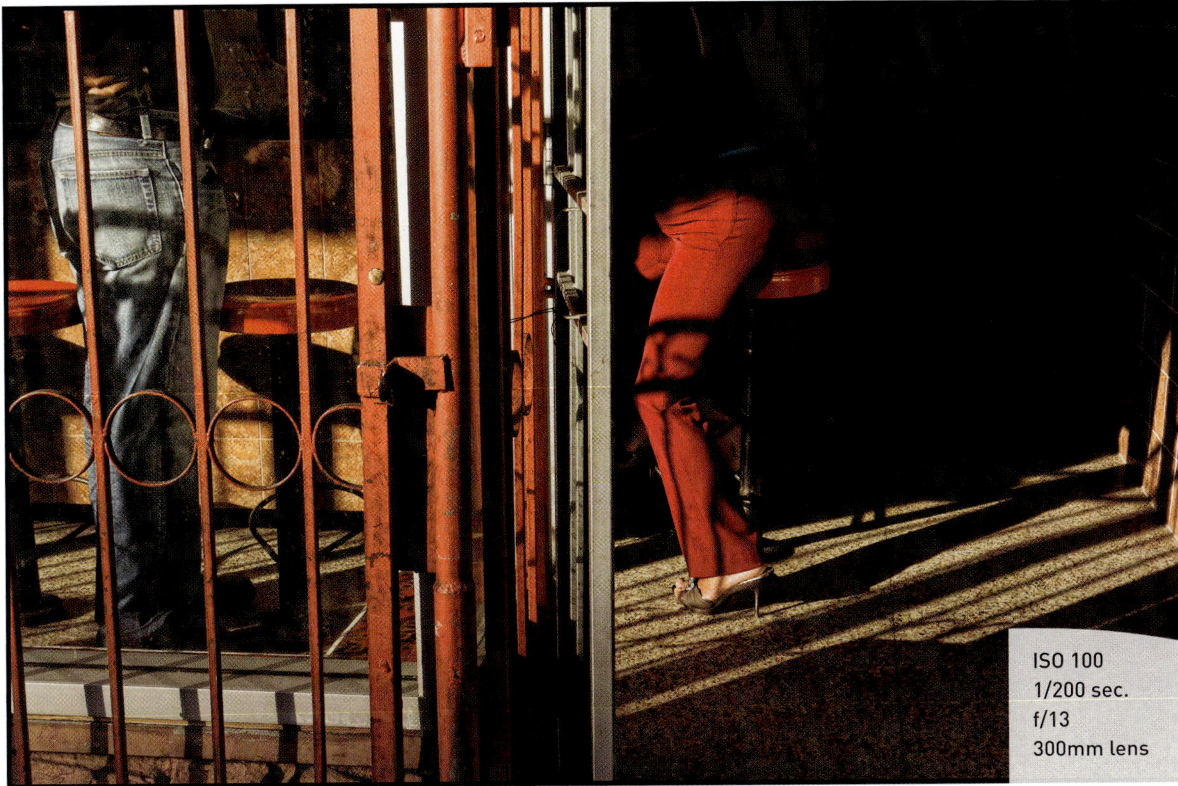

- **Partial:** Partial metering evaluates a more restrictive area of what you see in the viewfinder, only 6.2 percent. This is a good metering mode to use when your subject is severely backlit because it will disregard the rest of the frame for determining exposure.

- **Spot:** Spot metering is the most restrictive of the metering modes, using only 1.5 percent of what you see in the viewfinder. The point located at the center of the area will disregard all other areas of the frame. This is a good method to use when you're faced with a high-contrast lighting situation and you want to bias the exposure for the highlights (**Figure 3.10**).

FIGURE 3.10
By pre-visualizing
this shot as a high-
contrast scene
and using the spot
meter, I could bias
the exposure for the
highlights, allowing
the shadows to go
into a deep black.

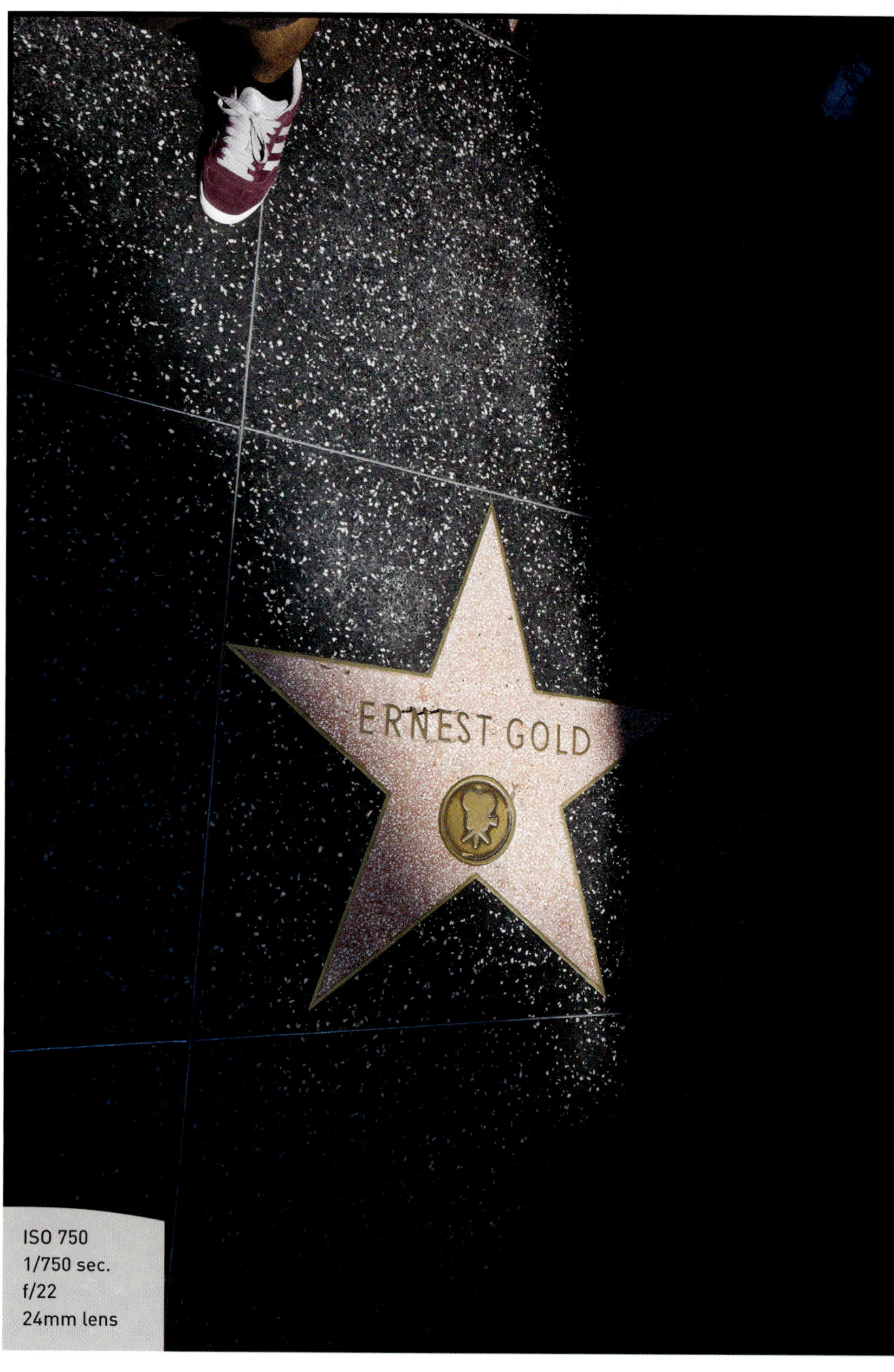
ERNEST GOLD
ISO 750
1/750 sec.
f/22
24mm lens

Although evaluative metering is my preferred metering mode, I use the other metering modes when confronted with high-contrast lighting situations, such as a backlit subject or when a shaft of light illuminates a subject. By biasing the exposure for the highlights, I ensure that I retain detail in this area of the shot. This may result in some areas of shadow going completely black, but I like the result. If you want to retain some shadow detail, you may instead want to use center-weighted average because it considers more of the viewfinder area than partial and spot metering do.

TO SET THE METERING MODE, FOLLOW THESE STEPS:

1. Turn on your camera, press the Mode Dial lock release button, and then turn the Mode Dial to your preferred exposure mode (P, Av, Tv, or M).

2. Press the shutter button halfway to activate the meter.

3. Press the Metering mode selection/White balance selection button.

4. Rotate the Main Dial to rotate through the four metering modes: evaluative, partial, spot, and center-weighted average.

HOW I SHOOT: A CLOSER LOOK AT THE CAMERA SETTINGS I USE

For the great majority of the images I make, I'm using Aperture Priority and Manual. On occasion, I use Program or Shutter Priority modes, but they aren't part of my regular playbook.

A large majority of my work involves travel and street photography, as well as portraits. So, for many of those images, I'm concerned with controlling my depth of field. If I'm shooting a landscape image, I use a small aperture to maximize depth of field or a wide aperture to achieve a shallow depth of field. In this exposure mode, I'm constantly monitoring my shutter speed to ensure that my image sharpness isn't negatively impacted by a too-slow shutter speed.

If I'm facing a challenging lighting situation or if I simply need to maintain a consistent exposure, I choose manual exposure mode. This is a good exposure mode when I want to purposely underexpose or overexpose an image for creative effect, especially when working with high-contrast directional light (**Figure 3.11**).

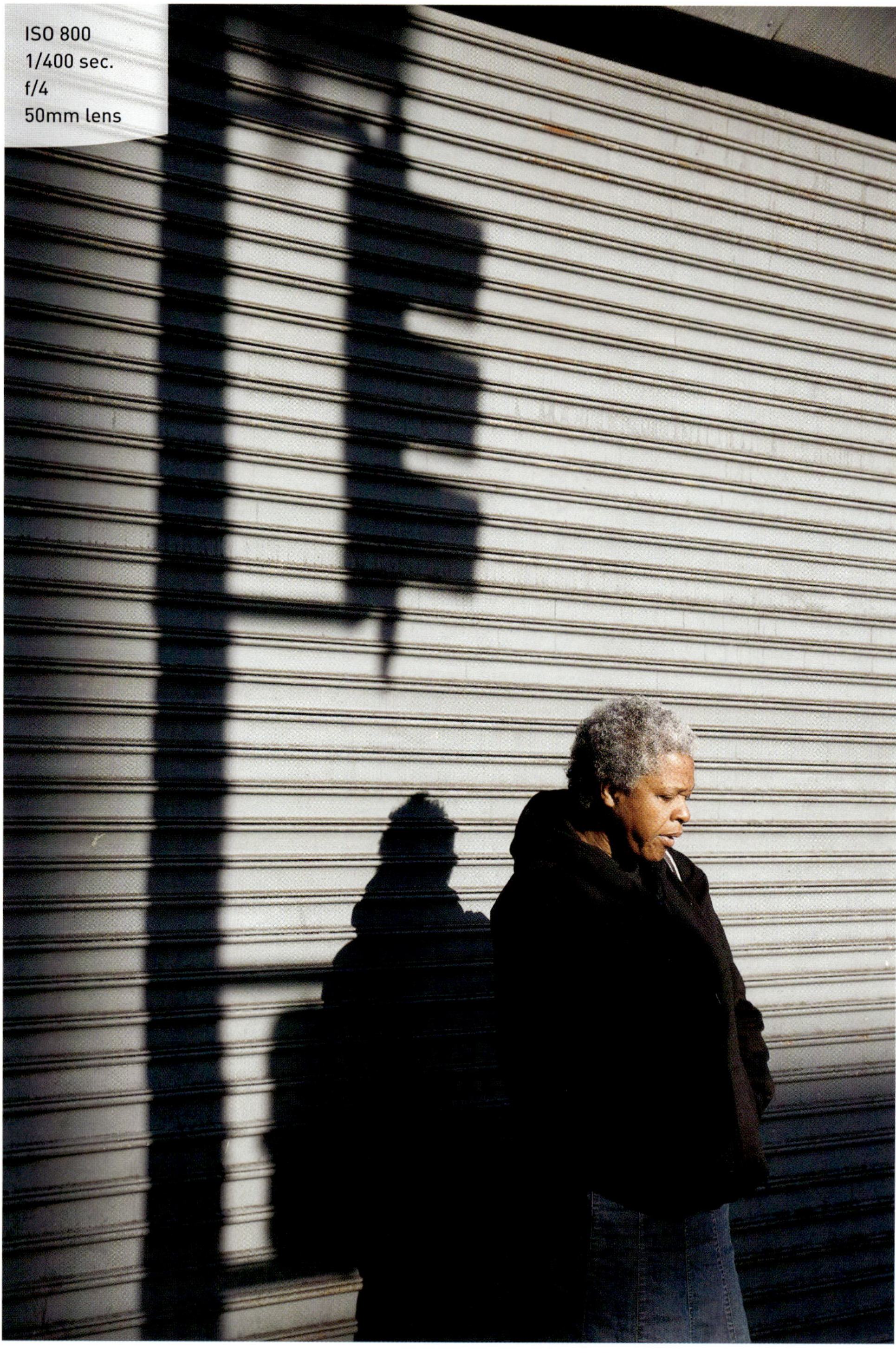

FIGURE 3.11
Setting the camera for a high ISO in a moderate- to low-light situation helps to produce a sharp and well-exposed image without concern for camera shake due to using a too-slow shutter speed.

I often make my f-stop my first consideration when determining my exposure. So, instead of having to worry about both aperture and shutter speed, I only have to think about changing my shutter speed, which is a big advantage when things are rapidly changing in front of me.

When starting off a new series of images, I take a test shot and review the image, especially to note whether the Highlight Alert is warning me of areas of overexposure. If it does, I assess whether the area has important highlight information that I want to retain, and then apply some degree of exposure compensation. Then I take another photograph to evaluate the exposure. If I'm happy with the results, I continue shooting.

The majority of the time, you'll find that the camera will deliver a good exposure. For those times when it falls short or doesn't fit your vision for the scene, exposure compensation is the best way to improve the result, followed by your choice of metering method. You'll gain confidence with handling exposure as you continue shooting and become increasingly familiar with your camera.

Chapter 3 Assignments

The information covered in this chapter will define how you work with your camera from this point on. Sure, there may be times when you just want to grab some quick pictures and you'll resort to the Scene Intelligent Auto mode or Program mode, but to get serious with your photography, you should learn how to use the other exposure modes as well.

Starting Off with Program Mode

Set your camera on Program mode and start shooting. Become familiar with the adjustments you can make to your exposure by turning the Main Dial. While shooting, make sure that you keep an eye on your ISO.

Learning to Control Time with Shutter Priority Mode

Find some moving subjects and then set your camera to Shutter Priority mode. Have someone ride a bike back and forth in front of you or photograph cars as they go by. Start with a slow shutter speed of around 1/30 second and then try shooting with faster and faster shutter speeds. Keep shooting until you can freeze the action. Now find something that isn't moving, like a flower, and work your shutter speed from something fast, like 1/500 second, down to about 1/4 second. The point is to see how well you can handhold your camera before you start introducing camera shake into the image.

Controlling Depth of Field with Aperture Priority Mode

The name of the game with Aperture Priority mode is depth of field. Set up three items in a line extending away from you, an equal distance apart. I would use chess pieces or something similar. Now focus on the middle item and set your camera to the largest aperture that your lens allows (remember, large aperture means a small number, like f/3.5). Now, while still focusing on the middle subject, start shooting with ever-smaller apertures until you're at the smallest f-stop for your lens. If you have a zoom lens, try doing this exercise with the lens at the widest and then the most telephoto settings. Now move up to subjects that are farther away, like telephone poles, and shoot them in the same way. The idea is to get a feel for how each aperture setting affects your depth of field.

Giving and Taking with Manual Mode

Go outside on a sunny day and, using the camera in Manual mode, set your ISO to 100, your shutter speed to 1/125 second, and your aperture to f/16. Now press the shutter button to get a meter reading. You should be pretty close to that zero mark. If not, make small adjustments to one of your settings until it hits that mark. Now is where the fun begins. Start moving your shutter speed slower, to 1/60 second, and then set your aperture to f/22. Now go the other way: Set your aperture to f/8 and your shutter speed to 1/500 second. Now review your images. If all went well, all the exposures should look the same. This is because you balanced the light with reciprocal changes to the aperture and shutter speed. Now go back to the original setting of 1/125 second at f/16 and try just moving the shutter speed without changing the aperture. Just make 1/3-stop changes (1/125 to 1/100 to 1/80 to 1/60), and then review your images to see what a 1/3 stop of overexposure looks like. Then do the same thing going in the opposite direction. It's hard to know if you want to overexpose or underexpose a scene until you've actually done it and seen the results.

Getting Comfortable with Exposure Compensation

Photograph a white subject against a light or white background in Program, Aperture Priority, or Shutter Priority mode. After your initial exposure, take several different exposures with +1, +2, and +3 exposure compensation. Compare the images to see how the white values look, paying particular attention as to when areas of highlight are overexposed, as indicated by the Highlight Alert. Create a series of similar images using a dark subject against a dark background, but instead apply –1, –2, and –3 compensation and note the difference in tonality and colors.

Discovering Metering Methods

Place your subject in front of a large window through which a lot of light is passing through. Photograph your subject using the evaluative, partial, spot, and center-weighted average metering modes and compare the results. Note how the shutter/aperture combination may have changed when using Program, Shutter Priority, or Aperture Priority exposure modes.

Share your results with this book's Flickr group!

Join the group here: www.flickr.com/groups/Canon5DMarkIIIFromSnapshotstoGreatShots

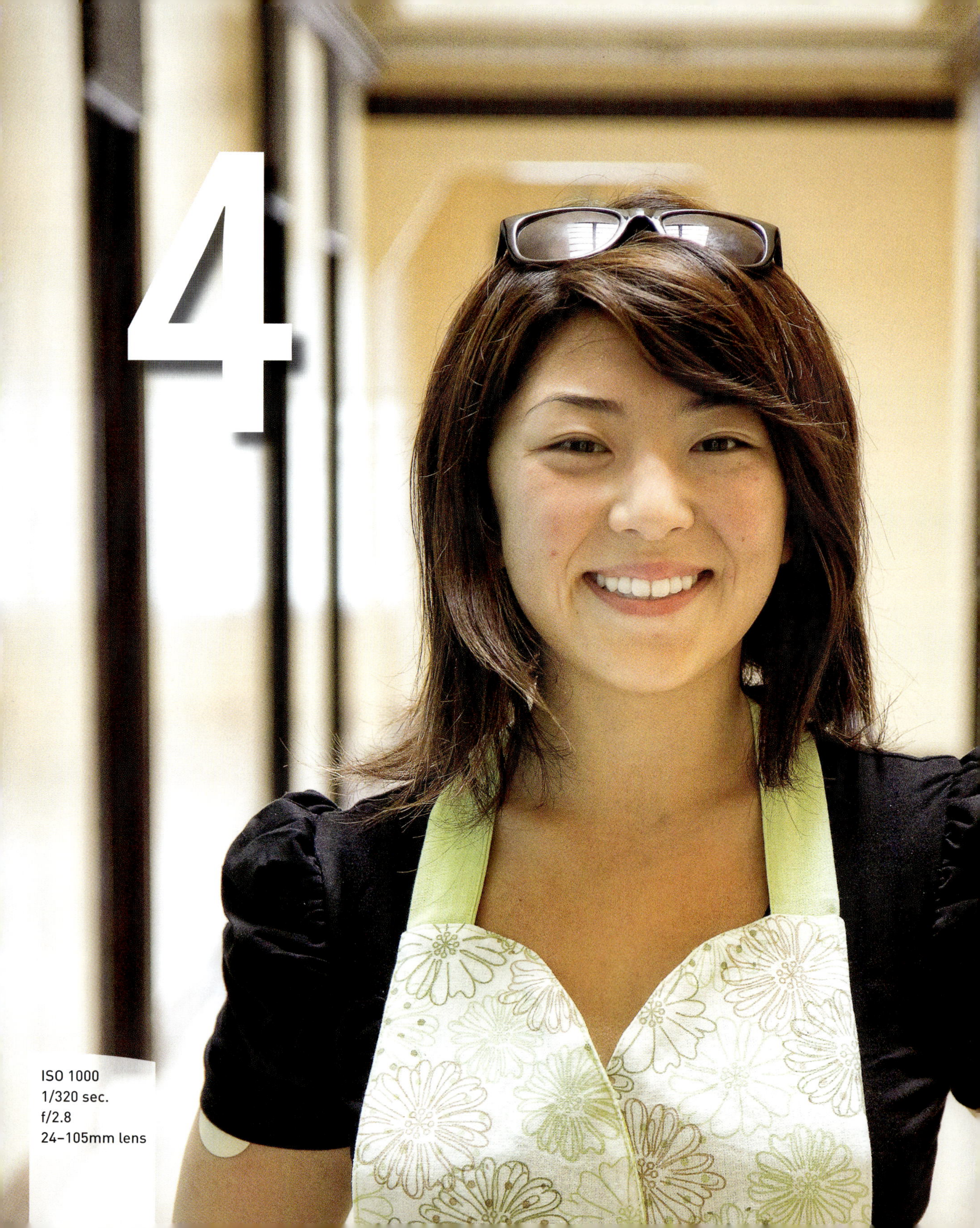

4
ISO 1000
1/320 sec.
f/2.8
24–105mm lens

That Wonderful Face

SETTINGS AND FEATURES TO MAKE GREAT PORTRAITS

People are the most-often photographed subject with any camera, and no less so with the 5D Mark III. This camera offers a range of versatility and control that you might not have enjoyed with your previous camera, which should make photographing people easier and more fun. Getting good portraits is about much more than having the correct settings on your camera. It's also about being aware of your subject, the background, and the lighting. In this chapter, I tell you how to consider all those factors in order to make great photographs of people—whether they're family, friends, or a great subject you meet on the street.

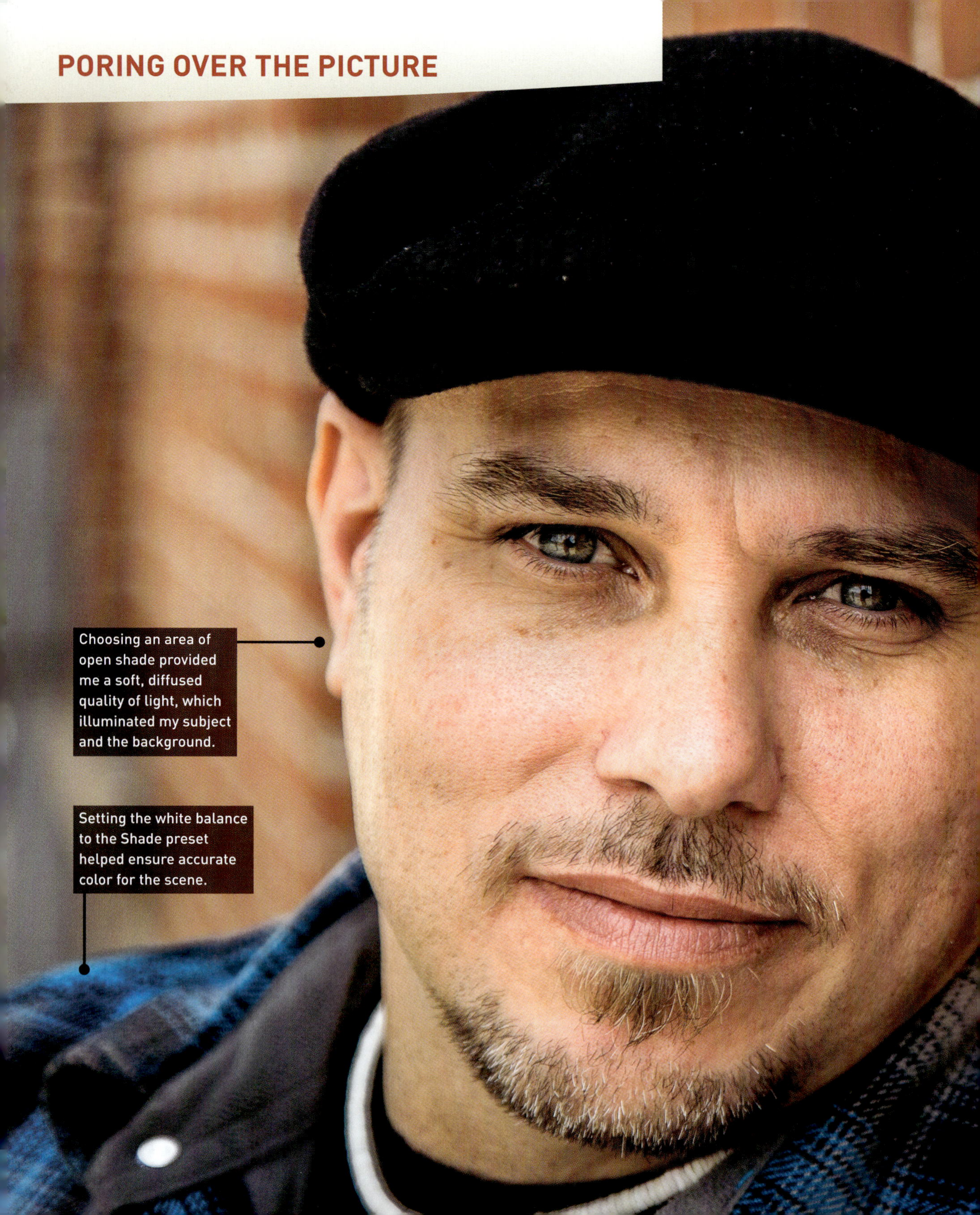
Choosing an area of open shade provided me a soft, diffused quality of light, which illuminated my subject and the background.

Setting the white balance to the Shade preset helped ensure accurate color for the scene.

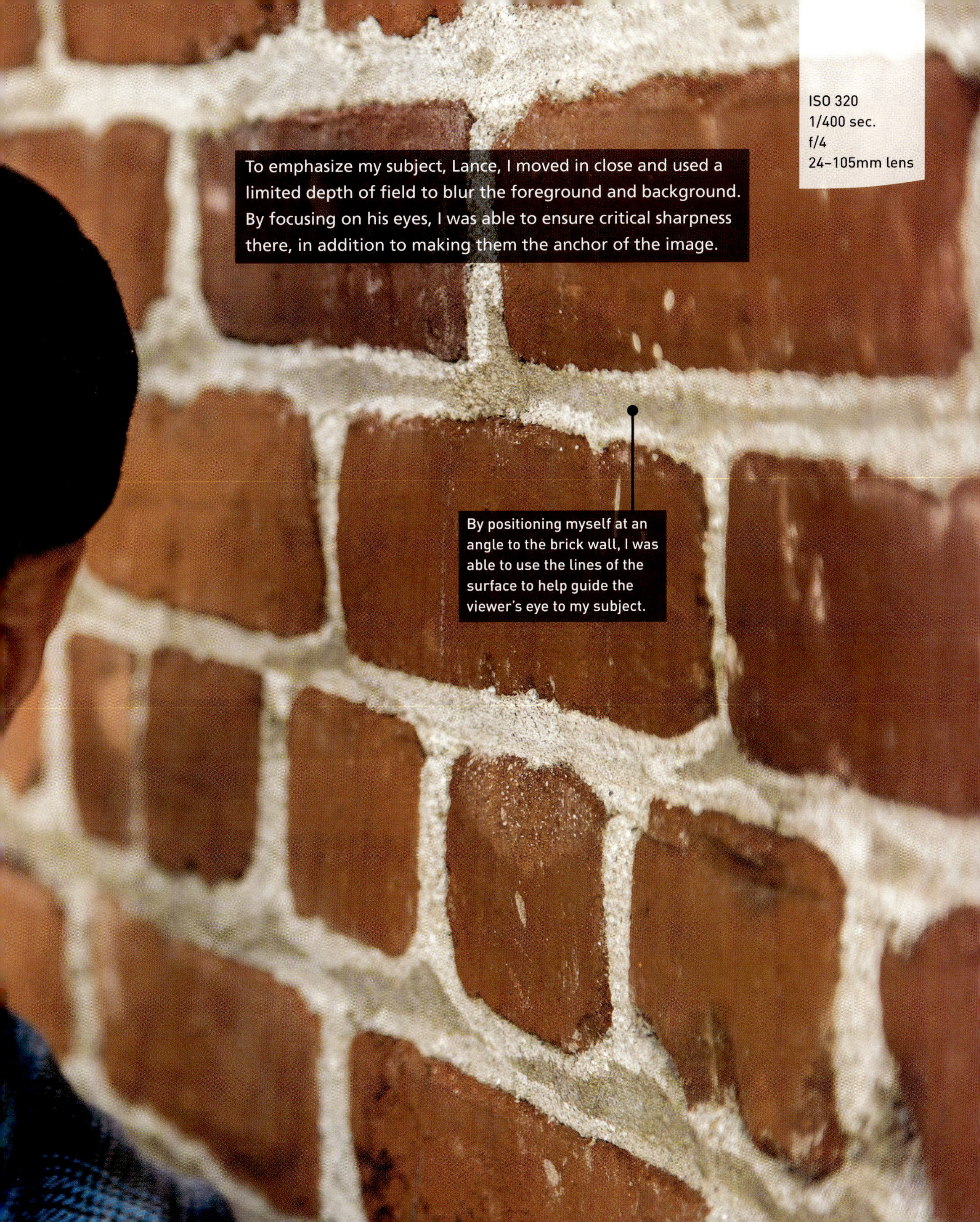
ISO 320
1/400 sec.
f/4
24–105mm lens
To emphasize my subject, Lance, I moved in close and used a limited depth of field to blur the foreground and background. By focusing on his eyes, I was able to ensure critical sharpness there, in addition to making them the anchor of the image.
By positioning myself at an angle to the brick wall, I was able to use the lines of the surface to help guide the viewer's eye to my subject.

PORING OVER THE PICTURE

The background is often as important to a photograph as the subject. A poor background, as well as bad lighting, can ruin an image. In this image, I used the frame within a frame created by the paint on the wall to "contain" my subject. The contrast between the color of his suit and the light blue background helps to draw the viewer's eye to my subject and his expression.

By using Aperture Priority mode, I was able to control depth of field. I still paid attention to my shutter speed in order to ensure that camera shake didn't reduce sharpness.

A moderate telephoto lens provides a focal length that can render the subject, well, free of the distortion that might occur with wider focal-length lenses, particularly at close distances.

Making or placing my subject in the brightest area of the frame helps to draw the viewer's eye.

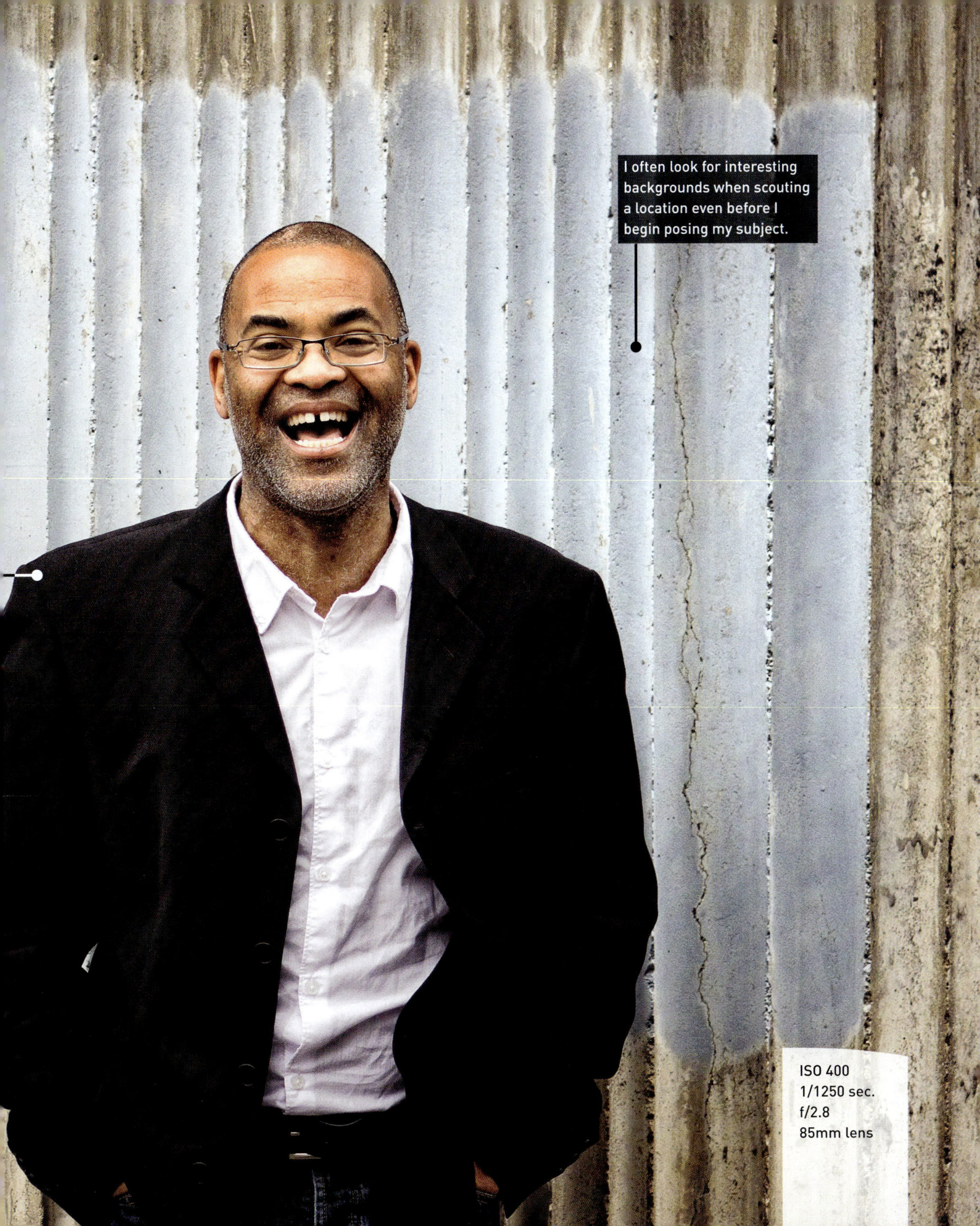

I often look for interesting backgrounds when scouting a location even before I begin posing my subject.

ISO 400
1/1250 sec.
f/2.8
85mm lens

APERTURE PRIORITY MODE

Of the exposure modes mentioned in the previous chapter, Aperture Priority will most often be the best choice for creating portraits. Because it provides you complete control over depth of field, Aperture Priority mode allows you to control the look of your image, whether it's a tightly framed headshot or an environmental portrait, such as this image of a parking attendant (**Figure 4.1**). The choice of aperture will either allow you to throw the background dramatically out of focus or render much of the frame acceptably sharp. The choice of aperture achieves more than simply a good exposure; it also becomes the means by which you begin to creatively control the look of your photograph.

Now, don't think that you have to use a crazy-fast lens (such as an f/1.2 or f/2.8) to achieve great results and get a blurry background. Often an f-stop of f/4 or f/5.6 will be sufficient, and you might even find that having an extremely wide-open aperture gives you too little depth of field for a portrait, since you want most of the face to appear sharp.

I often shoot my portraits with a working aperture of f/4 or f/5.6 in order to get most of the face tack sharp. Though I sometimes use lenses with wider apertures for portraits, it's often only when I'm seeking that unique look provided by such a shallow depth of field.

GO WIDE FOR ENVIRONMENTAL PORTRAITS

Portraits can be about more than simply creating a headshot. A great portrait can be as much about the space that a subject inhabits as it is about the subject itself. For such images, a wide focal length and a moderate aperture such as f/5.6 or smaller can provide the kind of depth of field needed to reveal the details of the subject and the space that he or she inhabits.

A wide-angle lens can be any focal length from 35mm or wider. Such lenses not only include more in the frame, but they also provide a more generous depth of field than telephoto lenses do. A wide-angle lens can be especially beneficial when you're working in a very tight, enclosed environment.

However, be careful about using a wide-angle lens very close to your subject, because it can lead to some distortion. Keep your subject away from the edge of the frame. This will reduce the distortion, especially with very wide-angle lenses.

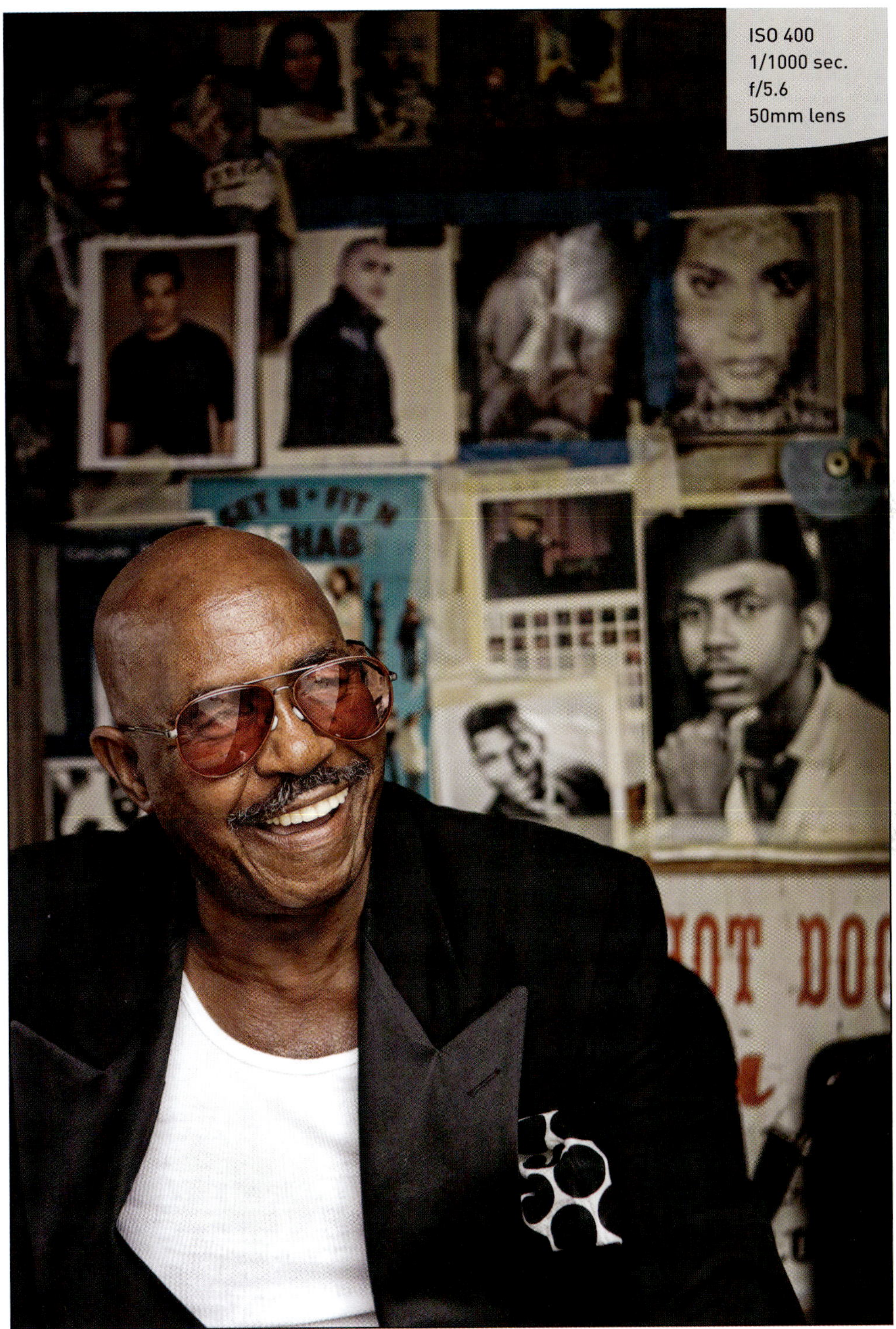

FIGURE 4.1
A 50mm lens and the choice to place my subject off-center allowed me to include this personalized booth of a parking attendant.

LIGHTING AND BACKGROUND

Whenever I make a portrait, the two biggest considerations revolve around lighting and background. Even before I've exposed a single frame, I'm thinking about the quality of light that I have to work with and where I'm going to place my subject. When I don't consider these two factors carefully, the result is often a lackluster portrait. Even if I have the most beautiful subject in the world in front of my lens, bad lighting and a distracting background will reduce the impact of the photograph.

Though I produce portraits using a wide variety of lighting, including direct sunlight, I often look for an area of open shade. Open shade is an area where shade is being produced by a building or a tree. I look for a spot where the direct sunlight is transitioning into an area of shade. Then I place my subject just at the cusp of that shaded area so that the subject has the benefit of some of the reflected light; this creates an image that is both bright and contrasty. Such lighting often eliminates the harsh, distracting shadows commonly found in photographs made using direct sunlight, particularly during the middle of the day.

The other big consideration I make is with respect to the background. Many great portraits are ruined by distracting elements in the background, such as tree branches, cars, or other brightly colorful elements. Such elements can pull the viewer's attention away from the subject and to the background, thus diminishing the impact of the portrait. So, I often try to choose as simple and as clean a background as I can find. This often calls for me to move my subject into a better location. I won't hesitate to ask my subject to move if it means I'll be able to make a better photograph (**Figure 4.2**).

WHITE BALANCE AND ISO

When shooting in open shade, I often set my white balance to the Shade preset. This adjusts the white balance to maintain a flattering look to the skin. Otherwise, if the white balance is left on the AWB or Sunny preset, the subject will look a tad blue, because the area of shade naturally has a bluish colorcast. By setting my white balance for the Shade preset, a little warmth is added to compensate for that coolness in the quality of light.

I also increase my ISO. It may increase to 200 to 400, depending on the quantity of light and what's happening with my shutter speed. If I'm using the lens and a wide aperture, such as f/4 or wider, I may only need to increase my ISO to 200 in order to achieve a reasonable shutter speed. However, I won't hesitate to increase it to

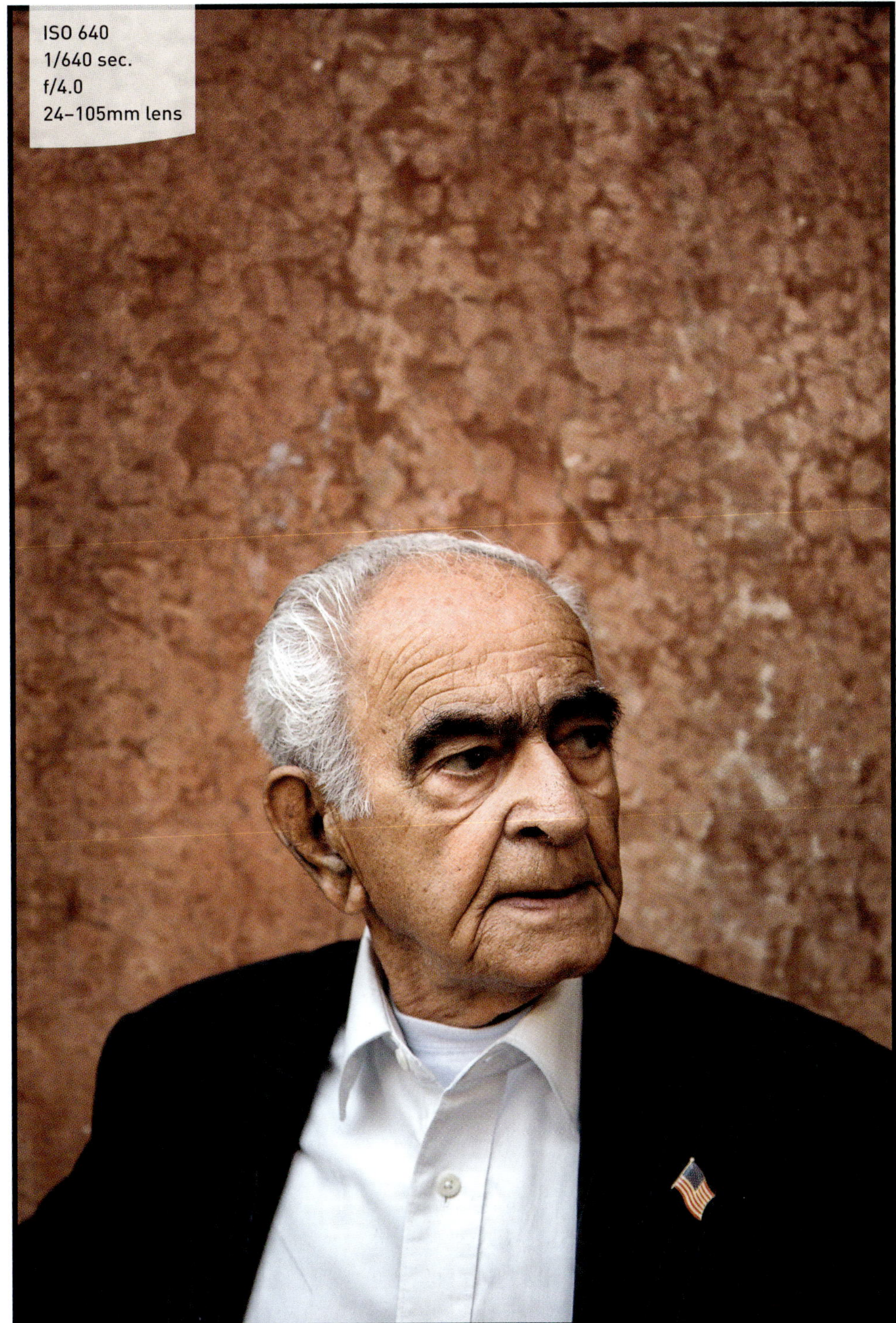

I moved this subject from an area of open shade but with a cluttered background. I repositioned him against this wall that served as a better background, free of distractions.

ISO 400 or even higher if it means that I can use a reasonable shutter speed in order to ensure sharpness. If I fail to increase the ISO, which I unfortunately do forget to do on occasion, the shutter speed will be too slow and there will be a drop in sharpness. It may not be immediately evident when I'm shooting the images, but it will be painfully obvious when I enlarge the image on my computer screen.

If I move the subject into an area of direct sunlight, I set the white balance to the Daylight preset (**Figure 4.3**) and I may decrease my ISO to 100 or 200. When we move indoors where the illumination is primarily tungsten light bulbs, I'll change my white balance to the Tungsten light preset and increase my ISO to at least 800. In each situation, I'm evaluating the light that I have to work with, and adjusting the ISO and the white balance accordingly. From there, I can adjust my aperture, making sure that my shutter speed isn't too slow. If it is, I'll open up my aperture and/or increase the ISO.

With these considerations made, I'm free to focus on my composition and on building a rapport with my subject.

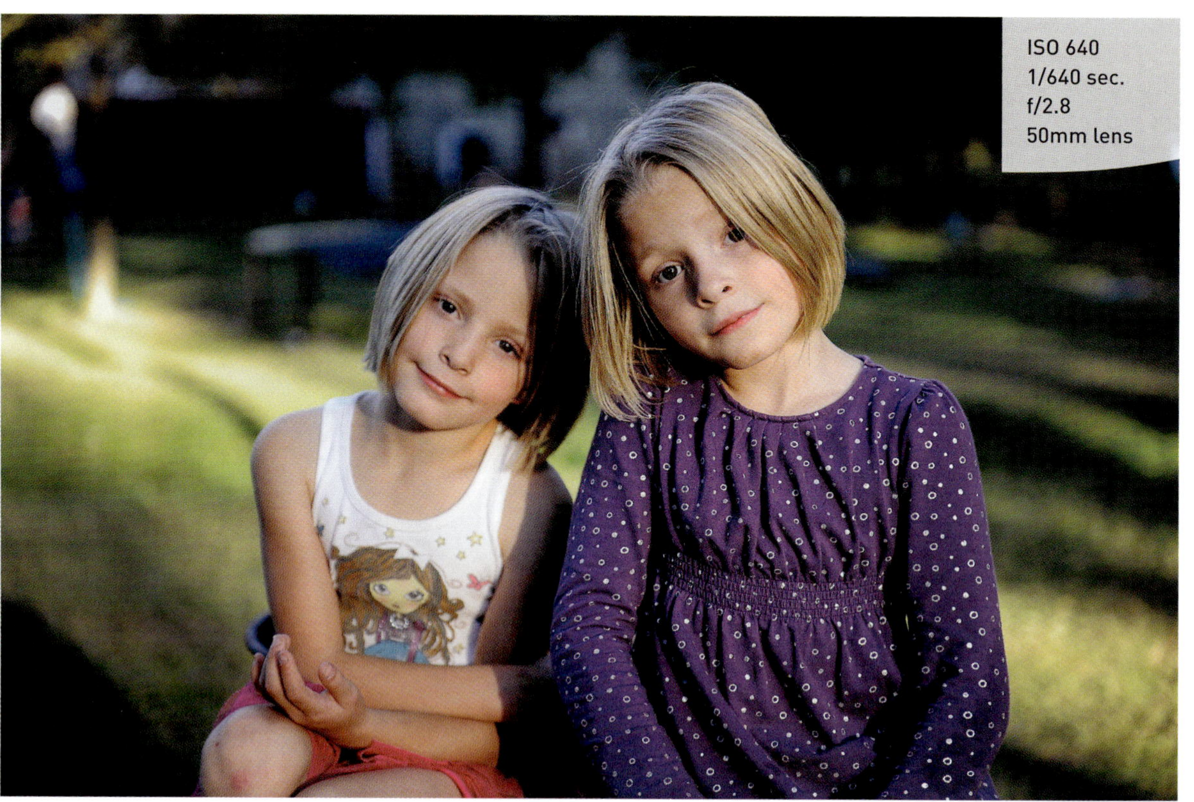

PORTRAIT METERING

The 5D Mark III offers four different metering modes by which the light of the scene can be measured to help you achieve an accurate exposure. Evaluative metering does much of the heavy lifting for my photography. Even in relatively complicated lighting situations, I've found that evaluative metering does a great job in giving me accurate exposures. When I don't like the result it's giving me, I often use the exposure compensation feature to increase or decrease the exposure and achieve the look that I'm going for. However, I sometimes use the partial, center-weighted average (**Figure 4.4**), or spot meter when I want to emphasize my subject for the basis of my exposure.

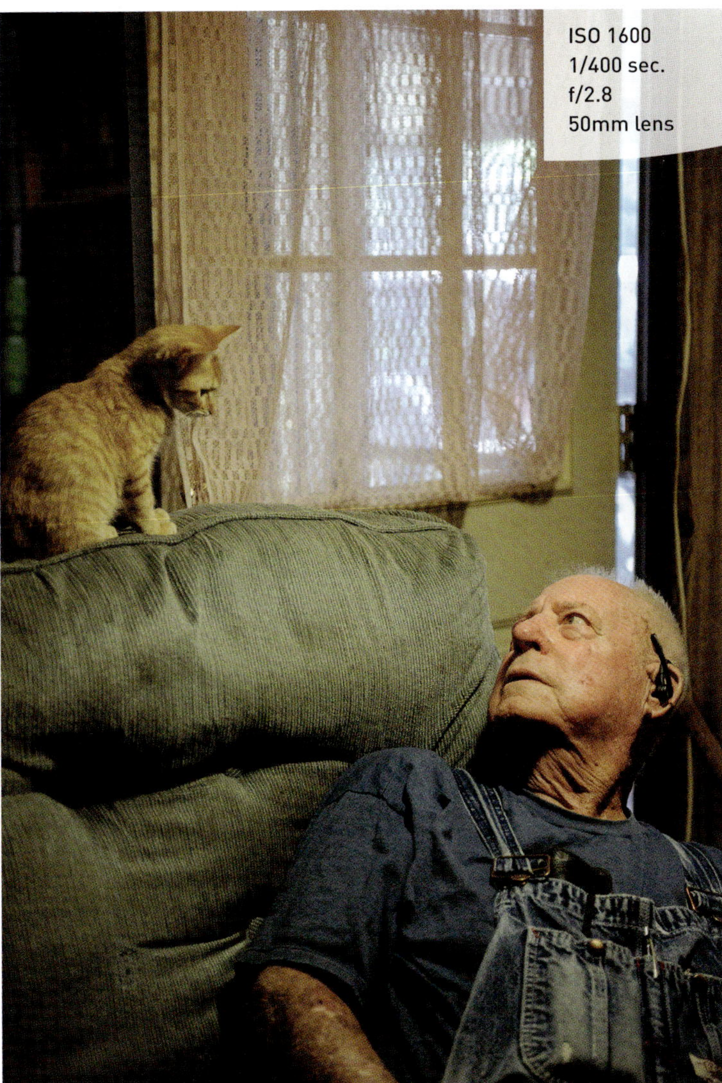

FIGURE 4.4
This low-light scene was illuminated by a few lamps and called for metering the scene using center-weighted average metering to ensure a good exposure for this interaction between man and cat.

If I have a severely backlit subject, which means the area behind the subject is considerably brighter, I may use the partial, center-weighted average, or spot mode to isolate the exposure on my subject. This may result in the background being blown out or overexposed, but if the background is of little importance, I'll be okay with that. I want to make sure that my subject is well exposed in order to retain the important details of the face.

THE AE LOCK FEATURE

One of the available options is the ability to lock your exposure. You can lock the setting in your camera temporarily if you want to recompose your image—for example, if you're in an environment where there is sufficient lighting on your subject, but the background is significantly brighter or darker (**Figure 4.5**). The metering in your camera is continuous, meaning it will change depending on where the center of the viewfinder is pointed. If you compose the image so the person is off-center, the camera will meter the wrong part of the scene.

To correct this, you can meter for one part of the image (in your subject), lock those settings down so that they don't change, and then recompose the scene and take your photo.

For more on how to use the AE lock feature, turn to Chapter 3.

FOCUS: THE EYES HAVE IT

In a portrait, nothing is more important than the eyes. They eyes are the very first place we look when looking at an image of a person. As a result, the eyes need to be one of the sharpest elements in the frame. If the eyes aren't in focus, the viewer's experience of the photograph can be diminished. It's important to be very much in control of where the camera is focusing, because despite how sophisticated the auto-focus technology of the camera is, it doesn't guarantee that the eyes of the subject will always be the sharpest element in the frame.

When it comes to making a portrait, this is a perfect time to control how many of the AF sensors are used for focus detection. For example, choosing the single-point AF mode would be a good choice for a portrait because it would allow you to choose a single focus point that would focus on the eyes of the subject. I did this for this

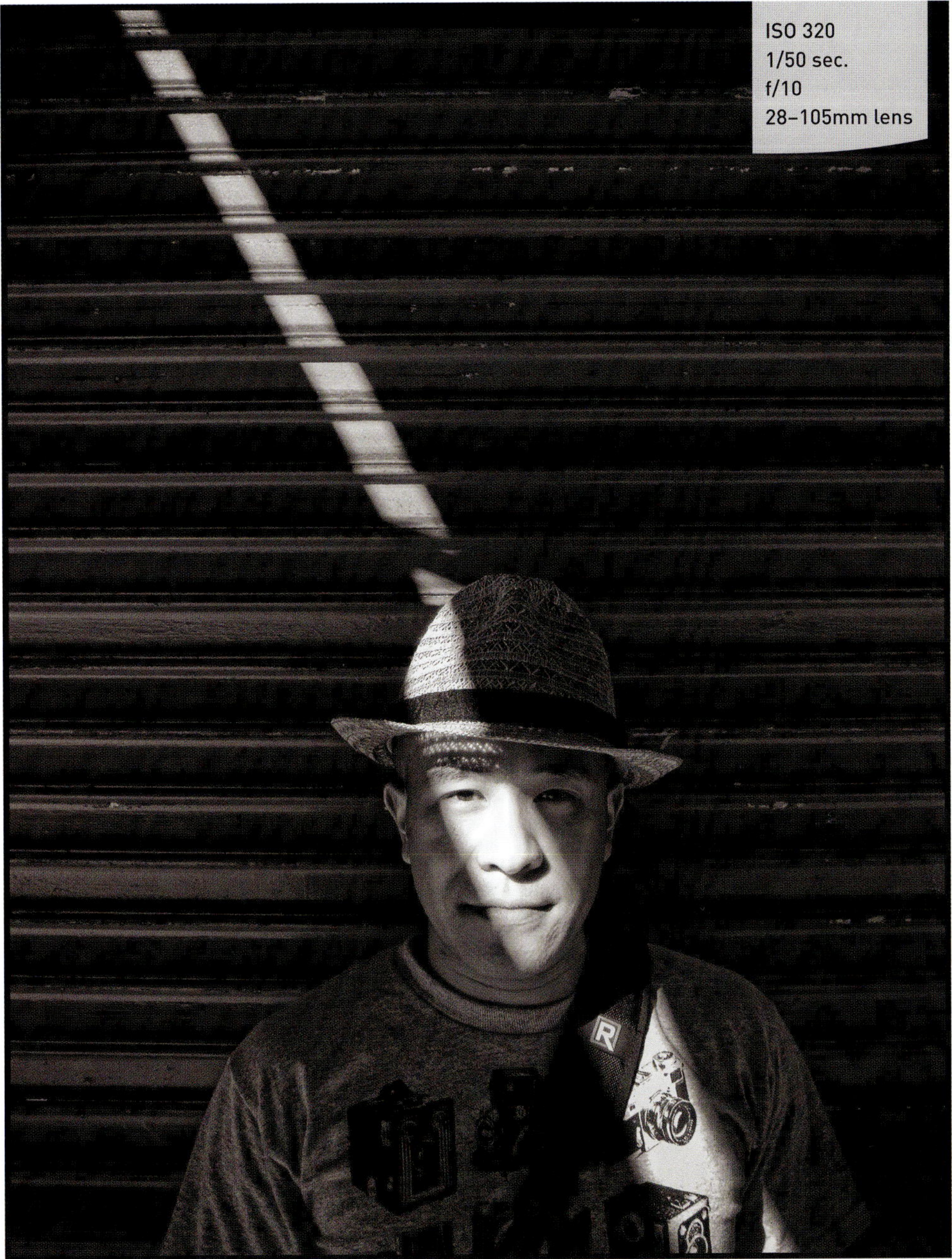

FIGURE 4.5
Because so much of the scene includes shadows, it was important to lock the exposure based on the highlights in order to ensure that they weren't overexposed.

portrait of a Passion play actress (**Figure 4.6**). Controlling which AF sensors are used is particularly important if you're using a wide aperture that can result in a very narrow depth of field. Otherwise, the camera could focus on the nose or the shirt, which could result in the eyes being slightly soft, which you always want to avoid.

If you're making candid portraits or if the subject is moving, you may be best served by a more moderate aperture, such as f/5.6 or f/8, which will provide you a more generous depth of field. This may require you to increase your ISO in order to maintain a reasonable shutter speed, but it will help ensure that your subject is sharp.

As you change the composition of your photograph, the focus point may need to be changed accordingly. If the subject is slightly turned away from the camera, it's best to focus on the eye closest to the camera.

TO SET UP FOR ONE-SHOT FOCUSING MODE, FOLLOW THESE STEPS:

1. Press the AF mode selection/Drive mode selection button.
2. Rotate the Main Dial to change the focusing mode to One Shot.

TO SET UP FOR SINGLE-POINT AF MODE, FOLLOW THESE STEPS:

1. Press the AF point selection button.
2. While looking through the viewfinder, repeatedly press the AF area selection mode/Multi-function button to cycle through the AF area selection modes, and choose the single-point AF mode.

TIP

I typically use the single-point AF for focus selection. I find it easier to place that point directly on the location where my critical focus should be established and then recompose the shot. Even though the single point can be selected from any of the focus points, it typically takes longer to figure out where that point should be in relation to my subject. By using the center point, I can quickly establish focus and get on with my shooting. If I have the benefit of a great depth of field, such as when I'm photographing a group, I choose zone AF or the AF point expansion mode for focus detection.

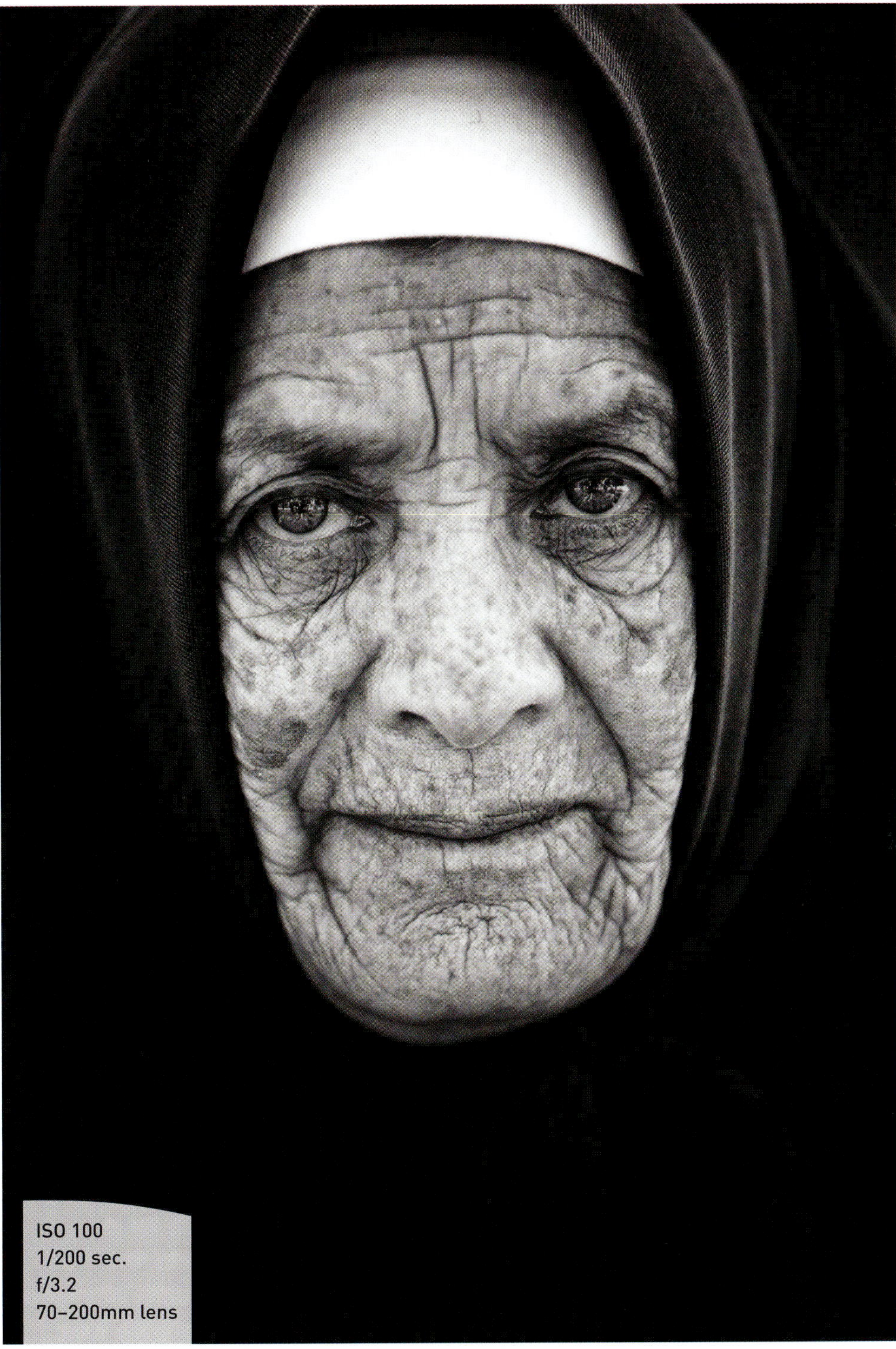

The use of a telephoto lens combined with a wide aperture resulted in a shallow depth of field. So, I made sure to detect and lock the focus on the eyes in order to produce this portrait of a Passion play actress.

1. Press the AF point selection button.

2. Using the multi-controller, choose your active autofocus sensor. You also can use the Main Dial and Quick Control Dial to move to an active sensor.

3. To shoot using this focus point, place that point on your subject's eye, and press the shutter button halfway, until the focus point flashes and you hear the chirp.

4. While still holding down the shutter button halfway, recompose and take your shot.

ORIENTATION-LINKED AF POINT

You can designate separate focus points based on whether you're holding the camera vertically or horizontally. This helps reduce time having to change the AF point for your subject. It's a great help when you're frequently changing camera orientation during a shoot.

To set up an orientation-linked AF point, follow these steps:

1. Press the Menu button and, using the Main Dial, select the AF 4 menu screen.

2. Using the Quick Control Dial, select Orientation linked to AF Point, and press the Setting button.

3. Using the Quick Control Dial, select Select Separate AF points, and push the Setting button.

FOCUS LOCK

Locking focus is one of the most important things to learn with an autofocus camera, especially when making portraits. Locking focus ensures that your subject remains the point of focus as you refine your composition, compose with your subject off-center, or change camera orientation. It's an important tool to prevent another part of the subject or the background from being in focus, such as the fence that served as a background in this portrait (**Figure 4.7**).

You can lock focus by either holding down the shutter button halfway or pressing and holding the AF start button. If you've been using autofocus DSLRs for years, you'll likely be used to holding down the shutter button halfway. If you find it difficult to do without taking a photograph, the AF start button is a welcome alternative. Not only will it allow you to lock focus, but it also will allow you to engage focus without unintentionally making a photograph.

You can completely separate any autofocus function from the shutter button, which many photographers, especially sports photographers, prefer to do. When you do this, autofocus is activated only when the AF start button is pressed. Locking the focus becomes as simple as releasing pressure on the AF start button. Autofocus will only resume when you reapply pressure to the AF start button. You can then assign the shutter button to meter the scene only when it's depressed halfway.

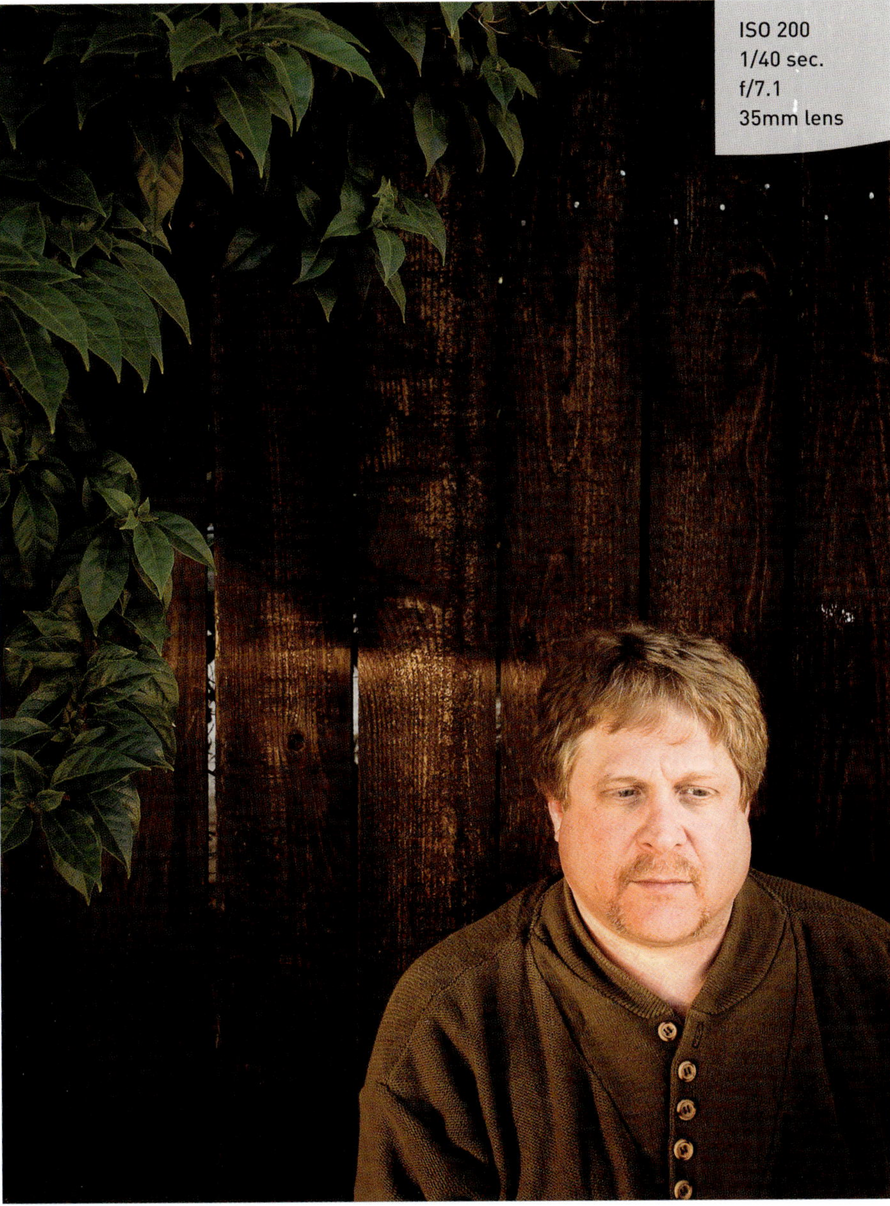

FIGURE 4.7
To create a more interesting composition, I posed my subject off-center and used the foliage to balance the entire composition. I focused on him, locked the focus, and recomposed the shot in order to keep him as sharp as possible.

1. Press the Menu button and, using the Main Dial, select the Customer Function 2: Display/Operation menu screen.

2. Using the Quick Control Dial, select Custom Controls, and push the Setting button.

3. Using the Quick Control Dial, select AF-On, and push the Setting button.

4. Select the AF icons on the far left, and press the Setting button.

5. Using the Quick Control Dial, select the shutter button icon, and press the Setting button.

6. Choose the Metering icon, which appears in the center, and press the Setting button.

TIP

If you aren't accustomed to working this way, I highly recommend that you practice before shooting something important. It's easy to forget that you've disabled autofocus from the shutter button, which can result in a lot of out-of-focus photographs.

HOW TO BUILD A COMPOSITION

Now, that I've chosen a location that provides the best lighting and background and I've sent my white balance, ISO, shutter speed, and my focus points appropriately, I can focus more on my composition. All the technical considerations have been made, so I don't have to be distracted by them. The only time I need to reconsider the technical details is if the lighting changes or I move my subject into a different area. Otherwise, I can just focus on the subtle differences in my subject's expression or body language, which can give me that special something that results in a great portrait.

Though most of our portraits may simply involve a composition where the subject is put in the very center of the frame, we actually have a lot of choices. You can put the subject in the center of the frame, off-center, or sometimes even at the extreme edges of the frame. The placement of your subject within the frame and the perspective from which you shoot your subject can make or break an image. For example, when I want to make the environment as important as my subject, I'll position the subject off-center to include more of the background in the composition (**Figure 4.8**).

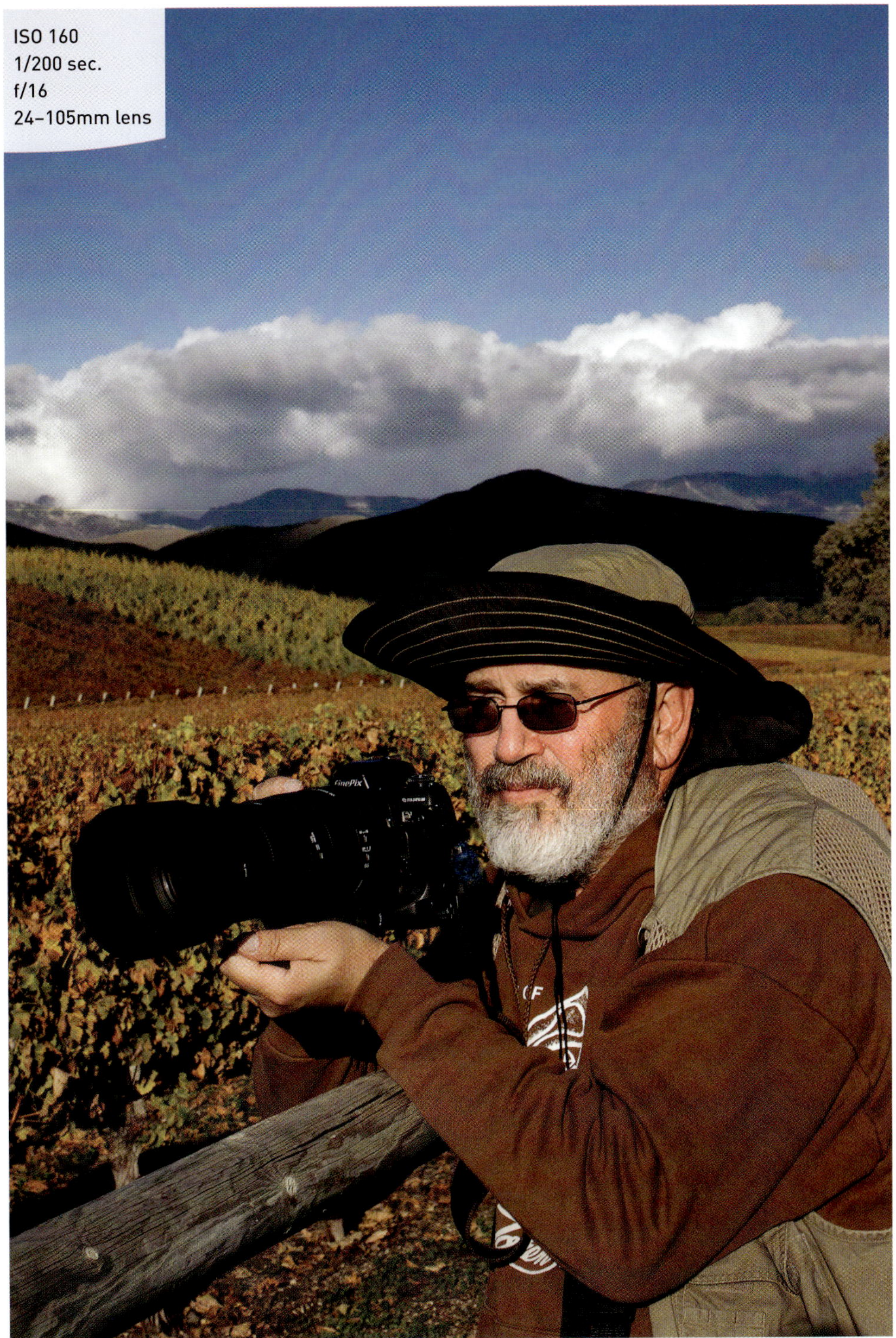

FIGURE 4.8
I wanted to create a composition that provided a sense of place for this portrait of my friend Paul. By orienting the camera vertically and including the vineyard and sky, I produced a sense of where we were during this great day of shooting.

Here are a few tips to help you create some amazing portrait compositions.

THE RULE OF THIRDS

One of the most basic rules of composition, the "rule of thirds," is a very good principle to work with when photographing people. Imagine a tic-tac-toe board, with two lines spaced evenly down the center of the frame both horizontally and vertically. Your goal is to place the subject, or part of your subject, on one of the intersecting lines. You're basically trying to keep the person off-center without pushing him or her too close to the edge of the frame.

This same rule can be used quite effectively when making a tightly framed photograph of the face, where you place each eye at one of those intersecting points in order to help create a balanced composition, as I did for this portrait of master photographer Joel Meyerowitz (**Figure 4.9**).

The great thing about the 5D Mark III is that you can add a grid overlay to your viewfinder and LCD (when shooting in Live View) to help you with composition. You'll need to set up the appearance of the grid lines for the viewfinder and the LCD monitor separately. The latter is enabled when you're using the camera in Live View mode (in which you're using the LCD monitor to compose your photograph).

TO SET UP THE GRID DISPLAY IN YOUR VIEWFINDER, FOLLOW THESE STEPS:

1. Press the Menu button and turn the Main Dial to access the Set-up 2 menu screen.

2. Use the Quick Control Dial to scroll down to VF grid display. Press the Setting button.

3. Use the Quick Control Dial to enable the VF grid display. Press the Setting button.

TO SET UP THE GRID DISPLAY FOR LIVE VIEW, FOLLOW THESE STEPS:

1. Press the Menu button and turn the Main Dial to access the Shoot 4: LV menu screen.

2. Use the Quick Control Dial to scroll down to Grid Display. Press the Setting button.

3. Use the Quick Control Dial to select the 3x3 or other grid pattern. Press the Setting button.

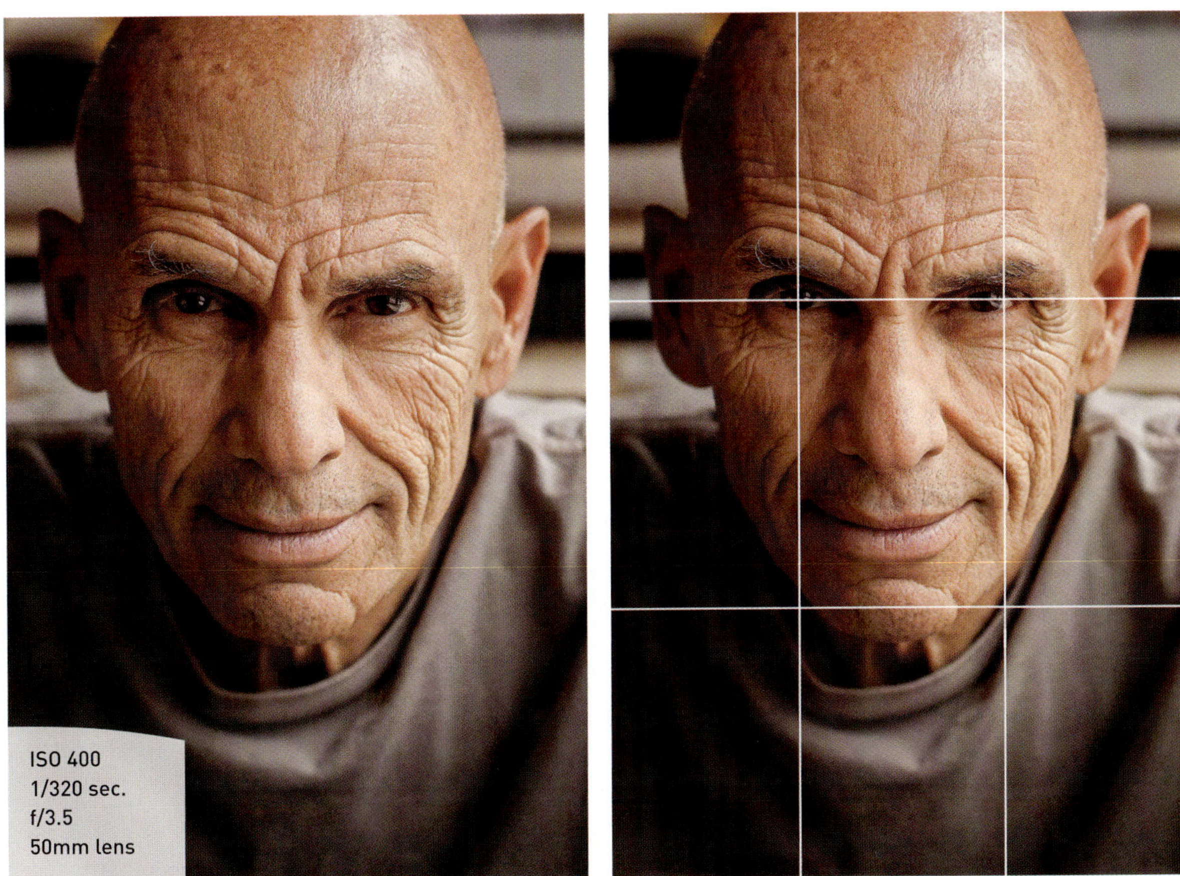

FIGURE 4.9
For my photograph of master photographer Joel Meyerowitz, I used the rule of thirds to build the composition and placed his eyes in the top third of the frame.

REMEMBER

The rule of thirds is a "rule," not a "law." Don't think that every photograph you make has to adhere to the rule of thirds. It's a great tool to use to build a composition, but sometimes breaking the rules can result in a better photograph.

PERSPECTIVE

Perspective, the position from which the photographer chooses to make a photograph, is important for any image, but especially when making a portrait. The point of view from which you choose to make the photograph is the very point of view that will impact the way the viewer experiences the photograph and the subject.

Photographers often make photographs from their own eye level, but it's important when making a portrait to consider the eye level of the subject, especially when you're photographing children (**Figure 4.10**). Try photographing the subject at his or her own eye level. This creates a sense of equality between the viewer and the subject, which can help create a sense of intimacy. If you want to give the subject a sense of power and authority, position the camera below the subject's eye level and shoot up slightly.

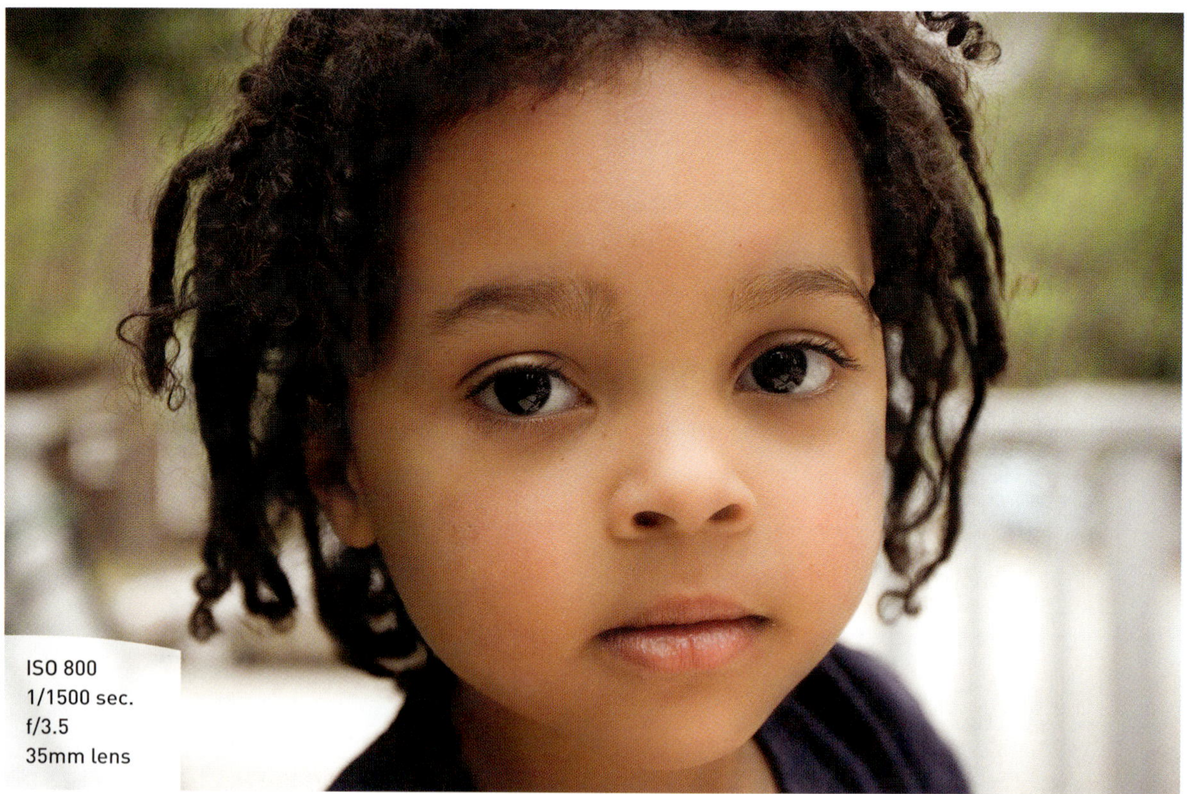

FIGURE 4.10
Getting down to the child's eye level allowed me to create a photograph that was more intimate than what would have been created by looking down on him.

CAMERA ORIENTATION

Camera orientation is another consideration to make when making a portrait. It can dramatically change how the viewer experiences the photograph and the environment the subject is in. A horizontal orientation can be good if you want to include a good amount of the environment in the scene, even if the background is thrown out of focus. It not only can provide a sense of place, but also can help to draw the viewers' attention to the subject.

A vertical composition can help emphasize the subject more by eliminating areas of the background. This can help emphasize the face and the expression, while eliminating distracting elements in the background that might pull the viewers' attention away from the person.

CLASSIC BLACK-AND-WHITE PORTRAITS

There is a certain classic look to black-and-white portraiture (**Figure 4.11**). By eliminating color in emphasizing dark and light tones, we can experience a portrait subject in a very different way than we do with a traditional color photograph.

Though I preferred to shoot color images and then later convert the images to black and white, the 5D Mark III allows you to see the captured image as a black-and-white image on your camera's LCD monitor when you shoot in the Monochrome picture style. If you're shooting JPEGs, the saved file will be a black-and-white image. If you're shooting raw, the original raw file will still be in color, allowing you to convert the shot into black and white using your favorite photo-editing application.

Whether you shoot and capture raw files or JPEGs, setting the display for black and white can be a great educational tool to begin to learn to see the world in black and white.

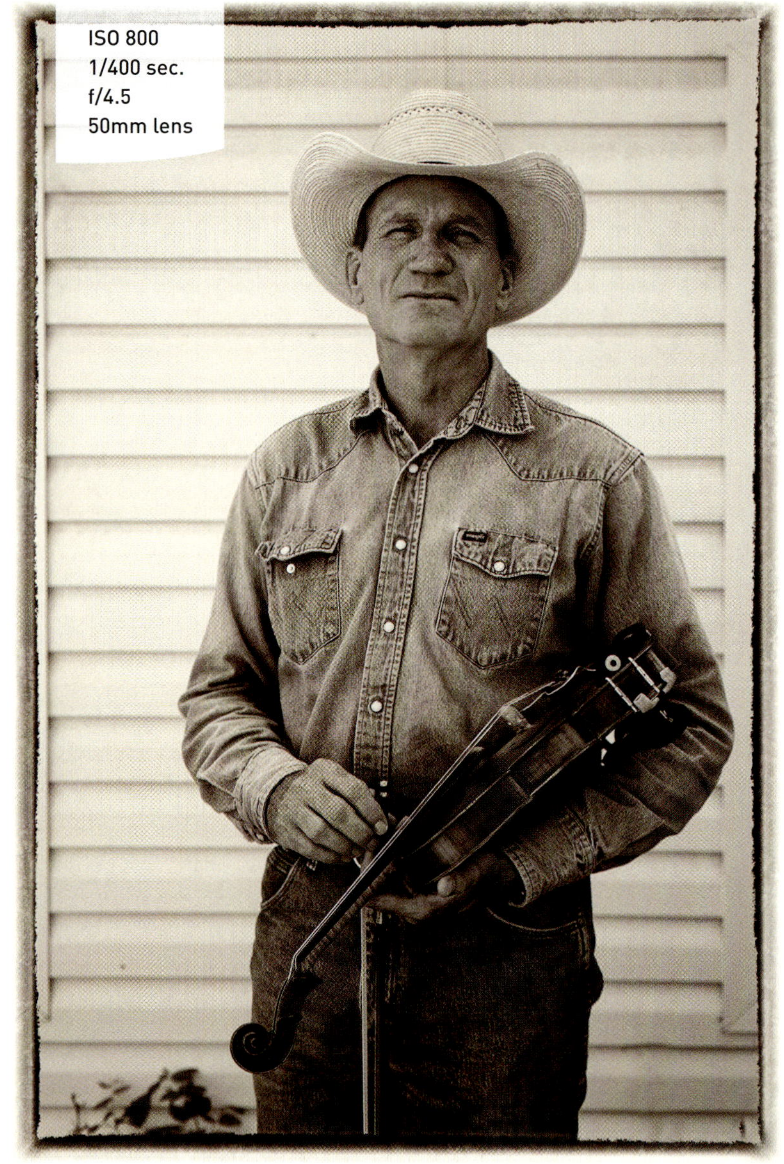

TO SET YOUR PICTURE STYLE TO MONOCHROME, FOLLOW THESE STEPS:

1. Press the Creative Photo/Comparative playback (Two-image display)/Direct print button, and use the Main Dial to select the Picture Style mode. Press the Setting button.

2. Use the Quick Control Dial to select Monochrome Picture Style. Press the Setting button.

Your camera will continue to shoot with the Monochrome picture style until you change it to another setting.

TO CUSTOMIZE THE PICTURE STYLE SETTINGS, FOLLOW THESE STEPS:

1. When you're in the Picture Style section of the menu where you selected Monochrome, press the Info button located to the left of your viewfinder.

2. Use the multi-controller to highlight the setting you want to change, and press the Setting button.

3. Use the multi-controller to move the cursor to a new position on the scale (the default setting will remain marked with a gray arrow) or to select a different filter, and press the Setting button.

4. Perform the same process for the other options. Then press the Menu button to return to the regular menu screen. You can now start shooting with your new settings.

TIPS FOR SHOOTING BETTER PORTRAITS

Before we get to the assignments for this chapter, I thought it might be a good idea to leave you with a few extra pointers on shooting portraits that don't necessarily have anything specific to do with your camera. Entire books cover subjects like portrait lighting, posing, and so on, but here are a few pointers that will make your people pictures look a lot better:

- **Choose a good quality of light.** I often prefer an area of open shade. However, one way to determine whether you're shooting your subject in bad light is simply to pay attention to what's happening with the shadows. If you see dark and harsh shadows appearing on the subject's face, particularly beneath the brow, chin, or nose, you're likely working with high-contrast light, which is rarely flattering for a subject. If you find yourself in such a lighting situation, move your subject into an area of open shade where the lighting will be much more flattering and pleasing.

- **Find a clean and simple background.** A common mistake is to photograph a subject but not pay attention to what's happening in the background. Such images can include huge distractions, which compete with the subject for the viewer's attention. Look for clean and simple backgrounds that are free of clutter. This will help the viewer focus completely on the subject.

Continued ➤

- **Choose an appropriate focal length**. Though you can use virtually any focal length for a portrait, I often prefer to use a focal length between 50mm and 135mm for most of the portraits that I make. I find that this focal length range renders the subject well, free of the distortion that might be found with a wider focal length. With longer telephoto lenses, I can throw the background out of focus and use the limited depth of field to emphasize my subject.

- **Pay attention to camera orientation**. Make images with the camera oriented both vertically and horizontally. Carefully consider what you include in the frame. If you believe that an element in the background is distracting, find a way to eliminate it. Remember that if anything in the frame doesn't serve the subject, you need to get rid of it.

- **Keep your eyes on the shutter speed**. You must be constantly vigilant with respect to your shutter speed. Many great portraits are ruined because of camera shake. So, whenever you're shooting in a lighting situation other than direct sunlight, make it a point to note your shutter speed and, if necessary, increase your ISO so that you can shoot with a fast-enough shutter speed to ensure a sharp photograph.

- **Don't ask people to smile**. Most people will put on a forced smile when the camera is pointed at them. Some smiles are very sincere and natural, but others look forced and uncomfortable. If they're the latter, don't hesitate to suggest that the subject not smile; tell the subject to relax and look directly into the camera's lens. This can result in a good portrait, which renders the subject in a very natural and sincere way.

- **Get down to the subject's eye level**. When photographing children, I always try to get down to their eye level. Moving from the adult point of view to a kid's point of view can make a remarkable difference in a photograph. Such images provide a level of intimacy that can't happen otherwise. So, don't hesitate to get on the floor with the kids, which will dramatically change the dynamic between you and them and, consequently, the photographs.

- **Photograph when they aren't looking**. Candid moments can be just as revealing as images where the subject is looking directly at the camera. Using a photojournalistic approach, a photographer can reveal the dynamics of relationships between people that are often missing in more traditional photographs. Being a fly on the wall and capturing images where people are interacting and reacting with each other can reveal more about the relationships than any other kind of image.

Chapter 4 Assignments

Experiment with Depth of Field

Using the longest focal length that you have available (for example, a 70mm focal length or longer), create a portrait. Try to find an area of open shade that has a simple and clean background. Set your camera to Aperture Priority mode and the white balance to the Shade preset. Choose the widest aperture available on your lens. Remember to observe your shutter speed and increase your ISO until you can achieve a shutter speed at which you can reliably handhold. Make a few photographs, and then shoot at a more moderate aperture, such as f/5.6, and compare the results. Again, stay aware of your shutter speed so that the image doesn't suffer from camera shake.

Observe the Quality of Light

Photograph your subject under a variety of lighting conditions: under direct sunlight, open shade, indoors using artificial light, and with window light. Observe the differences not only with respect to your exposure and white balance, but also the presence of shadows and how they fall on the subject and on the overall scene.

Learn to Handle Exposure Extremes

Position a subject in front of a bright window. Photograph your subject using all four metering modes: evaluative, partial, spot, and center-weighted average. Compare the images to see which of the metering modes provides you a better exposure under this extreme kind of lighting situation.

Create Creative Compositions

Create a series of portraits in which you position your subject in different areas of the frame. Create images with the subject in the very center of the frame, as well as images using the rule of thirds. Also, experiment with positioning your subject at the extreme edges of the frame, as well as shooting from different perspectives, both above and below the subject.

Shoot in Black and White

Enable the Monochrome picture style and create a series of black-and-white portraits. Photograph your subject in a variety of lighting conditions and see how the contrast changes as a result of your choice of lighting.

Share your results with this book's Flickr group!

Join the group here: www.flickr.com/groups/Canon5DMarkIIIFromSnapshotstoGreatShots

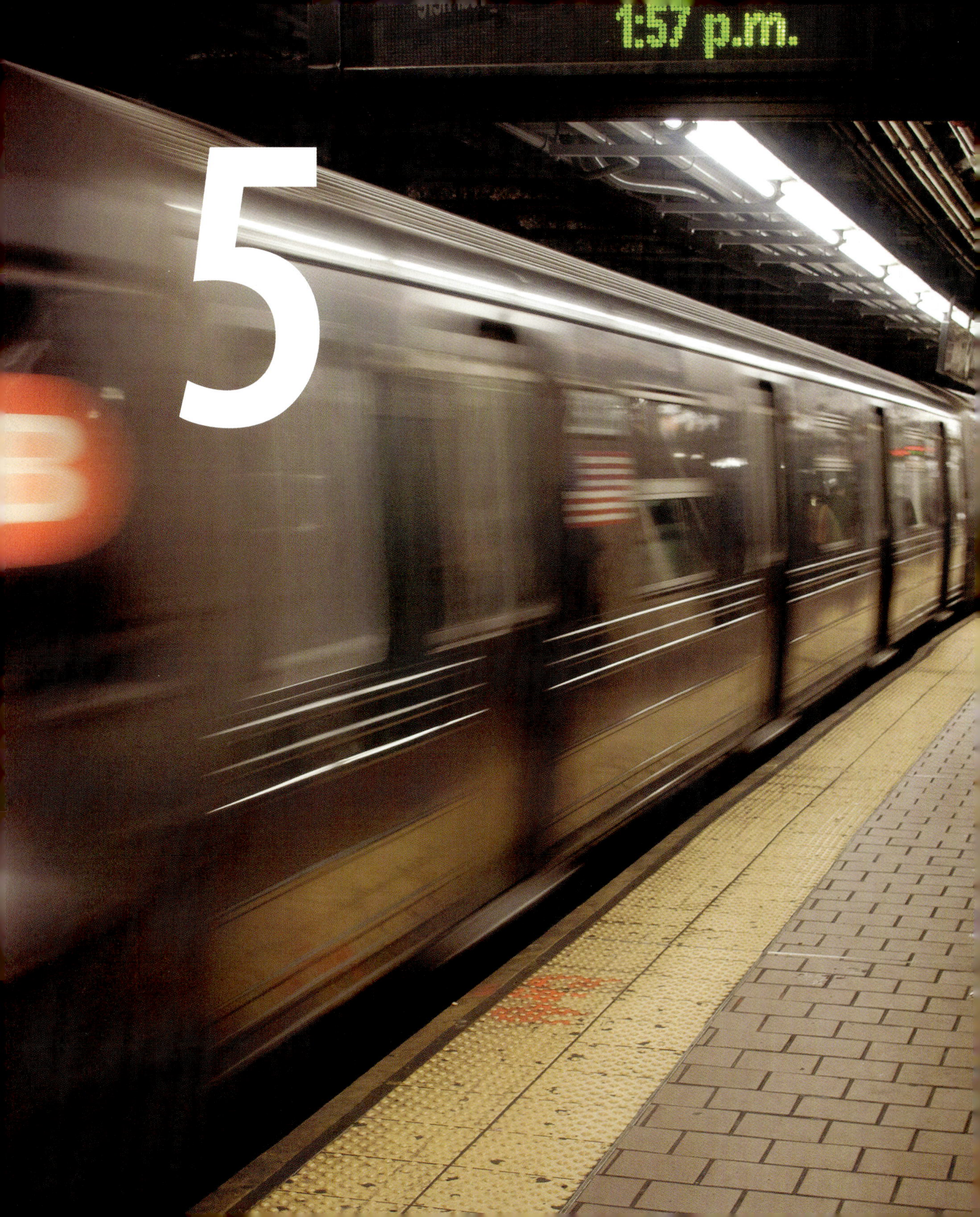

5

Moving Targets

TRICKS TO CAPTURING MOTION

Photographing moving subjects is likely the most challenging type of photography that's out there. The fast-moving action demands not only a lot of concentration, but also a lot of confidence with the camera. Merely having a professional-level camera is no guarantee that you can get a great shot of that one unforgettable and pivotal moment. It requires a balance of awareness and timing and technical know-how to really pull it off consistently. Capturing motion is more than just sports photography. There is movement everywhere, and how you capture that movement can result in some great photographs.

ISO 400
1/10 sec.
f/5
24–105mm lens

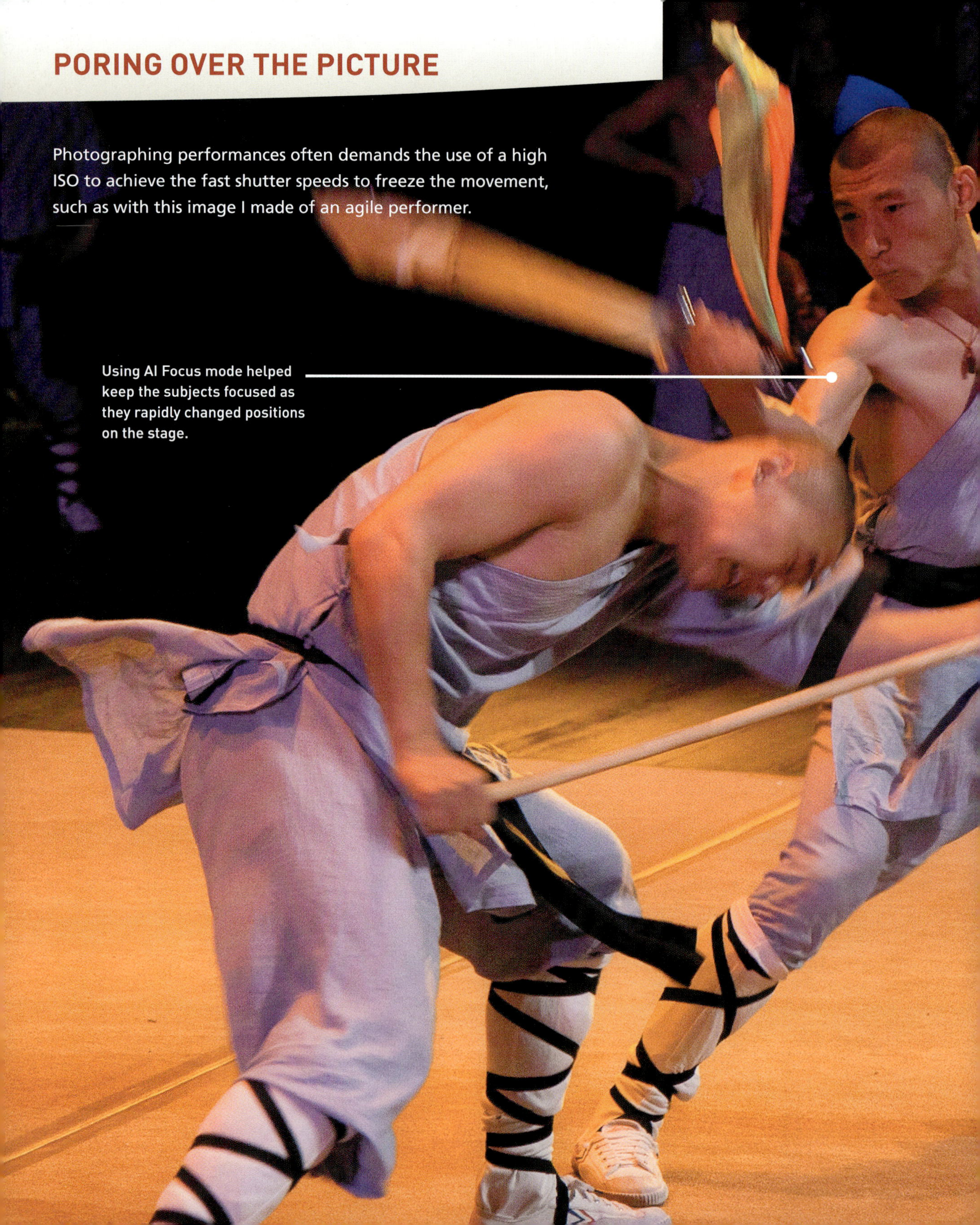

PORING OVER THE PICTURE

Photographing performances often demands the use of a high ISO to achieve the fast shutter speeds to freeze the movement, such as with this image I made of an agile performer.

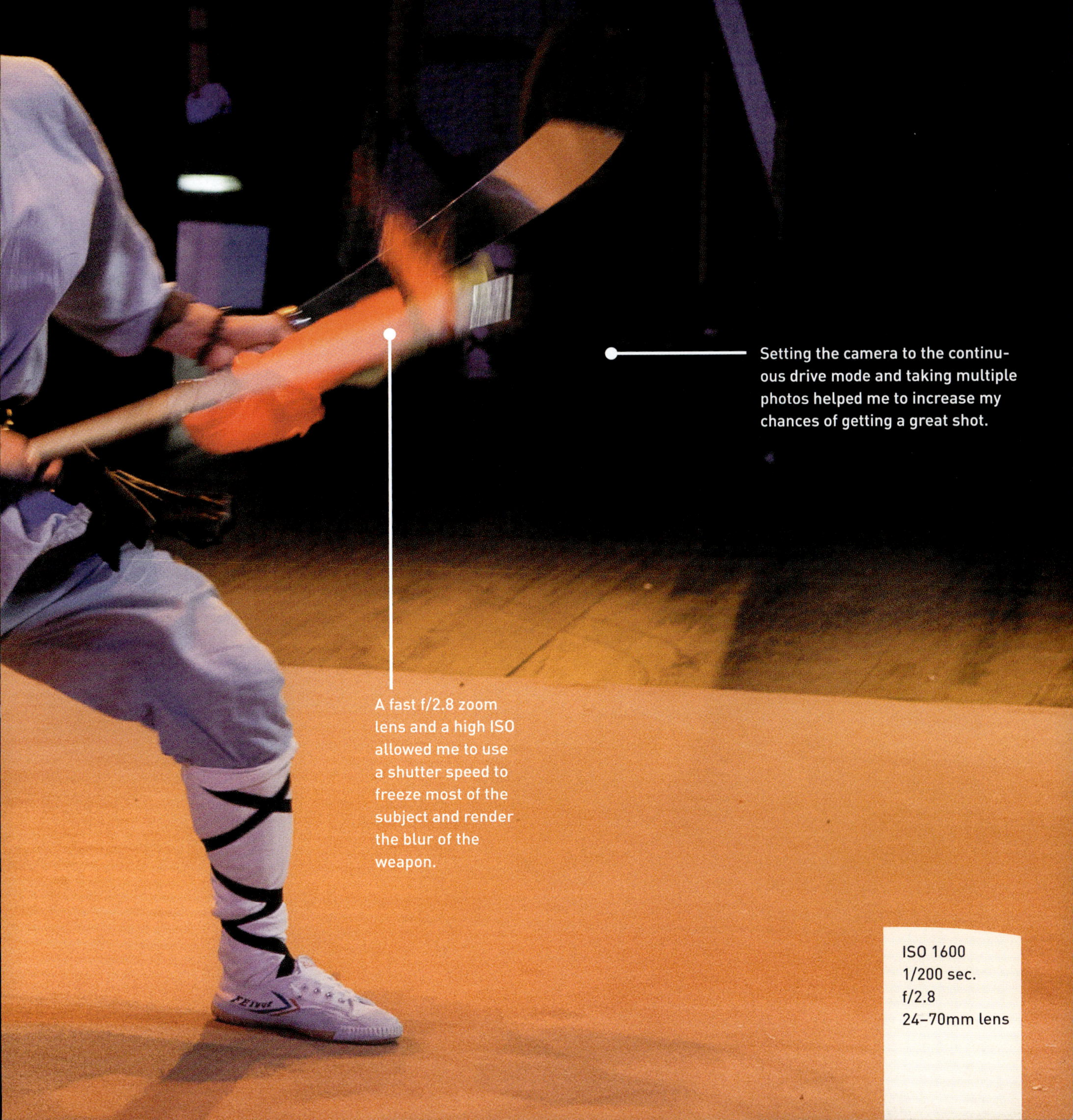

Setting the camera to the continuous drive mode and taking multiple photos helped me to increase my chances of getting a great shot.

A fast f/2.8 zoom lens and a high ISO allowed me to use a shutter speed to freeze most of the subject and render the blur of the weapon.

ISO 1600
1/200 sec.
f/2.8
24–70mm lens

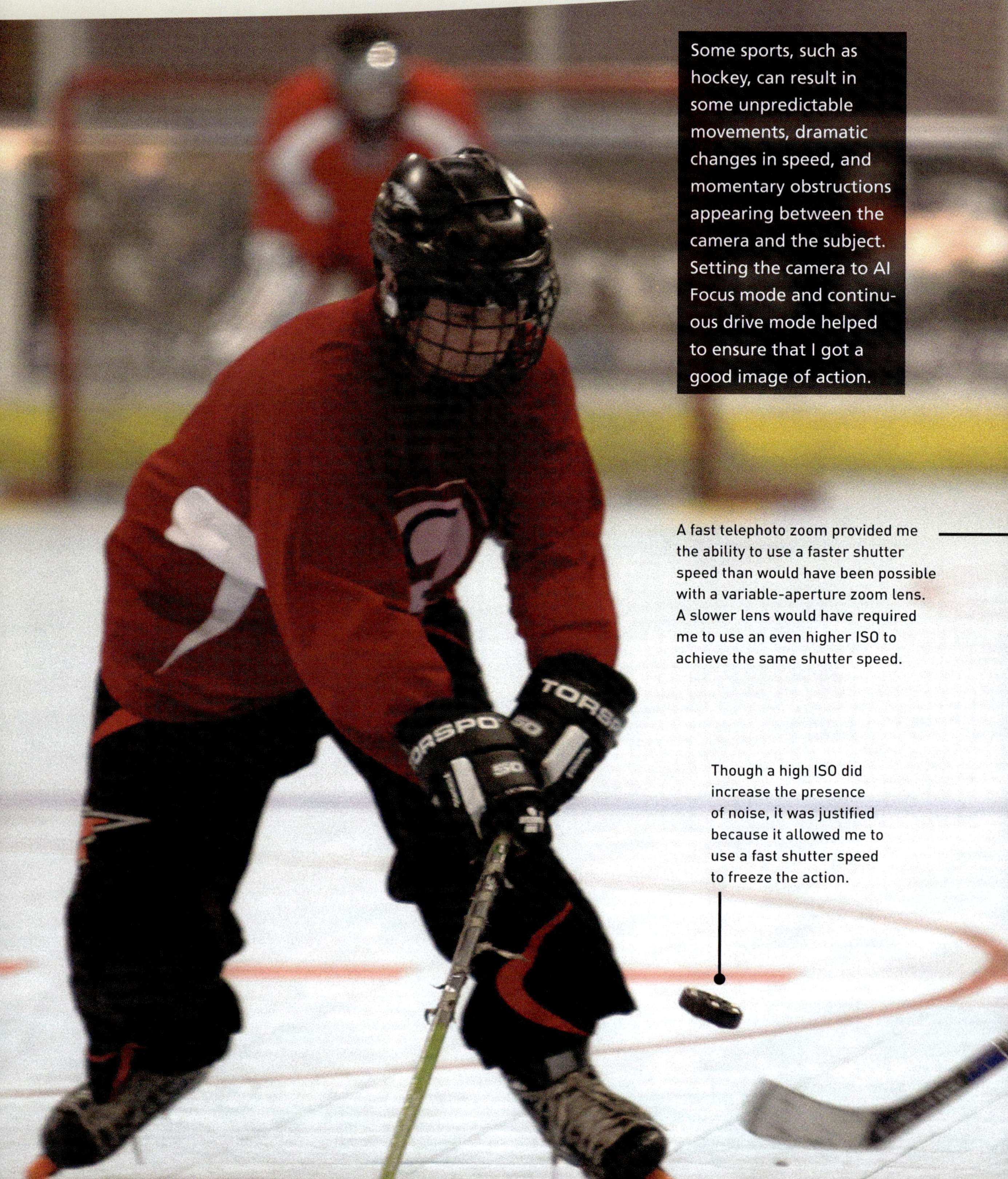

Some sports, such as hockey, can result in some unpredictable movements, dramatic changes in speed, and momentary obstructions appearing between the camera and the subject. Setting the camera to AI Focus mode and continuous drive mode helped to ensure that I got a good image of action.

A fast telephoto zoom provided me the ability to use a faster shutter speed than would have been possible with a variable-aperture zoom lens. A slower lens would have required me to use an even higher ISO to achieve the same shutter speed.

Though a high ISO did increase the presence of noise, it was justified because it allowed me to use a fast shutter speed to freeze the action.

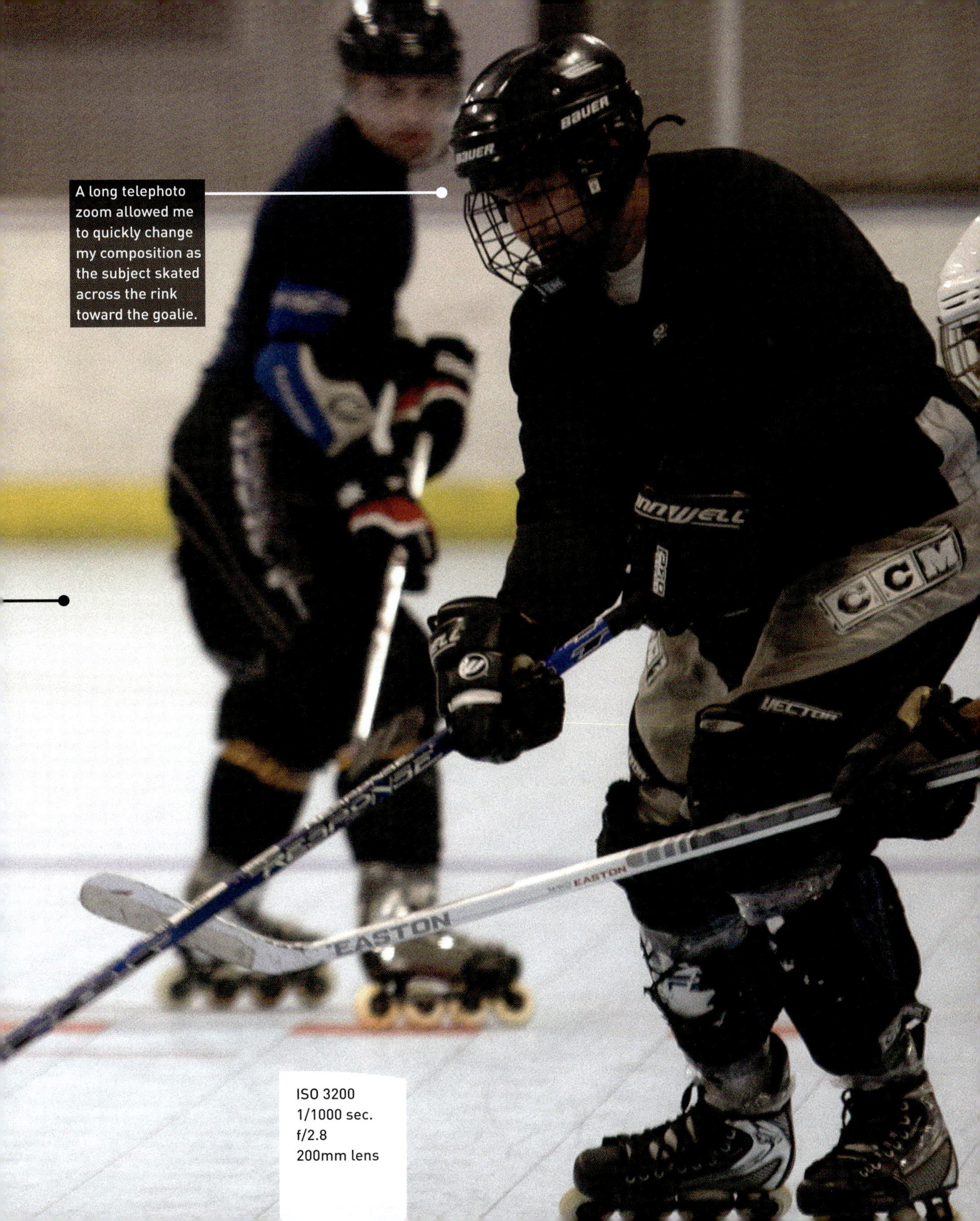
A long telephoto
zoom allowed me
to quickly change
my composition as
the subject skated
across the rink
toward the goalie.
ISO 3200
1/1000 sec.
f/2.8
200mm lens

THE THREE QUESTIONS TO ASK YOURSELF WHEN YOU'RE PHOTOGRAPHING MOVEMENT

Throughout this book, I've talked about the importance of shutter speed for exposure and sharpness, but when it comes to action or movement, shutter speed takes on a different and very important role. Shutter speed is how you can render the action. You can freeze the fast movement of a horse galloping toward the finish line or make a speeding car into an abstract of color and light. The choice of shutter speed controls how you capture the subject and visually render the action.

Many photographers want to freeze the action, which calls for shutter speeds of 1/500 second or faster. There is no one ideal shutter speed, but a shutter speed in this vicinity will provide you the ability to freeze action. The "best" shutter speed for any action will be influenced by the direction the subject is moving, how fast the subject is moving, and how far you are from the subject. And those factors are the subjects of the three questions you need to start with when you're photographing action.

WHICH DIRECTION IS MY SUBJECT MOVING?

Typically, the first thing that people think about when taking an action shot is how fast the subject is moving, but the first consideration should be the direction of travel. Where you're positioned in relation to the subject's direction of travel is critically important in selecting the proper shutter speed:

- **If the subject is moving across your viewfinder,** you need a faster shutter speed to keep that lateral movement from being recorded as a streak across your image. Alternatively, if you *want* to show the movement of the subject (**Figure 5.1**), you can use a slower shutter speed.

- **If your subject is moving perpendicular to your shooting location, either toward you or away from you,** you can use a slower shutter speed because the camera sees the subject as more stationary.

- **If your subject is moving in a diagonal direction,** both across the frame and toward or away from you, you need a shutter speed in between the two.

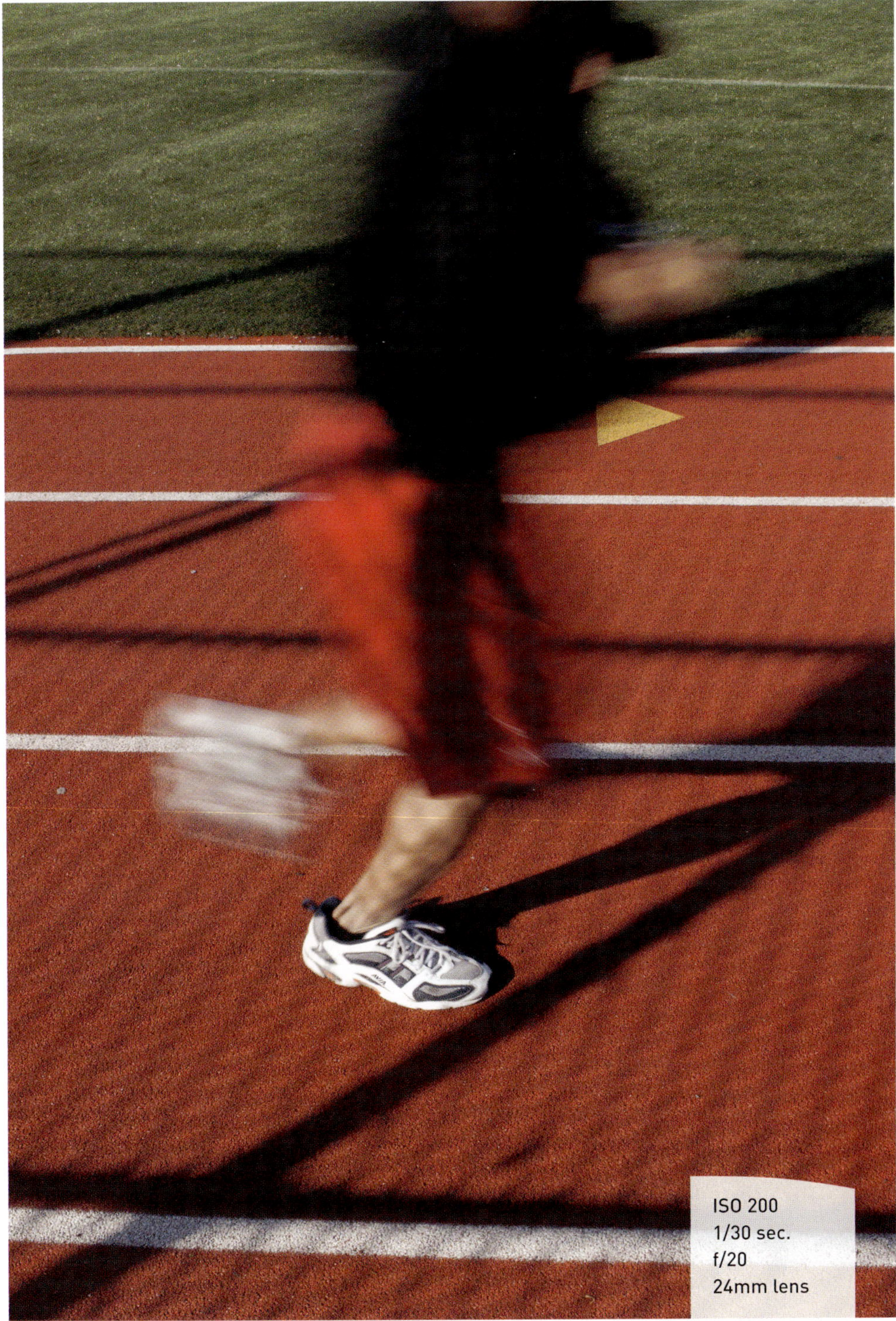
ISO 200
1/30 sec.
f/20
24mm lens

FIGURE 5.1
This runner was moving across the frame and demonstrates the direction of travel. The proximity of the camera to the subject and the shutter speed can impact how the motion is rendered.

HOW FAST IS MY SUBJECT MOVING?

After the angle of motion has been determined, you can assess the speed at which the subject is traveling. The faster your subject moves, the faster your shutter speed needs to be in order to freeze that subject. A person walking across your frame might only require a shutter speed of 1/60 second, while a skateboarder (**Figure 5.2**) traveling in the same direction would call for 1/500 second. That same skateboarder traveling toward you at the same rate of speed, rather than across the frame, might require a shutter speed of only 1/125 second. You can start to see how the relationship of speed and direction comes into play in your decision-making process.

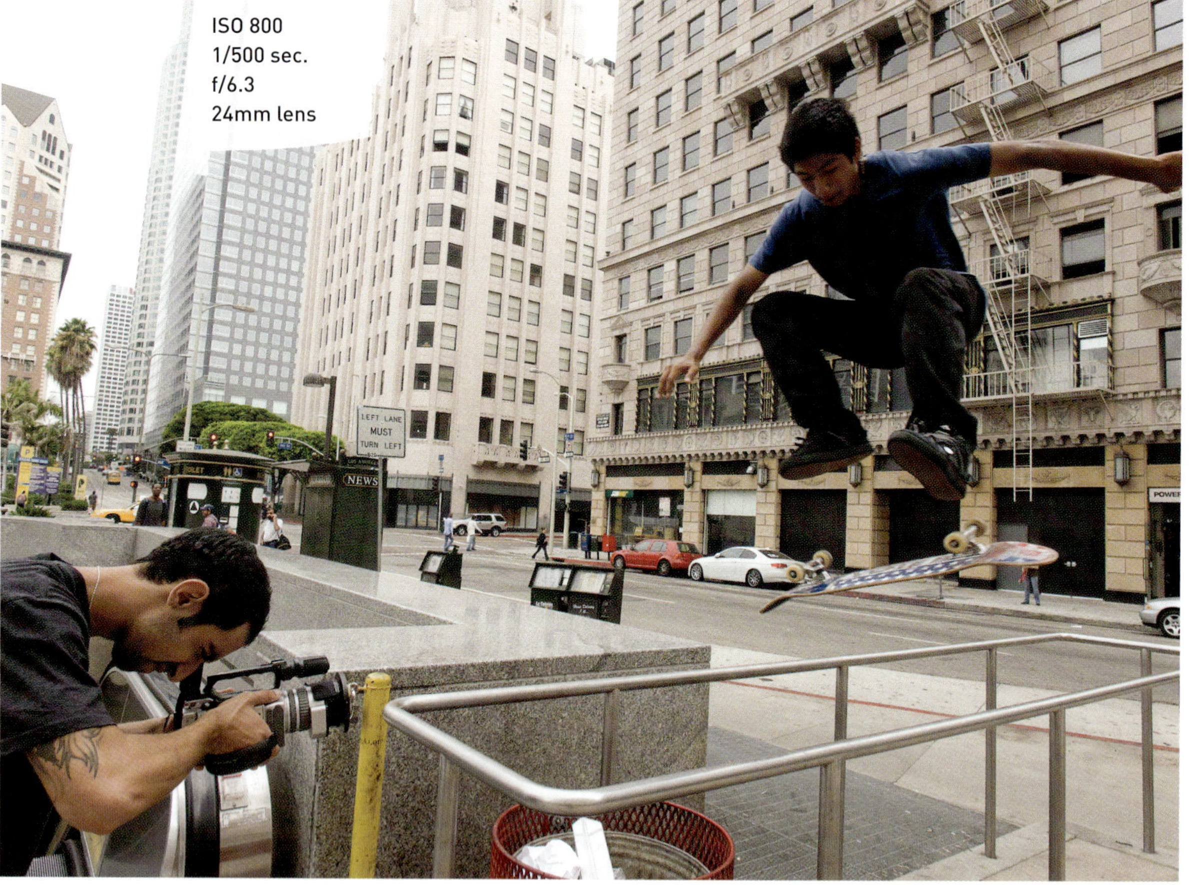

FIGURE 5.2

A fast-moving subject moving very close to the camera requires a faster shutter speed in order to freeze the movement, as with this image of a skateboarder.

HOW FAR AM I FROM MY SUBJECT?

One final factor to keep in mind when photographing moving subjects is their distance from the camera.

Imagine that you're standing on top of a tall building looking down at the street below. You can watch the cars moving with little effort. In other words, your eyes don't have to move very far to see cars travel from one block to another—you don't have to turn your head much to follow the cars.

Now imagine yourself on the sidewalk directly next to the street, and try to follow those cars traveling at the same speed. You would need to move your head from left to right to keep your eye on a car. Standing on the street requires a lot more movement on your part to keep up with the moving traffic (**Figure 5.3**).

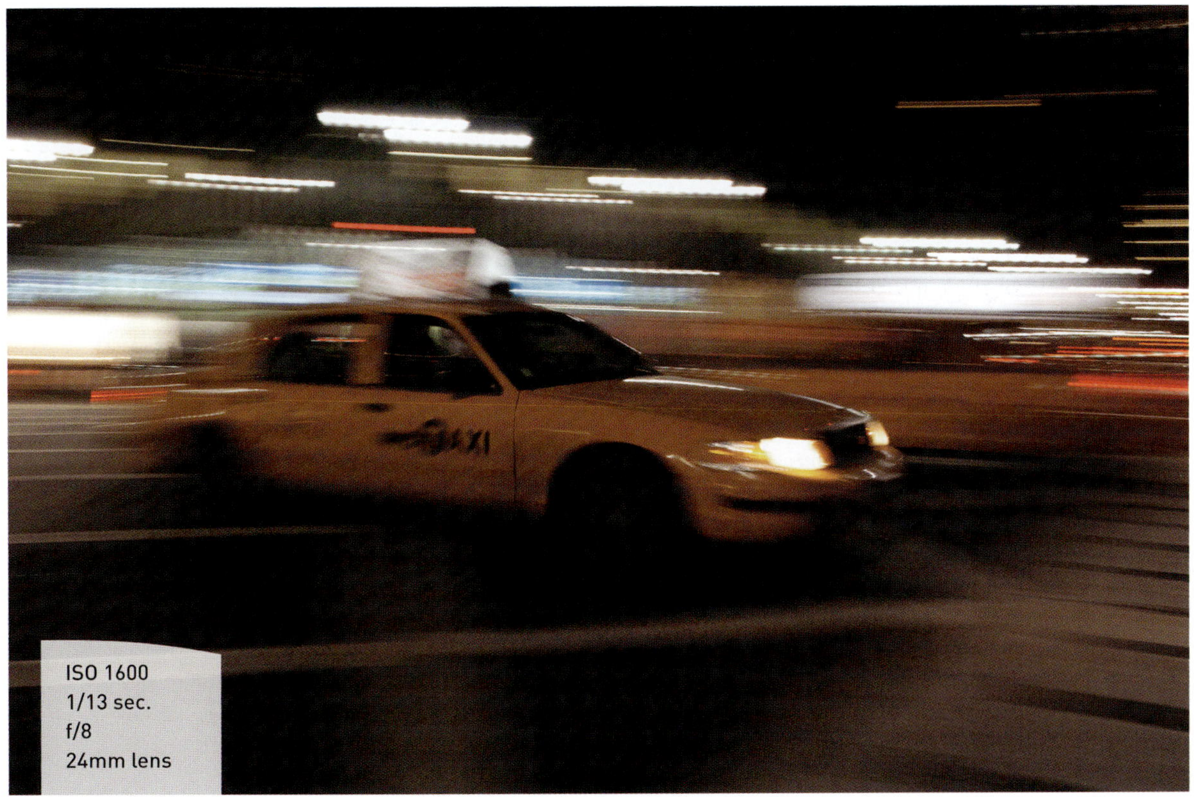

FIGURE 5.3
The close proximity of the cab and my use of a slow shutter speed while panning the camera allowed me to capture the energy and motion of the vehicle, resulting in a more creative take on a common sight in New York City.

FIGURE 5.4

The distance of the plane allowed me flexibility in how to capture it. In this case, I used a very fast shutter speed, which kept the plane sharp and rendered only a slight blur of the propellers.

Now imagine you're holding your camera and trying to photograph the cars in both of these two scenarios. Although the subject is traveling at the same speed in both instances, the movement of your camera will affect the shutter speed required in order to freeze the action. Photographing a fast-moving subject that is farther from you requires a slower shutter speed than if you were standing a few feet away from it, because the perceived speed is much slower (**Figure 5.4**).

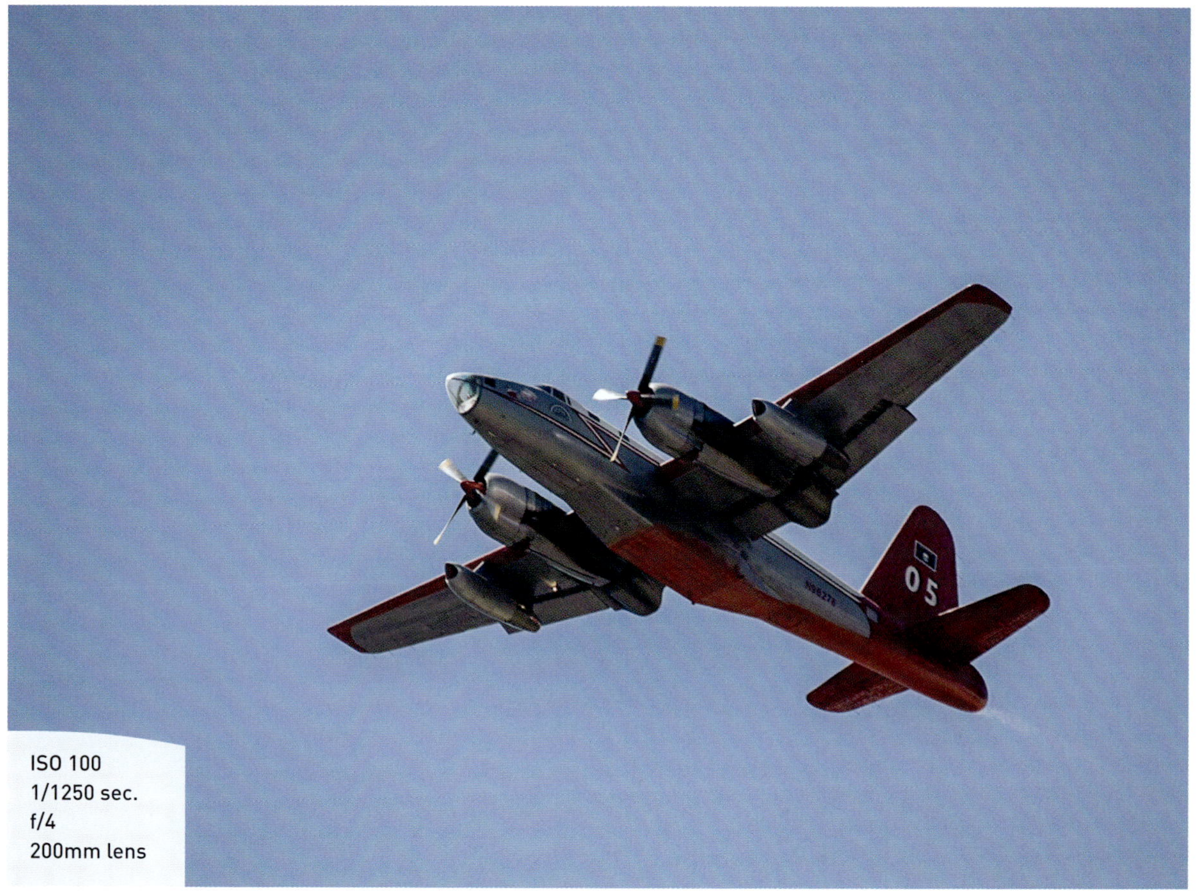

ISO 100
1/1250 sec.
f/4
200mm lens

WHAT EXPOSURE MODES CAN DO FOR YOUR MOTION PHOTOS

The choice of exposure mode does more than just provide you a good exposure; it also allows you to choose how much control you want over the aperture and shutter speed to control the look of your image. In portraiture, you often want to control your depth of field, so aperture is important. When it comes to action, shutter speed allows you to control how movement is captured.

USING SHUTTER PRIORITY MODE TO STOP MOTION

Although the choice of aperture is a critical consideration for portraits and landscape photography, in sports and action it's the shutter speed that's critical. So, it makes sense that Shutter Priority mode is the best exposure mode to use. You set the shutter speed to capture the action in the way you see fit, and the camera controls the aperture (**Figure 5.5**).

However, if you expect to use a fast shutter speed, you'll require a good deal of light. The lens will likely be set for a wide aperture. If light levels are very low, even the widest aperture of the lens may not be enough to produce a good exposure at low ISO. This will require you to increase the ISO in order to achieve an aperture that will give you a correct exposure, as well as allow you to use the fast shutter speed that you need.

So, if you find yourself photographing in a typical high school gymnasium, for example, which wasn't designed with photographers in mind, you'll likely need to increase your ISO to 800 or even higher because the light levels are low. If you don't increase the ISO, the shutter speed will be too slow to freeze the fast-moving action on the court.

You'll know if the aperture won't be enough to provide you a correct exposure when the aperture value on the LCD panel and in the viewfinder flashes. This is an indication to you that you'll need to increase the ISO in order to maintain your current choice of shutter speed.

In general, you want to keep your ISO as low as possible in order to reduce the presence of noise, but when it comes to action photography, noise is less important. If you don't get a sharp photograph of the action, it won't matter that the resulting photograph doesn't have much noise. If the action is unintentionally blurred, the image is useless. Here's the good news, though: the 5D Mark III has low noise at high ISO settings. So, don't hesitate to increase the ISO if it ensures you the fast shutter speed that you need.

FIGURE 5.5
I needed a very fast
shutter speed to
freeze the motion
of this motorcyclist
because of his
proximity to the
camera.

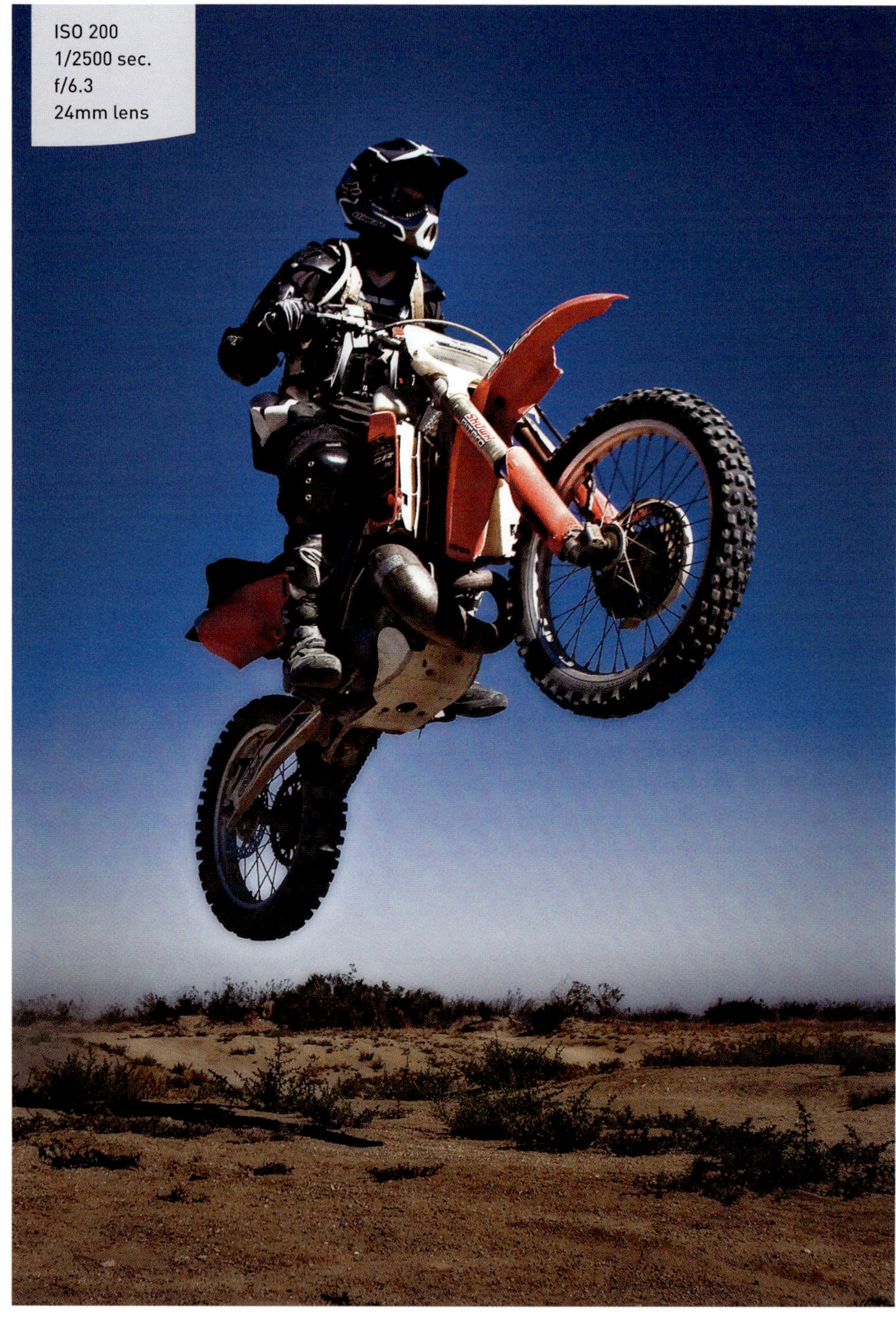
ISO 200
1/2500 sec.
f/6.3
24mm lens

USING APERTURE PRIORITY MODE TO ISOLATE YOUR SUBJECT

One of the benefits of working in Shutter Priority mode with fast shutter speeds is that, more often than not, you'll be shooting with the largest aperture available on your lens. Shooting with a large aperture allows you to use faster shutter speeds, but it also narrows your depth of field.

To isolate your subject in order to focus your viewer's attention, a larger aperture is required. The larger aperture reduces the foreground and background sharpness— the larger the aperture, the more blurred the foreground and background will be.

I'm bringing this up here because, when you're shooting most sporting events, the idea is to isolate your main subject by having it in focus while the rest of the image has some amount of blur. This sharp focus draws your viewer right to the subject. Studies have shown that the eye is drawn to sharp areas before moving on to the blurry areas. Also, depending on what your subject matter is, there can be a tendency to get distracted by a busy background if everything in the photo is equally sharp. Without a narrow depth of field, it might be difficult for the viewer to establish exactly what the main subject in your picture is.

Let's look at how to use depth of field to bring focus to your subject. In the previous section, I told you that you should use Shutter Priority mode for getting those really fast shutter speeds to stop action. Generally speaking, Shutter Priority mode will be the one you use most often for shooting sports and other action, but sometimes you'll want to ensure that you're getting the narrowest depth of field possible in your image. The way to do this is by using Aperture Priority mode.

So, how do you know when you should use Aperture Priority mode as opposed to Shutter Priority mode? It's not a simple answer, but your LCD monitor can help you make this determination. The best scenario for using Aperture Priority mode is a brightly lit scene where maximum apertures will still give you plenty of shutter speed to stop the action.

For example, say you're shooting a soccer game in the midday sun. If you've deter-mined that you need something between 1/500 and 1/1250 second for stopping the action, you could just set your camera to a high shutter speed in Shutter Priority mode and start shooting. But you also want to be using an aperture of, say, f/4.5 to get that narrow depth of field. Here's the problem: If you set your camera to Shutter Priority and select 1/1000 second as a nice compromise, you might get that desired f/stop ... but you might not. As the meter is trained on your moving subject, the light levels could rise or fall, which might actually change that desired f-stop to something higher, like f/5.6 or even f/8. Now the depth of field is extended, and you'll no longer get that nice isolation and separation that you wanted.

To rectify this, switch the camera to Aperture Priority mode and select f/4.5 as your aperture. Now, as you begin shooting, the camera holds that aperture and makes exposure adjustments with the shutter speed **(Figure 5.6)**. This technique works well when you have lots of light—enough light so that you can have a high-enough shutter speed without introducing motion blur.

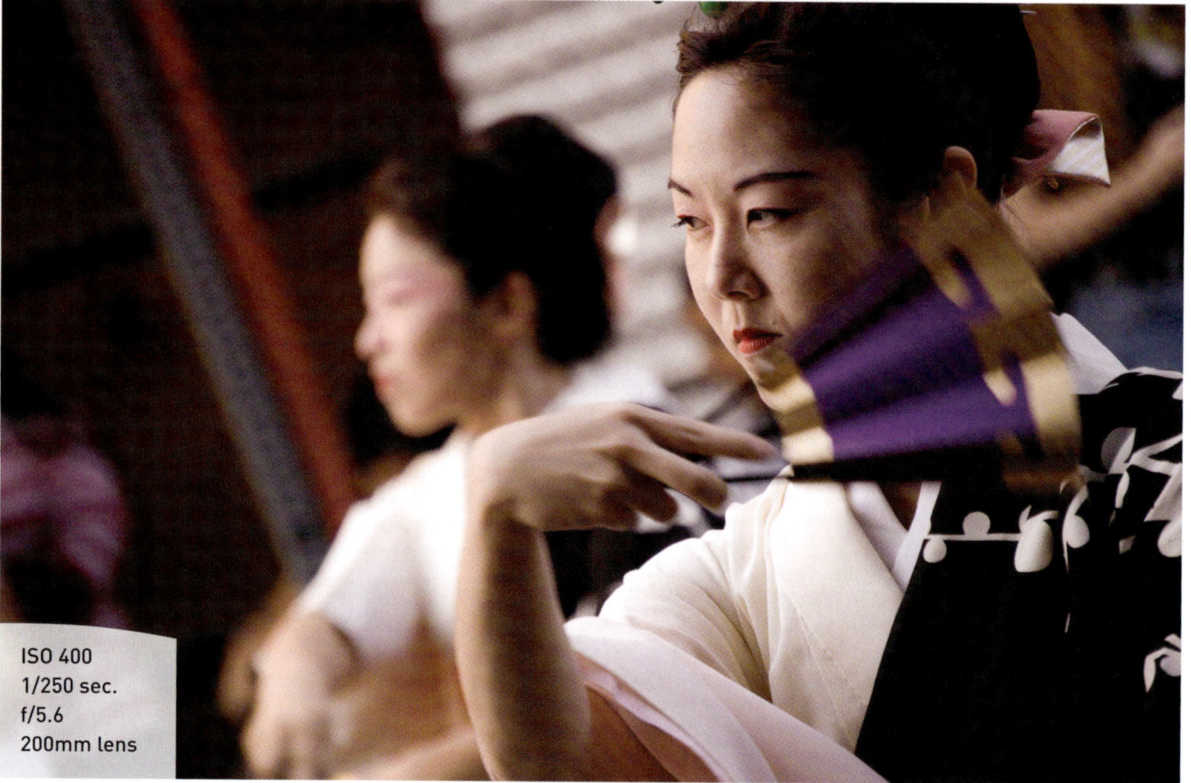

FIGURE 5.6
By selecting a large aperture setting, this geisha is nicely separated from the background, while the moderate shutter speed keeps her sharp but renders the movement of the fan with a slight blur.

KEEPING IT IN FOCUS

With the exposure issue handled for the moment, let's move on to a subject of equal importance: focusing.

CHOOSING A FOCUS MODE

The 5D Mark III has several focus modes to choose from. To get the greatest benefit from each of them, you need to understand how they work and the situations where each mode will give you the best opportunity to grab a great shot.

AI SERVO AF

Because we're discussing subject movement, your first choice is going to be AI Servo AF mode. (The AI stands for Artificial Intelligence.) AI Servo uses all the focus points in the camera to find a moving subject and then lock in the focus when the shutter button is completely pressed. Unlike One-Shot AF mode, which works best for stationary subjects, AI Servo AF mode will help track your subject in the frame and give you better focus results.

TO SELECT AND SHOOT IN AI SERVO AF MODE, FOLLOW THESE STEPS:

1. Press the AF mode selection/Drive mode selection button.

2. Rotate the Main Dial until AI Servo appears on the LCD panel.

3. Locate your subject in the viewfinder, and then press and hold the shutter button halfway to activate the focus mechanism.

4. The camera will maintain focus on your subject, as long as the subject remains within one of the focus points in the viewfinder or until you take a picture.

NOTE

The AF mode is used to select the method with which the camera will focus the lens. This is different from the AF point mode, which determines where you want the lens to focus using a cluster of small points that are visible in the viewfinder.

When using AI Servo AF mode, you have the choice of using the AF point mode in automatic or selecting a group of AF points or individual AF points. To select a focus point or using the AF point mode, follow these steps:

1. Press the AF point selection button.

2. Press the AF area selection mode/Multi-function button repeatedly to cycle through your options for AF Select Area.

3. Use the multi-controller to select the group or individual focus point for focus detection. You also can use the Main Dial and Quick Control Dial to make a selection.

AI FOCUS AF

If you're going to be changing between a moving target and one that's still, you should consider using the AI Focus AF mode. This mode mixes both the One-Shot AF and AI Servo AF modes for shooting a subject that goes from stationary to moving without having to adjust your focus mode.

When you have a stationary subject, simply place your selected focus point on your subject, and the camera will focus on it. If your subject begins to move out of focus, the camera will switch to AI Servo AF mode and track the movement, keeping a sharp focus.

For example, suppose you're shooting a football game. The quarterback has brought the team to the line and he's standing behind the center, waiting for the ball to be hiked. If you're using the AI Focus AF mode, you can place your focus point on the quarterback and start taking pictures of him as he stands at the line. As soon as the ball is hiked and the action starts, the camera will switch to AI Servo AF mode and track his movement within the frame. This technique can be a little tricky at first, but once you master it, it'll make your action shooting effortless. Using this mode, you can identify your subject for the camera so that it knows exactly which subject to maintain as the priority for your focus selection.

To select AI Focus AF mode, simply follow the same steps listed for selecting AI Servo AF, but instead select the AI Focus AF mode.

MANUAL FOCUS

I use the autofocus modes for the majority of my shooting, but sometimes I like to fall back on manual focus. This usually happens when I know when and where the action will occur and I want to capture the subject as it crosses a certain plane of focus. Manual focus is especially useful in sports like motocross or horse racing

(**Figure 5.7**), where the subjects are on a defined track. By prefocusing the camera, all I have to do is wait for the subject to approach my point of focus and then start firing the camera.

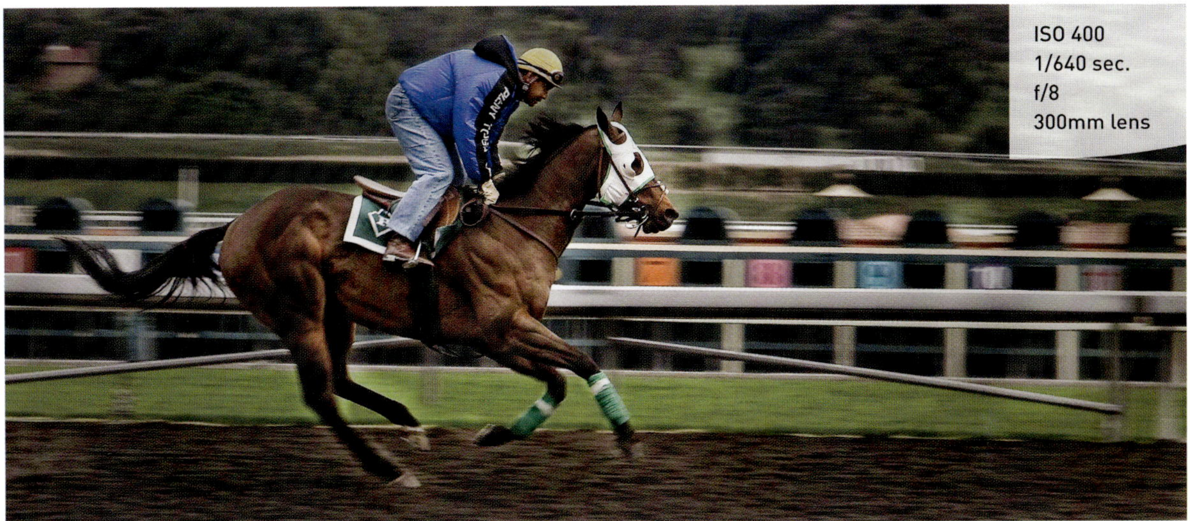

FIGURE 5.7
Prefocus the camera to a point where you know the subject will be, and start shooting right before the subject gets there.

CUSTOMIZING AF PERFORMANCE

Not only is the 5D Mark III's autofocus system faster than that of the 5D Mark II, but it also provides much greater flexibility and control. Depending on the action or the sport that you're photographing, the subjects will travel at different speeds; they may change directions abruptly; or they may have other elements, such as another player, that may obstruct your view of them while photographing. Each of these factors can make accurate focus a challenge. However, the 5D Mark III makes it possible to adjust the autofocus performance with just those things in mind, making it far easier to achieve consistently sharp photographs.

The following functions are preset cases that customize the AI focus performance of the camera for different types of action:

- **Case 1: Versatile multipurpose setting:** This is a general mode, which can handle a great majority of movement shots. This mode can accommodate subjects that temporarily stray from the active AF points or when a new subject comes into the frame. The camera can easily track the movement of a subject as the subject moves left, right, up, or down within the active autofocus sensors.

- **Case 2: Continue to track a subject, ignoring possible obstacles:** This mode emphasizes the subject on which the camera has begun tracking focus. If a momentary obstruction or another element enters the active AF sensors, the camera will continue to calculate focus for the primary subject.

- **Case 3: Instantly focus on subjects suddenly entering AF points:** This mode allows you to switch to another moving subject and begin tracking it, allowing you to achieve effective focus even as your subject matter changes. If another element moves in front of your subject, the camera will refocus on the element closer to the camera.

- **Case 4: For subjects that accelerate or decelerate quickly:** This mode is ideally suited for subjects whose speed can change dramatically during a movement, including a sudden stop.

- **Case 5: For erratic subjects moving in any direction:** This mode is good for subjects that can dramatically change position within the frame, whether up or down, left or right. This setting is optimized for use with AF point expansion, Zone AF, or 61-point automatic selection AF.

- **Case 6: For subjects that change speed and move erratically:** This mode offers maximum adaptability for tracking subjects whose direction and speed of movement can rapidly change. This setting is optimized for use with AF point expansion, Zone AF, or 61-point automatic selection AF.

1. Press the Menu button and turn the Main Dial to access the AF1: AF Configure menu screen.

2. Rotate the Quick Control Dial to select one of the AF Cases and press the Setting button.

CUSTOMIZING AF FUNCTION

You can further customize the camera to suit your unique shooting needs when using AI Servo AF. Customizing the autofocus function determines whether confirmation of focus, releasing the shutter, or a balance of the two will be the priority.

For example, some photographers who shoot football may prefer to weight the priority to release to ensure that they get a shot, even if it isn't tack sharp, because it may be an important moment in game play. They don't want to lose an important moment waiting for the camera to nail the focus. This may result in some images being slightly out of focus, but it may make the difference between getting and not getting the all-important shot.

By default, the camera sets an equal weight between focus confirmation and the release. However, you have the ability to bias the performance either way for the first and subsequent images when shooting continuously.

AI SERVO 1ST IMAGE PRIORITY

This setting controls how the camera will perform for the first image captured during a continuous burst when shooting in AI Servo AF:

1. Press the Menu button and turn the Main Dial to access the AF2: AI Servo menu screen. Rotate the Quick Control Dial to select AI Servo 1st image priority. Press the Setting button.

2. Rotate the Quick Control Dial counterclockwise to select Release to make taking the picture the priority. Rotate the Quick Control Dial clockwise to make focusing the priority.

AI SERVO 2ND IMAGE PRIORITY

This setting controls how the camera will perform with subsequent images made during a continuous burst when shooting in AI Servo AF:

1. Press the Menu button and turn the Main Dial to access the AF2: AI Servo menu screen. Rotate the Quick Control Dial to select AI Servo 2nd image priority. Press the Setting button.

2. Rotate the Quick Control Dial counterclockwise to select Release to make taking the picture the priority. Rotate the Quick Control Dial clockwise to make focusing the priority.

ONE-SHOT AF RELEASE PRIORITY

This setting controls how the camera will perform in Single shooting mode when the camera will fire only once on pressing the shutter button. By default, the camera is biased for focus confirmation, which is recommended. However, you also can set this for release priority.

1. Press the Menu button and turn the Main Dial to access the AF3: One Shot menu screen. Rotate the Quick Control Dial to select One-Shot AF release priority. Press the Setting button.

2. Rotate the Quick Control Dial counterclockwise to change from the camera default of focus priority and to instead select Release, thus making taking the picture the priority.

SELECTING YOUR AF POINTS

If you prefer to change and select your active AF points when using Single-point AF, you might find it tedious to have to navigate across all 61 autofocus sensors to reach a single sensor. In this situation, you actually can reduce the number of sensors that will be active, resulting in less effort to choose individual autofocus sensors or groups of sensors. You have four choices to select from (**Figure 5.8**):

- **61 Points:** All 61 autofocus points are selectable.

- **Only cross-type AF points:** These will vary based on the maximum aperture of your lens.

- **15 Points:** Only 15 major AF points will be manually selectable.

- **9 Points:** Only 9 major AF points will be manually selectable.

If the camera is set for automatic AF point selection, the camera will still use all 61 autofocus points for detection.

To set selectable AF points, follow these steps:

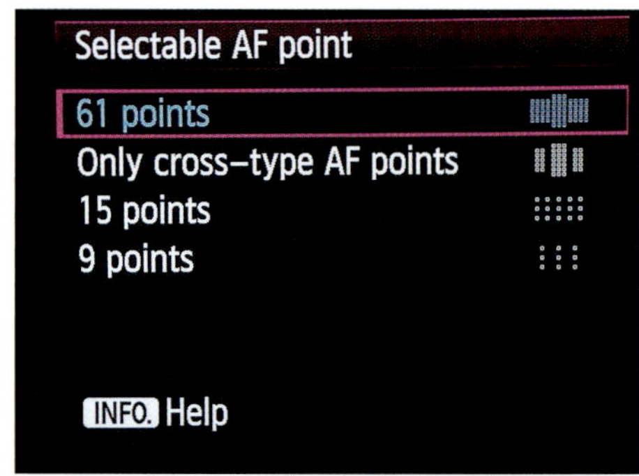

FIGURE 5.8

Choosing how many AF points are active can prove a big convenience if you prefer to choose your AF points manually using Single-point AF mode.

1. Press the Menu button and turn the Main Dial to access the AF4 menu screen. Rotate the Quick Control Dial to select Selectable AF point. Press the Setting button.

2. Rotate the Quick Control Dial to the number of AF points you want active. Press the Setting button.

DRIVE-MODE OPTIONS

The drive mode determines how fast your camera will take pictures. The single drive mode is for taking one photograph at a time. With every full press of the shutter button, the camera takes a single image. The continuous drive mode allows for a more rapid capture rate—think of it like a machine gun. When you're using the continuous drive mode, the camera continues to take pictures as long as the shutter button is held down (or until the memory buffer fills up).

When in AI Servo AF mode, you can set your camera's drive mode to three settings:

- **Single shooting:** Pressing the shutter button will result in only one shot being taken.

- **High-speed continuous shooting:** A maximum of six shots per second will be captured while maintaining pressure on the shutter button.

- **Low-speed continuous shooting:** Three shots per second will be captured while maintaining pressure on the shutter button.

The continuous drive mode isn't just suitable for sports—it can help to capture the telling moment in everyday life (**Figure 5.9**) or create a series of images that tell a complete story.

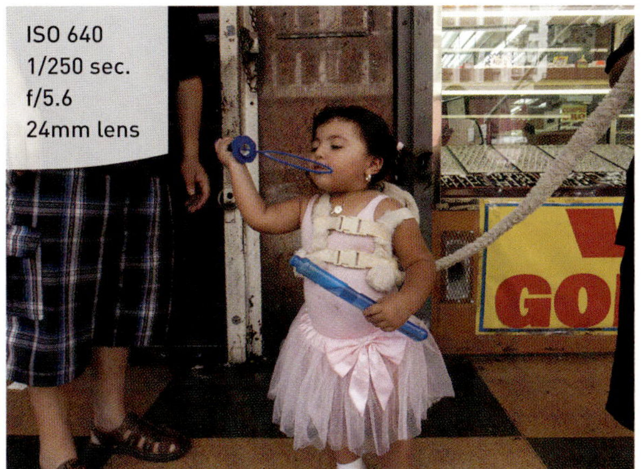

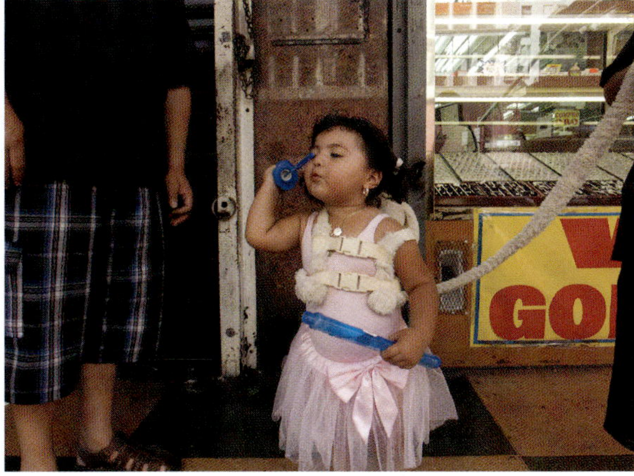

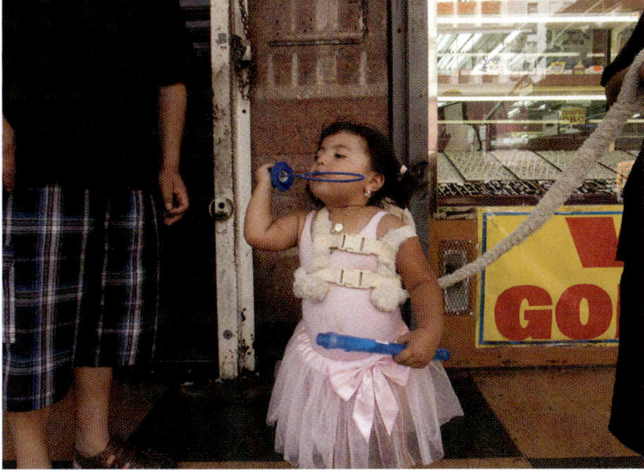

FIGURE 5.9
The continuous drive mode allowed me to capture this series of images of a young girl attempting to blow bubbles.

1. Press the AF mode selection/Drive mode selection button.

2. Rotate the Quick Control Dial while looking at the LCD panel to select between
   single shooting, high-speed continuous shooting, and low-speed continuous
   shooting. The icon that looks like stacked-up rectangles is the continuous mode.
   Press the Setting button to lock in your change.

3. To shoot, just press the shutter button and hold until the desired number of
   frames has been captured.

> **NOTE**
>
> Your camera has internal memory, called a "buffer," where images are stored while they're
> being processed prior to being moved to your memory card. Depending on the image
> format you're using (RAW, JPEG, RAW+JPEG), the buffer might fill up and the camera
> will stop shooting until space is made in the buffer for new images. If this happens, you'll
> see "Busy" appear in the viewfinder and on the LCD monitor. The camera readout in the
> viewfinder tells you how many frames you have available.

CHOOSING A LENS

An important consideration with autofocus performance will be your choice of lens.
Though the 5D Mark III offers 61 autofocus sensors, how many are active and how
they perform will be the result of the speed of your lens. Fast lenses with maximum
apertures of f/2.8 and faster offer the greatest access to all types of autofocus sensors, including cross-type sensors for improved autofocus performance. Slower lenses,
such as variable-aperture zooms (for example, f/4–5.6), will result in some autofocus
sensors not being active, as a result of their lower light-gathering capability.

If you intend to shoot a lot of action or sports, especially in low-light conditions, you
should consider investing in fast lenses such as a the 70–200 f/2.8 or 300mm f/2.8
(depending on the sport that you're shooting).

CREATING A SENSE OF MOTION

Shooting motion isn't always about freezing the action. Sometimes you want to convey a sense of motion so that the viewer can get a feel for the movement and flow of an event. Two techniques you can use to achieve this effect are panning and motion blur.

PANNING

Panning has been used for decades to capture the speed of a moving object as it moves across the frame. It doesn't work well for subjects that are moving toward you or away from you. Panning is achieved by following your subject across your frame, moving your camera along with the subject, and using a slower-than-normal shutter speed so that the background (and sometimes even a bit of the subject) has a sideways blur, but the main portion of your subject is sharp and blur-free.

The key to a great panning shot is selecting the right shutter speed: too fast and you won't get the desired blurring of the background; too slow and the subject will have too much blur and won't be recognizable. Practice the technique until you can achieve a smooth motion with your camera that follows along with your subject (**Figure 5.10**).

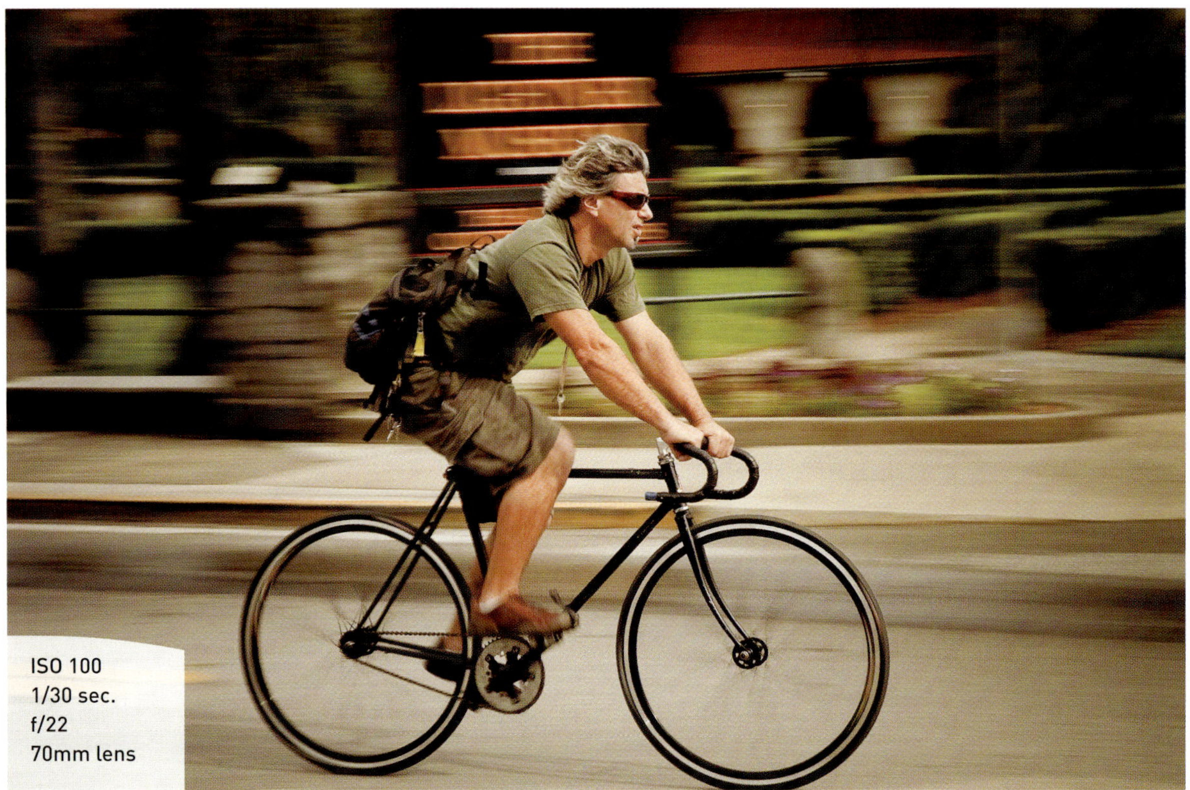

TIP

When panning, be sure to follow through even after the shutter has closed. This will keep the motion smooth and give you better images.

MOTION BLUR

Another way to let the viewer in on the feel of the action is to simply include some blur in the image. This isn't accidental blur caused by choosing the wrong shutter speed. This blur is more exaggerated, and it tells a story.

Just as in panning, there is no preordained shutter speed to use for this effect. It's simply a matter of trial and error until you have a look that conveys the action. The key to this technique is the correct shutter speed combined with keeping the camera still during the exposure. You're trying to capture the motion of the subject, not the photographer or the camera, so use a good shooting stance or even a tripod.

A great way to use this technique is to have a static background to serve as a contrast element to the blurred movement of the subject (**Figure 5.11**).

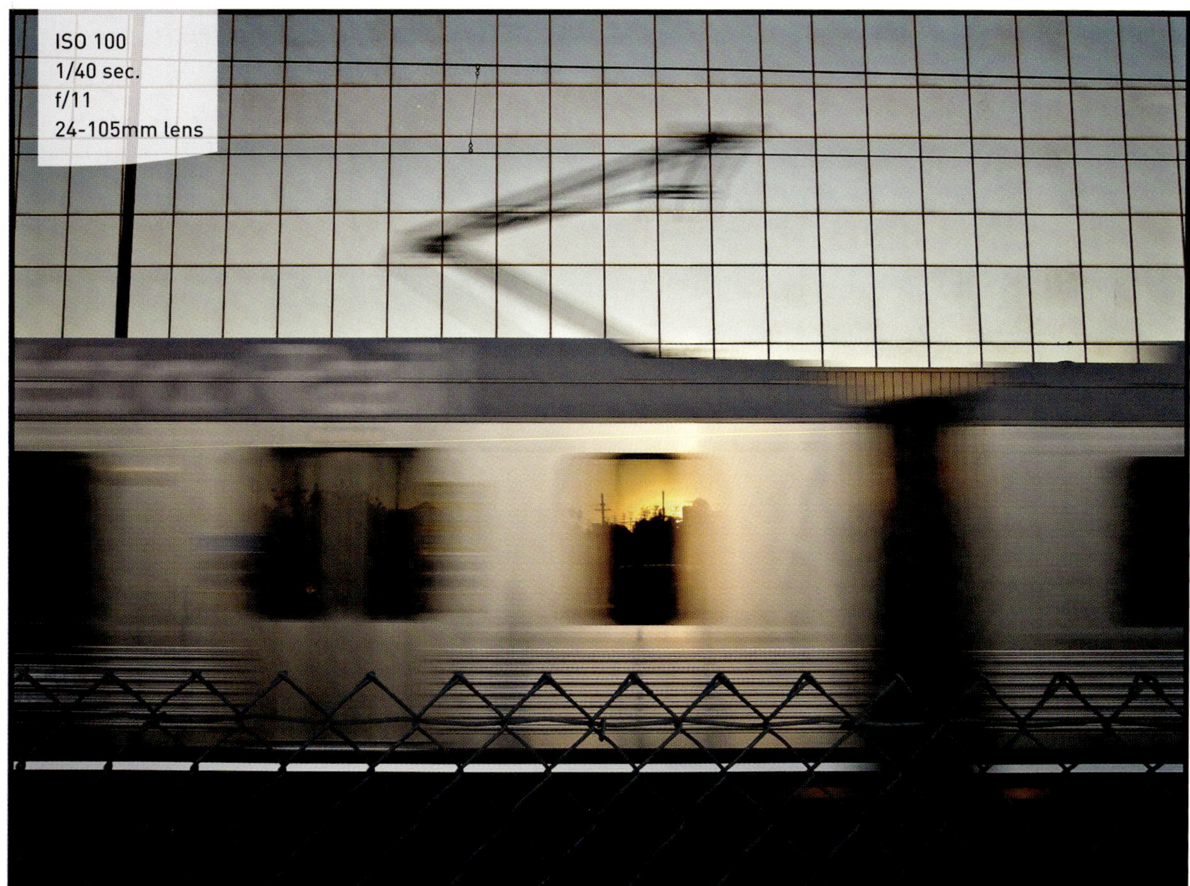

FIGURE 5.11
The blur of the Metro car is made that much more dramatic by the static elements in the frame, including the fence in the foreground and the office building in the background.

Sometimes I want to render motion as an abstraction. I don't want to freeze the action. In fact, I don't even want to make the subject recognizable. Instead, I want to use the subject's motion to explore color and tone. This can sometimes involve not only a slow shutter speed, but also panning the camera or even zooming the lens in or out during the duration of the exposure.

This triptych of images (**Figure 5.12**) was made while riding on a train. Another train was moving on the opposite track and I used a slow shutter speed to render our combined motions into a continuous blur of color. I combined three of the images into a triptych.

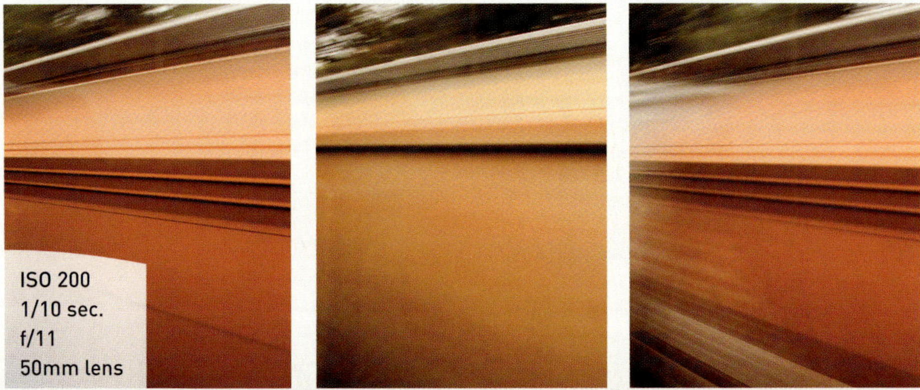

FIGURE 5.12
A series of images of a passing train through the window of another train provided the opportunity to create a series of abstractions that use movement and color to produce an interesting series.

Chapter 5 Assignments

The Mechanics of Motion

For this first assignment, you need to find some action. Explore the relationship between the speed of an object and its direction of travel. Use the same shutter speed to record your subject moving toward you and across your view. Try using the same shutter speed for both to compare the difference made by the direction of travel.

Wide Versus Telephoto

Photograph a subject moving in different directions, but this time, use a wide-angle lens and then a telephoto lens. Check out how the telephoto setting on the zoom lens will require faster shutter speeds than the lens at its wide-angle setting.

Get a Feel for Focusing Modes

In this chapter, I cover two different ways to autofocus for action: AI Servo and AI Focus. Starting with AI Servo AF, find a moving subject and get familiar with the way the mode works. Change from AF point selection to a single-point selection.

Now repeat the process using AI Focus AF. The point of the exercise is to become familiar enough with the two modes so that you can decide which one to use for the situation you're photographing.

Anticipate the Spot Using Manual Focus

For this assignment, you need to find a subject that you know will cross a specific line that you can prefocus on. A street with moderate traffic works well for this exercise. Focus on a spot on the street that the cars will travel across. Don't forget to set your lens for manual focus. To do this right, you need to set the drive mode on the camera to the continuous mode. Now, when a car approaches the spot, start shooting. Try shooting in three- or four-frame bursts.

Follow the Action

Panning is a great way to show motion. To begin, find a subject that will move across your path at a steady speed and practice following it in your viewfinder from side to side. Now, with the camera in Shutter Priority mode, set your shutter speed to 1/30 second and the focus mode to AI Servo AF. Pan along with the subject and shoot as it moves across your field of view. Experiment with different shutter speeds and focal lengths. Panning is one of those skills that takes some time to get a feel for, so try it with different types of subjects moving at different speeds.

Feel the Movement

Instead of panning with the motion, use a stationary camera position and adjust the shutter speed until you get a blurred effect that gives the sense of motion while still being able to identify the subject. There is a big difference between a slightly blurred photo that looks like you just picked the wrong shutter speed and one that looks intentional for the purpose of showing motion. Just like panning, it will take some experimentation to find just the right shutter speed to achieve the desired effect.

Share your results with this book's Flickr group!

Join the group here: www.flickr.com/groups/Canon5DMarkIIIFromSnapshotstoGreatShots

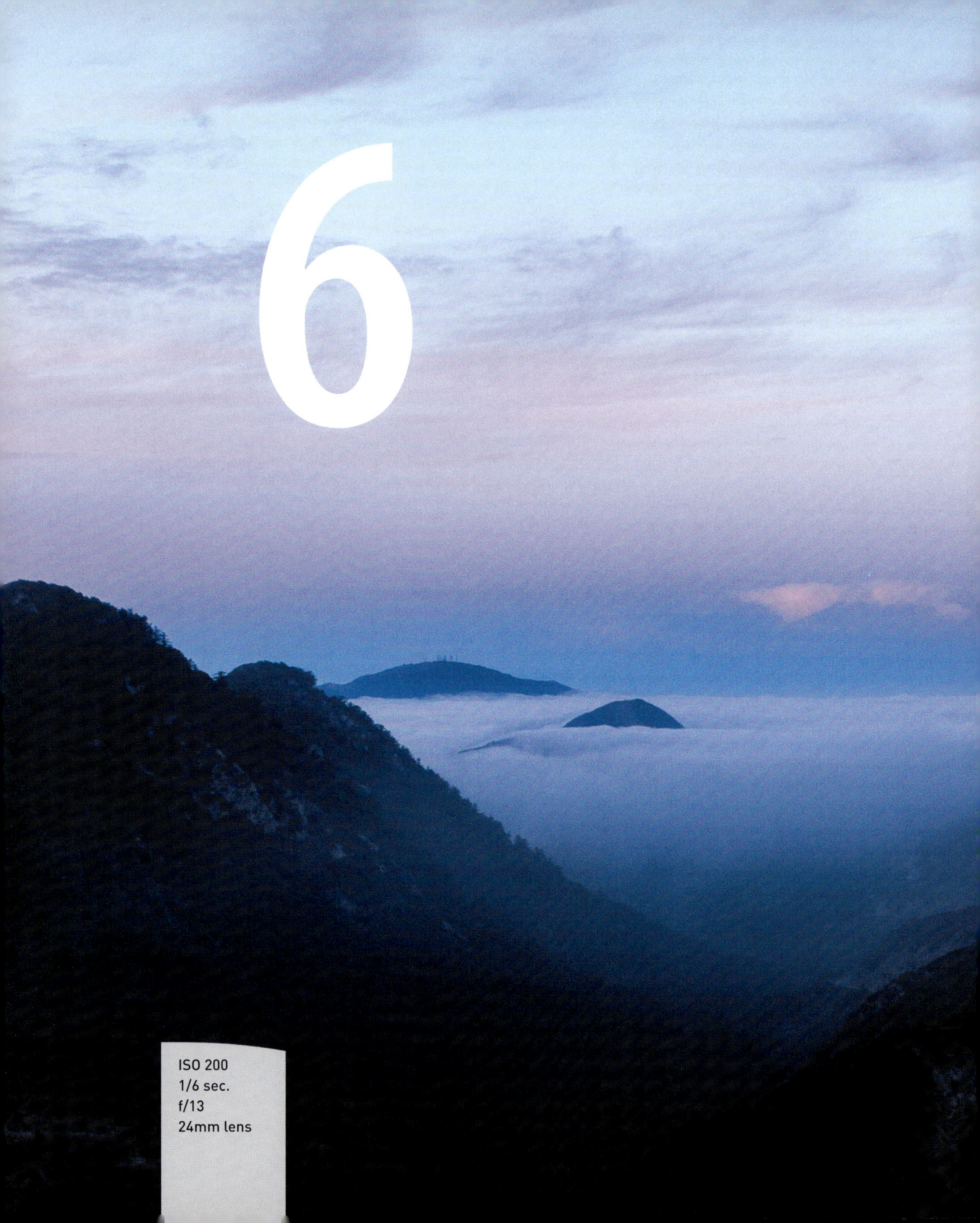
6
ISO 200
1/6 sec.
f/13
24mm lens

Landscape Photography

GETTING THE MOST OUT OF YOUR LANDSCAPE PHOTOGRAPHY

The natural world has been a popular subject of photography since photography was created, and it's no less so today. The opportunity that the landscape provides to capture beautiful scenes with beautiful light is a challenge, but it can be one of those most gratifying types of photography to master.

In this chapter, I outline some of the features of the 5D Mark III that will improve not only your landscape photography but also your chances of pulling off that unforgettable shot.

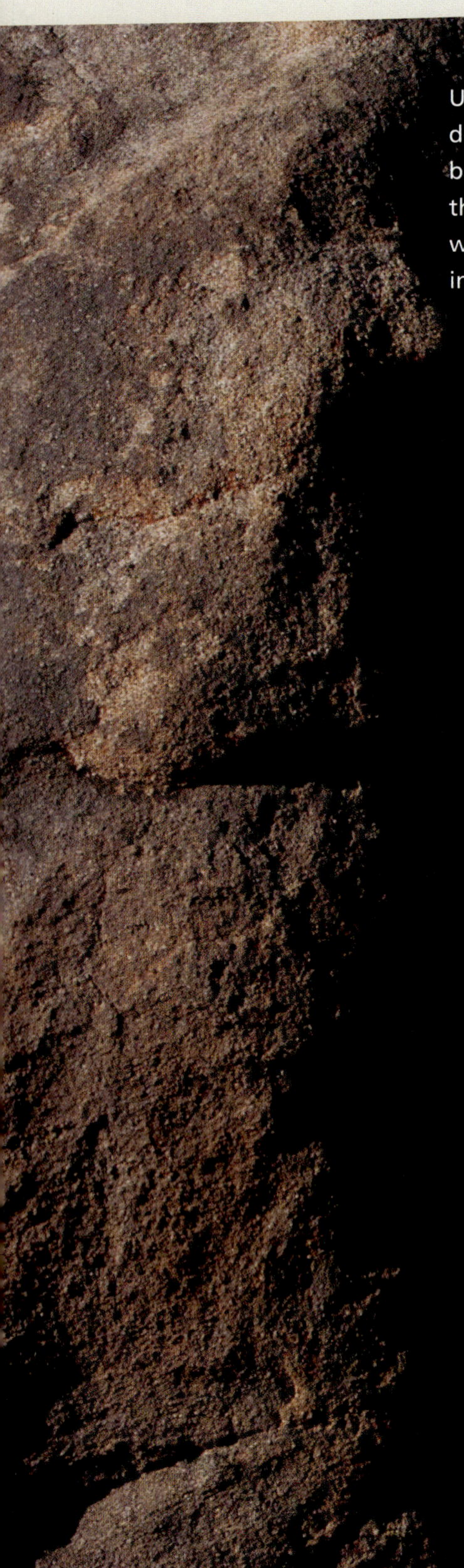

Using a wide-angle lens with a small aperture can provide a deep depth of field that renders both the foreground and the background sharp. The layering of a composition with elements that are close to and far from the camera delivers an image with a sense of depth and weight to it. It also can provide interesting visual contrast among shapes, textures, and colors.

By including the presence of the dark shadow, I emphasized the brighter area of the frame, which was my main point of interest.

I used a sturdy tripod and a remote release to ensure the sharpness of the image.

ISO 200
1/50 sec.
f/18
29mm lens

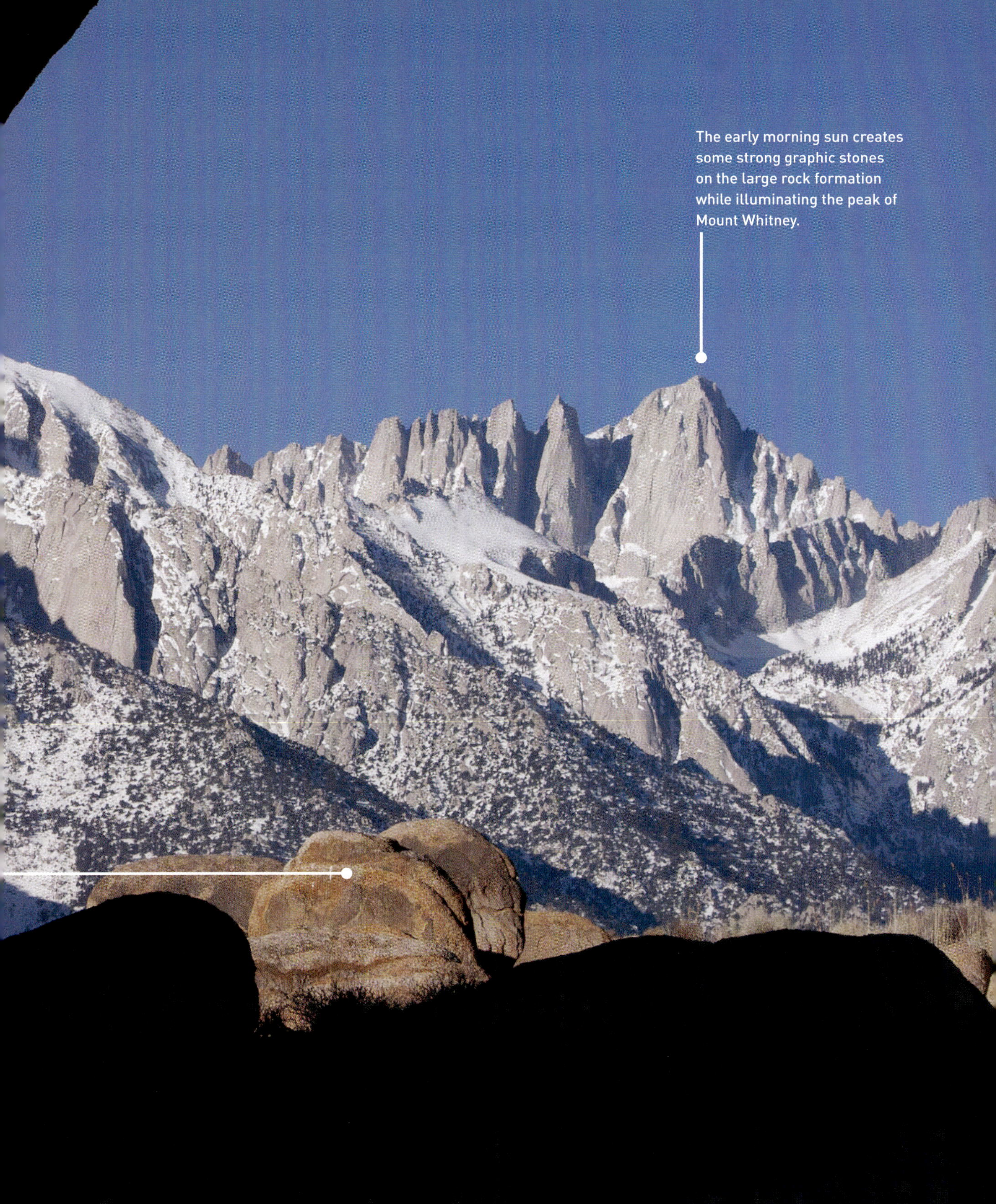

The early morning sun creates some strong graphic stones on the large rock formation while illuminating the peak of Mount Whitney.

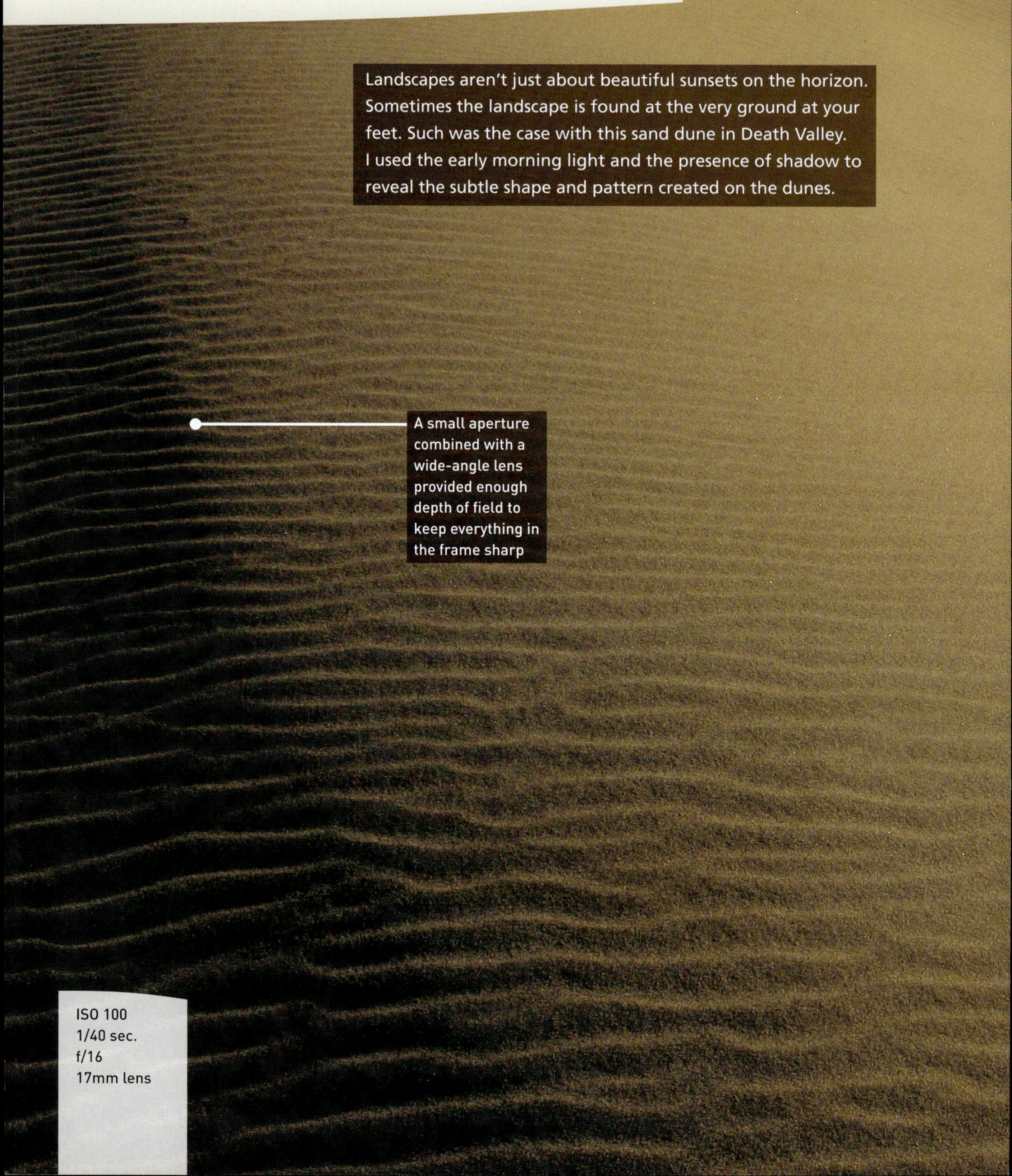

Landscapes aren't just about beautiful sunsets on the horizon. Sometimes the landscape is found at the very ground at your feet. Such was the case with this sand dune in Death Valley. I used the early morning light and the presence of shadow to reveal the subtle shape and pattern created on the dunes.

A small aperture combined with a wide-angle lens provided enough depth of field to keep everything in the frame sharp

ISO 100
1/40 sec.
f/16
17mm lens

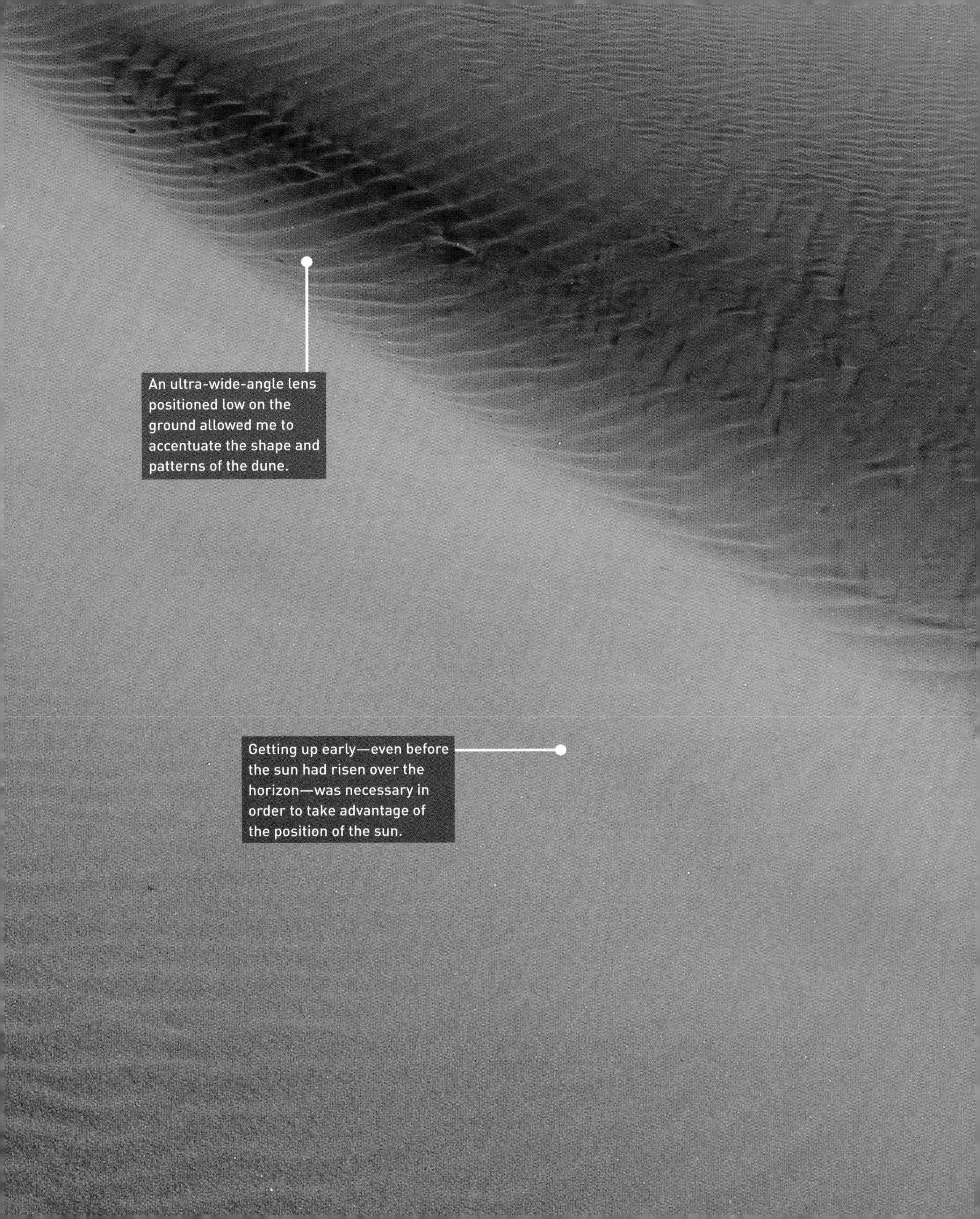

An ultra-wide-angle lens positioned low on the ground allowed me to accentuate the shape and patterns of the dune.

Getting up early—even before the sun had risen over the horizon—was necessary in order to take advantage of the position of the sun.

SHARP AND IN FOCUS: USING TRIPODS

Besides your camera and lens, the most important tool for your landscape photography will be a tripod (**Figure 6.1**).

Many of the best landscape photographs are made at sunrise or sunset, a time when the light levels are relatively low. This will require relatively slow shutter speeds in order to achieve a correct exposure. However, the slow shutter speeds can result in camera shake and a soft image. So, a tripod is essential in order to keep the camera stable at the moment of exposure.

And because a small aperture will likely be used in order to maximize depth of field, this also will have an impact on your shutter speed. So, if you're using a small aperture such as f/16 or f/22, the resulting shutter speed will be pretty slow. This again will require the use of a tripod to ensure sharpness.

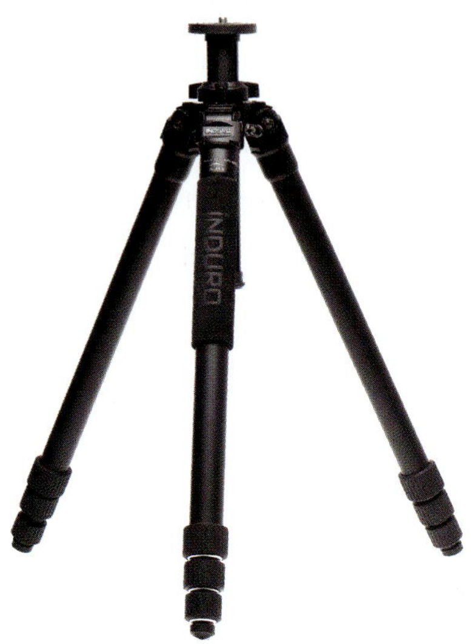

FIGURE 6.1

A good, reliable tripod, such as this tripod from Induro, is likely the second most important tool behind your camera for achieving sharp landscape images. (Image courtesy of InduroGear.com)

If I can make one suggestion about buying a tripod, it's to invest in as good a tripod as you can afford. Practically every photographer can tell you about having to buy several cheap tripods before realizing they needed to invest in a good-quality set of legs. Many of us have spent money on several sets of inexpensive tripods only to come to realize that if we had spent the same amount on just one good-quality tripod, we would've saved ourselves some grief and cash.

TIP

One of the benefits of using a tripod is that it forces you to slow down, which can be a very good thing. Carefully considering what you include or exclude from the frame is one of the biggest considerations you can make when creating a landscape photograph. Using a tripod forces you to carefully evaluate everything in the frame, increasing the likelihood of making a good photograph.

The quality that's possible with your 5D Mark III can easily be negated by the wrong tripod. So, invest in a good and sturdy tripod that fits your needs and budget. I prefer carbon fiber tripods because they're both sturdy and lightweight. Carbon fiber tripods are more expensive than aluminum ones, but for backpacking and heavy traveling, the lesser weight of the carbon fiber tripods is well worth the price.

The other consideration is the tripod head. Though some tripods may come with a pan-and-tilt head, I prefer using a ball head (**Figure 6.2**). Ball heads give you great flexibility and control. There are many different designs, but whichever one you choose should include a quick-release plate that you attach to the bottom of your camera. This allows you to quickly remove the camera from the ball head when you want to make a photograph without the tripod.

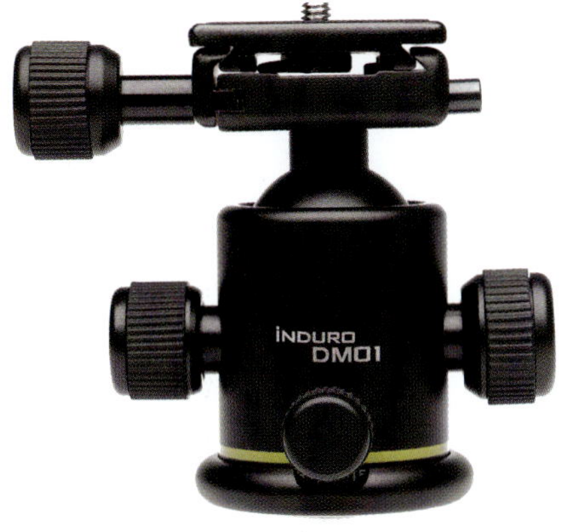

FIGURE 6.2
A ball head, such as this one from Induro, allows you to position the camera into virtually any position quickly and precisely. (Image courtesy of InduroGear.com)

TRIPOD STABILITY

Most tripods have a center column that allows the user to extend the height of the camera above the point where the tripod legs join together. This might seem like a great idea, but the reality is that the higher you raise that column, the less stable your tripod becomes. (Think of a tall building that sways near the top.) To get the most solid base for your camera, always try to use it with the center column at its lowest point so that your camera is right at the apex of the tripod legs.

IS LENSES AND TRIPODS: THEY DON'T MIX

If you're using image stabilization (IS) lenses on your camera, remember to turn this feature off when you use a tripod. Image stabilization can actually **create** movement when the camera is already stable. To turn off the IS feature, just slide the Stabilizer selector switch on the side of the lens to the Off position.

EXPOSURE MODES

When I'm photographing landscapes, Aperture Priority mode is my preference. Because I'm in control of the aperture, I can control the amount of depth of field. I sometimes use Manual exposure mode if the lighting is particularly complicated, but for the great majority of the images that I make, Aperture Priority is more than sufficient.

I still pay attention to what's happening with my shutter speed, even though I'm using the camera on a tripod. Though the image may not be as susceptible to the kind of camera shake that could occur if I were handholding the camera at such slow shutter speeds, I still check my shutter speed every time I start to photograph a new subject or scene. To completely eliminate the issue of camera shake, I fire the camera using a remote release or set my camera for the 2-second self-timer.

TIP

Even though many landscape photographs are shot with a small aperture, don't feel obligated to shoot at f/11 or f/16. You can make a landscape shot that is just as effective by using a limited depth of field with the lens set for wide aperture. Remember to experiment and play!

ISO

Though you'll often be shooting under low-light conditions, a tripod allows you to shoot at lower ISOs than you would if you were handholding the camera. Because of the stability provided by the tripod, you can shoot at a low ISO and still produce a good image. The use of a low ISO will help minimize the presence of noise, thus providing you with the best-possible image.

WHITE BALANCE

Getting accurate white balance is important with any photograph, but especially when shooting landscape images. So many different colors and tones exist within the frame that you'll want to ensure that those colors captured by the camera are an accurate reflection of what you saw in the original scene. This is why using white balance presets can really help to ensure that you get an accurate result.

AWB is influenced by all the colors and tones in the scene, and even the slightest shifting of the camera position can result in a difference in white balance. On the other hand, you'll likely get slightly different results of the same sunset if you're using the Daylight white balance preset. The Daylight preset will give you a more consistent rendering of color. Then, if you want to adjust the white balance from there, you know that your point of reference or your starting point is an accurate representation.

If you want to preview the look of the image before exposing a single frame, you can enable Live View mode and compare the white balance settings:

1. Press the Start/Stop button to activate Live View mode.

2. With Live View mode activated, press the Metering mode selection/White balance selection button and turn the Quick Control Dial to select a white balance preset that looks most appropriate for your scene.

3. Press the Start/Stop button again to exit Live View mode.

PICTURE STYLES

If you're recording and saving your files as JPEGs, the choice of Picture Style can be important. The Landscape Picture Style will increase contrast and color saturation, as well as increase the sharpness. This helps produce a JPEG that will look very good straight out of the camera without any further enhancements in your photo-editing software.

So, if you intend to produce JPEGs, make sure to set your Picture Style to Landscape. Just remember to reset it to Standard after you're done so that other images that you make in the future won't be adjusted for this particular Picture Style.

When shooting landscapes, I always look for great color and contrast. This is one of the reasons that so many landscape shots are taken in the early morning or during sunset. The light is much more vibrant and colorful at these times of day and adds a sense of drama to an image. You can help boost this effect, especially in the less-than-golden hours of the day, by using the Landscape Picture Style. This style will add some pop to your landscapes without the need for additional processing in any software.

TO SET UP THE LANDSCAPE PICTURE STYLE, FOLLOW THESE STEPS:

1. Press the Picture Style button and rotate the Quick Control Dial to select Picture Style. Press the Setting button.

2. Rotate the Quick Control Dial to select the Landscape Picture Style. Press the Setting button.

THE ELECTRONIC LEVEL

The inclusion of an electronic level helps ensure that your horizon lines will remain straight. Even the most eagle-eyed photographer can have a difficult time ensuring that horizon line is straight in the composition. This is why many photographers have a small bubble level that they either place on the tripod or hook up to the hot shoe of the camera.

However, the 5D Mark III offers a built-in electronic level (**Figure 6.3**) that you can enable in order to make sure that the horizon line is not slightly tilted in the frame. When the electronic level is activated, you can set the vertical and horizontal tilt and properly level your camera for landscape photography. You also have the option of viewing this feature on the LCD monitor or through the viewfinder.

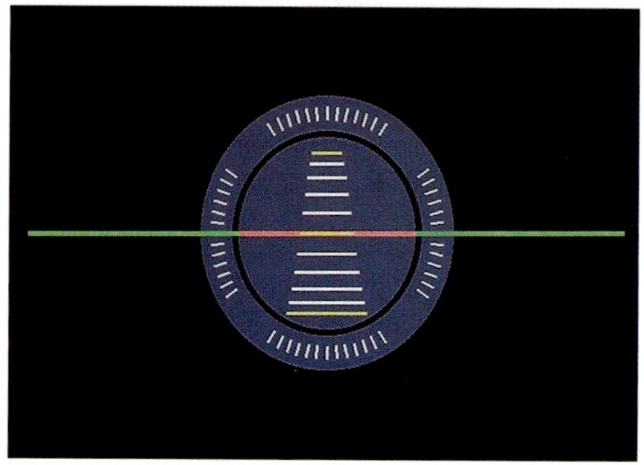

FIGURE 6.3
When the electronic level is enabled, you can view the indicator on the camera's LCD monitor to adjust the position of the camera to keep your horizon lines level.

TO SET UP THE ELECTRONIC LEVEL IN THE LCD MONITOR, FOLLOW THESE STEPS:

1. Press the Menu button and use the Main Dial to select the Set-up 3 menu screen. Then use the Quick Control Dial to scroll down and select Info button display options. Press the Setting button.

2. Make sure that there is a check mark next to the electronic level. If there isn't, use the Quick Control Dial to scroll to it and then press the Setting button. Use the Quick Control Dial again to scroll down to Okay, and then press the Setting button.

3. Press the Info button until the electronic level appears on the LCD monitor. (To view the electronic level when using Live View, press the Info button until it appears on the LCD monitor.) The image is level when the horizontal and vertical indicators turn from red lines to green.

TO SET UP THE ELECTRONIC LEVEL IN THE VIEWFINDER DISPLAY, FOLLOW THESE STEPS:

1. Press the Menu button and use the Main Dial to scroll to the Set-up 2 menu screen. Then use the Quick Control Dial to highlight the VF display. Press the Setting button.

2. Use the Quick Control Dial to enable the VF grid display function. Press the Setting button.

3. Now look through the viewfinder as if you were going to take a photograph. Press the M-Fn button (located next to the shutter button). Small black squares appear around the AF points. You'll know that the camera is level both vertically and horizontally when the only AF point visible is the one in the center. To exit from this mode, press the shutter button halfway.

THE GOLDEN HOUR

In landscape photography, the quality of light is essential to making beautiful photos. Many photographers will tell you that their favorite time of day to take outdoor foregrounds is during the first and last hour of sunlight, also referred to as the "golden hour." This is because the light is coming from a very low angle to the landscape, creating shadows and providing depth and character (**Figure 6.4**). The light also adds color to the earth and the sky, and clouds in the image further add to the color.

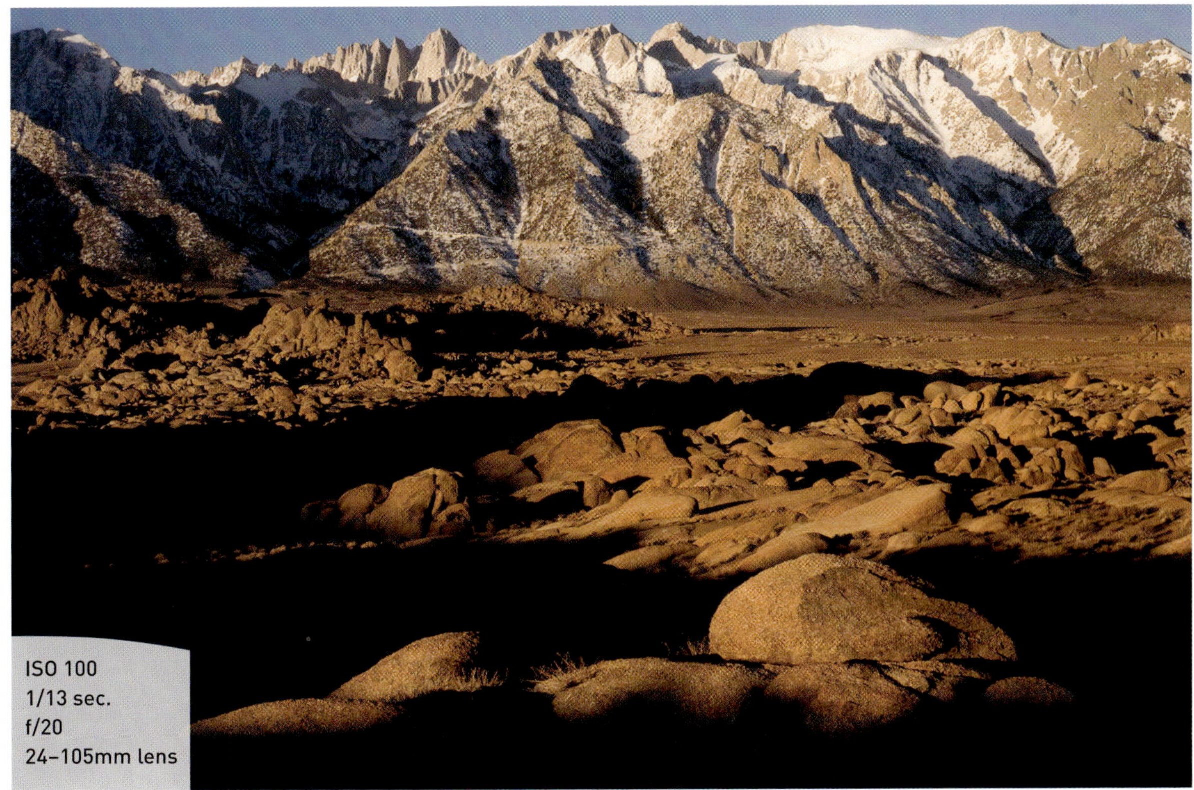

FOCUSING

For landscape photographs, you often want everything in the frame to appear sharp. This includes elements in the foreground, as well as elements in the distant background. As a result, you have to be careful about what you choose as your focus point. If you focus solely on an element on the distant horizon, this may result in an image in which the foreground elements are soft or out of focus, even though you're using a small aperture in order to maximize depth of field.

Hyperfocal distance (HFD) is the closest point of focus to the lens where the remaining distance (out to infinity) is acceptably in focus. Combining HFD with a small aperture will help you achieve a great depth of field, ideal for many landscape photographs, such as this image made in Death Valley (**Figure 6.5**). A simple way to achieve this is to focus on an object that is about one-third of the distance into your frame. This method is the one used by most working pros and is the easiest to remember and apply while shooting.

I manually select a single AF point or a group of AF points that will target an area in the foreground that's about one-third of the distance into my frame. This results in the area immediately in front of that focus point and beyond it being acceptably sharp in the final photograph, assuming I'm using a small aperture and a wide-angle lens to maximize depth of field.

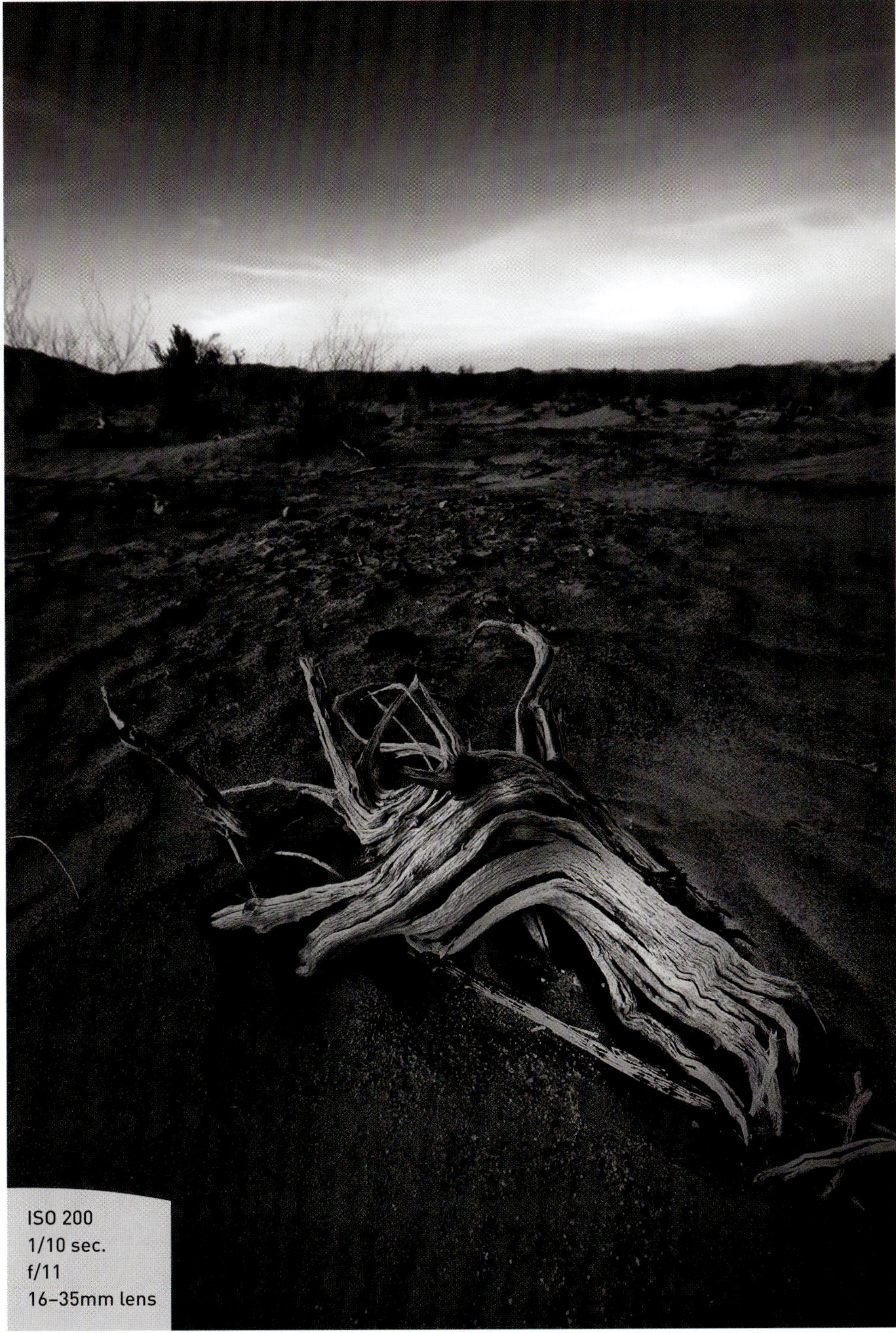

By detecting focus on an area one-third into the frame and using a small aperture with a wide focal length, I had enough depth of field to keep both the dead tree trunk and the horizon sharp. Using a tripod allowed me to use a low ISO.

DEPTH-OF-FIELD PREVIEW

When you view the image in the viewfinder, you don't always see the correct depth of field, and you might be tricked into thinking that you have more or less depth of field than you actually have. You can address this problem by using your camera's depth-of-field preview button. This easy-to-use feature works when you look through the viewfinder and press the depth-of-field preview button located on the front of the camera

Your viewfinder will darken, but don't worry: If you carefully examine the frame, you'll see how much of the scene will appear sharp. It's the equivalent of squinting your eyes in order to see better. The depth-of-field preview may take a little getting used to, but it can be an indispensable tool in ensuring that much of your frame is rendered sharp.

THE BEST OF BOTH WORLDS

There's no denying that the autofocus features on the 5D Mark III are great, but sometimes it just pays to turn them off and go manual. This is especially true if you're shooting on a tripod. Once you have your shot composed in the viewfinder and you're ready to focus, chances are, the area you want to focus on isn't going to be in the area of one of the focus points. Often, this is the case when you have a foreground element that's fairly low in the frame. You could use a single focus point set low in your viewfinder and then pan the camera down until it rests on your subject. But then you would have to press the shutter button halfway to focus the camera and try to recompose and lock down the tripod. It's no easy task.

You can get the best of both worlds by having the camera focus for you, and then switching to manual focus to comfortably recompose your shot:

1. Set up your shot and find the area that you want to focus on.

2. Pan your tripod head so that your active focus point is on that spot.

3. Press the shutter button halfway to focus the camera, and then remove your finger from the button.

4. Switch the camera to manual focus by sliding the switch on the lens barrel from AF to MF.

5. Recompose the composition on the tripod, and then take the shot.

The camera will fire without trying to refocus the lens. This works especially well for wide-angle lenses, which can be difficult to focus manually.

COMPOSITION

As a photographer, your job is to lead the viewer through the image. You accomplish this by using the principles of composition. Composition is the arrangement of elements in the scene that draws the viewer's eye through your image and holds his or her attention. As the director of this viewing, you need to understand how people see, and then use that information to focus their attention on the most important elements in your image.

There is a general order in which we look at elements in a photograph. The first is brightness. The eye wants to travel to the brightest object within a scene. So, if you have a bright sky, it's probably the first place the eye will travel to. The second order of attention is sharpness. Sharp, detailed elements will get more attention than soft, blurry areas. Finally, the eye will move to vivid colors while leaving the dull, flat colors for last. It's important to know these essentials in order to grab—and keep—the viewer's attention and then direct them through the frame.

THE RULE OF THIRDS

When it comes to composition, the easiest place to begin is with the rule of thirds. Using this principle, you simply divide your viewfinder into thirds by imagining two horizontal and two vertical lines that divide the frame equally.

By placing your subject near these intersecting lines, you're giving the viewer space to move within the frame. The one thing you don't want to do is place your subject smack-dab in the middle of the frame. This is sometimes referred to as "bull's-eye" composition, and it requires the right subject matter for it to work. It's not always wrong, but it will usually be less appealing and may not hold the viewer's focus.

Generally speaking, when you shoot landscapes, you should position the horizon one-third of the way up or down in the frame (**Figure 6.6**). Splitting the frame in half by placing your horizon in the middle of the picture is akin to placing the subject in the middle of the frame; it doesn't lend a sense of importance to either the sky or the ground.

FIGURE 6.6
Placing the horizon
line at the top
third of the frame
allowed me to cre-
ate an interesting
composition of the
salt flat, which also
allowed me to limit
the presence of the
featureless sky.

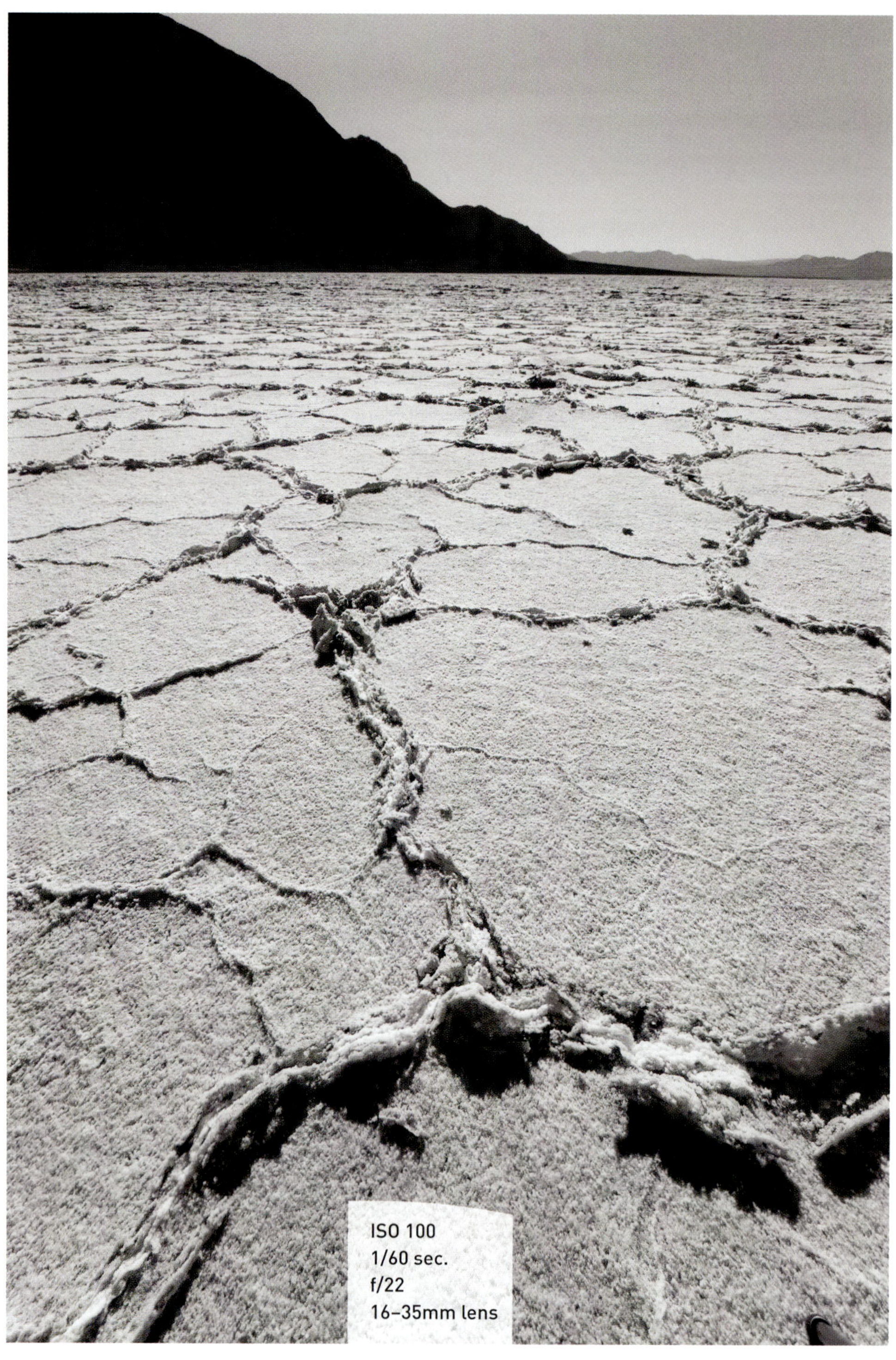
ISO 100
1/60 sec.
f/22
16–35mm lens

LOOKING DOWN

Good landscapes don't just have to be about sunset and cloudy skies. Sometimes, the best landscape images are right at your feet. This is a good place to look, especially on days when the skies are rather lackluster. Instead, you can focus on elements below the horizon line to make interesting photographs that explore texture, shape, color, and patterns.

One way of finding great such subject matter in such situations is to pay attention to the interplay of light with the landscape. For example, in this image of the sand dunes (**Figure 6.7**), I carefully observed how the early morning light revealed the shapes and textures of the sand, as well as created distinctive shadows.

The weather doesn't always cooperate, so it's important to be flexible, look for other photographic opportunities, and make the most of them when we can. Simply looking at the landscape at your feet can help you to come away with a memorable and satisfying photograph.

FIGURE 6.7
By paying attention to the early morning light effect on the sand dunes, I was able to create a satisfying landscape even though I don't include the sky or the horizon.

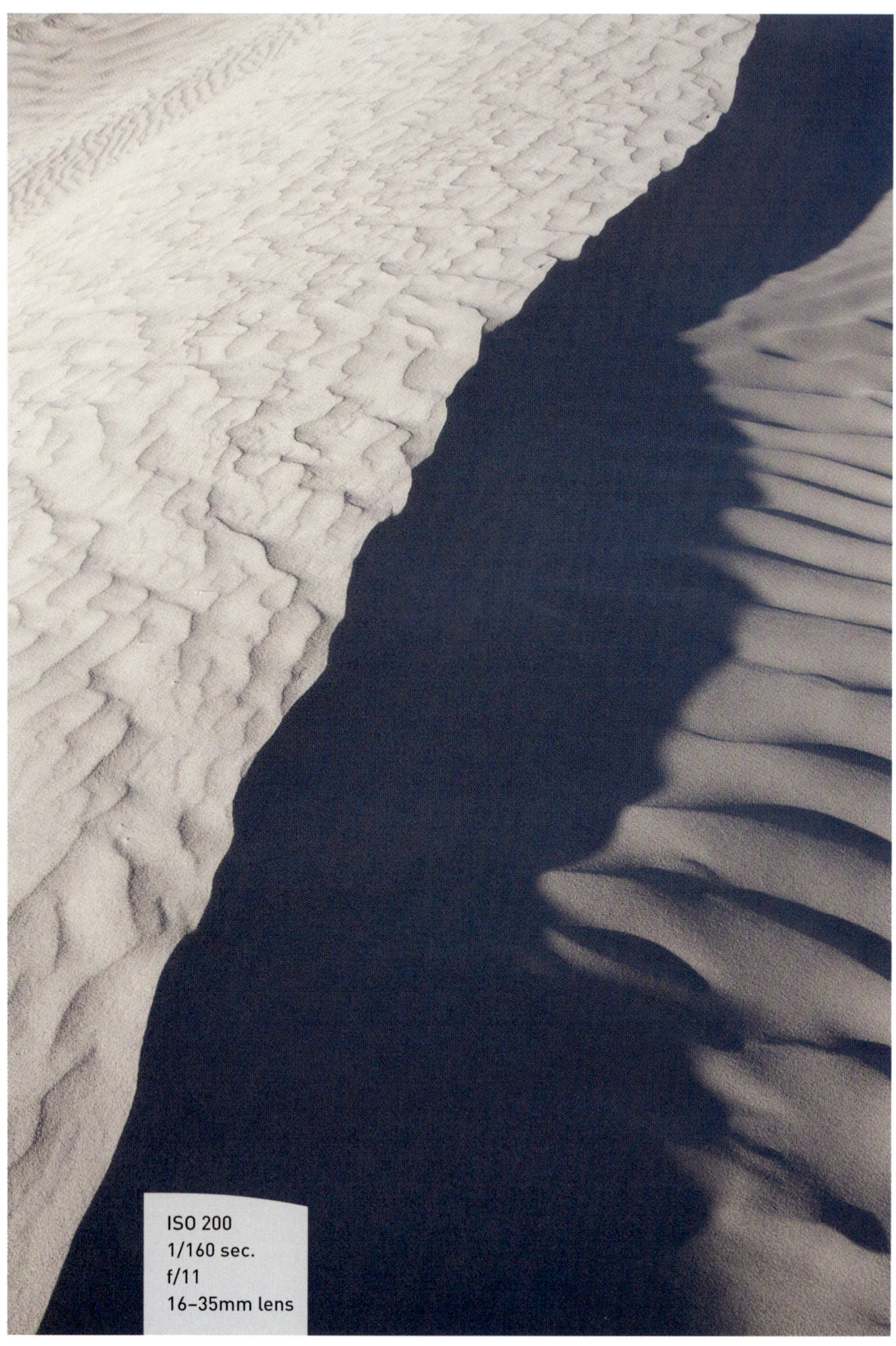

ISO 200
1/160 sec.
f/11
16–35mm lens

Chapter 6 Assignments

Experiment with White Balance and Picture Style

Set up your camera and use the Daylight white balance and Landscape Picture Style settings. Then turn on Live View mode and change the white balance to the other modes, previewing each image on the LCD monitor. Next, do the same with the Picture Style, and see how many different looks you can create with the same scene.

Level the Horizon

Set up your camera on a tripod and do your best to eyeball the horizon and get it level in your scene. Turn on the electronic level, either in the viewfinder or on the LCD monitor, and see how close you're getting your scene level. If you were off, go ahead and reposition the camera until it's level both vertically and horizontally. Don't forget to preview your composition before you take the shot. If you're eyeballing your composition without the aid of the electronic level, it's easy to make the mistake of creating a slightly tilted composition. So, save yourself time in having to fix this later in Photoshop, by using the electronic level.

Apply Hyperfocal Distance to Your Landscapes

Pick a scene that contains objects positioned near the camera, as well as something that is clearly defined in the background. Try using a wide to medium-wide focal length (18mm to 35mm). Use a small aperture and focus on the subject in the foreground. Then recompose and take a shot. When moving the camera position, use the object in the background as your point of focus and take another shot. Finally, find a point that is one-third of the way into the frame from near to far, and use that as the focus point. Compare all the images to see which method delivered the greatest range of depth of field from near to infinity.

Place Your Horizons

Find a location with a distinct horizon and, using the grid on the viewfinder or Live View on the LCD monitor, take three shots: one with the horizon in the top third of frame, one with the horizon in the middle, and one with the horizon in the bottom third of the frame. Compare each shot to see which is most visually striking.

Share your results with this book's Flickr group!

Join the group here: www.flickr.com/groups/Canon5DMarkIIIFromSnapshotstoGreatShots

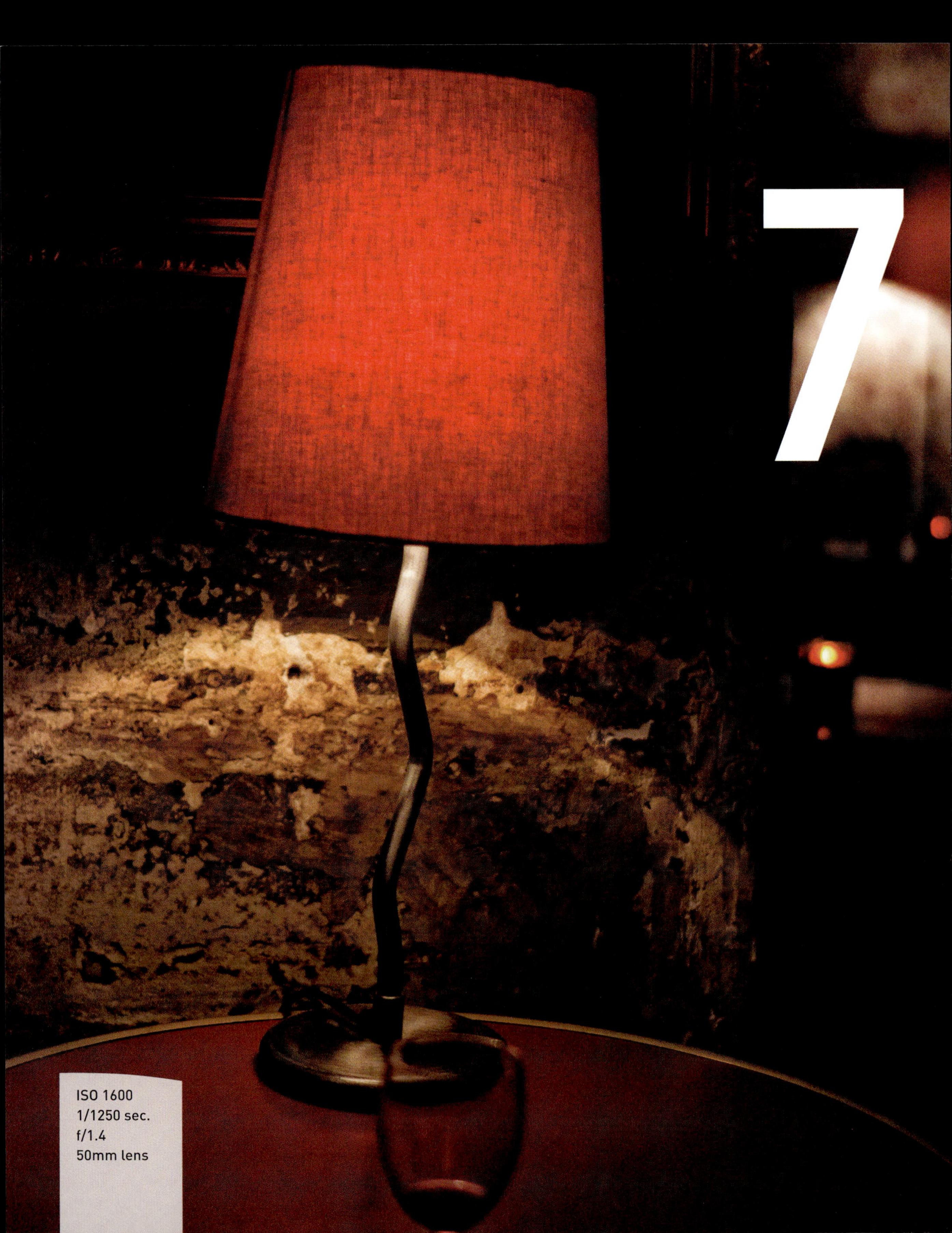
7
ISO 1600
1/1250 sec.
f/1.4
50mm lens

Low Lighting

SHOOTING WHEN THE LIGHTS GET LOW

The 5D Mark III is exemplary when it comes to shooting under low-light conditions. The camera's full-frame sensor, combined with its Digic 5+ image processor, provides you the ability to shoot at high ISOs while maintaining excellent image quality, detail, and color fidelity. Where photographers were once obligated to use flash, it's now possible to produce amazing images even under the most challenging lighting situations.

PORING OVER THE PICTURE

Long time exposures at twilight provide a great opportunity to balance the waning light of the sun with the light of office buildings and speeding vehicles. The use of a long shutter speed helps to create a streaming of light, which serves as a counterpoint to the graphic lines of the cityscape.

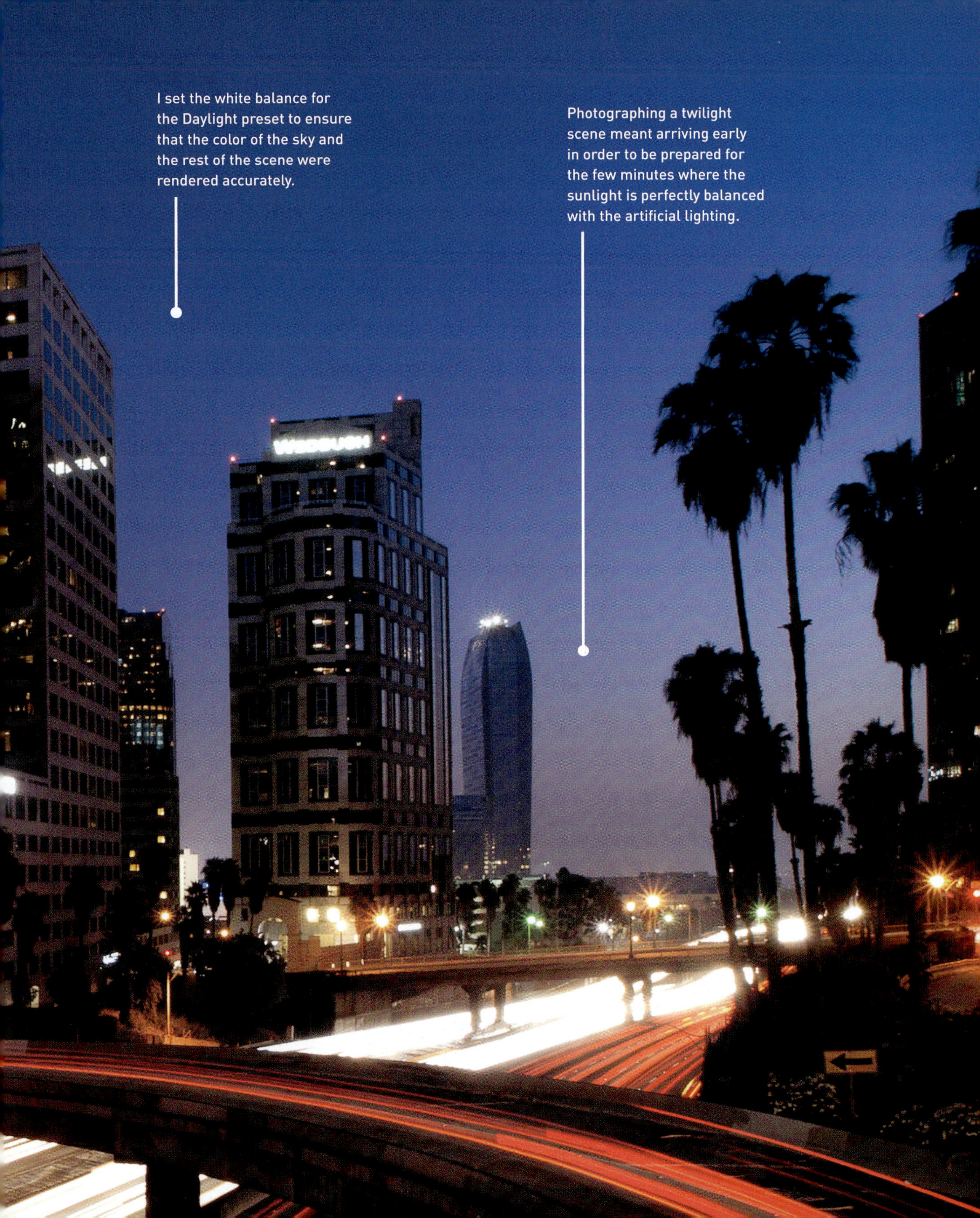

I set the white balance for the Daylight preset to ensure that the color of the sky and the rest of the scene were rendered accurately.

Photographing a twilight scene meant arriving early in order to be prepared for the few minutes where the sunlight is perfectly balanced with the artificial lighting.

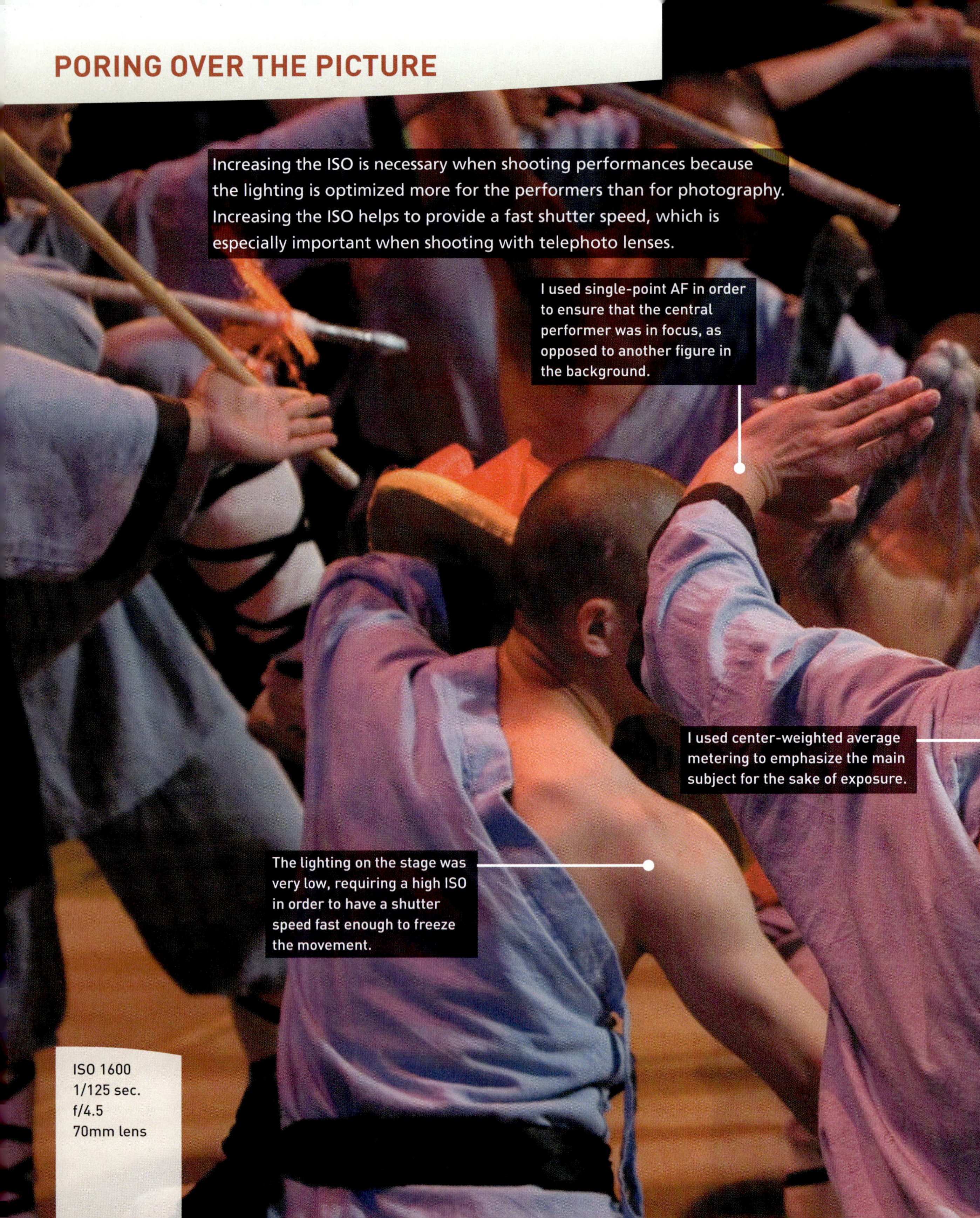

PORING OVER THE PICTURE

Increasing the ISO is necessary when shooting performances because the lighting is optimized more for the performers than for photography. Increasing the ISO helps to provide a fast shutter speed, which is especially important when shooting with telephoto lenses.

I used single-point AF in order to ensure that the central performer was in focus, as opposed to another figure in the background.

I used center-weighted average metering to emphasize the main subject for the sake of exposure.

The lighting on the stage was very low, requiring a high ISO in order to have a shutter speed fast enough to freeze the movement.

ISO 1600
1/125 sec.
f/4.5
70mm lens

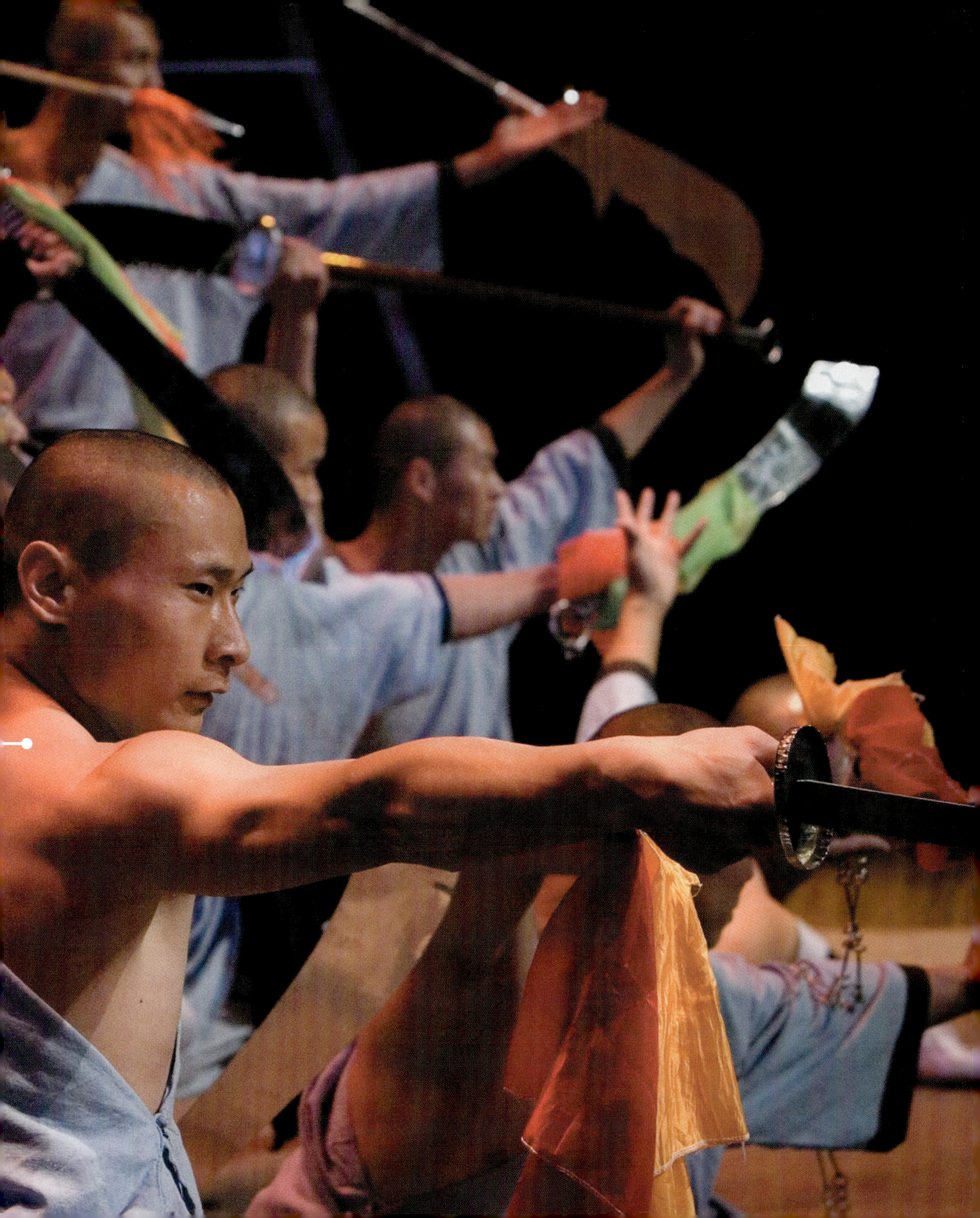

RAISING THE ISO: THE SIMPLE SOLUTION

As light levels drop, the ISO of the camera will likely need to be increased. Depending on the scene that you're photographing, you may need to increase your ISO to 800, 1600, 3200, or higher in order to achieve a good exposure with the shutter speed/aperture combination you prefer. Such was the case for this mariachi singer shot under very low light in a local restaurant (**Figure 7.1**)

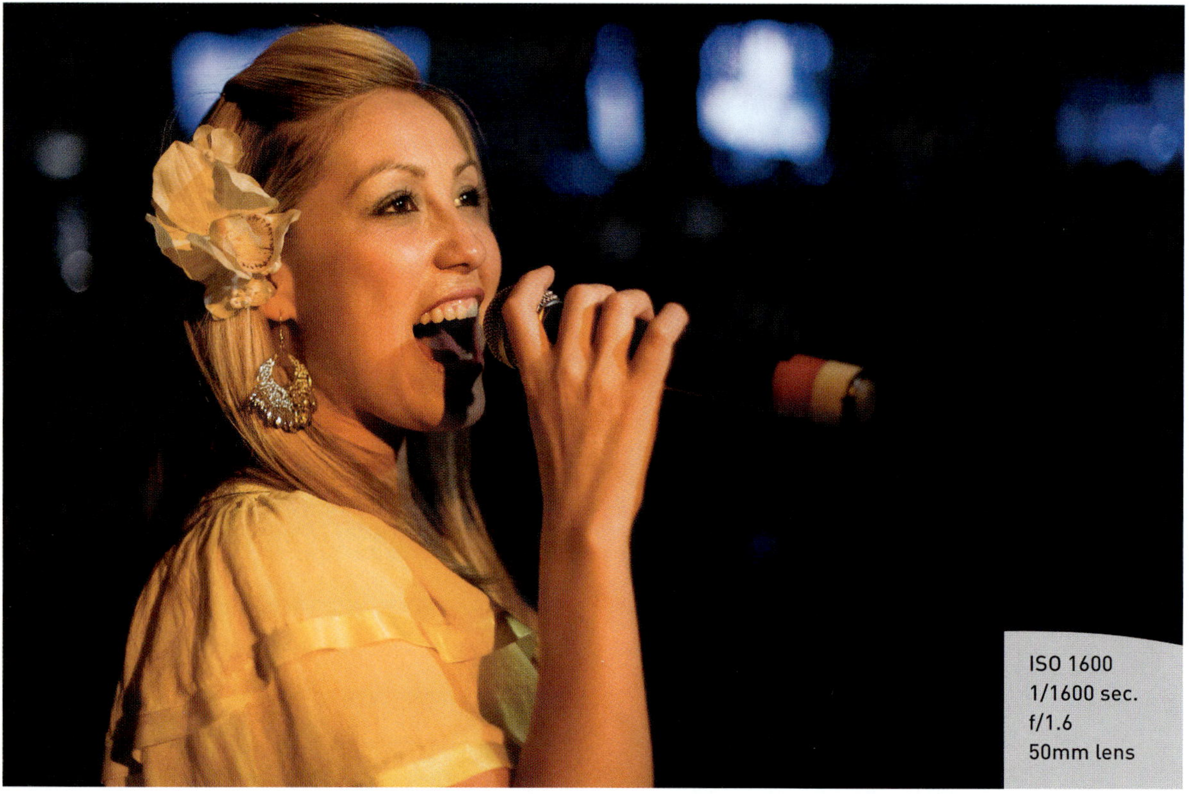

FIGURE 7.1
A fast 50mm lens provided me the ability to shoot a moderately high ISO to achieve a shutter speed fast enough to freeze the movement of the performer.

Shooting at such high ISOs was unthinkable just a few years ago, but DSLRs like the 5D Mark III have made it possible to produce quality images that can stand the scrutiny of big enlargement even at such high ISOs. So, don't hesitate to increase the ISO if the situation requires it.

Your choice to use a higher ISO often will be related to the shutter speed you're shooting at, which is especially important if you're handholding the camera. It might also be a consideration if you need a fast shutter speed to capture fast action in a venue with less than photo-friendly lighting. Whatever the case may be, the option to raise the ISO is one of the most important and indispensable tools available to you.

Whether it's photographing in a high school gymnasium, a theater stage, or a local restaurant, low-light conditions often require increasing the ISO in order to achieve a good result. Though general shooting may typically involve using an ISO range of between 100 to 800, indoor situations or night shooting can easily require you to shoot at ISOs of 1600, 3200, 6400 or even higher. Though such low-light conditions often are more the exception than the rule, it's important to understand when and why you'll want to increase the ISO.

TIP

Keep in mind that you may not always notice noise when viewing your images on the LCD monitor, because what you're seeing is a scaled-down version of the original. Using the zoom features on the back of the camera to preview your shots at 100 percent will give you a better idea of the amount of noise that higher ISO levels introduce to your images.

Though there will be an increase in noise as you boost the ISO, the 5D Mark III does offer a high ISO speed noise-reduction feature.

AUTO ISO

When the ISO setting is set to Auto (A), the camera will dynamically adjust the ISO as light levels increase and fall. This can be convenient for a situation in which the light is rapidly changing, but I recommend setting the ISO manually. Setting the ISO manually keeps you aware of what your light levels are and how the light is impacting your shutter speed. It also provides a level of consistency to your imagery with respect to noise, which may vary widely when using the Auto ISO feature.

Under extremely challenging lighting, the ability to increase the ISO beyond the standard range can help to get the shot. Though the ISO will increase the presence of noise, it can make the difference between getting and not getting the shot. If you find yourself in a situation where ISO 6400 isn't enough, you have the option of increasing your camera's ISO up to 102,400. This can be achieved by adjusting the ISO speed range.

TO SET UP THE ISO EXPANSION FEATURE, FOLLOW THESE STEPS:

1. Press the Menu button and turn the Main Dial to access the Shoot 2 menu screen.

2. Rotate the Quick Control Dial and select ISO speed settings. Press the Settings button.

3. Rotate the Quick Control Dial and select the ISO speed range. Press the Settings button.

4. With the minimum ISO speed range active (a red box will surround the window), rotate the Quick Control Dial to change the lowest ISO. Press the Setting button.

5. Rotate the Quick Control Dial to select the Maximum ISO window, and press the Setting button to make it active. Rotate the Quick Control Dial to set your maximum ISO, which can be as high as 102,400. Press the Setting button.

A word of warning about the expanded ISO settings: Although it's great to have these high ISO settings available during low-light shooting, they should always be your last resort. Even with high ISO speed noise reduction turned on, the amount of visible noise will be extremely high. I can't think of a situation where I ever need to use the 102,400 (H2) setting, but you might find yourself at a nighttime sporting event under lights, which would require ISOs of 3200 or 6400 to improve your shutter speeds and capture the action.

USING FAST GLASS

If you find yourself shooting under low-light conditions, you can usually assume that you'll be using your lens with the aperture at its widest setting (**Figure 7.2**). Such situations make the use of fast zooms or prime lenses a big advantage. Having a lens with a maximum aperture of f/2.8 or faster provides optics that are better at light-gathering in low light and also allows you to use faster shutter speeds without necessarily having to go to the highest ISO settings available on your camera.

If you're using a slower zoom lens, increasing the ISO will be absolutely necessary. So, if you find yourself frequently shooting under low-light conditions, it may be time to invest in a lens with a faster maximum aperture.

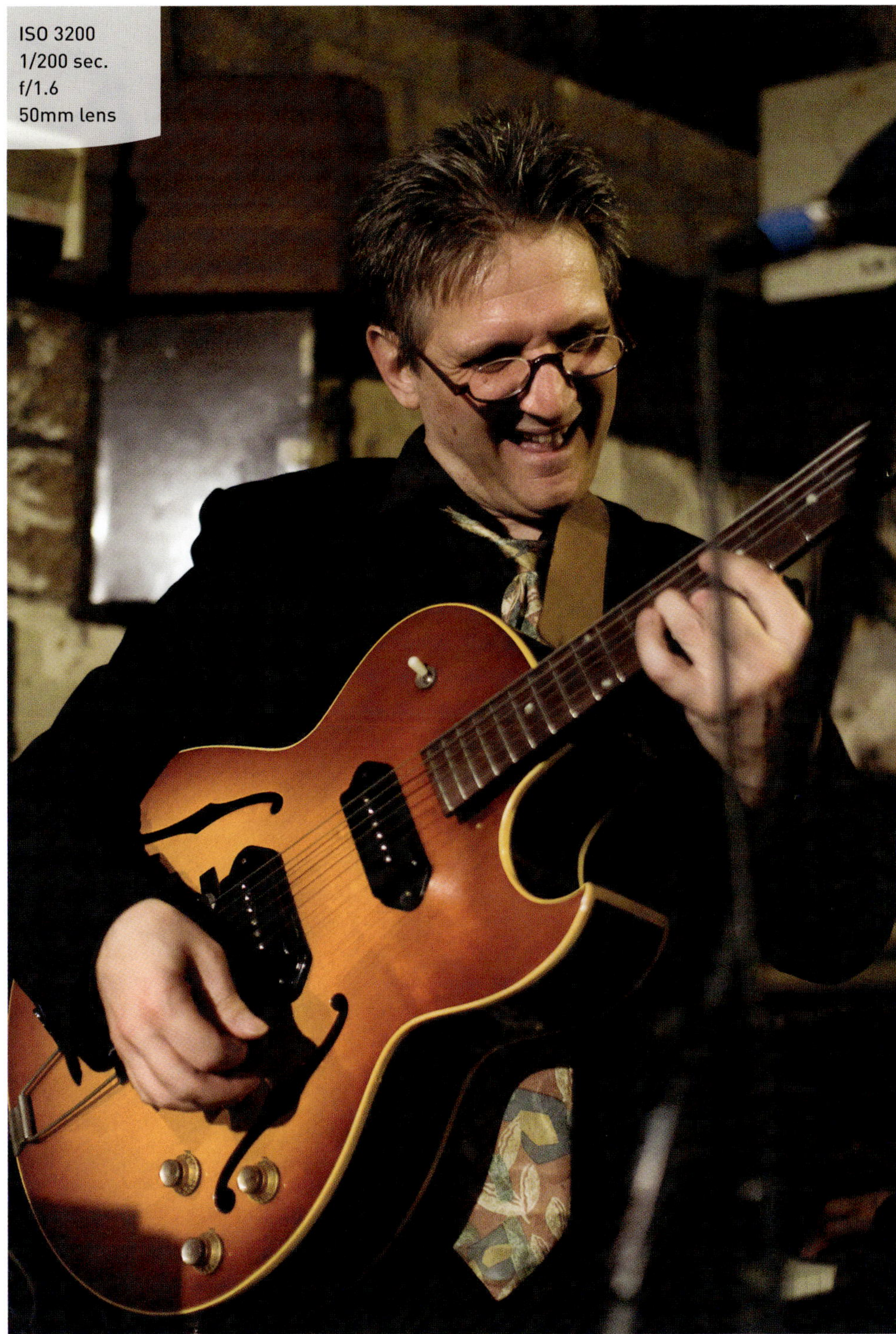

FIGURE 7.2
Having a lens with a fast maximum aperture provided the much-needed light-gathering capability for shooting under the extremely low light in this jazz club.

STABILIZING THE SITUATION

Many of today's Canon lenses come with a feature called image stabilization (IS). If you happen to have one of these lenses, you have a little extra help keeping yourself stable while doing any type of handheld photography. This is extremely useful in situations where the light is low and, to prevent camera shake, you need to set your shutter speeds slower than you normally would when shooting without a tripod. Most people can hold the camera steady at 1/60 second or faster. The longer the focal length, the faster your shutter speed needs to be in order to keep your images sharp and free of camera shake.

The Canon IS lenses contain small gyro sensors and servo-actuated optical elements that correct for camera shake and stabilize the image. The IS function is so good that you can improve your handheld photography by two or three stops—meaning, if you're pretty solid at a shutter speed of 1/60 second, the IS feature lets you shoot at 1/15 second and possibly even 1/8 second. Of course, this only affects camera shake— it won't make a moving subject sharp.

NOTE

If you aren't handholding the camera and lens as stable as possible, you may lose the advantage of the image stabilization. So, don't assume that you can become lax in how you handle the camera when shooting. You want to use the technology as a fallback, not a crutch.

FOCUSING IN LOW LIGHT

One of the more obvious challenges you'll face when photographing under low-light conditions is that of achieving focus. Though the camera may perform nearly flawlessly when there is an abundance of light, it can struggle if there is insufficient contrast or detail, as is often the case when photographing under low-light conditions.

For example, if you point your camera at a blank sheet of white paper, the camera will likely wrack the lens back and forth trying to detect focus. If you find yourself in a situation in which the camera is acting this way, you can likely assume that there isn't enough light or detail for the camera to detect focus.

When facing such a situation, I often select the AF points manually and target an area of my subject that has a good amount of contrast. Then I achieve and lock focus. This is especially important to do if you're composing your subject off-center.

By locking the focus (either by holding down the shutter button halfway or by pressing and holding the AF start button), I can lock focus, recompose, and shoot.

If the subject doesn't have enough contrast, another alternative is to focus on another object that is approximately the same distance to the camera as the subject. I detect and lock focus, recompose for my subject, and make the photograph.

Another option is to use manual focus. If you're photographing anything that is difficult to focus on, like fireworks, you should set your camera's focusing manually. If you point the camera into the dark sky, the autofocusing system will just keep searching for—and not finding—a focus point. To set your focus manually, just flip the switch on the lens from AF to MF and rotate the front of the lens until your focus is set.

USING THE SELF-TIMER FOR SHARPER PHOTOGRAPHS

Whether you're shooting with a tripod or resting your camera on the counter, you can increase the sharpness of your pictures by taking your hands out of the equation. Whenever you use your finger to press the shutter button, you increase the chance that there will be a little bit of a shake in your image. If you don't have a cable release to trigger the shutter button, try setting up your camera to use the self-timer.

To turn on the self-timer, press the AF mode selection/Drive mode selection button and rotate the Quick Control Dial until the self-timer icon appears in the LCD panel. There are two self-timer modes to choose from: 2 seconds or 10 seconds. I generally use the 2-second mode to cut down on time between exposures.

USING FLASH

In many situations, you'll want to use an external flash unit to create your photographs. Canon offers a variety of different flashes, ranging from the 600EX to the 270EX II. The flashes vary in power, adaptability, and custom functions, but each can provide enough light to capture an average scene.

Higher-end flashes will provide you such features as wireless triggering, high-speed sync, and coverage for ultra-wide-angle lenses. Though the 5D Mark III is an advanced camera, you don't have to invest in the top-of-the-line flash, particularly if you don't use flash frequently. When considering a flash, give good thought to how much you expect to actually use it and how. You may find that a moderate-range flash, such as the 580EX II or 480EX II, may be more than adequate. I used the 580EX off-camera using a TTL cable for this portrait of a mustached pool player (**Figure 7.3**).

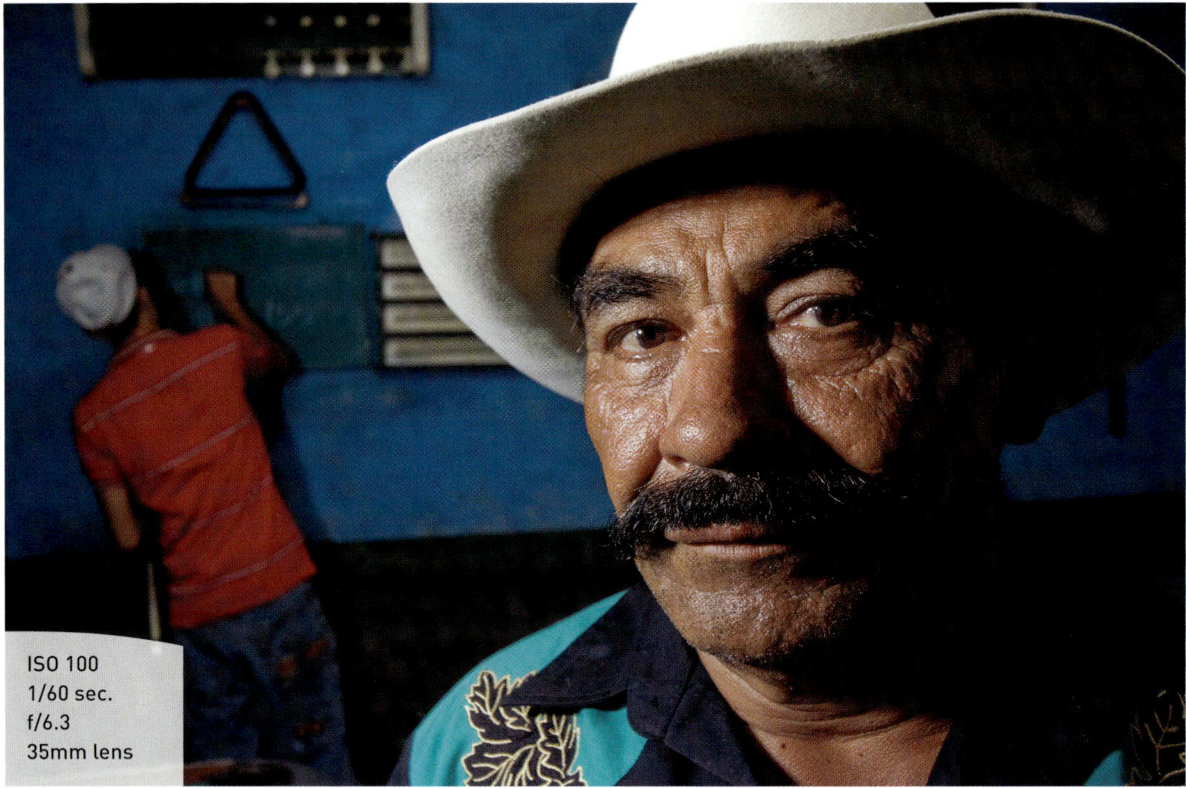

FLASH SYNC SPEEDS

The standard flash synchronization speed for your camera is between 1/60 and 1/200 second. A shutter speed faster than 1/200 second allows for the entire frame to be exposed during the brief duration of the flash. In fact, you'll find that your camera won't let you go beyond 1/200 second when the flash is activated.

NOTE

If you're using non-TTL studio strobes, take care not to set your shutter speed beyond the maximum sync speed of 1/200 second to avoid problems of an uneven exposure across the entire frame.

The key to great flash photography is controlling the shutter speed. The longer your shutter is open, the more ambient light you can let into your image. If you're photographing people during a sunset and you drop your shutter speed low enough to capture the light behind them, you can add beautiful colors to the background (**Figure 7.4**).

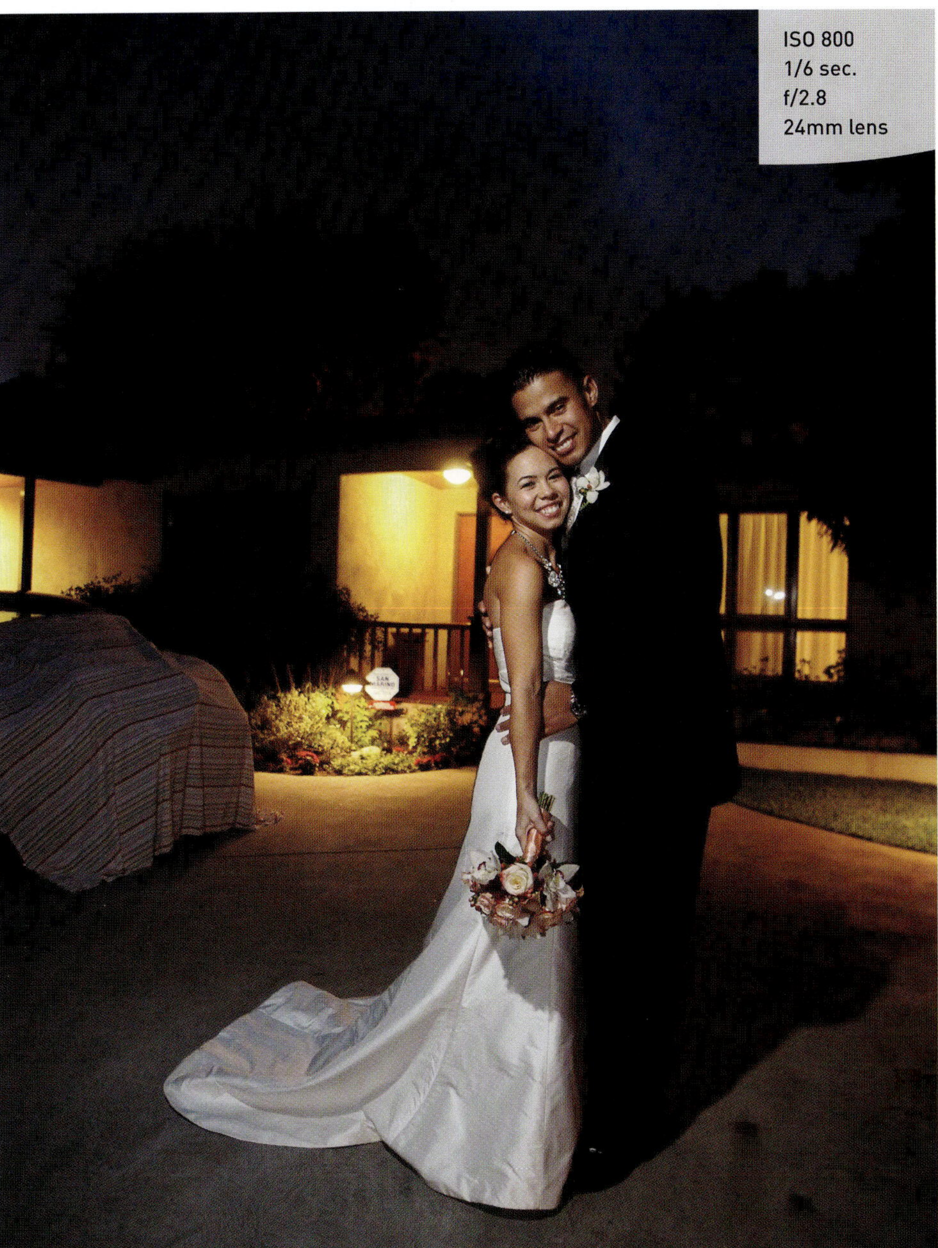

FIGURE 7.4
A very slow shutter speed mixed with flash allowed me to balance the flash output with the ambient light of the house where this young couple were celebrating their wedding.

Using different shutter speeds with the flash makes it possible to create some fun and creative shots as well. For example, I dropped the shutter speed considerably when photographing this dancer in a reception hall, which allowed me to capture some of the ambient light in the room. (**Figure 7.5**).

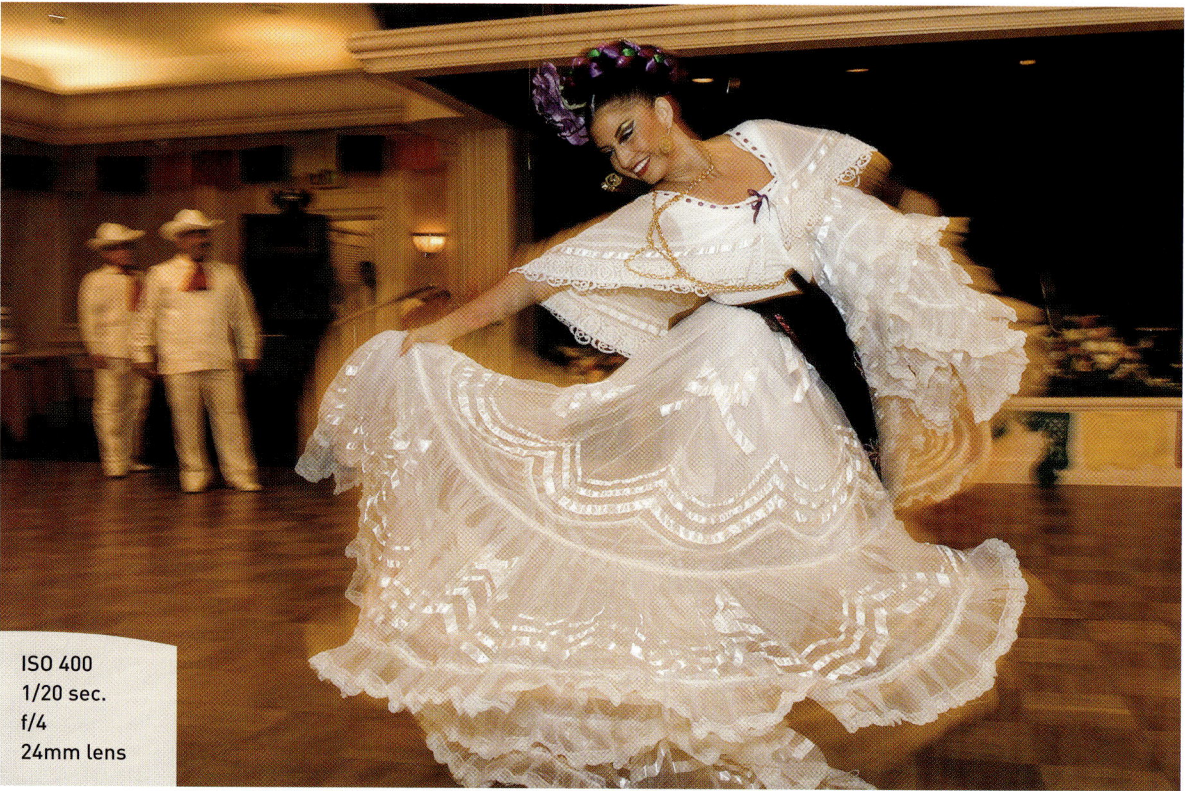

FIGURE 7.5
The use of a slow shutter speed allowed me to capture some of the ambient light in the scene, as well as create a slight ghosting at the edge of the subject's body and costume.

Let's take a look at how each of the camera modes affects the shutter speed when using your flash:

- **Program (P):** The shutter speed is automatically set between 1/60 and 1/200 second. The only adjustment you can make in this mode is to your exposure compensation by using the Quick Control Dial to change the f-stop.

- **Shutter Priority (Tv):** You can adjust the shutter speed from as fast as 1/200 second all the way down to 30 seconds. The lens aperture will adjust accordingly, but typically at long exposures the lens will be set to its largest aperture.

- **Aperture Priority (Av):** This mode has three custom settings for adjusting the shutter speed when using the flash, depending on your needs. The default setting is Auto, which sets the shutter speed for you.

1. Press the Menu button and use the Main Dial to select the Shoot 1 menu screen.

2. Rotate the Quick Control Dial to select the External Speedlite control. Press the Setting button.

3. Rotate the Quick Control Dial to select Flash sync. Speed in Av mode. Press the Setting button.

4. Use the Quick Control Dial to select your preference for shutter speed for sync flash. Press the Setting button.

FLASH EXPOSURE COMPENSATION

Canon flashes use a technology called E-TTL II (evaluative through the lens) metering to determine the appropriate amount of flash power to output for good exposure. When you press the shutter button halfway, the camera quickly adjusts focus while gathering information about the entire scene to measure the amount of ambient light. As you press down the shutter button completely, a pre-flash occurs to measure the light reflected off the subject that's been outputted from the flash. A determination is then made as to how much power is needed to accurately expose the subject while attempting to balance it to the ambient light exposure.

NOTE

This applies to the Program, Shutter Priority, and Aperture Priority modes. In Manual mode, this issue is left at the complete control of the photographer.

The default setting for the flash meter mode is invaluable. You can set the meter to average mode, but that should be avoided. Your best results will come from the E-TTL mode.

Sometimes the output of the flash will render your subject too light or too dark. Although the E-TTL system normally results in a good exposure, you may prefer to adjust the output of the flash to suit your own taste. Adjusting the flash output may help if the meter is having difficulty nailing the exposure. In this portrait of a roller derby athlete, I reduced the flash output by –2/3 to avoid overexposing her mouth guard (**Figure 7.6**). This is where Flash Exposure Compensation plays an important role, because it allows you to either increase or decrease the output of the flash in increments as small as 1/3 stop. You'll more than likely use this feature to reduce the flash output rather than increase it.

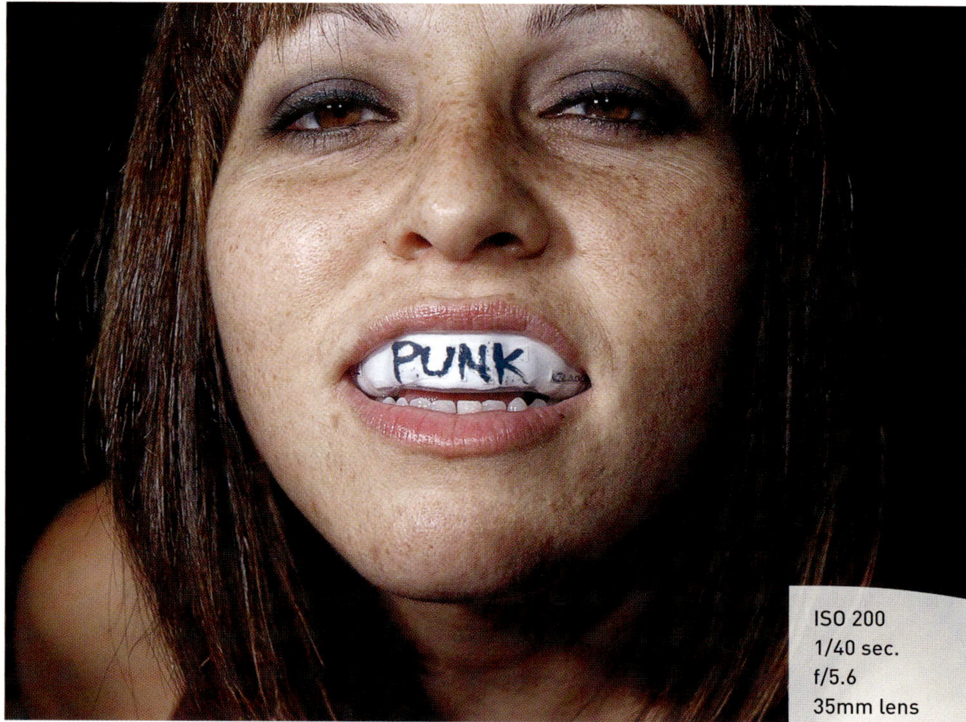

TO USE FLASH EXPOSURE COMPENSATION TO CHANGE THE FLASH OUTPUT, FOLLOW THESE STEPS:

1. Press the Q button to activate the Quick Control screen on the LCD monitor.

2. Use the multi-controller to move the cursor to the Flash Exposure Compensation icon, and press the Setting button.

3. Rotate the Main Dial or Quick Control Dial to adjust the flash compensation in 1/3-stop increments (left to subtract and right to add).

4. Press the shutter button halfway to return to shooting mode, and then take the picture.

5. Review your image to see if more or less flash compensation is required, and repeat these steps as necessary.

Increasing the flash output is not an option if the flash has already been outputting at full power. You know that your flash has done so if the indicator light on the back of the flash unit blinks rapidly after firing. This is also a warning that your subject may be underexposed if the subject was beyond the effective flash range. For such situations, you may need to either open the aperture or increase the ISO in order to achieve a correct exposure.

It's important to note that flash compensation will affect only the flash output, while exposure compensation will impact both the ambient light and the flash exposure. So, if you want to underexpose the ambient light while maintaining the same flash output, you need to make an adjustment on your flash to nullify the impact of exposure compensation. For example, if you apply a –1 compensation using exposure compensation, you would increase the flash compensation by +1 to keep the flash output the same, as I did for this portrait of two young women made at twilight (**Figure 7.7**).

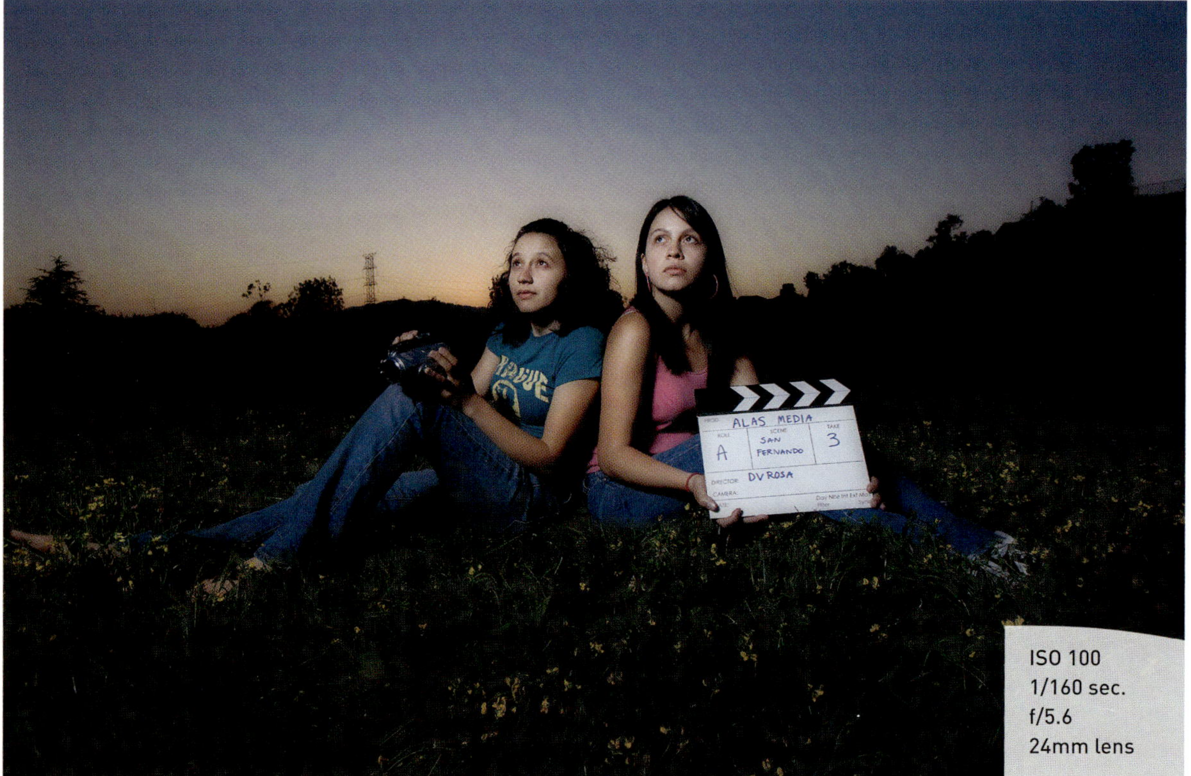

FIGURE 7.7
Being able to refine the flash output, especially when diffusing the flash through an umbrella, helped ensure an accurate flash exposure for this image.

FLASH SYNC MODES

The Canon 5D Mark III has two flash synchronization modes: 1st curtain and 2nd curtain. The term *curtain* relates to the opening and closing of the shutter. The first curtain refers to when the shutter is opened, and the second curtain describes the point just before the shutter is closed. (Visualize the curtain on a stage opening and closing; the amount of time it's open is how long your shutter speed is.)

Your external flash can resynchronize the fire during the first curtain or the second curtain. This applies only to shutter speeds of 1/30 second or slower, because faster shutter speeds are so quick that the mode wouldn't really matter. For longer exposures, I find that using a second curtain flash is usually a good option.

For example, imagine you're photographing a person running (say, from left to right) in a race. It's somewhat dark outside, maybe near sunset, so you might get away with a slower shutter speed of 1/15 second, but you also want to use your flash to freeze the subject in place. If you take your photo in 1st curtain sync mode, the flash will fire just as the shutter opens. The blurred subject will be exposed after this point until the shutter closes. In such an image, the flash will freeze the subject, but the streaking blur will appear in front of them. If you change your flash setting to 2nd curtain sync and take the same photograph, the flash will fire at the end of the exposure. So, the flash will freeze the subject at the end of the shutter duration and the blurred streak will be made to appear behind them for a more natural look.

TO USE 2ND CURTAIN SYNC, FOLLOW THESE STEPS:

1. Press the Menu button and turn the Main Dial to access the Shoot 1 menu screen.

2. Rotate the Quick Control Dial to select the External Speedlite control. Press the Setting button.

3. Rotate the Quick Control Dial to select the Flash function setting. Press the Setting button.

4. Select the 1st curtain sync icon on the far left. Press the Setting button.

5. Use the Quick Control Dial to select the 2nd curtain sync icon at the center of the screen. Press the Setting button.

NOTE

Rear-curtain sync using this camera control is accessible only when using the 270ЄX II 480ЄX II, 580ЄX II, and 600 flashes. Older flashes such as the 580ЄX are not compatible with this feature, though they will still provide Є-TTL metering.

Chapter 7 Assignments

Now that we've looked at the possibilities of shooting after dark, it's time to put it all to the test. These assignments cover the full range of shooting possibilities, both with flash and without. Let's get started.

Steady Hands?

It's important to understand just how powerful your IS can be in steadying your shots. Using an IS lens, find a subject and set your camera to Shutter Priority mode. With the IS enabled, take a few photos at 1/30, 1/15, and 1/8 second. Then turn off the IS feature and take the same shots with the same settings. Compare your images to see how much more camera shake you're creating in each shot.

Push Your ISO to the Extreme

Turn on the extended ISO feature. Now find a place to shoot where the ambient light level is low. This could be outside at night or indoors in a darkened room. Use the exposure mode of your choice and begin making a series of images. With each exposure increase the ISO one full stop (for example, from 200 to 400) until you get to 25,600. Make sure you evaluate the level of noise in your images, especially in the shadow areas. Only you can decide how much noise is acceptable in your pictures.

Get Rid of the Noise

With your camera set to record JPEGs, turn on the high ISO speed noise-reduction feature and repeat the preceding assignment. Find your acceptable limits with the noise reduction turned on. Also, pay attention to how much detail is lost in your shadows with this function enabled.

Long Exposures in the Dark

If you don't have a tripod, find a stable place to set your camera outside and try some long exposures. Set your camera to Aperture Priority mode and use the self-timer to activate the camera (this will keep you from shaking the camera while pressing the shutter button) or use a cable release if you have one. Shoot in an area that has some level of ambient light, whether a streetlight, traffic lights, or even a full moon. The idea is to get some late-night low-light exposures. For best results, perform this assignment and the next assignment in the same shooting session using the same subject.

Handle Focus Under Low Light

Go indoors into a low-light environment and find a subject with little contrast and detail. Attempt to focus on the subject as you would normally. If you experience difficulty, choose single-point AF and choose another area of the subject or another subject at the same distance and try to lock focus. Also, try focusing manually to achieve accurate focus and compare the results.

Get Creative with 2nd Curtain Sync

Now it's time for a little creative fun. Set your camera up for 2nd curtain sync and start shooting. Moving targets are best. Experiment with Shutter Priority and Aperture Priority modes to lower the shutter speeds and exaggerate the effect. Try using a low ISO so the camera is forced to use longer shutter speeds. Be creative and have some fun!

Share your results with this book's Flickr group!

Join the group here: www.flickr.com/groups/Canon5DMarkIIIFromSnapshotstoGreatShots

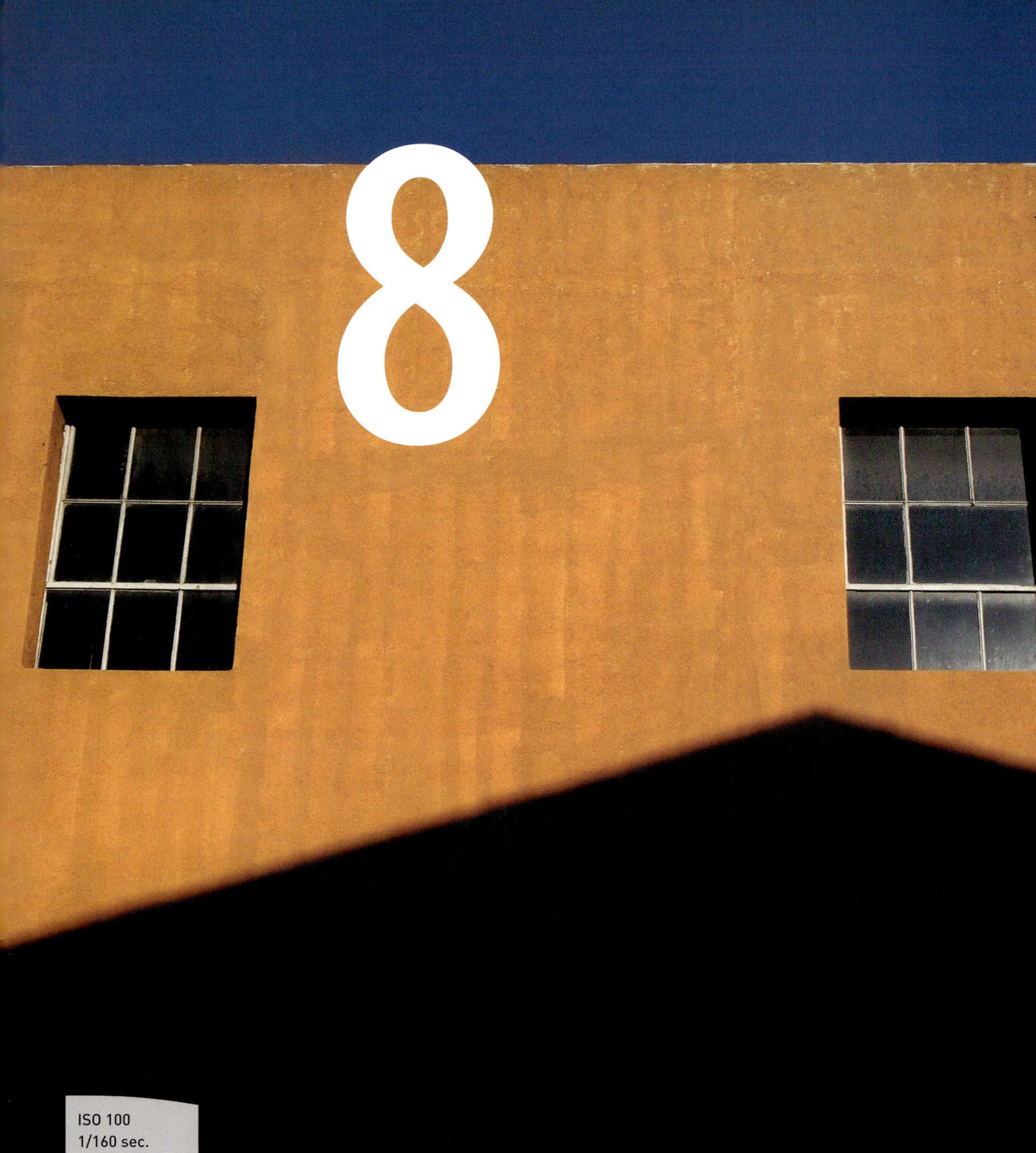
8
ISO 100
1/160 sec.
f/8
24–105mm lens

Creative Compositions

IMPROVING YOUR PICTURES WITH SOUND COMPOSITIONAL ELEMENTS

Creating good compositions involves more than always using the rule of thirds. It's a way of thinking that allows you to build photographs where you control the viewer's experience of the image. Composition is about understanding how people look at an image and how you can use those things to your advantage. In this chapter, I explain what those things are and how they can dramatically improve your photographs.

PORING OVER THE PICTURE

Being aware of what draws the human eye can allow you to make photographs of the most common and mundane objects, including a table and chair. Knowing that the eye is drawn to the brightest and most color-saturated elements in the frame allowed me to build a composition where the shape of the furniture and the shadow became the heart of the image, elevating it from more than just a snapshot.

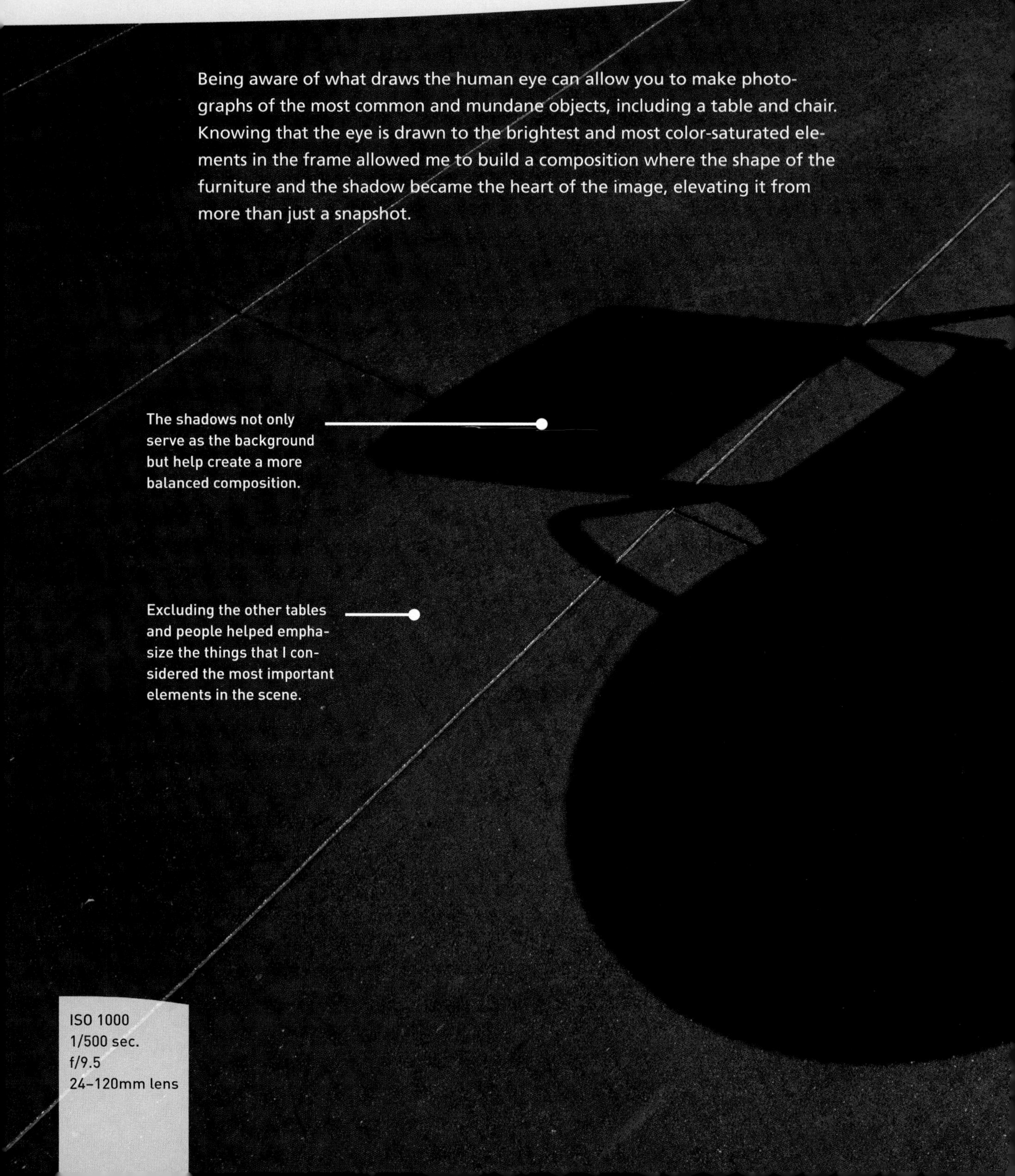

The shadows not only serve as the background but help create a more balanced composition.

Excluding the other tables and people helped emphasize the things that I considered the most important elements in the scene.

ISO 1000
1/500 sec.
f/9.5
24–120mm lens

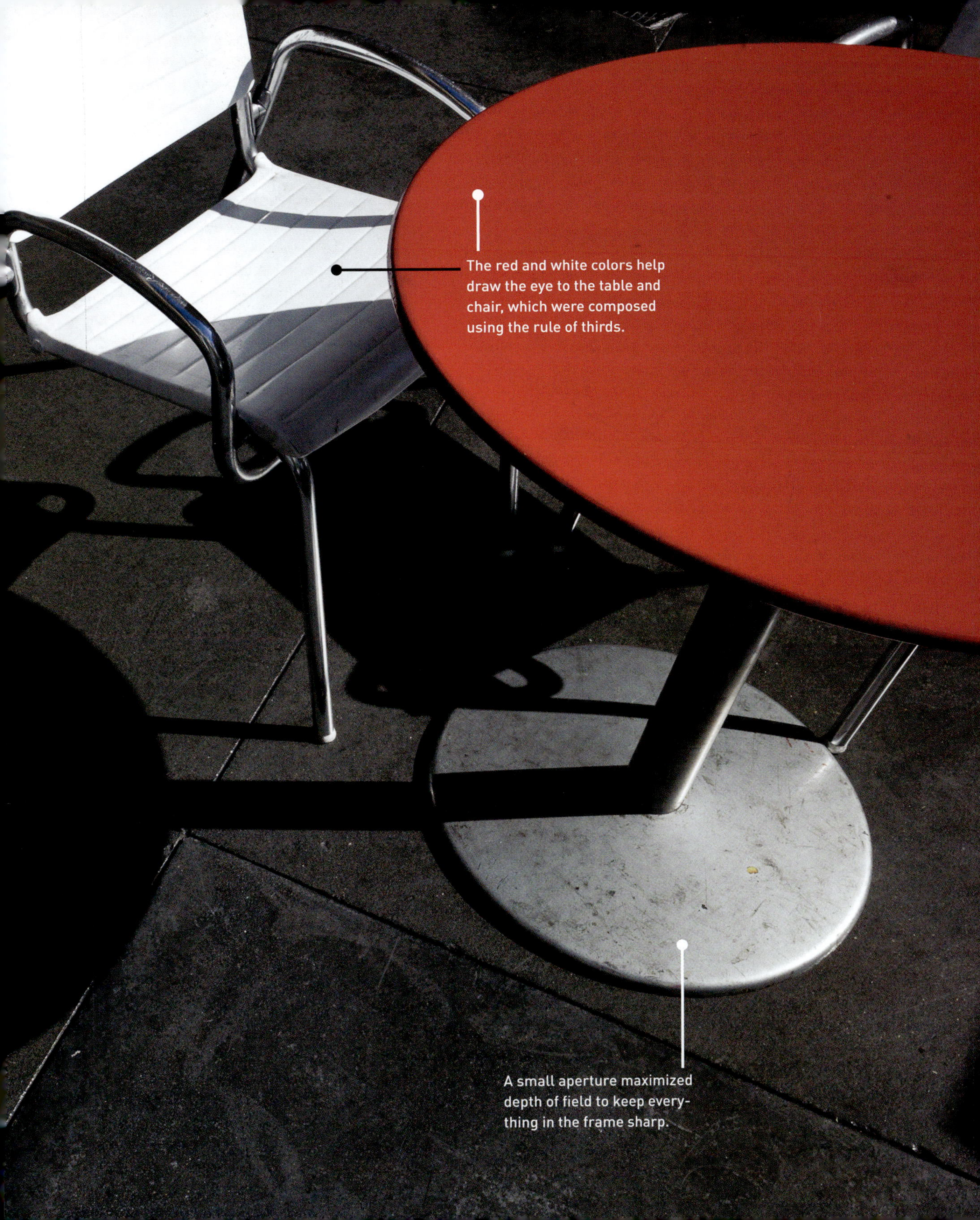

The red and white colors help draw the eye to the table and chair, which were composed using the rule of thirds.
A small aperture maximized depth of field to keep everything in the frame sharp.

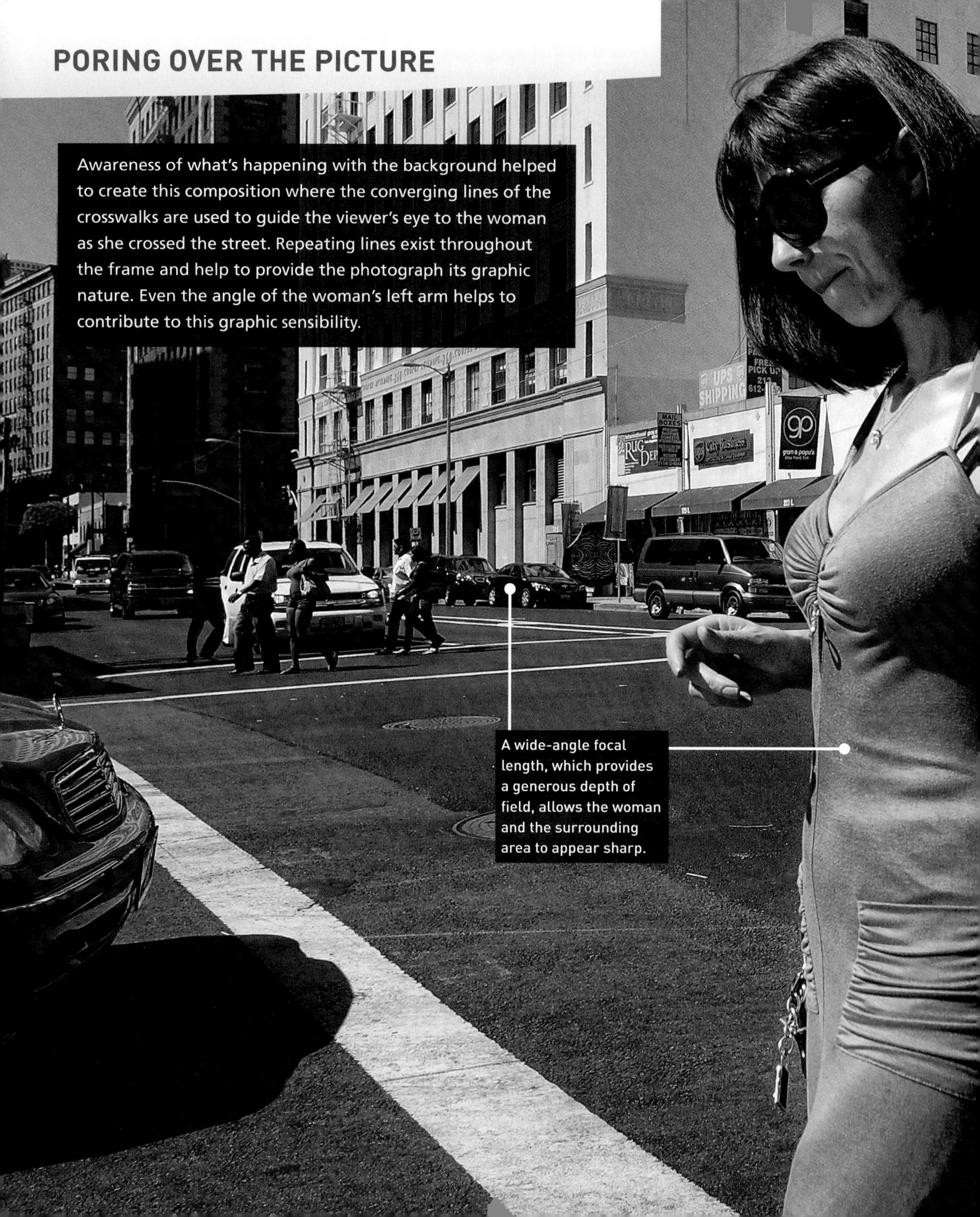

PORING OVER THE PICTURE

Awareness of what's happening with the background helped to create this composition where the converging lines of the crosswalks are used to guide the viewer's eye to the woman as she crossed the street. Repeating lines exist throughout the frame and help to provide the photograph its graphic nature. Even the angle of the woman's left arm helps to contribute to this graphic sensibility.

A wide-angle focal length, which provides a generous depth of field, allows the woman and the surrounding area to appear sharp.

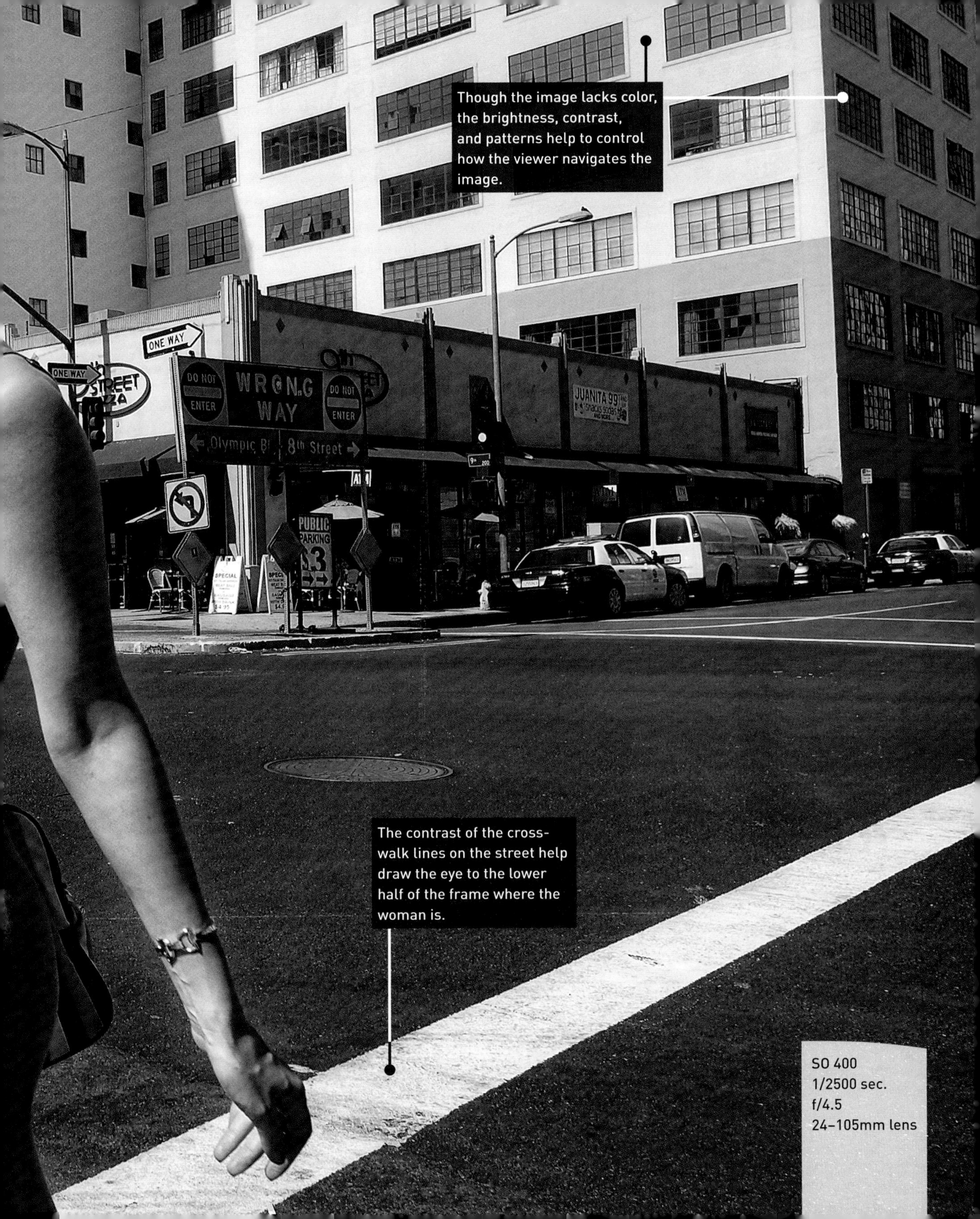

ONE WAY
ONE WAY
STREET PLAZA
DO NOT ENTER
WRONG WAY
DO NOT ENTER
JUANITA 99
Olympic Bl
8th Street
PUBLIC PARKING
$3
SPECIAL

Though the image lacks color, the brightness, contrast, and patterns help to control how the viewer navigates the image.

The contrast of the cross-walk lines on the street help draw the eye to the lower half of the frame where the woman is.

SO 400
1/2500 sec.
f/4.5
24–105mm lens

THE FIVE VISUAL DRAWS

There are five elements that will draw a viewer's attention in any image. Either individually or in combination with each other, these elements are often the very first things people look at within a photograph or any other kind of image.

BRIGHTNESS

Viewers' eyes are drawn to the brightest element in the frame. This is something that the great painters used to their advantage on their canvases, and it's something that we as photographers can take advantage of with any photograph. So, it's often best to ensure that the subject or a part of the subject is the brightest element in the scene, such as with this image of a girl playing with a balloon (**Figure 8.1**). Otherwise, if something in the background or a secondary element is brighter, it can compete with the subject for the viewer's attention.

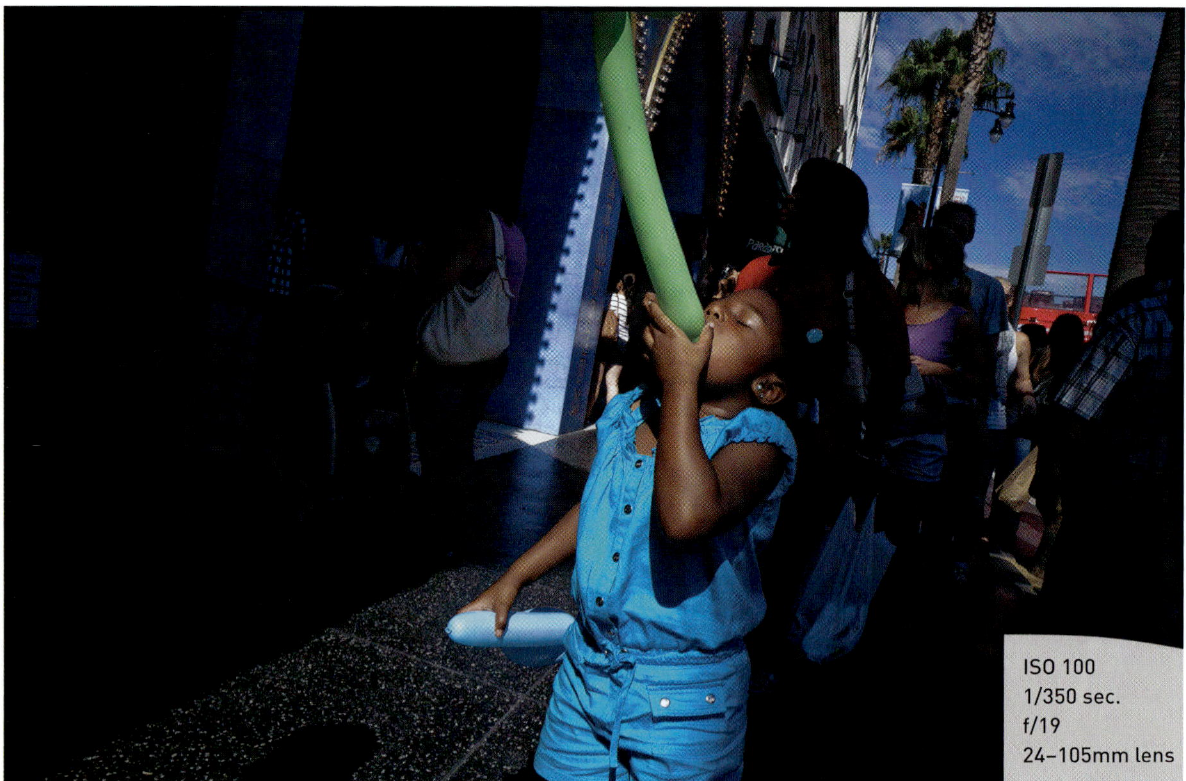

SHARPNESS

Though you're always concerned with the overall sharpness of image, the point of focus should be the sharpest element in the frame, as with this portrait of a well-dressed young man (**Figure 8.2**). If the subject is sharp and the background is out of focus, the viewer's eyes are immediately drawn to the element that's in focus. So, if the subject is slightly out of focus or unintentionally blurred, it can hamper the viewer's experience of the image.

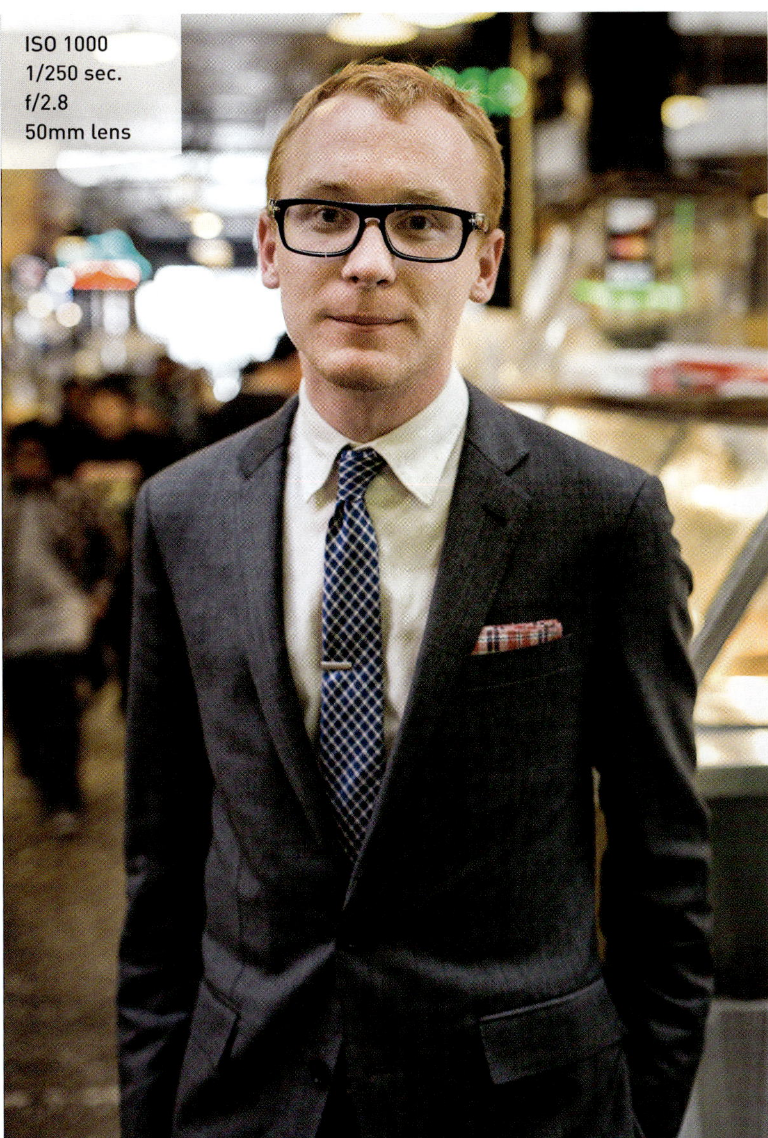

FIGURE 8.2
A shallow depth of field and precise focus on this young man helped to keep the viewer focused on his dapper appearance and expression.

CONTRAST

Areas where light meets dark can immediately draw the viewer's attention. Whether it's a silhouette or a contrast of shape or color, contrast can be a great device to draw the viewer's attention to a specific area in the frame. Contrast doesn't just have to be about light and dark (**Figure 8.3**); it also can be about color, such as the juxtaposition between the colors blue and yellow, which creates an amazing sense of resonance in a photograph.

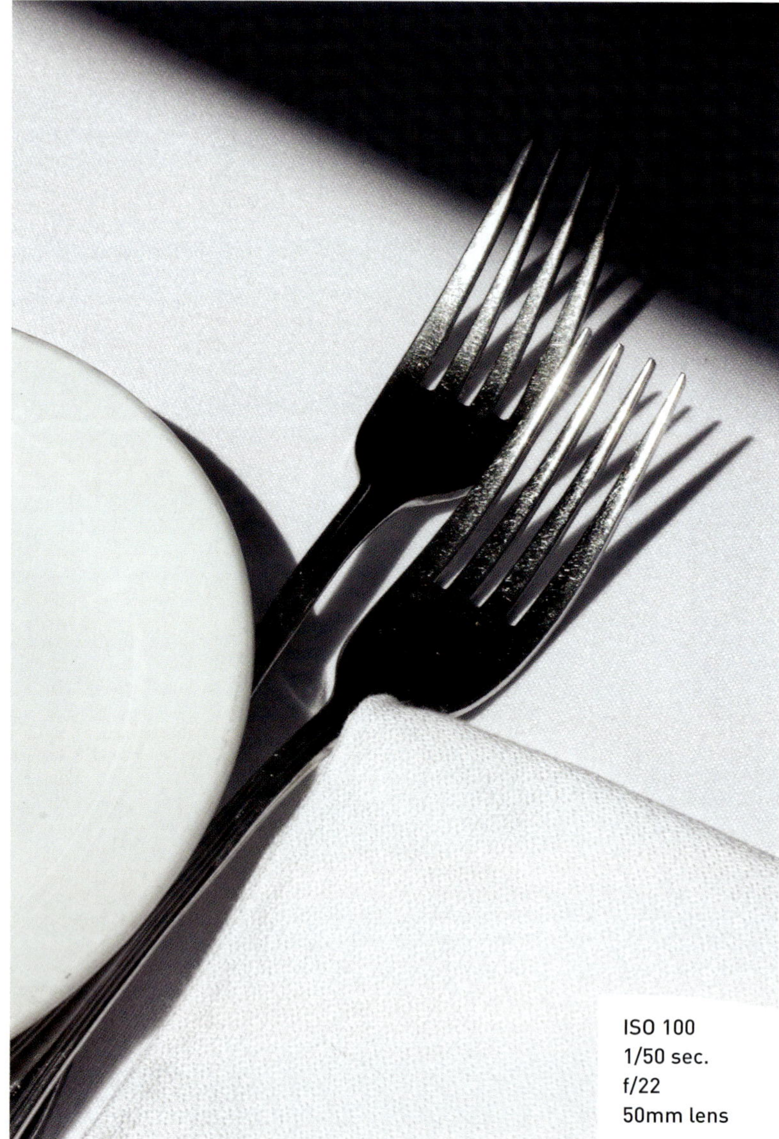

COLOR SATURATION

Saturated colors, such as the color red (**Figure 8.4**), can be a big visual draw. Saturated colors have a vibrancy to them that can easily catch the viewer's attention. Whether it's the clothing the subject is wearing or a door of a home in a small fishing village, color can become a key means of grabbing the viewer's attention.

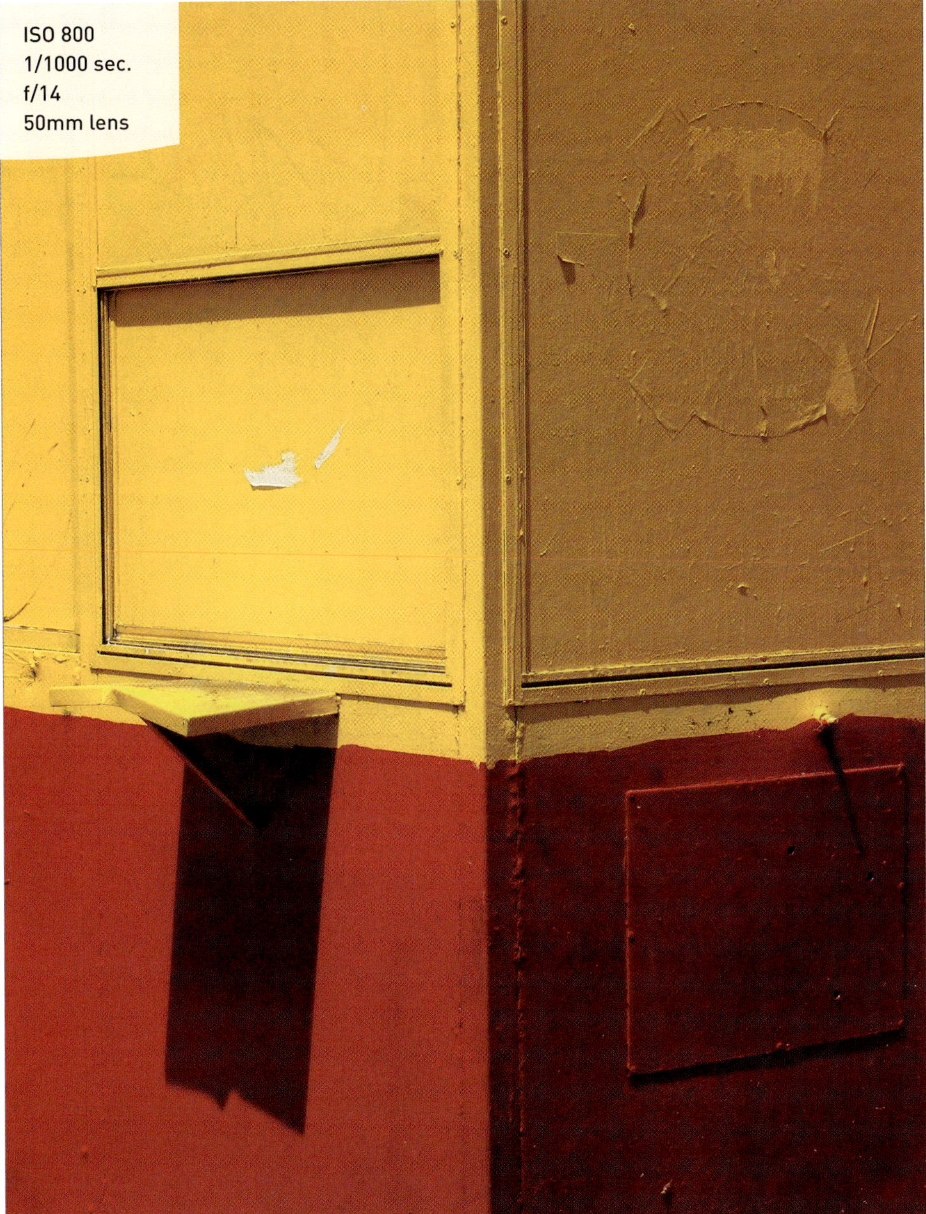

FIGURE 8.4
The hard light provided by direct sunlight emphasized the colors of this parking lot kiosk and created shadows that provided a sense of depth and shape to the structure.

You also can use color as a theme for your photography. I often create an image that is dominated by a single color as a background element (**Figure 8.5**). The background can act as a color contrast to my subject, resulting in a pleasing contrast, visual interest, and isolation.

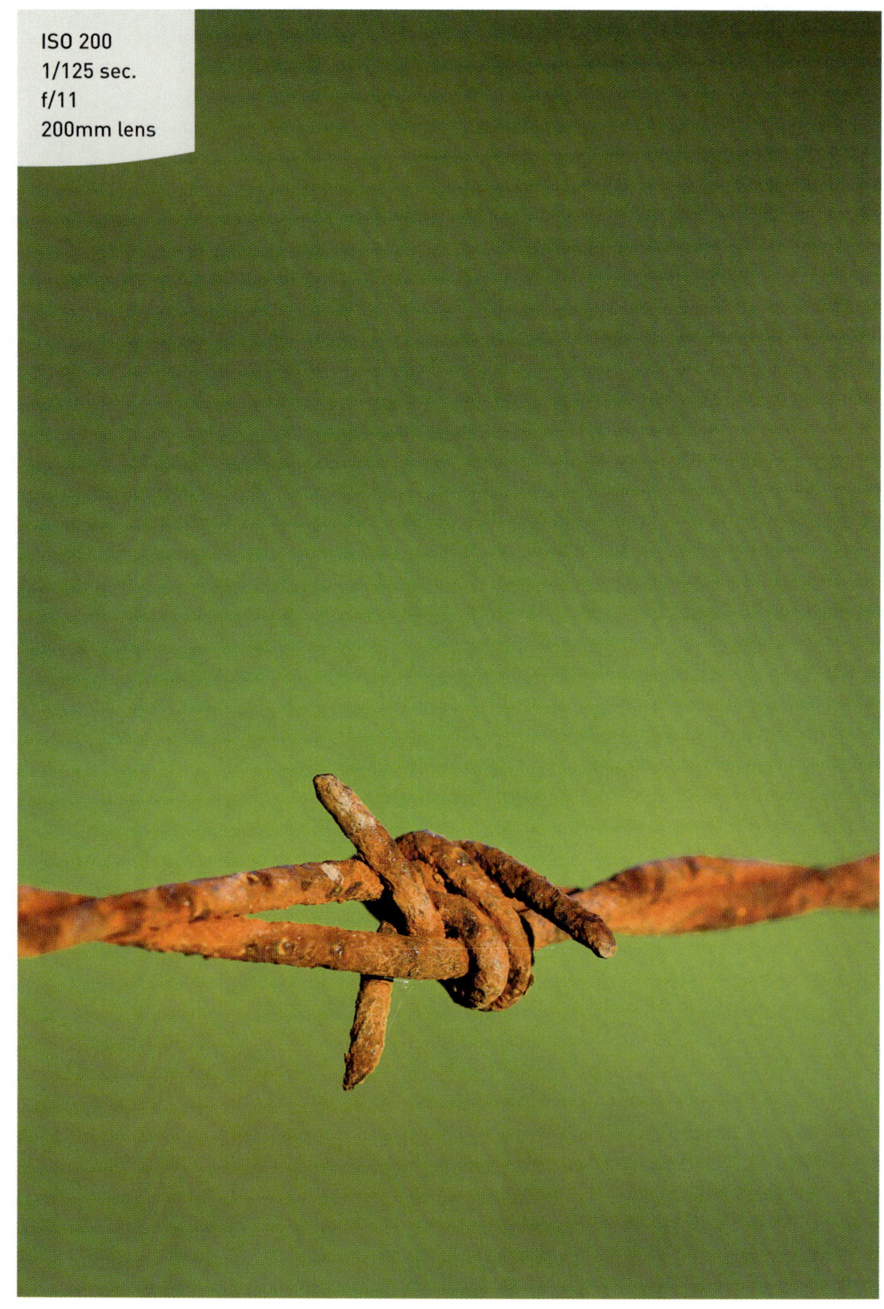

FIGURE 8.5
The saturated color of the barbed wire and the out-of-focus green foliage behind it created a contrast of color and sharpness that helped control how the viewer looks at the photograph.

PATTERN

Repeating patterns (**Figure 8.6**) often catch a viewer's attention. Our brains are wired to recognize patterns or repeating shapes and textures. The rhythm and flow that these patterns provide not only can be an interesting subject, but also can be used to control how the viewer navigates the entire photograph. It can help lead the viewer from the periphery of the image to the main subject.

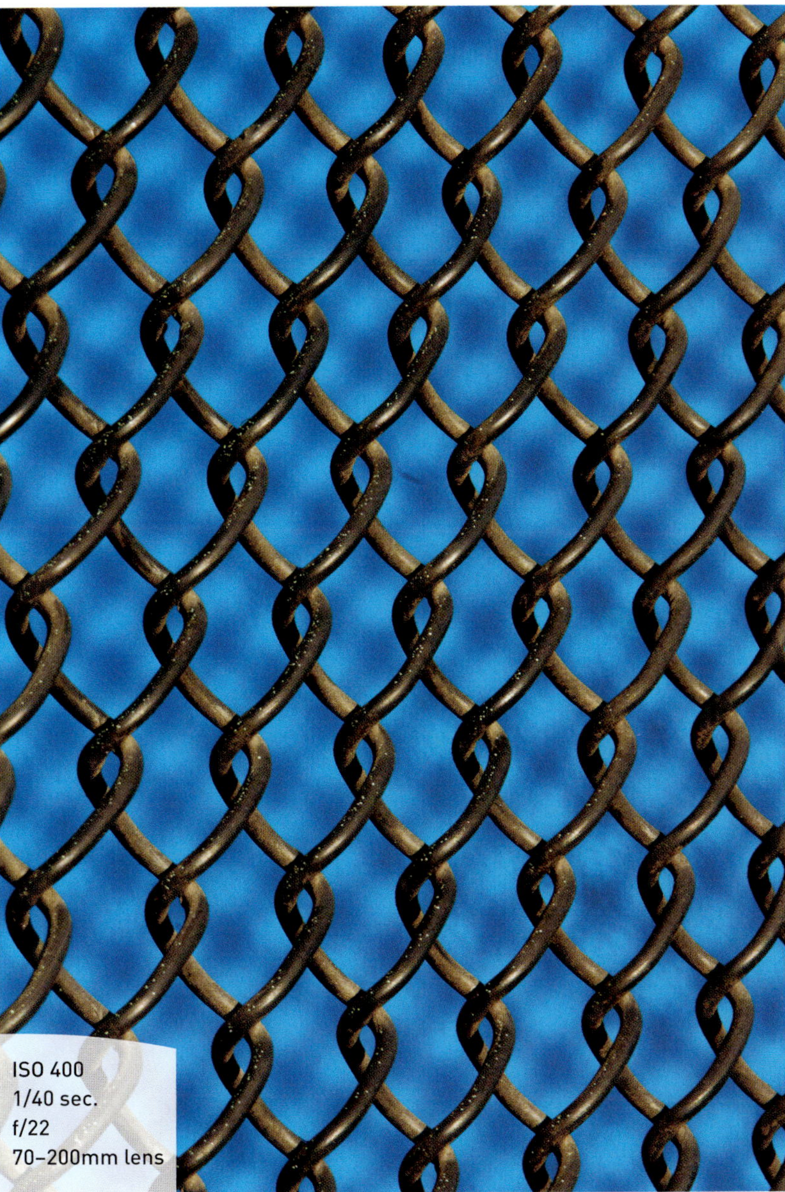

FIGURE 8.6
The color of the wall that lay behind this chain-link fence blended the visual draws of a strong saturated color, contrast, sharpness, and repeating pattern.

You also can introduce contrast through different geometric shapes that battle (in a good way) for the attention of the viewer. You can combine circles and triangles, ovals and rectangles, curves and straight lines, hard and soft, dark and light, and so many more shapes (**Figure 8.7**). You aren't limited to just one contrasting element either. Combining more than one element of contrast will add even more interest. Look for these contrasting combinations whenever you're out shooting, and then use them to shake up your compositions.

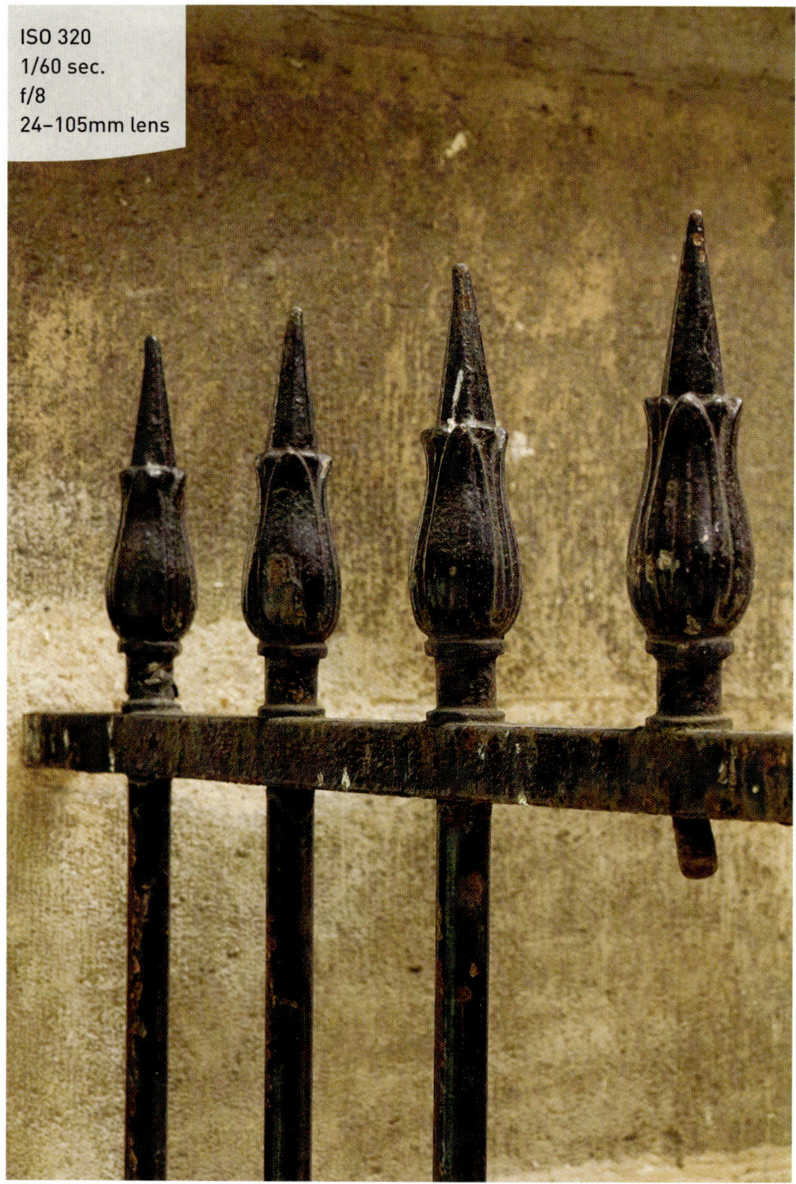

FIGURE 8.7
Breaking a pattern helps to emphasize the pattern itself, as with this image of an iron fence outside an old church.

WORKING TOGETHER

Many images fall apart when something other than the subject has one or more of the five visual draws. If you have a subject in the background that's brighter, has more contrast, and has more color saturation than your subject, that element becomes a big distraction. It results in the viewer's attention going back and forth between your main subject and the distraction, and it weakens the effectiveness of the image.

By creating a composition in which I'm aware of these different visual draws, I have better control over how a viewer experiences an image. In this image of the stairwell, I use my knowledge of pattern, brightness, contrast, and sharpness to help guide the viewer's eye not only down the stairwell but throughout the entire frame (**Figure 8.8**).

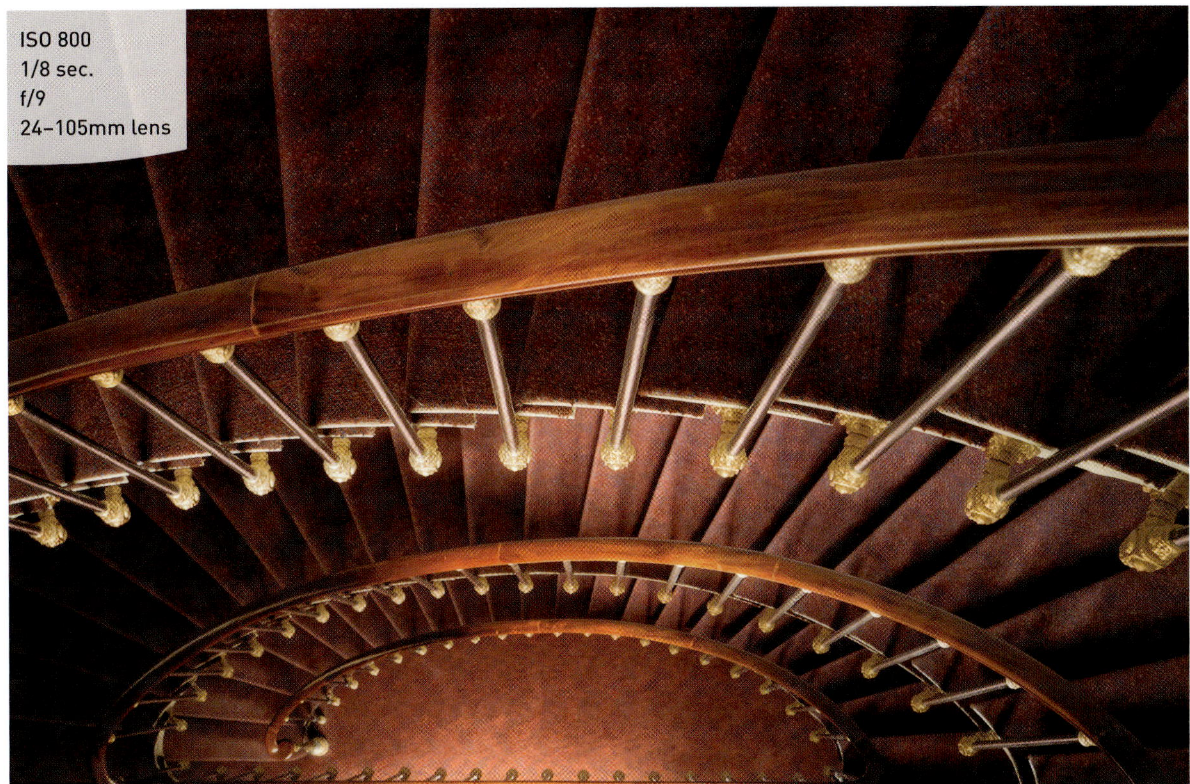

FIGURE 8.8

The visual draws of brightness, sharpness, contrast, color saturation, and pattern were all at play in this image of a hotel stairwell. The tight composition created a natural visual flow for the viewer to navigate.

DEPTH OF FIELD

Selective focus is a great way of emphasizing your subject. Using a wide aperture or a long telephoto lens can blur the background, as I often do for a portrait (**Figure 8.9**), while leaving your subject tack sharp. This allows the viewer to understand what the photographer considers the most important element in the frame. The background, even if it's blurred, can still provide a sense of place or provide an element of contrast.

FIGURE 8.9
The use of a wide aperture helped to throw the busy street out of focus and allowed me to focus on the face of this young woman.

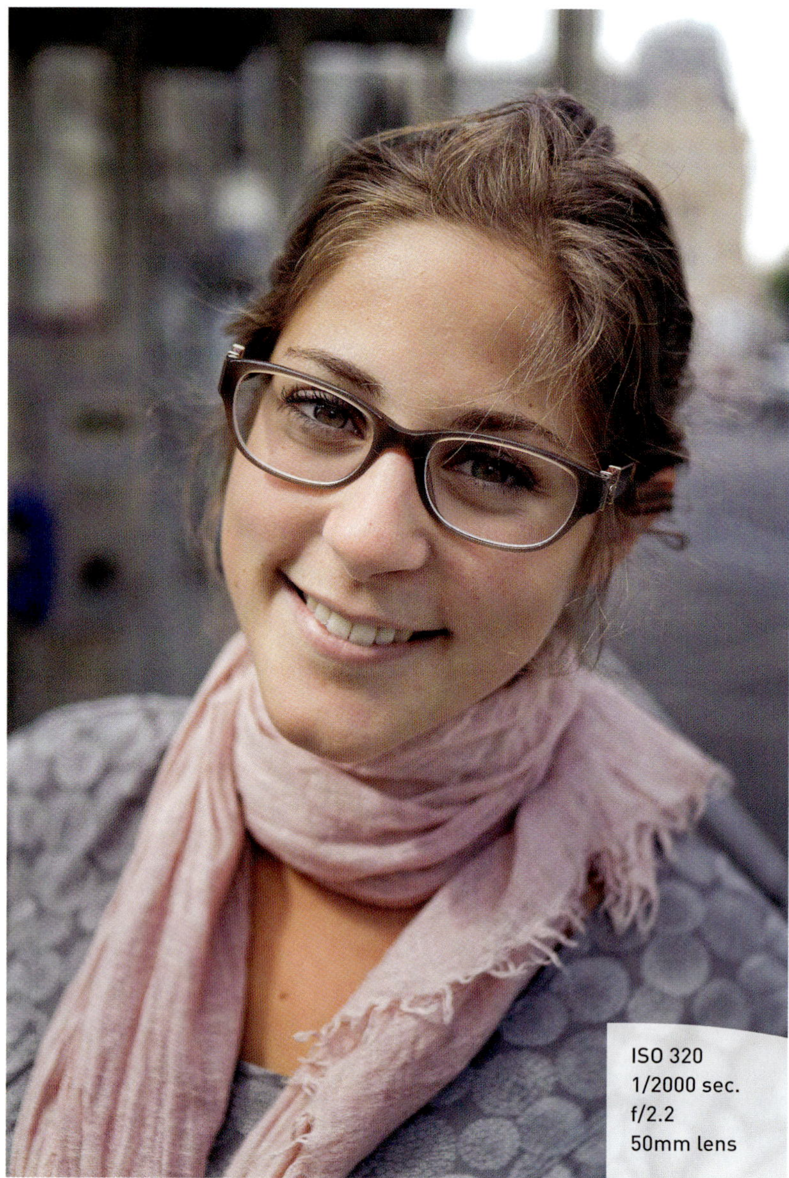

I use a small aperture to increase my depth of field when photographing a natural or urban landscape (**Figure 8.10**) where I want most of the frame to appear sharp. Though no one element is sharper than another, I'm using other visual draws such as pattern, brightness, color saturation, and contrast to create a successful composition.

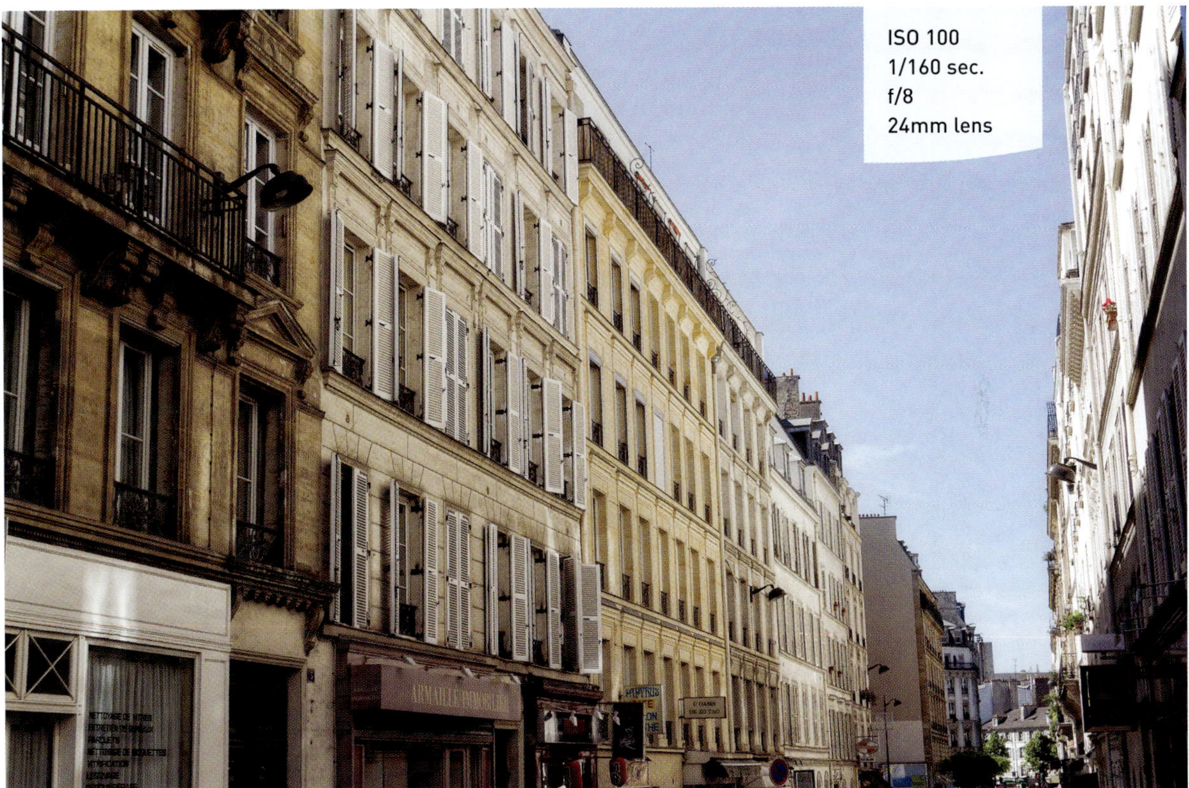

The depth of field provided by a wide-angle lens and a moderate aperture helped to emphasize the repeating pattern of the apartments, and the lines guide the viewer's eye to the end of the street.

BACKGROUNDS

More shots are ruined by the poor choice of a background then anything else. It's easy for photographers to get so myopic that they're only looking at the subject and not considering anything else that's happening within the frame. Remember, if something in your frame doesn't serve your subject, it doesn't need to be there. You can shift your position or your subject to eliminate those elements from the frame, especially if they're proving to be a distraction, as I did for this photograph of a plate of pasta at a busy restaurant (**Figure 8.11**). By avoiding clutter and distractions in the background, you're better able to have your main subject hold the viewer's attention.

FIGURE 8.11
Using a wide aperture to create a narrow depth of field to emphasize the ingredients of this delicious meal minimized the clutter and the activity of a busy restaurant.

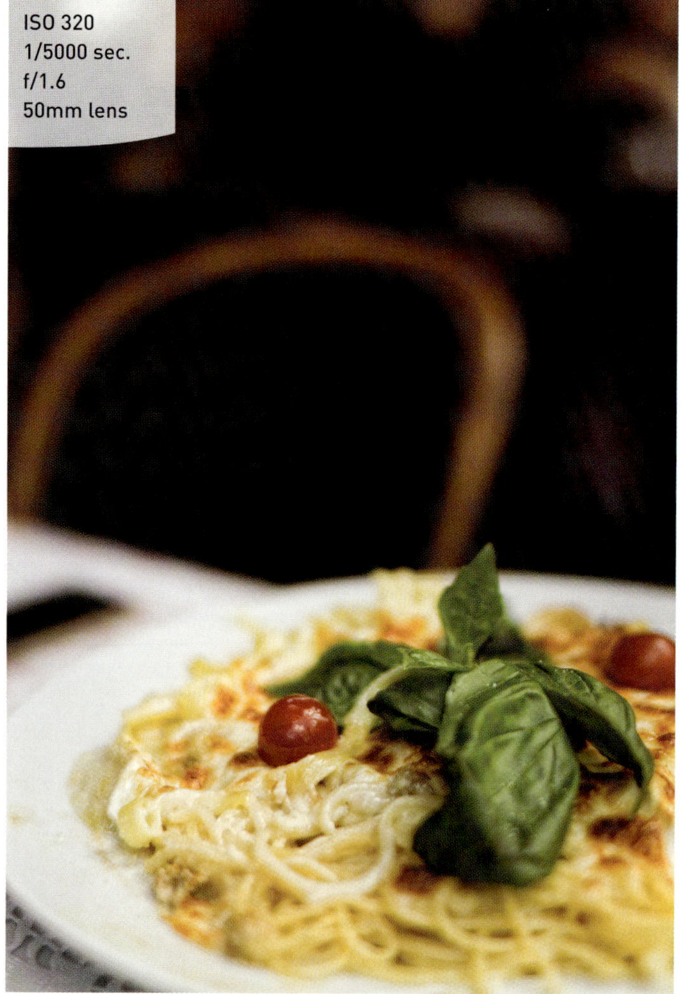

LEADING LINES

Finding ways to draw your viewer's eye toward the subject of your photo is important in a photographic composition. One way to do this is to incorporate leading lines in the image. You can use this technique to create a vanishing point on the subject itself or on some point in the horizon, such as in the photograph of the interior of a museum (**Figure 8.12**).

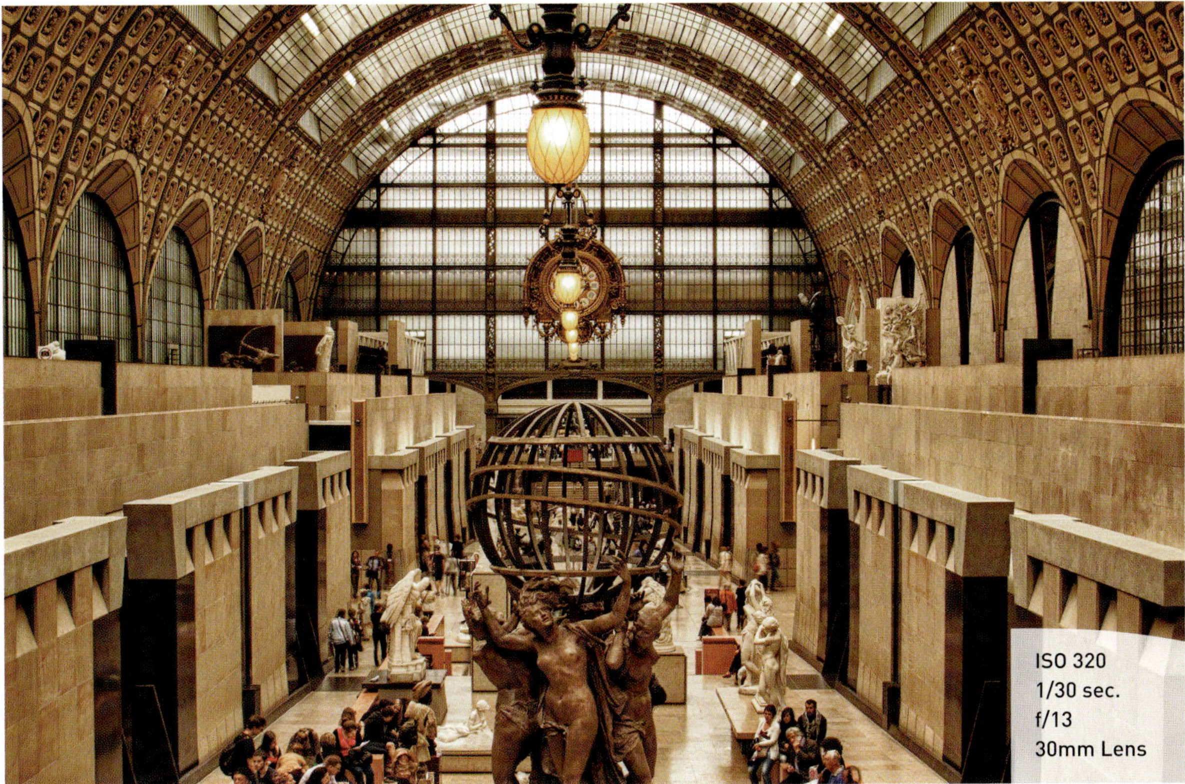

FIGURE 8.12
The leading lines and the repeating patterns that existed in the museum helped me to build a composition that flows naturally to the building's entrance.

Chapter 8 Assignments

Apply the shooting techniques and tools that you've learned in the previous chapters to these assignments, and you'll improve your ability to incorporate good composition into your photos. Make sure you experiment with all the different elements of composition and see how you can combine them to add interest to your images.

Learn to See Lines and Patterns

Take your camera for a walk around your neighborhood and look for patterns and angles. Don't worry so much about getting great shots as much as developing an eye for details.

Look for Brightness and Contrast

Look for scenes that are illuminated by direct sunlight and that are resulting in strong shadows. Create compositions that emphasize the bright areas of the scene.

Close in on a Clash of Colors

Look for and photograph scenes where colors contrast, such as blue/yellow or red/green. Create images that emphasize these conflicts of colors.

Use the Aperture to Focus the Viewer's Attention

Depth of field plays an important role in defining your images and establishing depth and dimension. Practice shooting wide open, using your largest aperture for the narrowest depth of field. Then find a scene that would benefit from extended depth of field, using very small apertures to give sharpness throughout the scene.

Lead Them into the Frame

Look for scenes where you can use elements as leading lines. Then look for framing elements that you can use to isolate your subject and add both depth and dimension to your images.

Share your results with this book's Flickr group!

Join the group here: www.flickr.com/groups/Canon5DMarkIIIFromSnapshotstoGreatShots

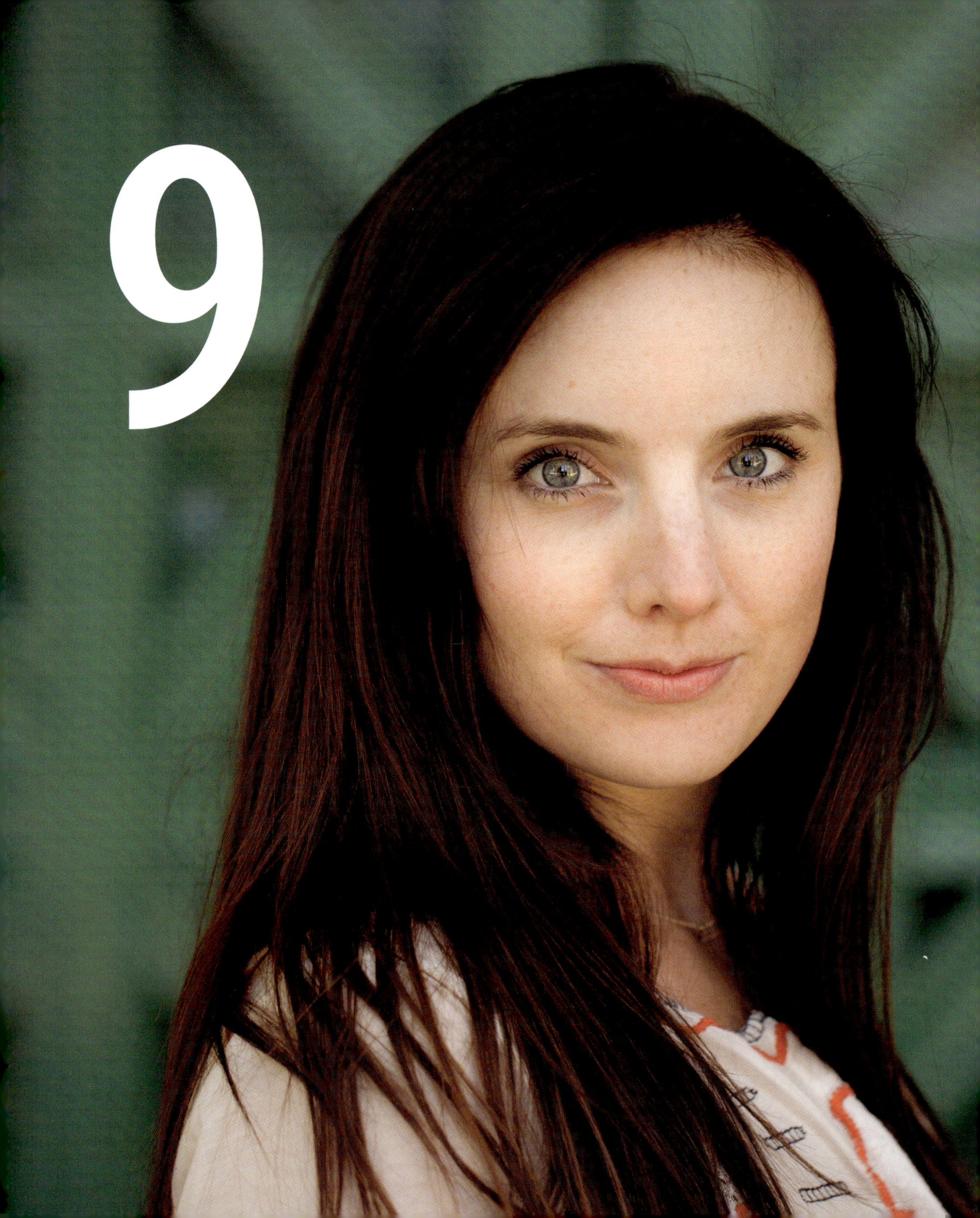

9

At the Movies

CREATING VIDEO WITH THE 5D MARK III

The introduction of the 5D Mark II revolutionized how photographers can capture video. The cinema-like look that was once the exclusive domain of expensive motion-picture film cameras suddenly was available at a fraction of the cost and with a significantly smaller camera body. Adopted by both professionals and enthusiasts, DSLRs have increasingly become one of the best ways to capture HD video content.

The 5D Mark III builds on the strength of the previous model and adds some important features. However, whether you're a seasoned videographer or just dabbling with the occasional video, you'll find that this camera has a lot to offer.

ISO 400
1/1000 sec.
f/2.8
100mm lens

CAMERA BACK

Creative Photo/Comparative playback
(Two-image display)/Direct print button
Menu button
Info button
Viewfinder eyepiece
Live View shooting/Movie
shooting switch
MENU
INFO.
AF-ON
START/
STOP
RATE
Q
SET
LOCK▶
Canon
Erase
button
Magnify/Reduce
button
Rating button
Playback button

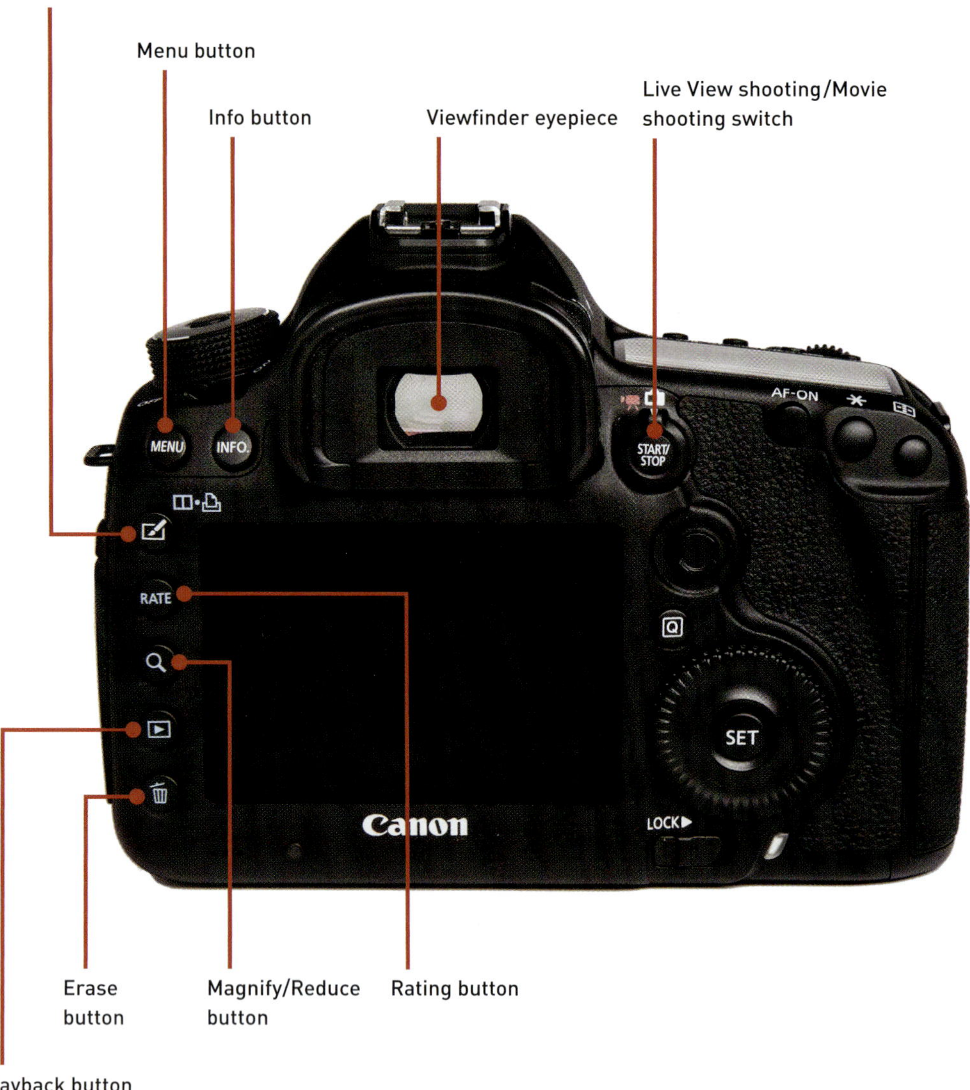

LCD MONITOR

Memory card
White balance and Picture Style
Focusing mode
AF point
Recording movie indicator
M
AF
N
OFF
RAW
1920
30
IPB
29:59
M
L
R
60
1.6
-3..2..1..·..1..2..3
[1059]
ISO 200
Exposure simulation
Battery check
ISO speed
Movie recording size
Shutter speed
Shots remaining
Audio sound levels
Aperture
Exposure compensation amount

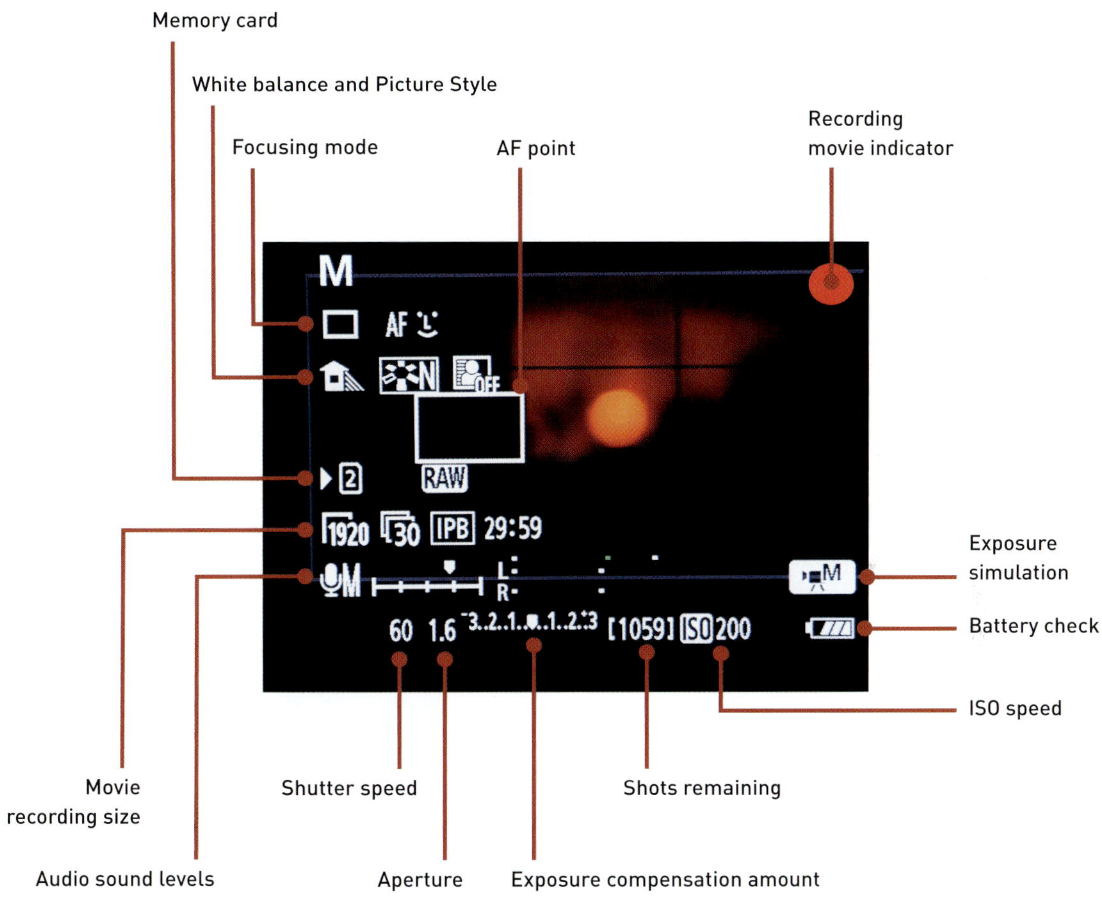

GETTING STARTED

It's important to note that, although the 5D Mark III produces exceptional-quality video, its primary purpose is that of a still camera. So, it lacks some of the advantages of a dedicated video camera such as a power zoom; speedy, continuous autofocus; and in-camera image stabilization. However, it does offer the versatility of removable lenses, high ISO performance, and incredible adaptability.

Because you're capturing motion as opposed to still images, camera stability becomes an even more important concern. A tripod, preferably one with a fluid head, is highly recommended because it helps reduce camera shake that can prove very distracting when watching video. If you intend to handhold the camera, a camera rig that includes a focusing mechanism can help you to hold the camera steady, as well as give you greater control for manually focusing the lens.

VIDEO QUALITY

One of the more important aspects of video to understand is resolution. You need to know what recording size you want to use, along with the frame rate, or frames per second (fps). The files are recorded as a .mov file and the quality and the resolution (size) of each file is measured in pixels. The fps is defined by how many frames (images) the camera records in a 1-second timeframe. It's important to set your video quality before beginning to record any video.

The 5D Mark III has three different sizes you can choose from (**Figure 9.1**):

- **1920 x 1080:** This is the full high-definition (HD) setting (16:9 aspect ratio). You have the option to record in 30 fps or 24 fps. Using this setting at 24 fps is a standard for recording motion pictures. This is often referred to as "1080p."

- **1280 x 720:** This is another HD setting with an aspect ratio of 16:9, but in a smaller resolution. It records movies at 50 fps or 60 fps and is often referred to as "720p." This is good for shooting website videos or if you want to create high-quality slow-motion effects with your movies using editing software.

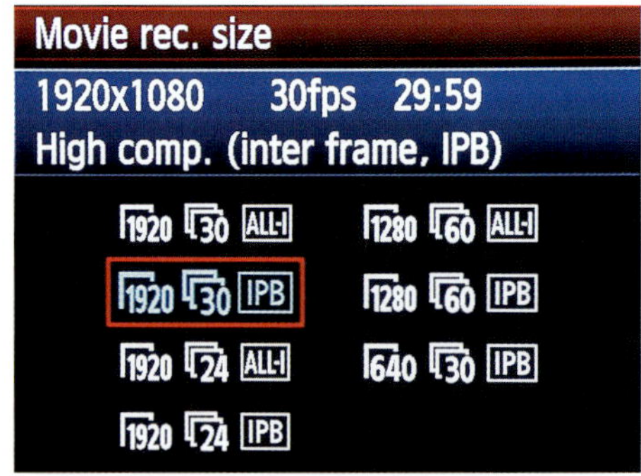

FIGURE 9.1

I recommend shooting at the highest resolution of 1920 x 1080 for recording video because you can always downsample the video clips for a lower-resolution output later.

- **640 x 480:** This setting is for standard definition (SD) recording and records in a 4:3 aspect ratio.

COMPRESSION METHOD

The camera offers two different compressions method for video: IPB and All-I:

- **IPB** applies compression to multiple frames to produce a smaller file, providing more space for recording. Think of it along the lines of the compression applied for producing a JPEG. If you don't intend to edit your videos and plan to simply upload the clips to your computer or a service such as YouTube, this should be your preferred mode of compression.

- **All-I** applies compression to each individual frame, which produces larger files than IPB but is more ideally suited for editing. It provides a superior file quality. This is my preferred method of compression whenever I'm shooting video.

SLOW MOTION

If you want to slow down your videos and create great high-quality slow-motion videos, you'll want to start by shooting at 720p. This setting records video at 60 fps, so when you bring it into your editing program, you can set it to play back at 50 percent speed, or 30 fps. Your video will play back half as fast as you originally recorded it without sacrificing image quality.

NTSC AND PAL

You can set your 5D Mark III in one of two formats: NTSC or PAL (**Figure 9.2**). NTSC is the standard format for broadcasting in North America, South America, and Asia; PAL is the standard format for most European countries and other parts of the world. The main difference between the two when shooting with the 5D Mark III is their frame rates (25/50 FPS for PAL and 30/60 FPS for NTSC).

Set your video format to the broadcasting standard for whatever country you're located in:

1. Set the camera to Video mode using the Live View/Movie Shooting switch.

2. Press the Menu button and use the Main Dial to get to the Shoot 4: Movie menu screen.

3. Access the movie recording size using the Quick Control Dial. Press the Setting button.

4. Use the Quick Control Dial and select your preferred movie-shooting mode. Press the Setting button.

5. Press the Menu button to go back to shooting video.

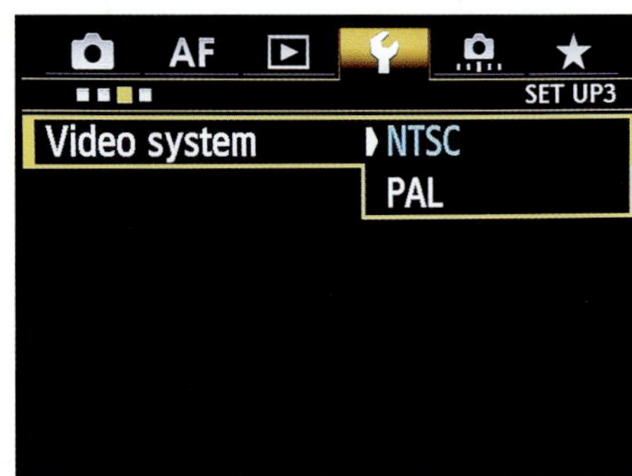

FIGURE 9.2

Make sure to set your camera for the broadcast standard where you live.

MEMORY CARDS

The choice of memory cards is very important when recording video. Because you're continually recording and saving large amounts of data, the speed by which the card reads and writes the data becomes critically important. If you're using a Compact Flash (CF) card, you should use a UDMA card for high-speed photography and video shooting. These cards are designed for high data-transfer speeds, which will limit the risk of dropped data. If you're using Secure Digital (SD) cards, use a card with a data transfer rate of 45 MB per second or faster.

Using less expensive and slower memory cards can hamper the performance of the camera for both still and video. It's best to invest in the fastest cards that you can afford to ensure the optimal performance of the camera. These fast cards can also cut down on the time it takes to download the files from the cards to your computer.

I recommend a memory card with a minimum capacity of 4 GB. Memory cards of 8 GB or 16 GB are also a good option. There are cards that offer capacities of 32 GB and higher, but make sure that such cards offer high data-transfer speeds.

SHOOTING AND PLAYBACK

Setting up your camera to shoot video has been much improved in the 5D Mark III with the addition of a dedicated button and switch for video. This makes it very easy to switch back and forth between video and stills. However, there are some other features and controls that are important to ensure that you capture the best video possible.

These features include the ability to play back your images on the camera (**Figure 9.3**), as well as take still pictures while recording video.

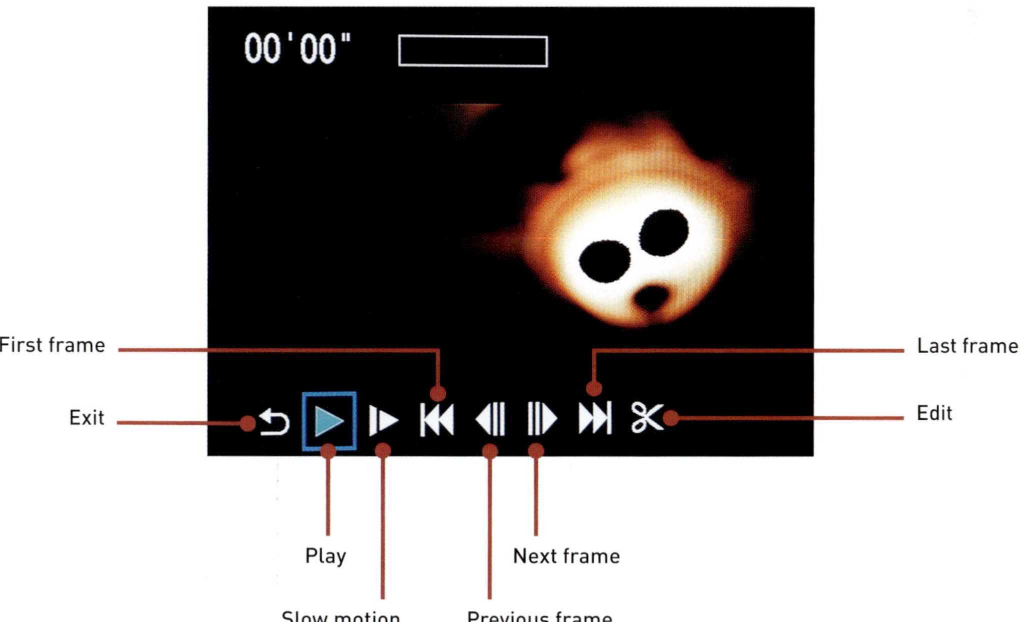

FIGURE 9.3
Use the Quick Control Dial to select the other options in the Playback mode. If you recorded sound with your movie, you can also use the Main Dial to adjust the sound volume during playback.

SHOOTING STILL WHILE RECORDING VIDEO

The 5D Mark III offers you the ability to capture a still image while you're recording video. Though it may not be a feature you use frequently, it's convenient because you don't have to switch back from the Video mode to the still mode in order to make a single photograph.

The image will be captured and saved based on the file format you choose for your still photographs. So, if you're shooting RAW, you'll see that displayed on the LCD monitor in Live View mode. This doesn't mean that the camera is recording a raw version of the video file, but rather that this is how the stills will be recorded.

If you want to make a still during video capture, simply press the shutter button and make a photograph. There will be a momentary pause during the recording and then the camera will return to recording video. When you play back your video file, there will be 1 second of a still image in the midst of your video, which you can include or edit out with your editing application.

RECORDING A MOVIE

TO RECORD A MOVIE, FOLLOW THESE STEPS:

1. Locate the Live View/Movie Shooting switch on the back of the camera and turn it to the red video camera setting. The LCD monitor will immediately go into Live View mode.

2. Compose and focus your scene and press the Start/Stop button to begin your recording. You'll notice a red dot appear in the upper right-hand corner of the LCD monitor. This indicates that video recording is in progress.

3. When you're finished recording, press the Start/Stop button. The red dot will disappear, indicating that you're no longer recording video.

PLAYING BACK A MOVIE

TO PLAY BACK A MOVIE ON YOUR CAMERA, FOLLOW THESE STEPS:

1. Press the Playback button located on the back of the camera.

2. Turn the Quick Control Dial until you reach one of your videos. You'll know it's a movie when you see the video camera icon in the upper-left portion of the LCD monitor. Press the Setting button.

3. To begin playback, press the Setting button. The play option on the bottom of the LCD monitor will be highlighted by default.

4. To stop or pause playback, press the Setting button again.

5. To exit from the playback screen, use the Quick Control Dial to select the exit option. Press the Setting button.

Viewing movies on your computer that were recorded with the 5D Mark III is simple. Just download the .mov file to your computer from the memory card or connect the camera to your computer using the USB cable. If you have a Mac, your movies will automatically play in QuickTime when you open the files (PC users can download the software online for free). The Canon Utility software that was included with your camera also has a program, Image Browser, that allows you to view still photos and play .mov files on your computer.

EXPOSURE

Controlling exposure for video is much the same as when you're creating still images, with one big, important difference. It's still a combination of the ISO, shutter speed, and aperture that allow you to control exposure. But the big difference is that you have less flexibility with respect to your choice of shutter speed.

The choice of shutter speed is directly related to the frame rate at which you're capturing video. The shutter speed should be double the frame rate you're using to capture video. So, for example, if you're shooting 24 fps, the recommended shutter speed will be 1/50 second. If you're shooting at 30 fps, the recommended shutter speed would be 1/60 second. This is the optimal shutter speed when producing video. If you set the shutter speed higher than that, it can negatively impact the quality of your video.

Because you need to "lock in" your shutter speed, the ability to control your exposure will largely be a result of your choice of aperture and ISO.

As with still photography, you can shoot in Auto or Manual mode. You can use the Scene Intelligent Auto, Program, Shutter Priority, or Aperture Priority modes, if you just want to capture a quick clip of video. However, I recommend using the camera in the Manual exposure mode in order to ensure the best possible results. In addition to giving you complete control over the ISO and the aperture, Manual mode also gives you the ability to change important settings on your camera, including audio recording levels, which are especially critical for producing quality video.

WHITE BALANCE

White balance is particularly important when shooting video, especially because it can be very difficult to correct color after the fact. You can do it, but there can be a loss of image quality, which results from having to dramatically shift colors. Though some color correction is always necessary with video, it's best when such changes are modest.

This is why using the white balance presets or, if time allows, a custom white balance, ensures that you're getting an accurate color rendering of the subject and the scene. AWB may be convenient, but if the camera moves during the recording of a clip, there can be slight changes to the white balance, and the resulting changes in color will be very difficult to correct in your editing application.

Because you're using the Live View mode, you can easily determine which white balance setting is best. As you're enjoying a live preview of the recorded image, you can easily cycle through the white balance presets or even set a specific Kelvin color temperature.

PICTURE STYLE

Picture Style is an important tool for shooting video. It impacts the final result in much the same way as it does with stills. Just keep in mind that once these settings are applied to the finished video, it isn't something that you can change after the video has been recorded.

If you intend to work with your video in an editing application, I suggest setting your Picture Style to neutral for flexibility (**Figure 9.4**). Otherwise, you can choose any of the other Picture Styles and upload and e-mail individual clips as-is.

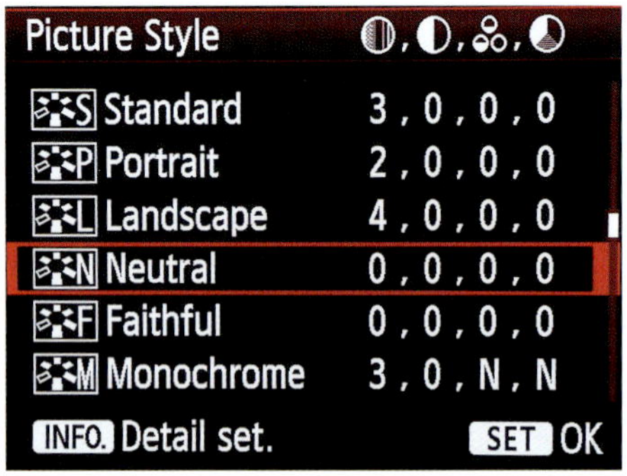

FIGURE 9.4
The Picture Style will be embedded into your video file and can be difficult to change later in your video-editing application.

COMPOSING VIDEOS

You'll find that the same rules of composition that apply to still photography will help you in creating compositions for video. Considerations for brightness, contrast, and sharpness, as well as the rule of thirds, will help you to create strong compositions. The 5D Mark III can help you with composing using the rule of thirds when you enable the grid display (**Figure 9.5**).

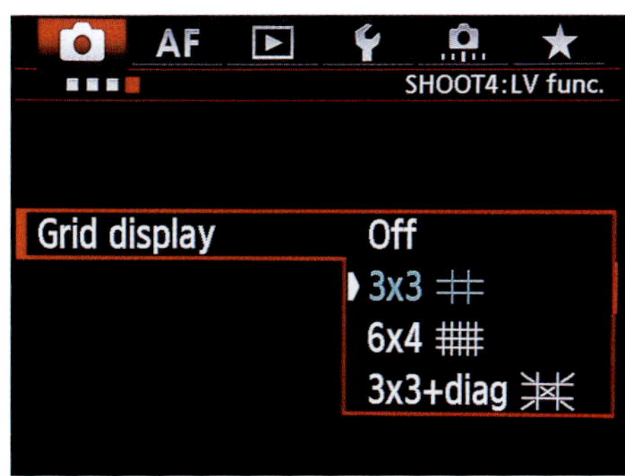

FIGURE 9.5
Enabling grid display can help greatly in making sure horizon lines are straight, which are as important in video as they are in still photographs.

TO SET THE GRID DISPLAY FOR VIDEO RECORDING, FOLLOW THESE STEPS:

1. Set the camera to Video mode using the Live View/Movie Shooting switch.

2. Press the Menu button and use the Main Dial to get to the Shoot 4: Movie menu screen. Use the Quick Control Dial to scroll down to Grid Display. Press the Setting button.

3. Use the Quick Control Dial to select the grid of your choice. Press the Setting button to lock in your change.

4. Press the Menu button to go back into movie-shooting mode. You'll now see a semitransparent grid over the LCD monitor.

When you're in Video mode, you'll notice a semitransparent mask covering parts of the LCD monitor. The space within the mask is the area that will be recorded; the semitransparent mask on either the top or bottom (HD) or left or right (SD) will not be recorded. This is extremely helpful when composing images for movies, because it tells you where the edges of the frame will be.

FOCUSING

Focusing for videos is slightly different than still-image focusing because you can't look through the viewfinder to set focus—it's all done on the LCD monitor. However, as with still photography, you can either manually focus or autofocus your lens. The 5D Mark III makes it easy to autofocus and gives you three different settings to choose from:

- **Live mode:** With live mode, the image sensor is used to focus. This method can take longer than focusing through the viewfinder (which uses the dedicated AF sensor).

- **Face-detection live mode:** This is the same as live mode focusing, but it focuses on the human face.

- **Quick mode:** With this setting, the dedicated AF sensor is used to set the focus; however, the Live View monitoring is momentarily interrupted in order for this to take place. This is the fastest method of focusing when in Live View or Video mode.

To use these focusing modes, just point the camera at your subject, use the multi-controller to select your focus point, and press the shutter button halfway. The focus point will flash green and you'll hear a beep when the camera finds the focus.

Using autofocus is easy and may even be convenient at times, but in my opinion the best video is created when focusing manually. This is because I don't want focus to be hunting or searching while I'm actually recording my video. That can be a big distraction. I prefer to set my focus before I actually begin recording.

Manually focusing also ensures that my subject is tack sharp at the moment of a recording, something that is especially critical when shooting with the 5D Mark III, which provides such a shallow depth of field. Achieving critical focus can be achieved easily by magnifying the image on the LCD monitor using the Magnify/Reduce button (**Figure 9.6**).

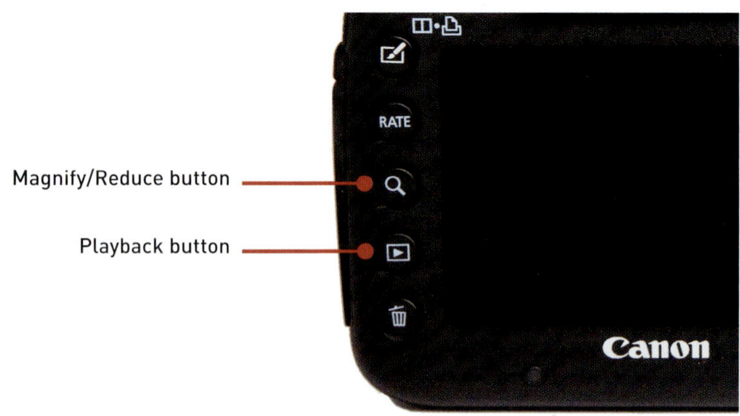

1. Set the camera to Video mode using the Live View/Movie Shooting switch. Make sure to select the Live Mode focusing option.

2. Use the multi-controller to select the area you want to focus on. When you have it set, press the Magnify/Reduce button once to zoom in. Pressing it once will magnify your image by a factor of 5 (5X), and pressing it twice magnifies the screen to a factor of 10 (10X).

3. Set the focusing switch on your lens to MF, and then turn the focusing ring of the lens until your image is in focus.

4. Press the Magnify/Reduce button until the image on the LCD monitor is back to normal view.

TIP

One of the big reasons to focus manually is that it eliminates the sound of the focus motor being picked up by the camera during recording. If sound is important, focusing manually before you start recording eliminates what could be a prominent audio distraction.

RECORDING QUALITY AUDIO

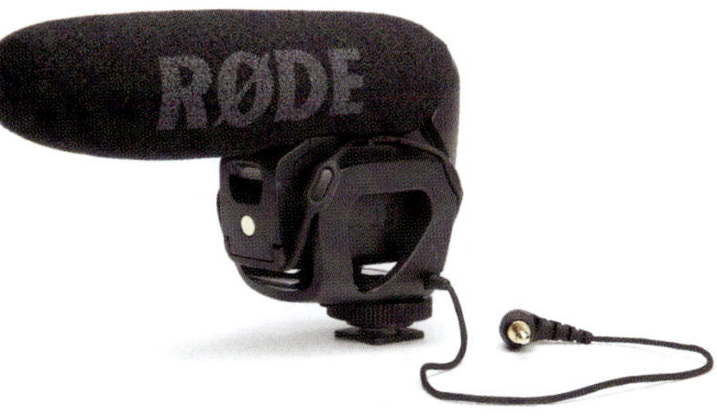

The 5D Mark III features a microphone, which is located on the front of the camera. It records monaural sound (sound recorded on a single channel). The audio quality might be acceptable at close distances, but the farther the subject, the poorer the sound will be because more ambient noise will likely be picked up. The microphone's proximity to the lens and the camera body also make it susceptible to picking up camera handling and focusing noise and even your own breathing. Nevertheless, it can be an important tool in your video making.

For significant improvement in audio, the 5D Mark III features an external microphone terminal located on the side of the camera, beneath the terminal cover. This allows you to connect an external stereo microphone, such as this model from Rode (**Figure 9.7**), which will be capable of producing much better audio than the built-in microphone. This can take the form of a shotgun microphone that can be seated on the camera's hot shoe and will pick up the audio of your subject, even though he may be a short distance away. This is the preferred method for recording audio in-camera.

FIGURE 9.7
An external shotgun microphone, such as this model from Rode, can help improve the quality of your audio, especially when your subject is at a distance from your camera.

If you have no interest at all in recording audio, you can disable the sound recording on the camera, but I don't advise doing that. It's too easy to forget that you aren't recording audio and, thus, ruin any subsequent shoots where audio is preferred.

EXTERNAL RECORDING DEVICES

Most professional videographers for whom sound is important will record audio using a device completely separate from the camera. This audio recorder is placed close to the subject and also may be connected to a shotgun or lavalier microphone. This will capture better audio than the camera is capable of recording. Though the camera will still record its audio, it's only used by the video editor as a reference track for syncing the audio from the digital recorder in a video-editing application such as Final Cut Pro or Adobe Premiere.

MONITORING AUDIO

A headphone terminal has been introduced in the 5D Mark III, which allows you to monitor sound while recording. This had been missing from the previous model and, in my opinion, it's one of the biggest improvements with respect to recording video. By plugging a set of headphones into the camera via the headphone terminal (**Figure 9.8**), you can monitor all the audio that's being recorded. It also can make you sensitive to distracting noises such as passing cars.

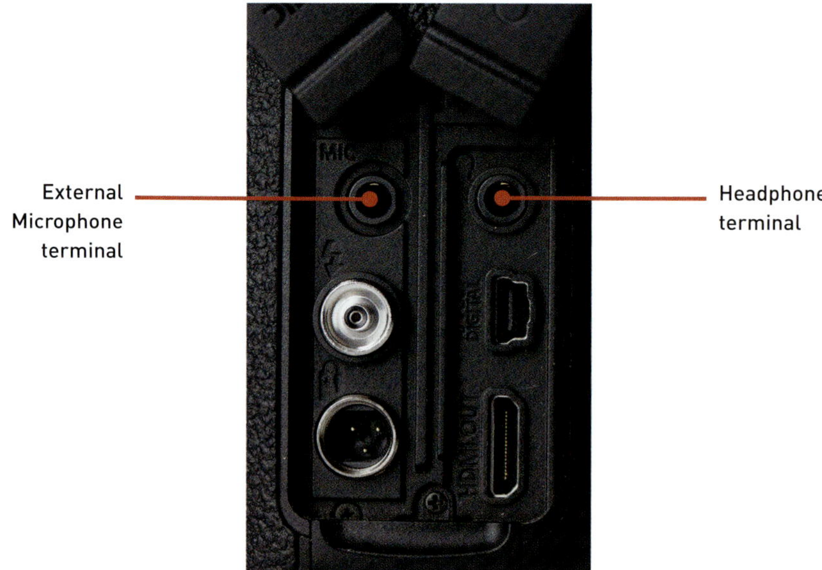

FIGURE 9.8
When recording audio is important to your video, make sure to wear a pair of over-the-ear headphones and plug them into the headphone terminal to monitor the quality of the audio.

If you're recording video with sound, you should always monitor your audio by wearing a set of headphones. Poor audio on a video will ruin it regardless of how beautiful or stunning the imagery. Wearing a set of headphones while recording ensures that the camera has been set correctly for audio levels.

I recommend that you wear a set of over-the-ear headphones rather than the ear buds you may have received with the purchase of an MP3 player. Over-the-ear head-phones provide a more accurate sense of the quality of the audio, which is especially important if you're recording interviews. Even if you're using the audio solely as a reference track, producing clean audio in-camera helps to produce more accurate syncing with an external audio recording.

ADJUSTING AUDIO LEVELS

You can increase or decrease the input sound levels coming in through the built-in microphone or the external microphone. Though the camera can be set to automati-cally adjust audio levels dynamically, I highly recommend that you set your audio levels manually.

If sound levels increase or decrease, the Auto sound recording setting will automati-cally increase or decrease the sensitivity of the microphone, often referred to as "gain." This will be based on the ambient sound level. This can result in an uneven quality of sound and a noticeable increase in signal noise when the gain is increased when the ambient sound level drops. In order to keep audio levels consistent throughout a clip, I recommend adjusting the audio levels manually via the camera's built-in interface (**Figure 9.9**).

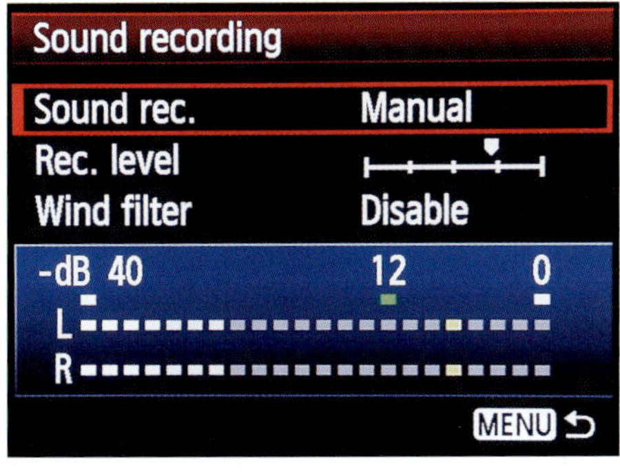

FIGURE 9.9
Adjust your audio levels manually before recording, in order to prevent peaking, which can result in distortion in your audio track.

1. Set the camera to Video mode using the Live View/Movie Shooting switch.

2. Press the Menu button and use the Main Dial to get to the Shoot 4: Movie menu screen. Use the Quick Control Dial to scroll down to Sound Recording and press the Setting button.

3. Use the Quick Control Dial to select the Auto, Manual, or Disable audio mode and press the Setting button. I recommend using the Manual audio mode.

4. With the Manual sound recording mode enabled, use the Quick Control Dial to scroll to Recording Level and press the Setting button.

5. Use the Quick Control Dial to increase or decrease the gain using the decibel (db) level indicators at the bottom of the screen as a reference. Try to keep audio levels at approximately −12 db and avoid having the scale peak into the red or to 0 db. Hit the Menu button twice to return to recording mode.

SILENT CONTROL

Occasionally, you'll want to change your aperture, ISO, or sound level while recording. To prevent the camera's microphone from recording the clicking of the button and dials, you can enable the camera's Silent Control mode to provide you quiet access to these settings while in the midst of recording.

By making the Quick Control Dial pressure sensitive, you can navigate between controls for your shutter speed, aperture, ISO, and audio levels. When the feature is enabled and you're recording, you can depress the Quick Control button, which will display the accessible control in the lower-left corner of the LCD monitor. You can then access each feature by lightly pressing the top or bottom of the Quick Control Dial. The setting will change to a blue color when active (**Figure 9.10**). You can then lightly touch the left or right area of the Quick Control Dial to make the desired changes.

FIGURE 9.10
Enabling the Silent Control on your camera will help minimize camera noise being picked up by the onboard microphone when you need to make changes to your recording settings.

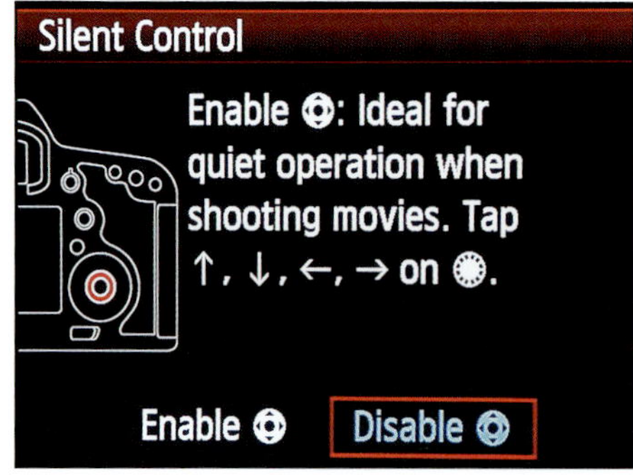

1. Press the Menu button and turn the Main Dial to access the Shoot 5: Movie menu screen.

2. Turn the Quick Control Dial to select Silent Control. Press the Setting button.

3. Turn the Quick Control Dial to Enable. Press the Setting button.

RECORDING GOOD VIDEO

If you've ever had to sit through a friend or family's vacation video, you know how tedious it can be to watch lengthy video clips that include a lot of jarring, shaky camera movements. Though the footage might be a reminder of a great vacation or event, few people want to spend an hour watching such poorly captured video. Here are some suggestions that will improve the quality of your video and may help you keep some good friendships.

PLAN YOUR SHOTS

One of the best ways to improve the quality of your video is simply to plan your shots. Instead of moving the camera around and recording everything that's in front of it, think ahead and consider exactly what you want to capture in a clip. Don't record everything while searching for your shot.

For example, if you're panning the camera from left to right, think of a starting point and an endpoint for that pan. Your audience doesn't need to see a lengthy pan shot in which the camera is moving back and forth—that can be both distracting and annoying. You can see great examples of simple pan shots in many TV shows and movies.

SHOOT SHORT CLIPS

A good video often consists of short clips edited together into a continuous piece. Though there are exceptions, the best videos are the result of interesting visuals put together in the editing room or, nowadays, on a computer. So, your ability to create good video will be the result of creating short clips that help to convey a certain part of the story. This can include a wide establishing shot, medium shots, close-up or detail shots, and shots that include camera movement. The more variety that you have, the better able you are to edit an interesting piece.

When it comes to shooting video, it's easy to produce clips that are too short. This should be avoided, because they'll limit your ability to apply transitions in your video-editing software. Even if it's just a detail shot of a baseball mitt, I suggest capturing approximately 10 seconds of video. This will provide enough footage at the beginning and end of the clip, which can have the benefit of a visual transition such as a fade-in or fade-out.

DON'T OVERSHOOT

If you have experience with a traditional video camera, you know that you can easily produce hours of footage. This may be great for capturing the entirety of an event, but it can be quite burdensome when it comes time to logging and editing that footage for a short piece. Having too much footage can result in the rapid depletion of space on your hard drive; plus, sorting through all that footage for a short 2- or 3-minute piece is challenging. If you're hoping to document an important event like a birthday party, think about the important moments that you expect to occur at that event and make a shot list of those moments that you want to make sure you capture. This can help you avoid shooting anything and everything and to focus only on the important storytelling moments.

HAVE A REASON TO MOVE THE CAMERA

Though some recent horror movies use hand-held cameras that visibly shake as they're being used, your video may not benefit from so much camera movement. It can be a dramatic device, but it also can quickly become irritating and distracting when overused. So, if you're handholding the camera, try to hold it as steady as possible and keep movements of the camera to a minimum. A tripod with a fluid head is highly recommended because it provides very clean and soft movements for panning and tilting.

WATCH THE LIGHT

Though the 5D Mark III provides excellent results under incredibly low-light situations, it's still best to shoot video using the best quality light available. You can shoot at high ISOs, but the video will have significant amounts of noise. So, just because your camera can record under certain lighting conditions, that doesn't mean you should record under those conditions, unless you specifically want that look for your final result.

Even professional TV and film productions that use the 5D use some lighting in order to improve the quality. Sometimes it can be as simple as moving your subject closer to a lamp in order to improve the amount of illumination falling on him.

REMEMBER

Just because the camera is capable of photographing under extreme low light doesn't mean that you have to give up being concerned with the quality of the light.

ACCESSORIZING

If you're serious about recording video with your 5D Mark III, you should consider investing in certain accessories. These accessories will help significantly in improving the quality of your video and sound.

FOCUSING RIG

The introduction of the 5D Mark II ushered in a whole new industry, which has created a variety of different contraptions on which the camera can be mounted. These rigs not only provide increased stability when the camera is being used without the benefit of a tripod, but also offer the ability to smoothly adjust focus while filming.

Such rigs come in a variety of different configurations and include shoulder rigs, Steadicam systems, and harness-style supports. Many of these are likely overkill if you only produce the occasional video clip. But if you find that you're producing a good amount of video, an investment in a focusing rig will be a good idea.

I personally use the IDC System Zero (**Figure 9.11**), which was designed by *National Geographic* photographer Bruce Dorn. It provides increased stability in a small compact design, in addition to providing a friction-based focus mechanism that allows me to manually focus my lens with ease. This minimizes any potential shaking or jarring that can occur when attempting to adjust the focus using the lens's focusing ring. Its components are easy to take apart and put in a camera bag. You can find out more by visiting www.idcphotovideo.com.

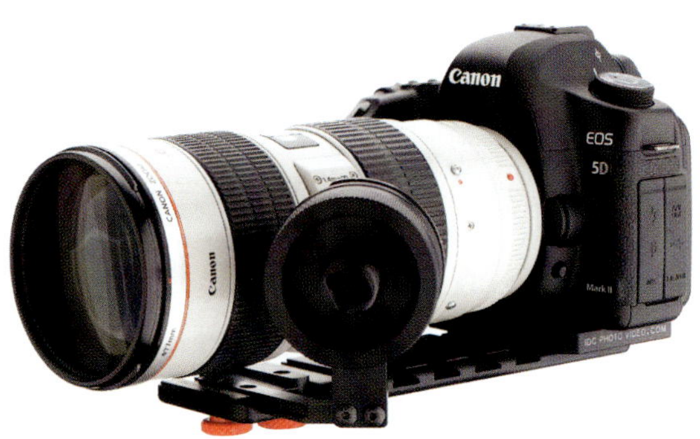

FIGURE 9.11
The IDC System Zero rig provides an ultra-portable and easily configurable rig, which provides for easy follow-focus and increased stability when handholding the camera.

OPTICAL VIEWFINDER

Though the LCD monitor on the 5D Mark III is bright and clear, it can be difficult to view under bright conditions. This is why having an optical viewfinder that sits over the LCD monitor can be a huge benefit. It provides a clear view of the monitor by eliminating glare, which can make it hard for you to evaluate the image for exposure or focus.

The Zacuto Z-Finder (**Figure 9.12**; www.zacuto.com) and the Hoodman Cinema Kit Pro (www.hoodmanusa.com) are two popular optical viewfinders to consider.

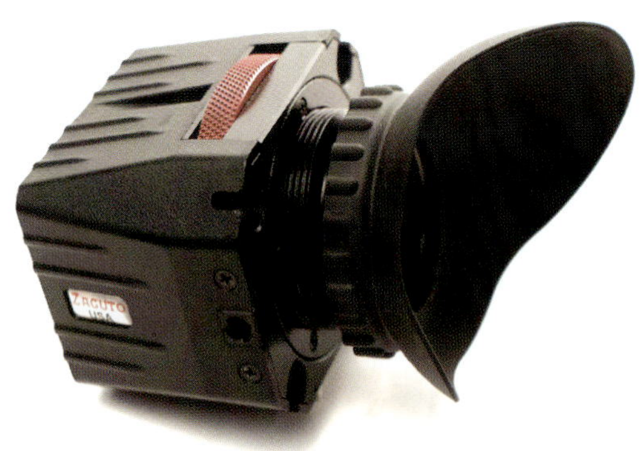

FIGURE 9.12
The Zacuto Z-Finder provides a magnified view of the LCD monitor, which helps in achieving focus and composing your shot. It helps to provide a clear view, free of glare.

NEUTRAL-DENSITY FILTER

Because you'll be limited in your ability to change your shutter speed, there will be times when controlling the ISO or aperture may not be enough to achieve the look that you're going for.

For example, in a bright, sunny situation, you may have to use a small aperture in order to achieve a correct exposure. However, if you want to produce an image with a shallow depth of field, you no longer have the option to increase the shutter speed to compensate for the use of a wide aperture.

For such situations, a neutral-density filter fitted on your lens can help reduce the quantity of light passing through the lens and, thus, provide you the means to use a wider aperture. These filters are available in a variety of strengths. I recommend buying a filter set, which provides varying degrees of light reduction.

Variable neutral-density filters are also available; they allow you to vary the degree of neutral density simply by rotating a ring, similar to one you would find on a polarizing filter.

EDITING VIDEO

Once you've recorded your movies, you might want to do a little more with them, such as assemble several video clips into a movie, or add sound or additional graphics or text. If so, you'll probably want to learn a thing or two about how to edit your videos using video-editing software. Many different software programs are available for you to choose from.

Inexpensive programs like iMovie or QuickTime Pro allow you to do basic editing of video clips. Other programs such as Final Cut, Sony Vegas, or Adobe Premiere will provide even more advanced editing options and allow you to add creative effects to your movies.

Using editing software is not required to play back and share movies created with your 5D Mark III, but it is a fun way to take your movies to the next level.

Chapter 9 Assignments

Get Familiar with Formats

It takes some time to discover the different movie recording sizes on your 5D Mark III. Set the camera to one of the HD settings (1920 x 1080 or 1280 x 720), and then change the setting to SD (640 x 480). Note the different aspect ratios (16:9 versus 4:3) in areas that are covered with the semitransparent mask. Shoot a few short videos in one recording size, and then play them back on your computer.

Play with White Balance and Picture Styles

Set your camera on a tripod and set it to movie-shooting mode. Set the exposure so you can see your scene properly, and then change the white balance, scrolling through all the different options, and watch the screen as you try each setting. Do the same with the Picture Styles, and pay attention to the colors in your scene as you make the changes.

Set Your Focus

Familiarize yourself with the different autofocus modes. Once you get the hang of it, set the lens to MF. Zoom in on the image on the LCD monitor by using the Magnify/Reduce button on the back of the camera to focus on a specific area of your scene.

Adjust Audio Levels

Find a subject whose sound level ranges from very soft to very loud. Record clips using both the automatic and the manual sound controls. Make sure to monitor the audio using headphones. Later, when listening to the audio on the computer, see what differences you can pick up in the quality of the audio between the two modes.

Shoot with Variety in Mind

Photograph someone doing something creative, such as playing a guitar or painting. Create a series of video clips that include a wide establishing shot, a medium shot, and close-up shots. Create a variety of different images, which you can later edit in your video-editing application.

Share your results with this book's Flickr group!

Join the group here: www.flickr.com/groups/Canon5DMarkIIIFromSnapshotstoGreatShots

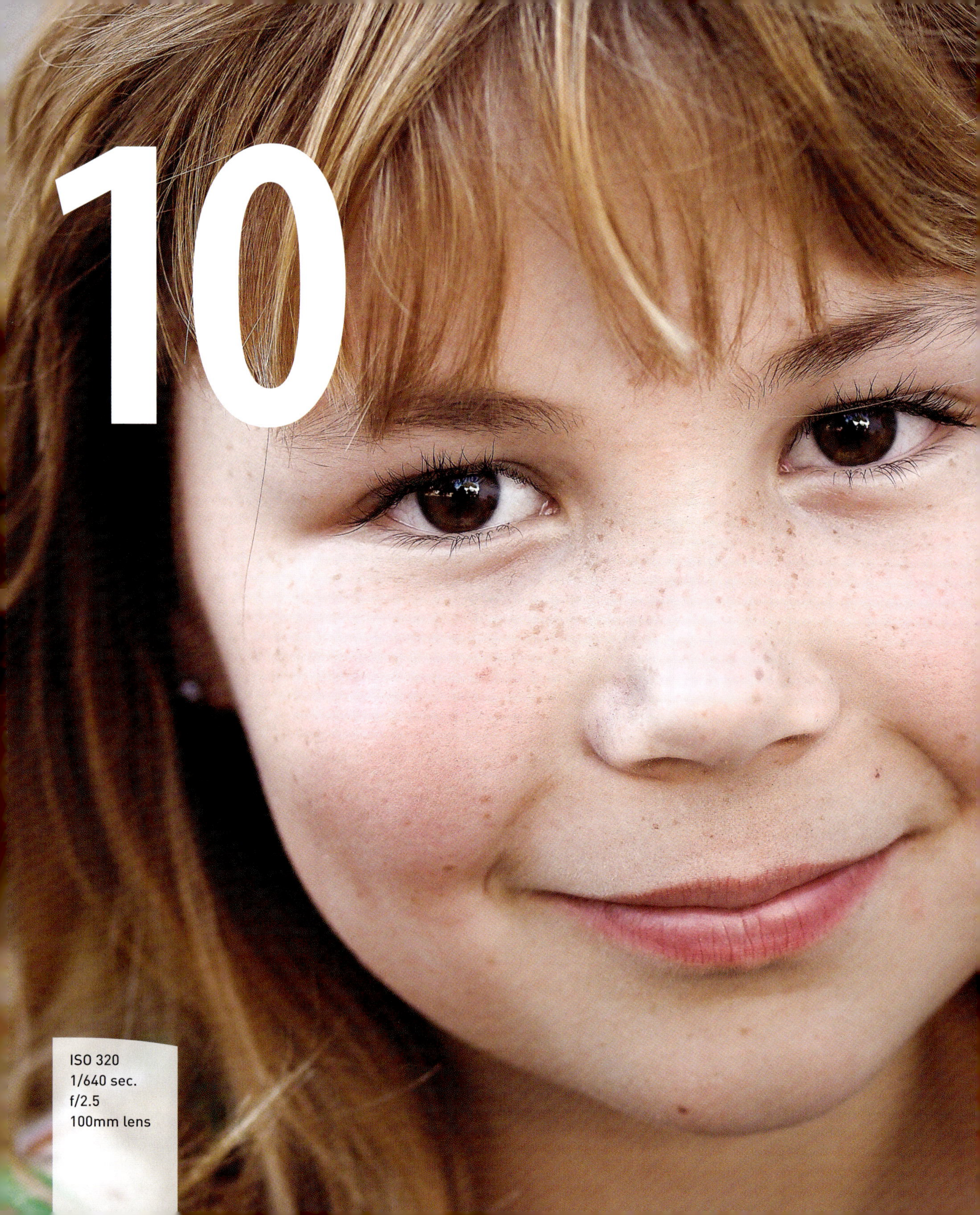
10
ISO 320
1/640 sec.
f/2.5
100mm lens

Advanced Techniques

DISCOVERING THE CREATIVE DIVERSITY IN YOUR DSLR

We have focused on a wide variety of features, but before we wrap things up, I'd like to discuss some other features that you may find valuable in your photography. Though you may not use these features frequently, they may help you pull off the shot.

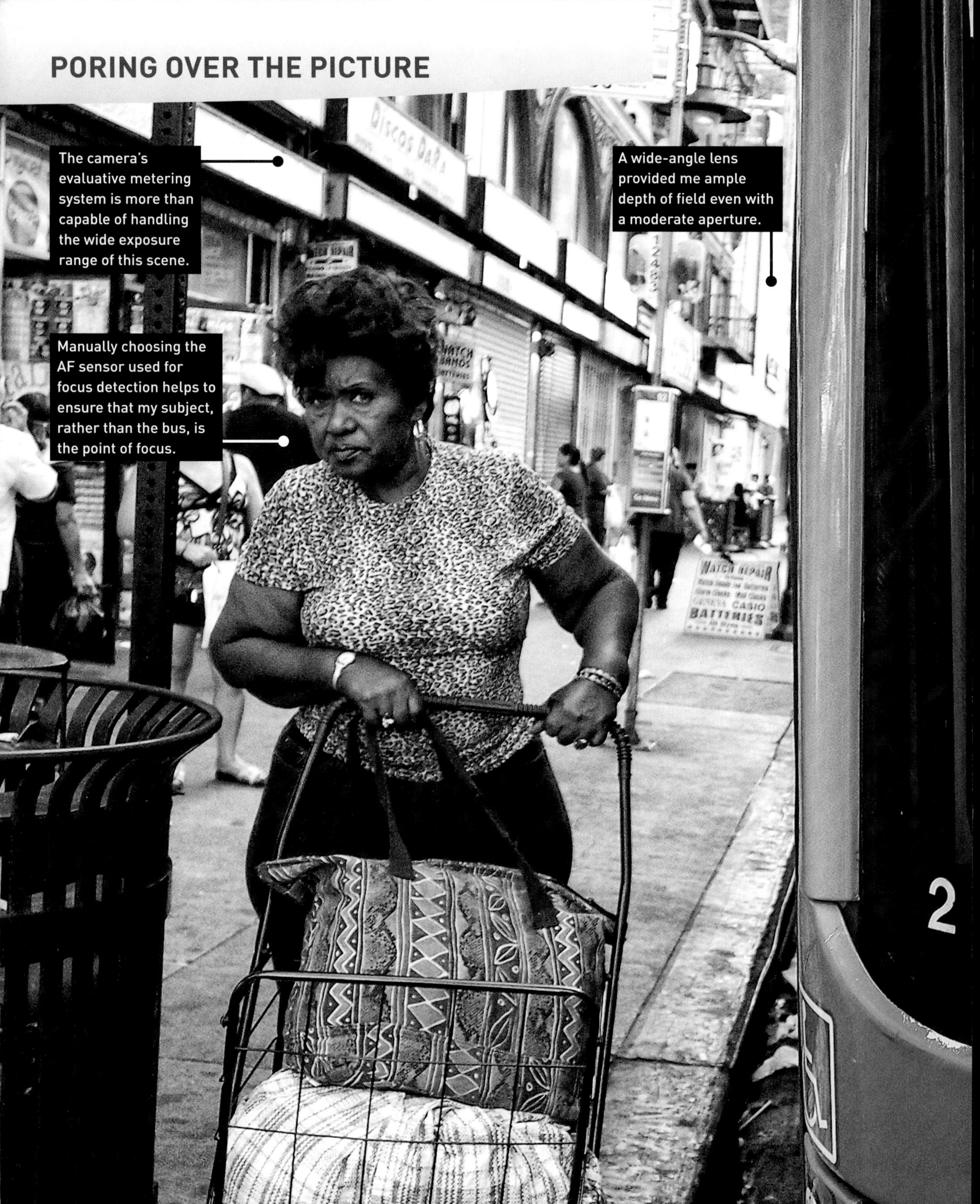
The camera's evaluative metering system is more than capable of handling the wide exposure range of this scene.

A wide-angle lens provided me ample depth of field even with a moderate aperture.

Manually choosing the AF sensor used for focus detection helps to ensure that my subject, rather than the bus, is the point of focus.

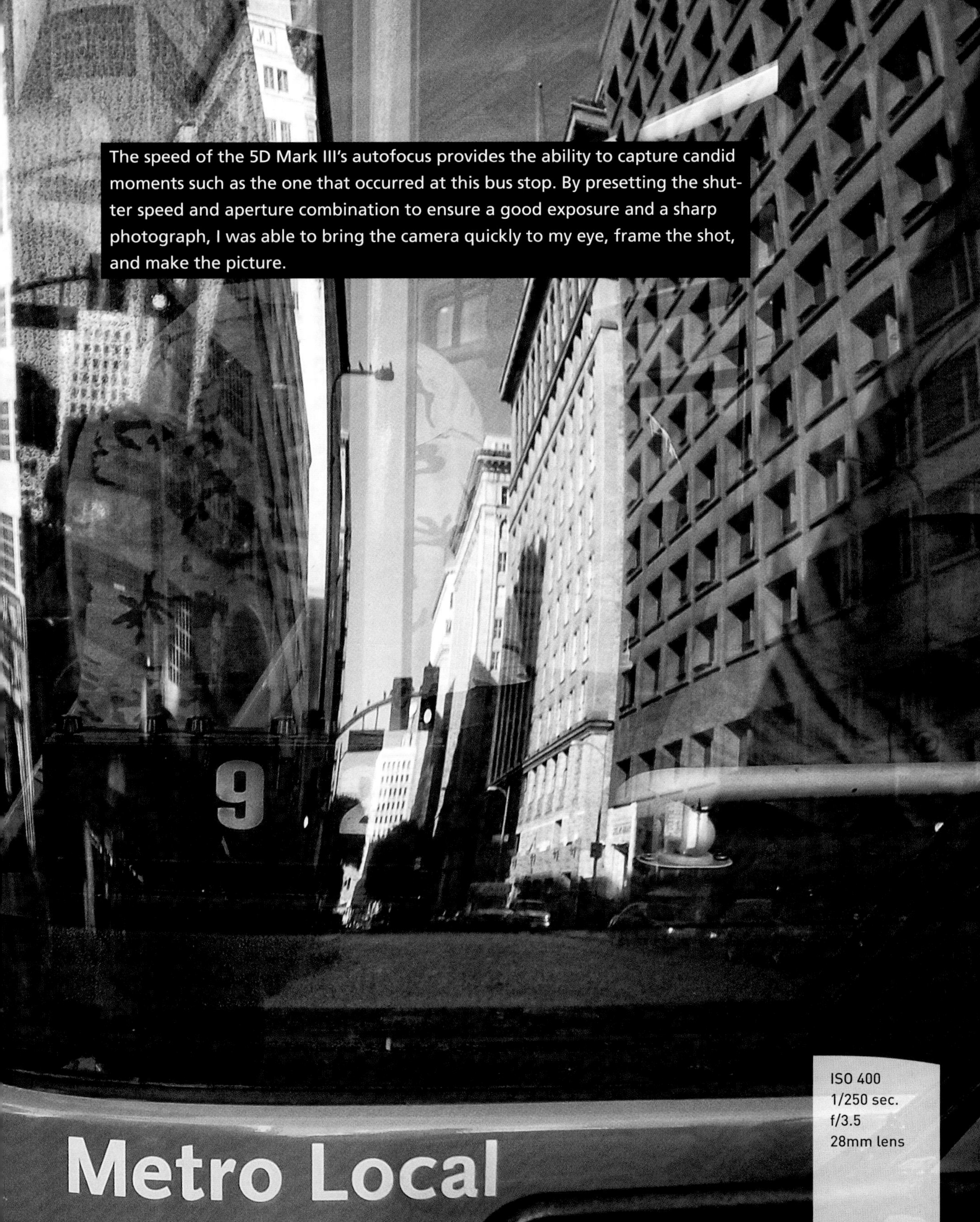

The speed of the 5D Mark III's autofocus provides the ability to capture candid moments such as the one that occurred at this bus stop. By presetting the shutter speed and aperture combination to ensure a good exposure and a sharp photograph, I was able to bring the camera quickly to my eye, frame the shot, and make the picture.

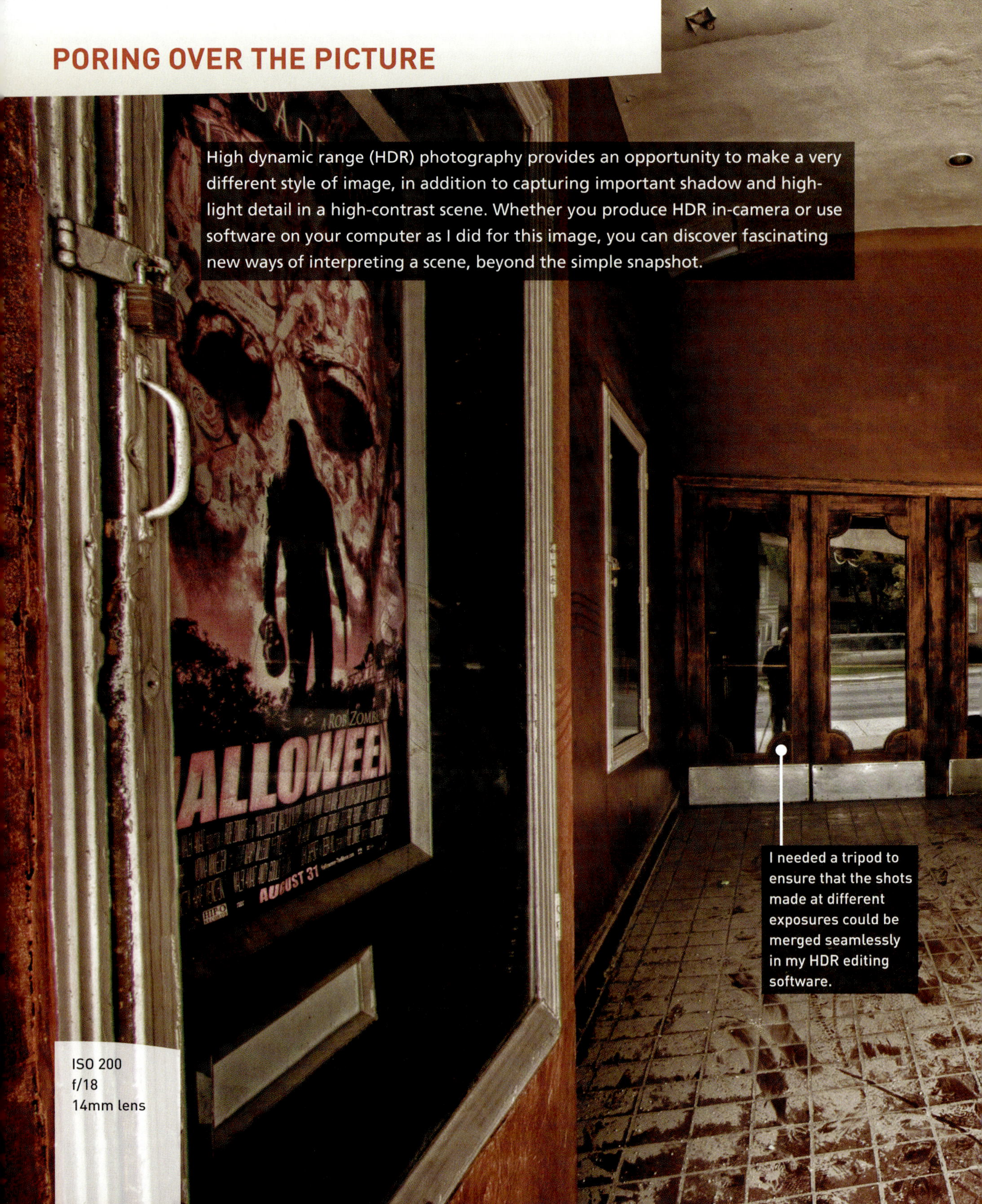

High dynamic range (HDR) photography provides an opportunity to make a very different style of image, in addition to capturing important shadow and highlight detail in a high-contrast scene. Whether you produce HDR in-camera or use software on your computer as I did for this image, you can discover fascinating new ways of interpreting a scene, beyond the simple snapshot.

I needed a tripod to ensure that the shots made at different exposures could be merged seamlessly in my HDR editing software.

ISO 200
f/18
14mm lens

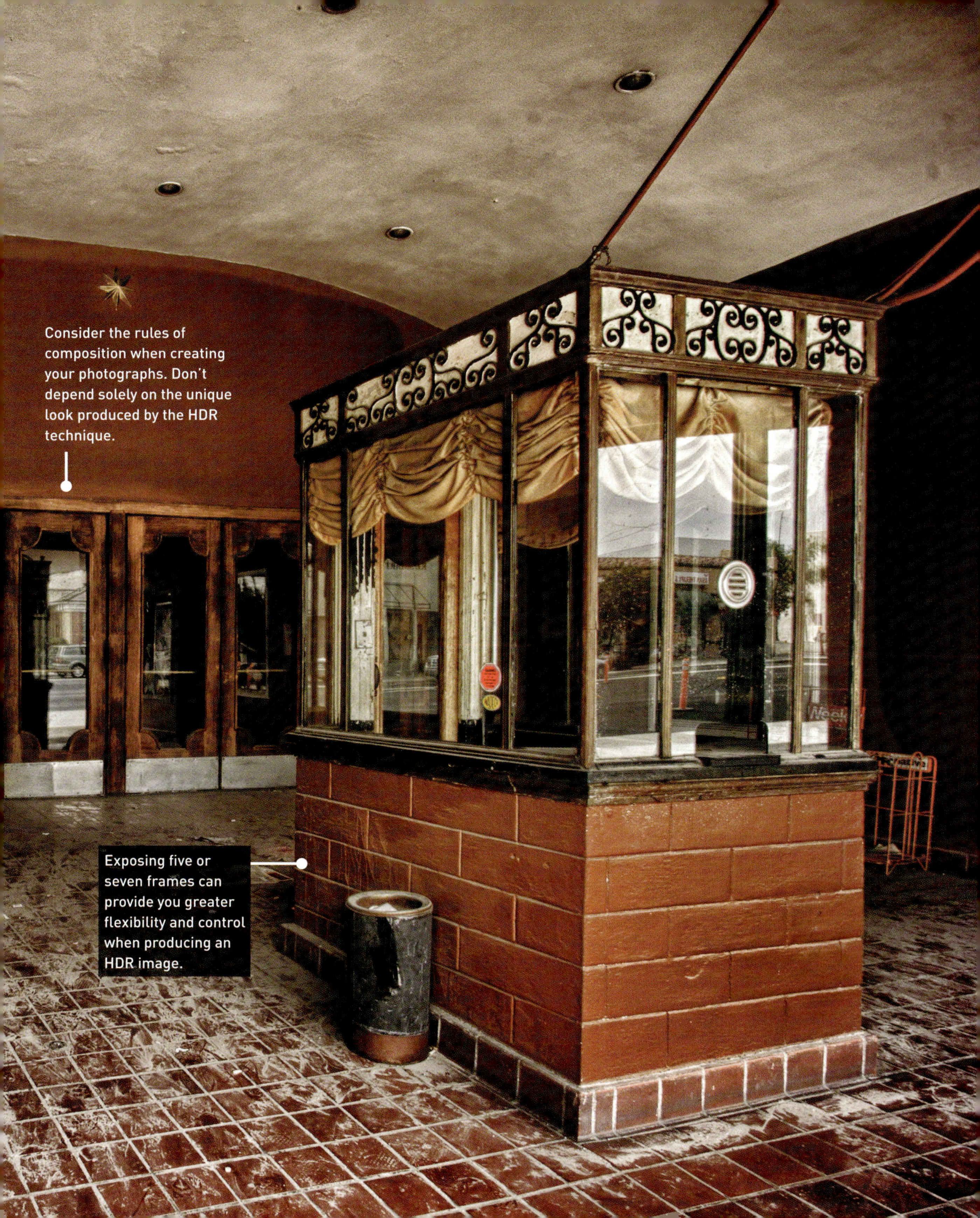
Consider the rules of composition when creating your photographs. Don't depend solely on the unique look produced by the HDR technique.

Exposing five or seven frames can provide you greater flexibility and control when producing an HDR image.

COPYRIGHT INFORMATION

Controlling the uses of your images is an important consideration for any photographer, whether professional or amateur. One of the ways that the 5D Mark III helps you with this is by giving you the ability to embed copyright info into the data file of the photograph or what is often referred to as IPTC data. This makes it very easy for someone who finds your image to look up your contact information if he's interested in using your image for publication.

This doesn't mean that a copyright symbol will be embedded on the actual photograph. Instead, the copyright information, including the image creator and copyright details (**Figure 10.1**), will be accessible through a photo-editing application such as Photoshop and will provide a resource for people interested in finding out who created the photograph.

FIGURE 10.1
Embedding your copyright information in the data file of your image can help provide people interested in your image valuable information regarding the ownership and the availability of that photograph.

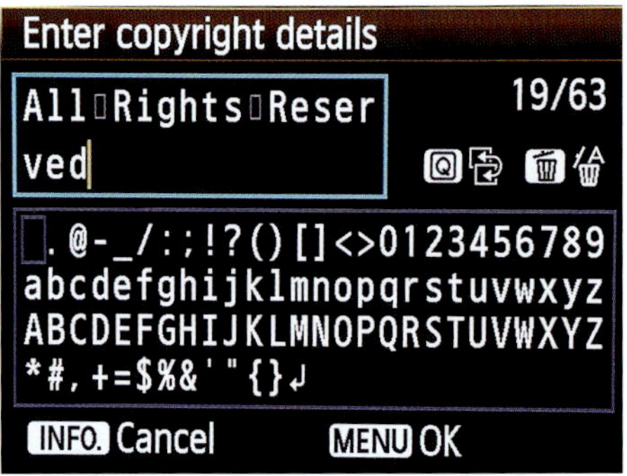

TO SET UP THE COPYRIGHT INFORMATION ON YOUR CAMERA, FOLLOW THESE STEPS:

1. Press the Menu button and turn the Main Dial to access the Setup 4 menu screen. Press the Setting button.

2. Use the Quick Control Dial to select Enter Author's Name. Press the Setting button.

3. Press the Quick Control button to access the text palette, which will be highlighted by a blue box. Turn the Main Dial or Quick Control Dial to select a character. Press the Setting button to add the character. If you make an error, press the Erase button.

4. Press the Menu button to finish entering the author's name.

5. Use the Quick Control Dial to select Enter Copyright Details and press the Setting button.

6. Press the Quick Control button to access the text palette, which will be highlighted by a blue box. Turn the Main Dial or Quick Control Dial to select a
   character. Press the Setting button to add the character. If you make an error,
   press the Erase button.

7. Press the Menu button to complete entering the copyright details.

RATING IMAGES

Rating images has always been an important part of organizing images on a computer. When you enable this function (**Figure 10.2**), the 5D Mark III allows you to
assign a rating to an image even before you've downloaded the files to your computer. Your image browser or photo-editing application will recognize this rating.
You can apply from one to five stars to an image.

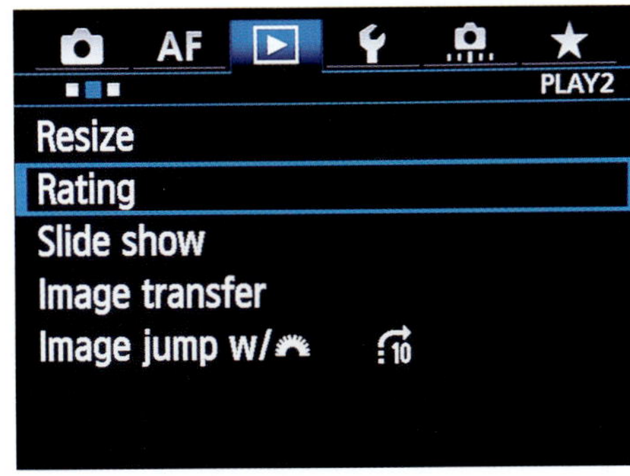

FIGURE 10.2
The rating of your images can
provide you a simple way for finding a single photograph from an
extensive shoot. Once embedded
in your file, an editing program
such as Photoshop or Lightroom
will recognize the rating.

Rating a preferred image in-camera can help to guide you to your preferred image
when it comes time to select and edit your images.

1. Press the Playback button and turn the Quick Control Dial to cycle through the recorded images or video clips.

2. Press the Rate button to assign a ranking. Each press of the Rate button will increase the rating count by one, up to a total number of five.

UPDATING FIRMWARE

Occasionally, Canon releases firmware updates to correct bugs, as well as to add features to your 5D Mark III. These updates are available for free download from the Canon website (http://usa.canon.com; **Figure 10.3**). If you find that your camera is using a firmware that isn't current (**Figure 10.4**), you can easily install a more recent version. The downloaded firmware update can then be saved to your memory card and installed on the camera to complete the firmware update.

TIP

Make sure to have a fully charged battery in your camera when performing a firmware update. If the camera's battery is exhausted during a firmware update, the camera can cease functioning and require a trip to a Canon service facility.

TO CHECK THE CAMERA'S CURRENT FIRMWARE VERSION, FOLLOW THESE STEPS:

1. Press the Menu button and rotate the Main Dial to access the Set-up 4 menu screen.

2. Turn the Quick Control Dial to access the firmware version number.

3. If this version is not the latest one listed on the Canon website, follow the steps in the next section to load the latest version.

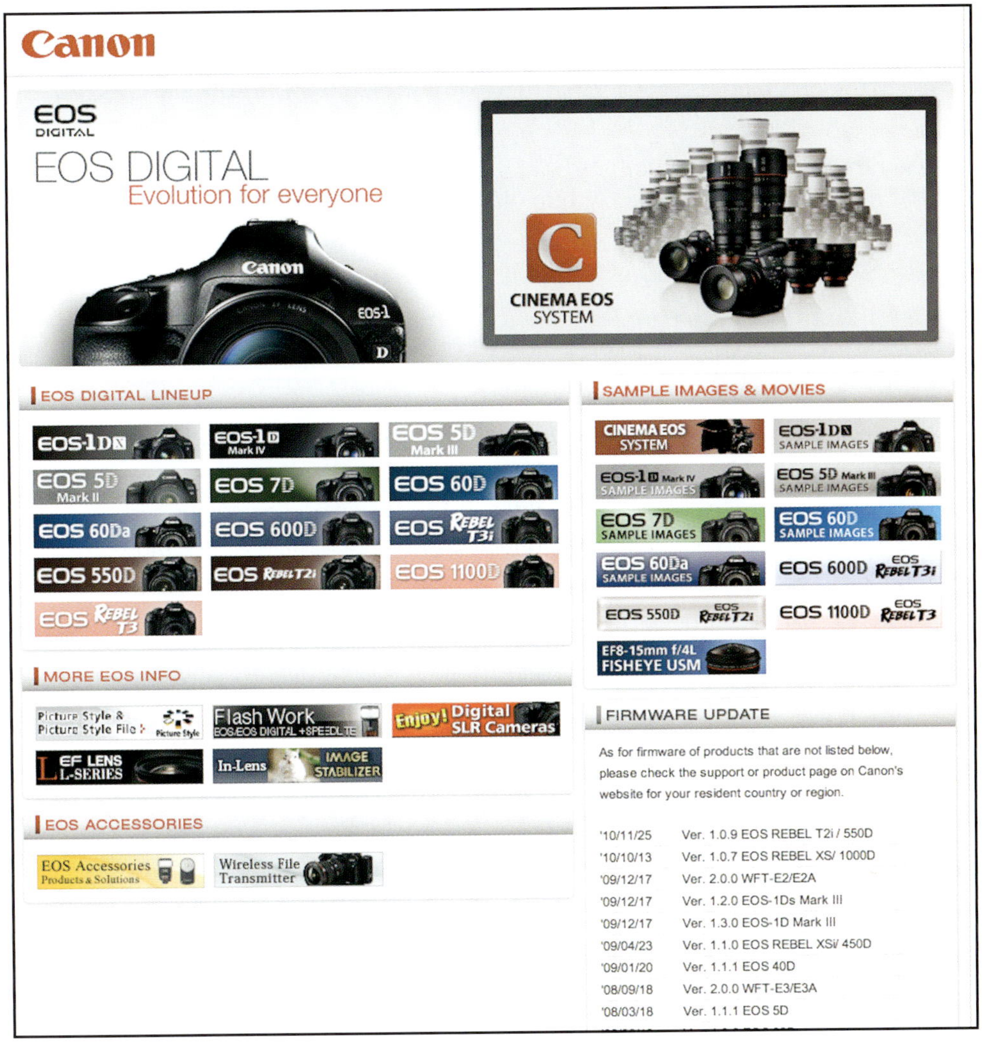

FIGURE 10.3
Updating the camera's firmware can remedy minor bugs, as well as expand the capabilities of your camera. Periodically visit the Canon website to check on new firmware releases.

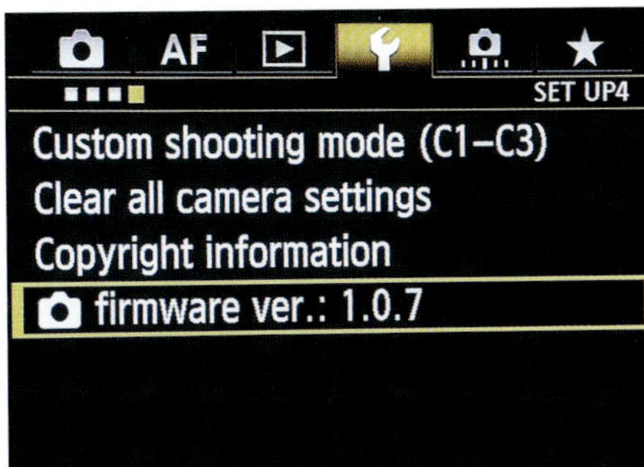

FIGURE 10.4
The Set-up 4 screen will reveal the current version of the camera's software and serve as the starting point for updating your camera.

1. Go to Canon's digital camera page (www.canon.com/deos-d/) and find the link to the Canon 5D Mark III.

2. From the Drivers and Downloads section, download the firmware update file that matches your operating system (Windows or Mac).

3. Extract the downloaded firmware file as per your operating system. (The firmware will be automatically extracted if you're using a Mac.)

4. Copy the uncompressed firmware file to a formatted, empty SD or CF memory card.

5. Press the Menu button and turn the Main Dial to access the Set-up 4 menu screen.

6. Rotate the Quick Control Dial and select the firmware version. Confirm your current firmware version. If it needs to be updated, press the Setting button.

7. The camera will confirm the current version of your firmware. To update the firmware, turn the Quick Control Dial and select OK. Press the Setting button.

8. The camera then asks you to select the new firmware version, which will already be highlighted in a yellow box (assuming it's the only firmware version on the memory card). Press the Setting button.

9. After you are asked whether you want to update the firmware, turn the Quick Control Dial to select OK. Press the Setting button.

10. When the firmware update is complete, press the Setting button.

REMEMBER

Don't turn off the camera or touch any buttons while the firmware is being updated.

MIRROR LOCKUP

If you're planning on taking a photograph with a long shutter speed, you're probably planning on using a tripod. Without the use of a tripod, camera shake is guaranteed. Using a tripod during long exposures is one way to ensure that the images are extremely sharp. Another factor that can affect the sharpness of the image comes from the mirror in the camera, which moves as it gets out of the way of the shutter. It doesn't seem like much, but that little slap of the mirror hitting the inside of the viewfinder housing can be enough to create vibrations during the exposure.

For the absolute sharpest images, you can set the camera to raise the mirror prior to exposing the photo. Unlike the regular process of exposure—where the mirror moves at the same time that the picture is taken—the mirror is locked into the raised position until the shutter is activated, thus further reducing the possibility of camera shake.

TO SET THE MIRROR LOCKUP FEATURE, FOLLOW THESE STEPS:

1. Press the Menu button and turn the Main Dial to access the Shoot 1 menu screen.
2. Turn the Quick Control Dial to select Mirror lockup. Press the Setting button.
3. Turn the Quick Control Dial to select Enable. Press the Setting button.
4. Exit the menu and set up your shot.
5. Press the shutter button completely to raise the mirror.
6. Press the shutter button a second time to activate the shutter and take the picture.

To further reduce the possibility of camera shake, use a shutter release cable or set the self-timer to 2 seconds. In self-timer mode, the mirror will lift when you press the shutter button, but the camera will fire automatically after 2 seconds, so you don't have to touch the camera again. Also, remember that the mirror lockup feature will remain active (even after turning the camera on and off) until you disable it in the menu.

BRACKETING EXPOSURES

There are a variety of reasons why you might want to take several versions of the same scene, but with different exposure values:

- You might want to ensure that you have a single image that has the best exposure.

- You might want images with different exposure values so that you can merge select areas of each image into a final composite.

- You may want to use all the images to produce an HDR image to expand the dynamic range of a photograph beyond the limits of the camera's sensor.

Bracketing allows you to program the camera to take two, three, five, or seven photographs at different exposure values (**Figure 10.5**). The camera handles each change of exposure automatically, eliminating the need for you to make an adjustment for each individual photograph.

The amount of exposure adjustment between individual images and the number of total images that you want for a bracketing series will depend on how wide an exposure range you believe you need to capture. For example, a very high-contrast scene might call for full-stop exposure changes for a total of five frames.

FIGURE 10.5
Producing multiple images at slightly different exposures can be a valuable tool for ensuring a good exposure or when creating HDR imagery.

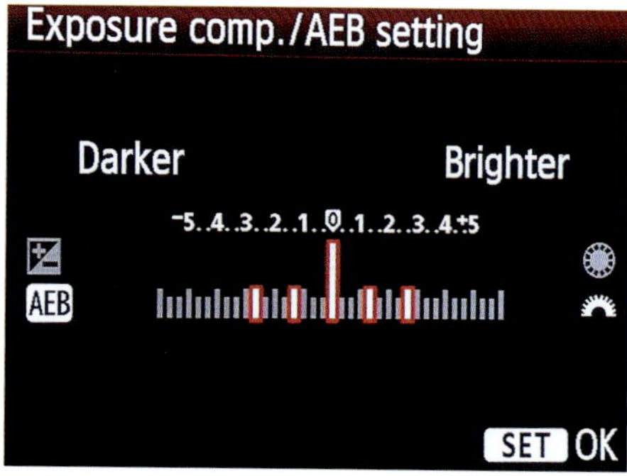

TO SET UP EXPOSURE BRACKETING, FOLLOW THESE STEPS:

1. Press the Menu button and turn the Main Dial to access the Shoot 2 menu screen.

2. Turn the Quick Control Dial to select Exposure Compensation/AEB. Press the Setting button.

3. Turn the Main Dial to select the increment of exposure change in 1/3-stop increments up to +/−3 stops. Press the Setting button to enable bracketing.

4. Press the AF mode selection/Drive mode selection button and select Continuous or Continuous High. (This allows the camera to take each image in rapid succession and stop when the bracket is complete.)

5. To disable autobracketing, turn off the camera or access the Exposure/AEB screen and turn the Quick Control Dial to set the camera back to recording a single image with no exposure change. Press the Setting button.

You can choose how many exposures will be created as part of the bracket. The 5D Mark III improves on the three-exposure bracket of the 5D Mark II and now makes it possible to do a five- and seven-exposure bracket, which is an advantage for photographers who shoot HDR images.

TO SET UP EXPOSURE BRACKETING, FOLLOW THESE STEPS:

1. Press the Menu button and turn the Main Dial to access the C.Fn1: Exposure menu screen.

2. Turn the Quick Control Dial to select Number of bracketed shots. Press the Setting button.

HDR PHOTOGRAPHY

High dynamic range (HDR) photography has become a popular type of digital photography for its ability to produce images that retain shadow and highlight detail in high-contrast scenes (**Figure 10.6**). Multiple images of the same scene using different exposure values are combined into a single image using software such as HDR Efex Pro, Photomatix Pro, or Photoshop.

Depending on how the files are processed, the image can appear very natural while capturing a wider tonal range than could be captured by the camera in a single exposure. The images also can be rendered to produce a very stylistic version of the scene. The latter has become quite popular and is the look that many people associate with HDR photography.

FIGURE 10.6
High-contrast scenes are ideal situations for creating an HDR image because of its ability to retain detail in both the bright highlights and the deep shadows.

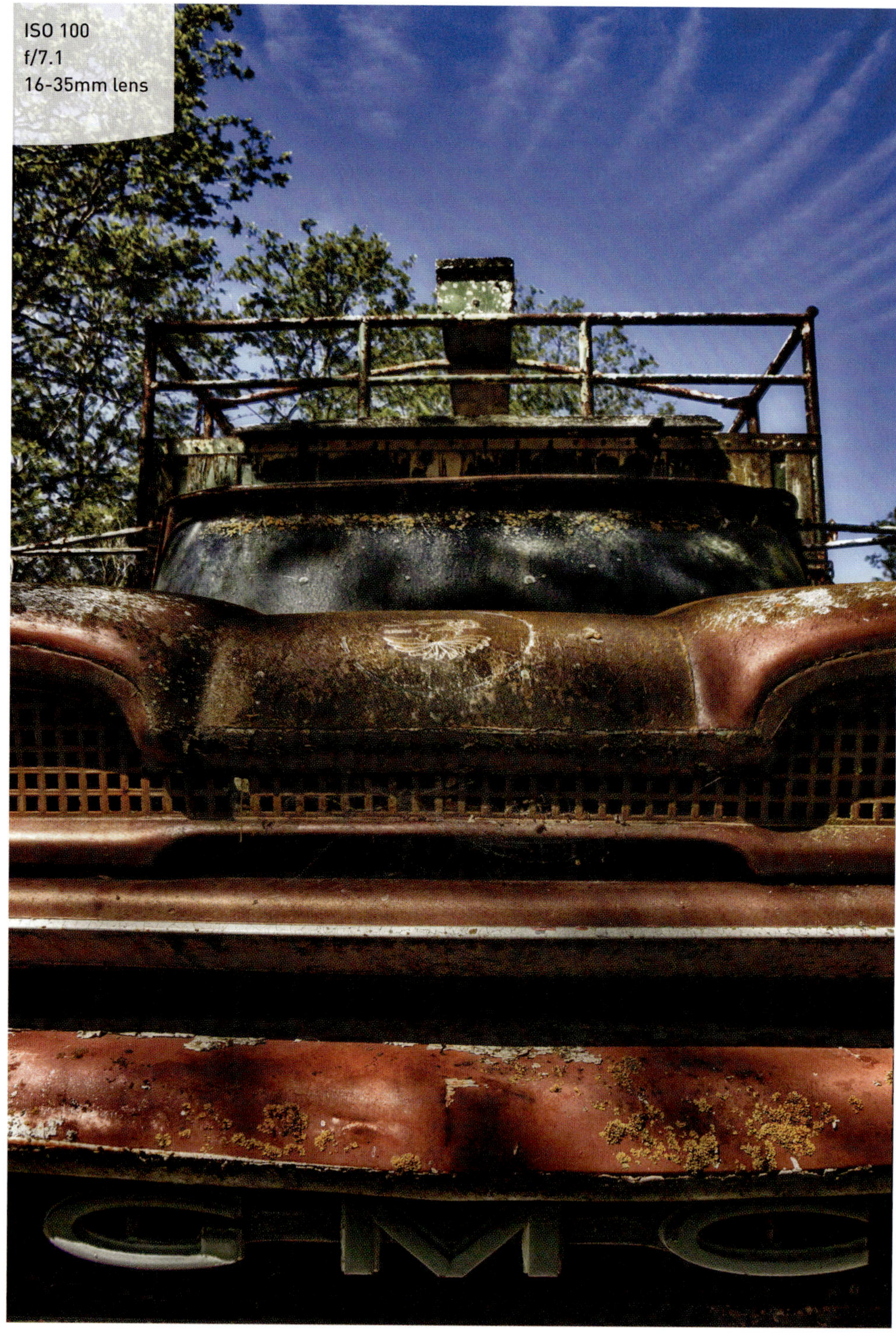

The 5D Mark III offers the ability to produce several different types of HDR images in-camera, eliminating the need for a computer or software. Though it doesn't provide the flexibility and control found in most HDR software, it is an easy and convenient way to produce a HDR look.

The camera features five different rendering effects for HDR images (**Figure 10.7**):

- **Natural:** Preserves the wide tonal range of the scene, retaining important details existing in the highlights and shadows.

- **Art standard:** Produces a more painterly effect by reducing contrast and gradation. The subject outlines have more clearly defined edges.

- **Art vivid:** Color saturation is increased above what appears with the art standard effect, creating a more graphic art look.

- **Art bold:** Achieves the greatest degree of color saturation to create a look similar to pop art.

- **Art embossed:** Produces the flattest-looking image, with color saturation, brightness, contrast, and gradation decreased considerably. It can produce an image that looks like a faded photograph, but with pronounced outlines of the subject.

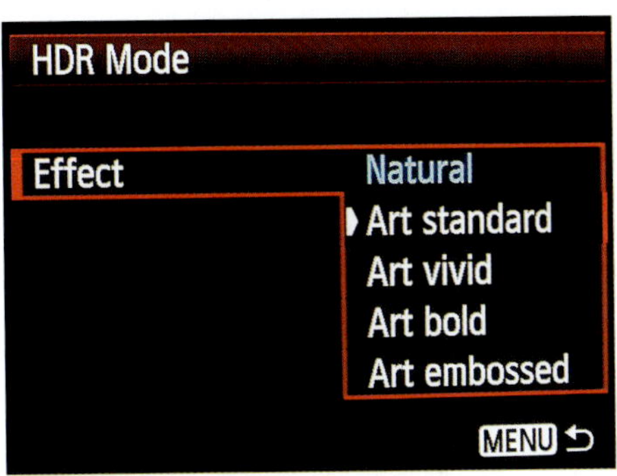

FIGURE 10.7
The choice of the HDR effect can result in an image that looks realistic to painterly. If you want greater control over the look of your HDR images, you might consider investing in HDR software.

TO SET UP FOR HDR PHOTOGRAPHY, FOLLOW THESE STEPS:

1. Press the Menu button and turn the Main Dial to access the Shoot 3 menu screen.

2. Turn the Quick Control Dial to select HDR mode. Press the Setting button.

3. Turn the Quick Control Dial to select Adjust Dynamic Range. Press the Setting button.

4. Select Auto or one of the full-stop exposure-bracketing options. Press the Setting button.

5. Turn the Quick Control Dial and select Effect. Press the Setting button.

Continued ➤

6. Use the Quick Control Dial to select the preferred Effect. Depress the Setting button.

7. Turn the Menu Dial and select Continuous HDR. Press the Setting button.

8. Turn the Quick Control Dial, select Every shot, and press the Setting button.

9. Use the Quick Control Dial to select 1 shot only if you want to produce only one HDR image or Every shot if you want to create several different HDR photographs. Press the Setting button.

10. Turn the Quick Control Dial to select Auto Image Align. Press the Setting button and choose Enable.

11. Use the Quick Control Dial to select Save Source Images. Press the Setting button.

12. Turn the Quick Control Dial to select All images, which will save all the original files, as well as the final HDR image, or select HDR image only to save only the HDR image.

MULTIPLE EXPOSURES

Multiple-exposure capability has been introduced with the 5D Mark III, providing another creative outlet. Though combining multiple images has been possible using applications like Photoshop, you can now achieve it in-camera. There is a certain level of unpredictability about this feature, but that's probably part of the allure because it provides a great opportunity for experimentation and playfulness, which can include photographing the subject both in focus and out of focus (**Figure 10.8**).

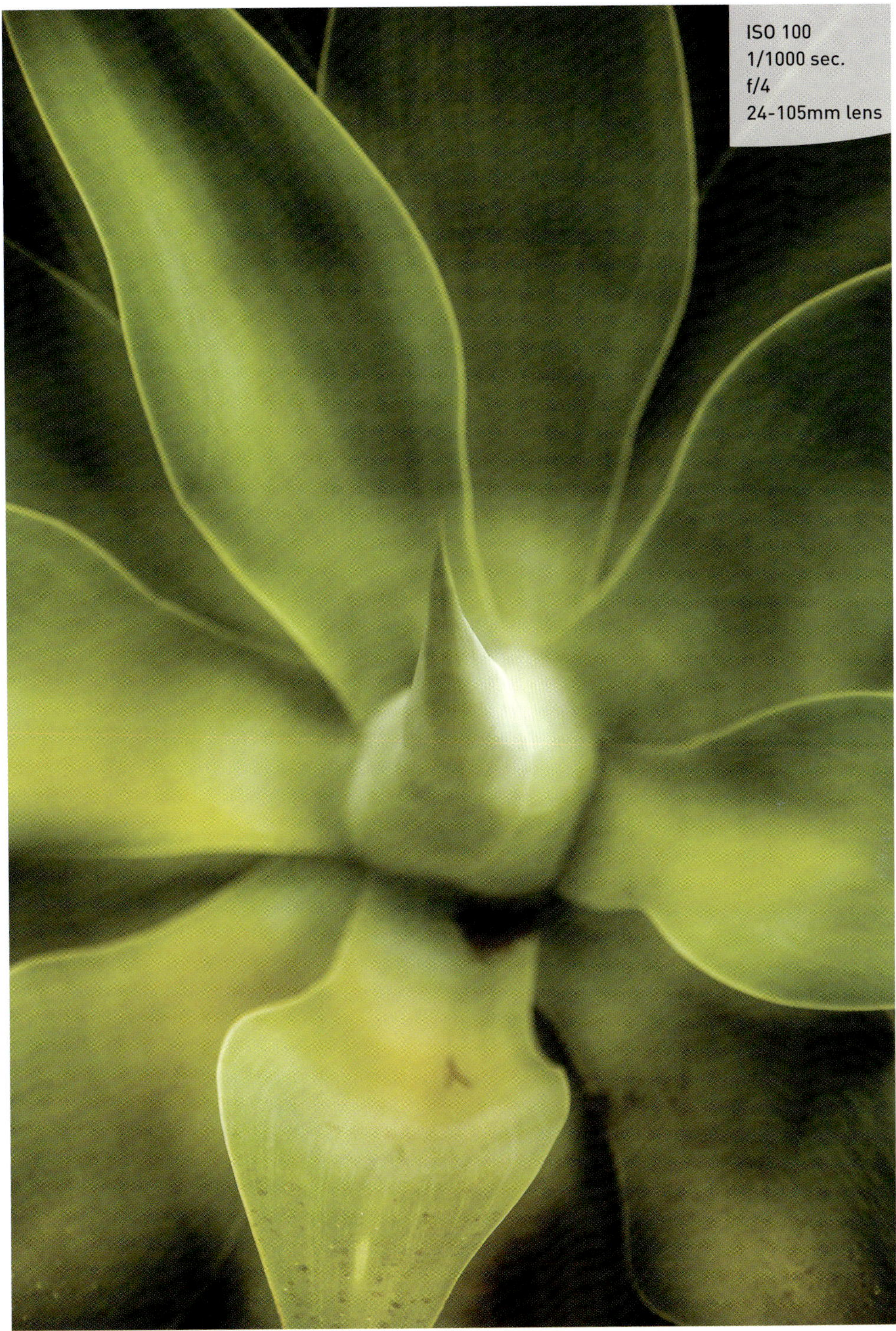

FIGURE 10.8
A simple multiple exposure can consist of taking an in-focus and out-of-focus image of the same subject. This creates an interesting painterly effect, with a graphic subject and good color.

When the function is accessed through the camera's Menu screen (**Figure 10.9**), you have the flexibility to produce a single multiple exposure or a series of them, depending on how you set your camera.

Using the Live View mode allows you to actually see the previously shot image(s) laid over the subject or scene you're about to photograph. This gives you incredible control over the look and composition of your final photograph.

The multiple-exposure setting provides several rendering options for you to choose from (**Figure 10.10**):

- **Additive:** The exposure of each image is added cumulatively to the image. For this setting, it's important to apply some negative compensation to each image based on the number of images used for a multiple exposure (2 images = –1 EV compensation, 3 images = –1.5 EV compensation, 4 images = –2 EV compensation).

- **Average:** Based on the number of exposures shot for the multiple exposures, the camera will automatically reduce exposure compensation for each frame.

- **Bright and Dark:** The brightness or darkness of the initial image is evaluated and overlaid with another image. Depending on whether you choose the bright or dark setting, the preferred tones are retained. This can result in an interesting blend of colors as the level of luminosity changes in areas of the frame.

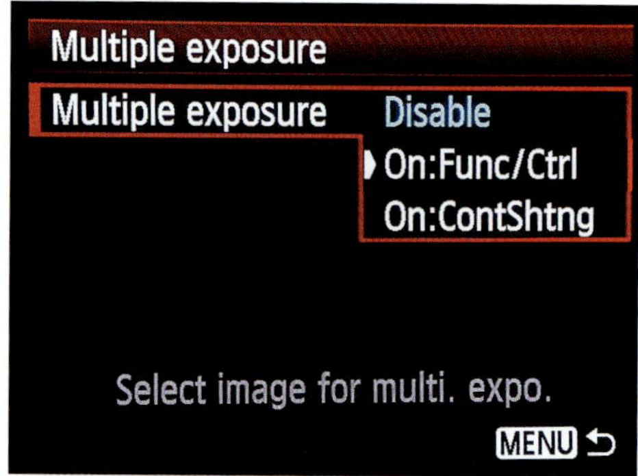

FIGURE 10.9
By activating the multiple-exposure function, you can expose a single frame multiple times to achieve a creative juxtaposition of imagery.

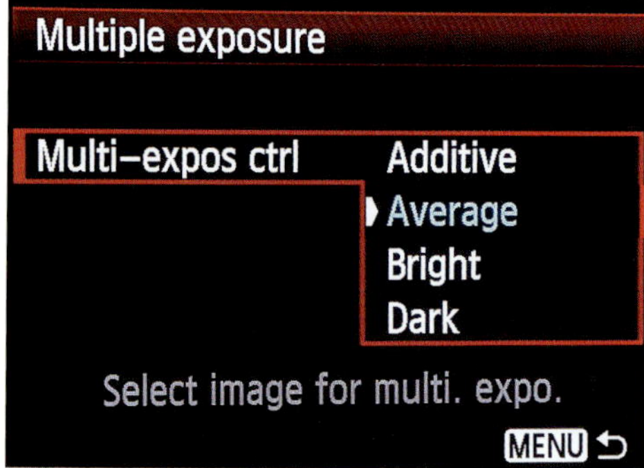

FIGURE 10.10
The camera provides several options for creating distinctive looks to the multiple images combined in-camera.

1. Press the Menu button and turn the Main Dial to access the Shoot 3 menu screen.

2. Turn the Quick Control Dial to select Multiple Exposure. Press the Setting button.

3. Turn the Quick Control Dial to select On: Function/Control or On: Continuous Shooting. (Live View is available only with On: Function/Control.) Press the Setting button.

4. Turn the Quick Control Dial to select Multiple Exposure control and press the Setting button.

5. Use the Quick Control button to select your preferred effect: Additive, Average, Bright, or Dark. Press the Setting button.

6. Turn the Quick Control Dial to select Number of exposures. Press the Setting button.

7. Turn the Quick Control Dial to create multiple exposures of up to nine images. Press the Setting button.

8. Turn the Quick Control Dial to select Save source image. Press the Setting button.

9. Turn the Quick Control Dial to select All images (to save the individual files and the completed multiple exposure) or Result Only (only the final multiple exposed file is saved). Press the Setting button.

10. Turn the Quick Control Dial to select Continue Multiple-Exposure. Press the Setting button.

11. Turn the Quick Control Dial to select 1 Shot Only (to create a single multiple exposure) or Continuously (to produce a series of multiple-exposure images).

TIP

If you find that you're unable to access the multiple-exposure option on your camera, it's likely because the HDR mode is enabled. Disable the HDR setting before attempting to shoot multiple exposures.

MY MENU

There are many items in the menu that you can change, but some you'll change more frequently than others. The My Menu function allows you to place six of your most used menu items in one place so that you can quickly get to them, make your changes, and get on with shooting. I frequently include access to the controls for formatting the memory card, checking the battery status, autoexposure bracketing, and picture style (**Figure 10.11**). Depending on what I'm photographing, I may change some of these settings to suit the demands of the shoot.

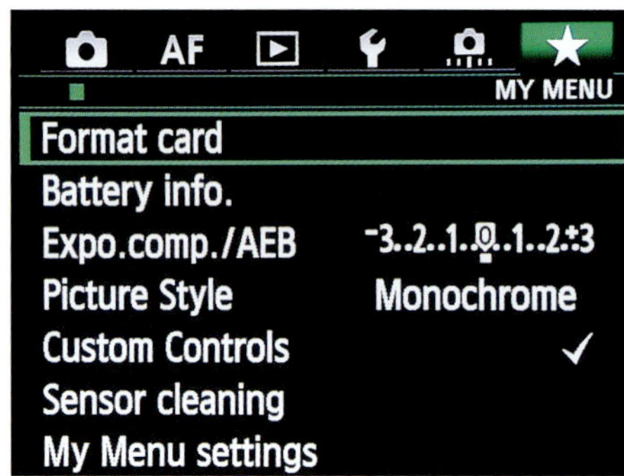

FIGURE 10.11
By placing my most frequently accessed controls in My Menu, I avoid having to navigate the extensive screens found on the 5D Mark III, which saves me lot of time.

Chapter 10 Assignments

Many of the techniques covered in this chapter are specific to certain shooting situations that may not come about very often. This is even more reason to practice them so that when the situation does arise, you'll be ready.

Adding Your Copyright Info

Input your copyright information so that all your images identify you as the photographer. Use your image-editing software to access the IPTC data to confirm that the data has been embedded.

Checking and Updating Your Firmware

Check the version of the firmware that is currently running on your camera. If there is a more up-to-date version, download it from the Canon website and install it into your camera. Make sure to fully charge your battery before attempting to update your firmware.

Nail the Exposure with Exposure Bracketing

Photograph a high-contrast scene that you imagine would be difficult to meter. Enable the autoexposure bracketing feature and produce a series of exposures. Vary the degree of compensation between frames, and try a series of three, five, or seven exposure brackets.

Enter the Magical World of HDR

Find a high-contrast scene with bright highlights and deep shadows and enable the HDR function of your camera. Create different versions of the subject using the five different built-in rendering styles.

Experiment with Multiple Exposures

Create a series of multiple-exposure images. Experiment with taking in-focus and out-of-focus images of the same subject. Also, try to combine very different subject matter into a single image. Remember to try the three rendering options and compare your results.

Share your results with this book's Flickr group!

Join the group here: www.flickr.com/groups/Canon5DMarkIIIFromSnapshotstoGreatShots

The camera used while writing this *From Snapshots to Great Shots* book was generously provided by B&H Photo.

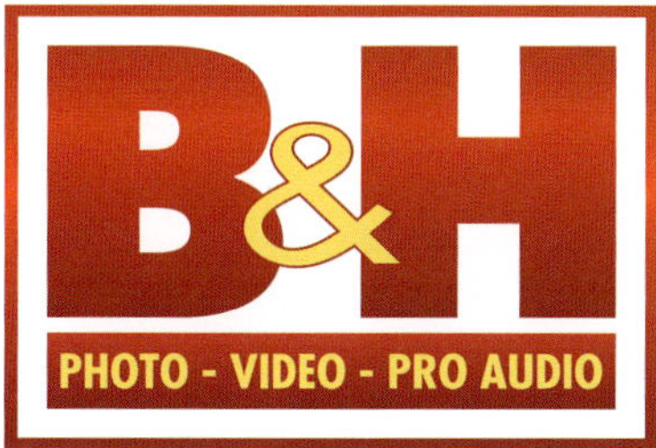

www.bhphotovideo.com

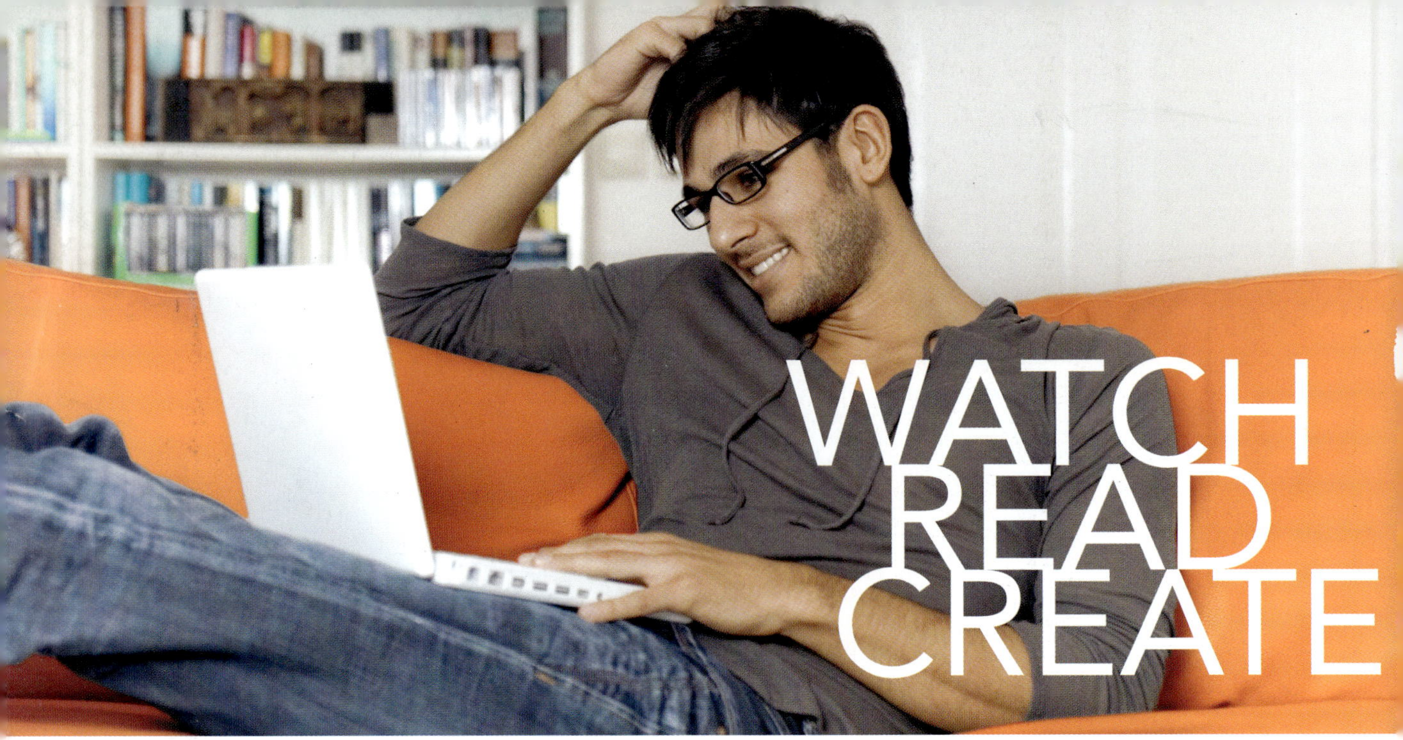

WATCH READ CREATE

Unlimited online access to all Peachpit, Adobe Press, Apple Training and New Riders videos and books, as well as content from other leading publishers including: O'Reilly Media, Focal Press, Sams, Que, Total Training, John Wiley & Sons, Course Technology PTR, Class on Demand, VTC and more.

No time commitment or contract required! Sign up for one month or a year.
All for $19.99 a month

SIGN UP TODAY
peachpit.com/creativeedge

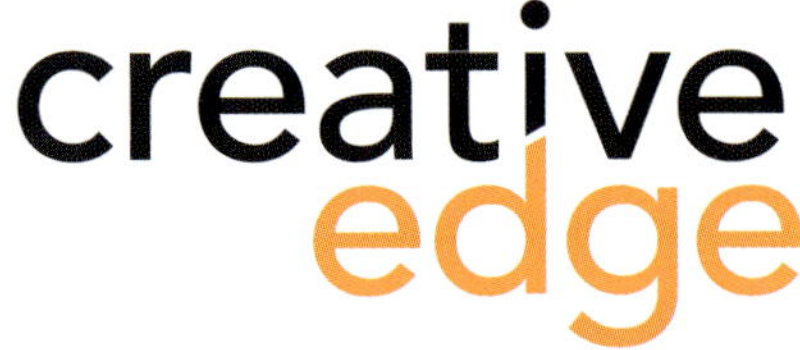